S0-GGH-330

The Phonology of Tone

Linguistic Models 17

Editors

Teun Hoekstra
Harry van der Hulst

Mouton de Gruyter
Berlin · New York

The Phonology of Tone

The Representation of Tonal Register

Edited by

Harry van der Hulst
Keith Snider

Mouton de Gruyter
Berlin · New York 1993

Mouton de Gruyter (formerly Mouton, The Hague)
is a division of Walter de Gruyter & Co., Berlin.

⊚ Printed on acid-free paper which falls within the
guidelines of the ANSI to ensure permanence and durability.

Library of Congress Cataloging-in-Publication Data

The phonology of tone : the representation of tonal register /
edited by Harry van der Hulst, K. Snider.
    p.   cm. — (Linguistic models ; 17)
  Includes bibliographical references and indexes.
  ISBN 3-11-013605-8 (alk. paper)
  1. Tone (Phonetics). 2. Register (Linguistics) 3. Prosodic
analysis (Linguistics) I. Hulst, Harry van der. II. Snider,
Keith L. III. Series.
P223.P47   1992
414'.6 — dc20   92-21565
                                                          CIP

Die Deutsche Bibliothek — Cataloging-in-Publication Data

The **phonology of tone** : the representation of tonal register /
ed. by Harry van der Hulst ; K. Snider. — Berlin ; New York :
Mouton de Gruyter, 1992
  (Linguistic models ; 17)
  ISBN 3-11-013605-8
NE: van der Hulst, Harry [Hrsg.]; GT

© Copyright 1992 by Walter de Gruyter & Co., D-1000 Berlin 30.
All rights reserved, including those of translation into foreign languages. No part of this
book may be reproduced in any form or by any means, electronic or mechanical, including
photocopy, recording, or any information storage and retrieval system, without permission
in writing from the publisher.
Printing: Gerike GmbH, Berlin. — Binding: Lüderitz & Bauer, Berlin. —
Printed in Germany.

Table of Contents

Affiliations ix
Preface and Acknowledgments xi

Keith Snider and Harry van der Hulst
Introduction
   1. Introduction 1
   2. Problems in representing tonal register 2
      2.1. Multiple tone heights 2
      2.2. The representation of contour tones 4
      2.3. The representation of register shifts 8
   3. The contributions to this volume 17
      3.1. Mary Clark: Representation of downstep in Dschang
          Bamileke 17
      3.2. Larry Hyman: Register tones and tonal geometry 18
      3.3. Bob Ladd: In defense of a metrical theory of
          intonational downstep 20
      3.4. Victor Manfredi: Spreading and downstep: prosodic
          government in tone languages 21
      3.5. John Stewart: Dschang and Ebrié as Akan-type tonal
          downstep languages 21
      3.6. Moria Yip: Tonal register in East Asian Languages . . . 22
   References 24

Mary M. Clark
Representation of downstep in Dschang Bamileke
   1. Downstep and tonal register 29
   2. A phonological representation for downstep: the
     floating-tone approach 32
   3. The tonal-feature approach 36
   4. Revision of Hyman's analysis 39
      4.1. Lexical tone and the tonal representation 39
      4.2. The class 1/9 associative 44
      4.3. The general associative construction 50
      4.4. Nouns with rising-tone stems 56
      4.5. The verbs 59
      4.6. Summary 61

5. The downstep rule, re-visited 62
6. Conclusion 71
References 72

Larry M. Hyman
Register tones and tonal geometry
1. Introduction 75
2. The proposal 76
3. H tone raising in Engenni 85
4. H tone raising in Mankon 89
5. Upstep in Kirimi (Cahi dialect) 94
6. Conclusion 103
References 105

Robert D. Ladd
In defense of a metrical theory of intonational downstep
1. Introduction 109
2. Background 109
   2.1. First digression–defining paralinguistic 113
   2.2. Second digression: phonetic models of vertical scale .. 116
      2.2.1. Phonetic models of downstep 118
3. The case against register tones 120
   3.1. Pierrehumbert and Beckman's arguments 120
   3.2. Problems with Pierrehumbert and Beckman's arguments 123
      3.2.1. Problems with the phonetic model of downstep . 123
      3.2.2. Problems with the function of paralinguistic effects 124
      3.2.3. Problems with experimental results on range expansion 125
      3.2.4. Problems with the definition of prosodic domains 127
4. Reassembling the pieces 128
References 130

Victor Manfredi
Spreading and downstep: Prosodic government in tone languages
1. Introduction 133
2. Tone and locality in Benue-Kwa 135
3. Prosodic government 149
4. Metrical tone classes 167
5. Prosodic typology 176
6. Prosody and syntax 178
References 179

Table of contents

John M.Stewart
Dschang and Ebrié as Akan-type total downstep languages
- 1. Introduction 185
- 2. Akan 188
  - 2.1. Total downstep, whole numbers, and integer-assigning algorithms 188
  - 2.2. Sequence structure conditions and the automatic rules which serve them 190
    - 2.2.1. "Downstep Displacement" in Kikuyu 190
    - 2.2.2. Low tone stepping in Akan 193
- 3. Dschang 196
  - 3.1. The distribution of downstep and upstep 196
  - 3.2. The tones of the associative form of the noun 202
  - 3.3. The tones of the associative construction 206
- 4. Ebrié 222
- 5. Conclusion 242
- Postscript 243
- References 244

Moira Yip
Tonal register in East Asian languages
- 1. Introduction 245
- 2. Register as a tonal feature 245
  - 2.1. Taiwanese 246
  - 2.2. Suzhou 247
  - 2.3. Fuzhou 248
  - 2.4. Cantonese 248
- 3. Register as a phonation feature 249
  - 3.1. Shanghai 249
  - 3.2. Tibetan 254
- 4. Register as an intonation feature 258
  - 4.1. Hausa 259
- 5. Intonation in East Asian languages 262
  - 5.1. Shanghai 262
  - 5.2. Mandarin 262
- 6. Conclusion 266
- References 266

Index of authors 269

Index of languages 275

Index of subjects 279

Affiliations

Mary Clark
 Department of English
 Hamilton Smith Hall
 Durham
 New Hampshire 03824-3574
 USA

Larry Hyman
 Department of Linguistics
 University of California
 Berkeley, CA 94720
 USA

Harry van der Hulst
 Department of General Linguistics
 P.O. Box 9515
 2300 RA Leiden
 The Netherlands

Robert Ladd
 Department of Linguistics
 University of Edinburgh
 Adam Ferguson Building
 George Square
 Edinburgh EH89LL
 Scotland

Victor Manfredi
 African Studies Center
 Harvard University
 270 Bay State Road
 Boston, MA 02215
 USA

Keith Snider
 Summer Institute of Linguistics
 7500 W Camp Wisdom Road
 Dallas, TX 75236
 USA

John M. Stewart
 7 East Barnton Gardens
 Edinburgh EH4 6AR
 Scotland

Moira Yip
 School of Social Sciences
 University of California at Irvine
 Irvine, CA 92717
 USA

Preface and Acknowledgments

All contributions to the present volume have been written on invitation by the editors. The invitation went out late 1988 and we received draft versions of the articles in the course of 1989 and 1990. The final versions as well as the introduction were completed in the second half of 1991.

We would like to thank all authors for their willingness to participate in this project and we believe that this collection of articles presents a comprehensive overview of the study of tonal register. The introduction will provide readers who are less familiar with the history of this subject and its major aspects with a suitable background in this area.

We would like to thank a number of people who helped us in various ways during the preparation of this book: Marc van Biezen, Alice den Heijer, Simone Langeweg and René Mulder.

Harry van der Hulst
Keith Snider

Issues in the Representation of Tonal Register

Keith Snider and Harry van der Hulst

1. INTRODUCTION*

Given that the majority of the world's languages is tonal, it is incumbent upon phonologists to strive towards the development of phonological theories which provide an adequate formal account of tonal phenomena. Efforts to this end have been many but the issues involved remain far from settled. In part, this is due to one aspect peculiar to tone, the fact that tonal oppositions are relative in nature; e.g., a phonetic Low tone can often be differentiated from a phonetic High tone only by comparing the two in a specific environment. This would be comparable to analyzing a vowel system in which a morpheme ending in [i] could be differentiated from one ending in [a] only by comparing each with a postposition that begins with a vowel of known quality.

The problem of establishing contrasts between elements which are only relative in nature is further compounded by the fact that there appear to be registers involved. Clements (1990:59) defines "register" as the "frequency band internal to the speaker's range, which determines the highest and lowest frequency within which tones can be realized at any given point in an utterance". Under certain conditions, this register can be shifted upward or downward, and this shift in register then re-establishes the fundamental frequencies at which the various affected tones are phonetically realized.

The present chapter includes a presentation of some major problems involved in formally representing tonal register phenomena. It also provides a discussion of various attempts to overcome these problems, and concludes with a summary of the proposals which form the content of the subsequent chapters in this book.

---

* We thank Larry Hyman, Victor Manfredi, and Jeroen van de Weijer for giving comments on an earlier version of this paper. We also thank all contributors to this volume for their help in writing section 3.

2. PROBLEMS IN REPRESENTING TONAL REGISTER

In this section, we wish to outline some of the major problems to be confronted in the representation of tonal phenomena. Although we focus on issues relating to register, our perspective is slightly broader than that. We first deal with the question how many *tone heights* must be distinguished. We next look at the matter of *contour tones* and, finally, we consider the problems involved in formally representing *shifts in tonal register*.

2.1. Multiple tone heights

Perhaps the most basic problem which confronts the tonologist is how to formally represent multiple tone heights, both in underlying and in derived representations. Here we specifically talk about *level* tones, i.e. tones which, from a phonological point of view, are not considered to be contours. It seems that at least four discrete levels of height need to be accounted for. In a paper devoted to this subject, Hyman (1986) lists Igede as having four underlying and four surface levels, Gwari as having three underlying but four surface levels (cf. Hyman and Magaji 1970), and Kagwe as having four underlying but three surface levels (cf. Koopman and Sportiche 1982). There are a few studies, however which report five discrete levels. One of the earliest and most convincing descriptions of such tone systems is that of the San Andres Chicahuaxtla dialect of Trique (Longacre 1952). Five levels are also assumed in the Copala dialect of Trique (Hollenbach 1984 and 1988), Miao-Yao (Chang 1953), Dan (Bearth and Zemp 1967 and Flik 1977), and Bencnon (Wedekind 1983). Cf. Anderson (1978) and Maddieson (1978) for general discussions of tonal systems.

Accounting for four discrete levels of tone can be optimally accomplished by assuming two binary features. One of the earliest proposals along this line was that of Gruber (1964), which appears in (1). This proposal shows resemblance to the more recent autosegmental approaches to tone, which we will discuss below. (1 is highest and 4, lowest):

(1)
	High	High2
1	+	+
2	+	−
3	−	+
4	−	−

This and other (early) proposals for representing tone are discussed elsewhere in the literature. We refer the interested reader to Stahlke (1977), Anderson (1978), Clements (1979, 1981, 1983), and Snider (1988).

A system using [±High] and [±Low] can only deal with a three-tone system, since [+High, +Low] is excluded. But even accounting for three levels poses problems for a two-feature system, when one considers the natural classes needed to account for the various types of assimilation in different languages. In some three-tone systems, for instance, the Mid tone seems to be more closely associated with the Low tone than with the High tone. One example of this is Ga'anda (Newman 1971) in which both Low tones and Mid tones cause following High tones to be downstepped. In other three-tone systems such as that of Moba (Russell 1986), the Mid tone is more closely associated with the High tone, and this may be seen in that the Mid tone, like the High tone, is downstepped following a Low tone.

(2) *Ga'anda*   *Moba*
     High Can be downstepped   High Can be downstepped
     Mid   Causes downstep   Mid   Can be downstepped
     Low   Causes downstep   Low   Causes downstep

Cross-linguistic evidence of this type indicates that we need to be able to distinguish two different representations for the Mid tone and thus four different tone levels. A system as in (1), which is capable of generating the four-way distinction, is therefore strongly favoured.

Accounting for five discrete levels of tone is more problematical than accounting for four. It is clear that a third feature of tone must be added to the system. One of the earliest proposals which involves three features is that of Wang (1967):

(3) | | High | Central | Mid |
     |---|------|---------|-----|
     | 1 | + | − | − |
     | 2 | + | + | − |
     | 3 | − | + | + |
     | 4 | − | + | − |
     | 5 | − | − | − |

By adding a third tone feature, however, the classic problem of overgeneration manifests itself, since three binary features allow for up to eight levels of tone. While languages with five discrete levels have been argued to exist, those with eight have not. A further problem which arises with feature systems of this nature is that there is no clear indication of how languages with fewer discrete levels should be described. As noted by Clements (1983:146-7), "a language with two tone levels can be described in ten different ways" using three binary features. We will not go into the question how a five-level system can be characterized in a principled way, although we believe that an extra feature is not called for.

2.2. The representation of contour tones

The problem of formally representing contour tones played a key role in the development of autosegmental theory. Prior to the appearance of Woo (1969), contour tones were widely perceived to be the result of some sort of modification of level tones; e.g. high-rising or high-falling (cf. Pike 1948). Woo's proposal for tone features was similar to Wang's in that she also used three binary features to account for multiple tone heights. A crucial difference, however, lies in their proposals for handling tonal contours. Whereas Wang proposed the additional binary features of [Rising] and [Falling], Woo claimed that contour tones are actually sequences of level tones. Working in pre-autosegmental times, she was then forced to conclude that contours could not occur on short vowels, but necessarily only occur over two or more segments or *tone bearing units*. The reason for this was that a single matrix could not contain a sequence of two tone features in SPE.

Woo's claim that contour tones are confined to sequences of tone bearing units has since been demonstrated not to be true, as argued by Leben (1971 and 1973) and Williams (1976) (but see Duanmu 1990). Initial steps were taken by Leben and Williams towards giving adequate representation to single segments which bear sequences of level tones. Following these steps, Goldsmith (1976) worked out a detailed alternative to the phonological model of Chomsky and Halle (1968), viz. *autosegmental phonology*.

In autosegmental phonology, the speech signal is not only "chopped" vertically into segments, but is also "sliced" horizontally into autosegmental sequences of features which represent some part of the speech signal. For example, one sequence would represent tonal features, whereas another sequence would represent, say, the rest. Each sequence is referred to as a *tier*, and matrices on each tier as *autosegments*. Coordination between two tiers is achieved by sets of *association lines* which appropriately "connect" autosegments of one tier with autosegments of another tier. The advantage of this approach, of course, is that it allows for "many-to-one" mappings, e.g. two or more tonal matrices can be associated with one single unit on the tier that represents the tone bearing unit, and vice versa.

Not only has autosegmental phonology proven valuable in the analysis of tone systems, but by assuming that other than tonal features also occupy separate autosegmental tiers, it has offered solutions to problems involving such things as nasalization and various types of vowel harmony. A logical extreme of autosegmental phonology is that every feature is represented on a separate tier. This view necessitates the postulation of a "central" tier to which all features characterizing one position in the syllable structure associate. This tier is referred to as the skeletal tier and its units are usually represented by Xs. Autosegmental phonology, then, resolves the problems raised by Woo and Leben by allowing representations of the following kind:

(4)

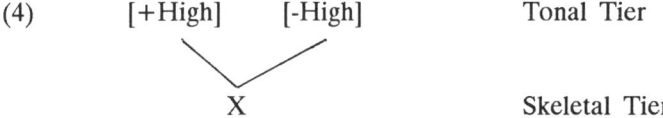

[+High]   [-High]   Tonal Tier

          X   Skeletal Tier

Structures such as that of (4) account for the contours found in African languages remarkably well. This success may be attributed to the fact that, for the most part, contours in African languages tend to occur more on the edges of morphemes and words than in the middle of such units. If tonal contours are in fact just a linear sequence of two different level tones which come to be associated with one tone-bearing unit (TBU), we then have a reasonable explanation for their predominant occurrence in edge environments. It is precisely at the edges of domains where we expect to find contours, either through the addition or spreading of a tone from a neighbouring morpheme or word to the peripheral TBU of an adjacent morpheme or word, or through the deletion of an initial or final vowel, in a sandhi context. If the tones remain while their TBU is deleted, they can associate to, for example, the TBU that caused the deletion.

While early autosegmental phonology provides a reasonable account of contour tones in African languages, problems arise when one tries to account for the contours of many East Asian languages. In an article devoted to the subject of contour tones, Yip (1989) points out that the contours of these languages are often *unitary contours*. Unitary contours differ from what we will call *composite contours* (or *tone clusters*) significantly in two ways. As units in their own right, they are realized on any TBU as freely as are level tones, thus differing from composite contours which are realized mainly on edges. (In as far as unitary contours occur in languages which favour monosyllabic words, this difference may be difficult to establish in all cases.) The second way unitary contours differ from composite contours is that unlike composite contours, which spread or reduplicate only one or the other of their composite parts, unitary contours have been claimed to spread or reduplicate as a unit (Chan forth.). While early autosegmental phonology provides a reasonable account for composite contour tones, the problem of providing a model which accounts (in a satisfactory manner) for both composite and unitary contour tones did not arise until later.

One of the important developments leading to a solution to the problem of representing unitary contour tones was the work of Yip (1980). Yip claimed that there are actually two tonal tiers associated with TBUs—a Tone Tier, and a Register Tier. Recognizing that tonal systems with five levels of height are somewhat special, she proposed that two binary features, [High] and [Upper], occupy two independent tiers that are associated with TBUs. Together, these features define four discrete levels of pitch as in (5) (cf. the proposal in 1).

(5)
	Tone Tier	Register Tier
1	+High (H)	+Upper
2	−High (L)	+Upper
3	+High (H)	−Upper
4	−High (L)	−Upper

Structurally, the features from each tier are associated directly with the TBUs (taken to be matrices containing all non-tonal features; the skeleton had not been developed in 1980). In (6), we illustrate a falling tone (taken from Yip 1980:32).

(6)   [−Upper]
            |
           pe?
           / \
          H   L

While Yip (1980) was an important development in tone theory, it still left unsolved the adequate representation of *both* composite and unitary contours. It was not until after the advent of feature geometry that further progress was made in this area.

Feature geometry refers to a claim worked out in detail in Clements (1985) and Sagey (1986) that the autosegmental tiers are not all linked to the skeletal tier directly. Rather, there is a hierarchical arrangement involved in the sense that autosegments on tiers which constitute a class (e.g. all tone features, all place features, etc.) associate to a tier intermediate between these autosegments and the skeletal tier. The units on tiers which merely group other tiers that bear features are called *class nodes*.

(7)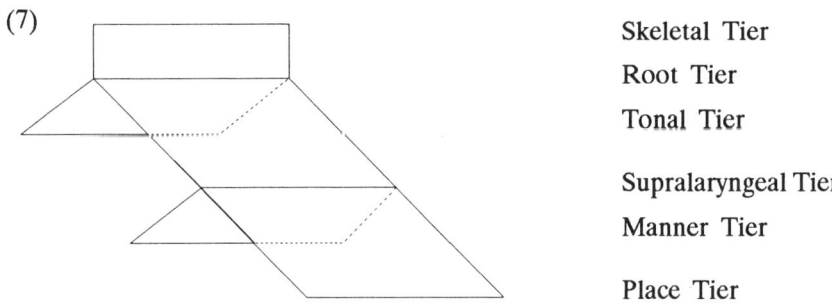

Skeletal Tier
Root Tier
Tonal Tier

Supralaryngeal Tier
Manner Tier

Place Tier

Except for the case of tonal features, we will not concern ourselves here with all the details of hierarchical arrangements of features and tiers. Detailed discussion of proposals on feature hierarchy can be found in Den Dikken and Van der Hulst (1988) and McCarthy (1988).

Adopting the notions of two tonal tiers (from Yip), and of feature geometry (from Clements and Sagey), several linguists (many independently of one another) have made proposals using the geometric structure of (8).

(8)

Tonal Tier 1
Tonal Tier 2
Tonal Node Tier
TBU Tier

Proposals along the lines of (8) have included Archangeli and Pulleyblank (1986), Hyman (this volume), Hyman and Pulleyblank (1988), Inkelas (1987, 1989), Inkelas and Leben (1990), Snider (1988, 1990) and Yip (this volume). It is not always clear whether the TBU tier is the root tier or the skeletal tier in these proposals, but we ignore that issue here.

Exploiting the feature geometry of (8), one can represent, say, a *composite* falling tone as in (9a), and a unitary falling tone as in (9b) or (9c), depending on whether or not the fall involves a change in register.

(9)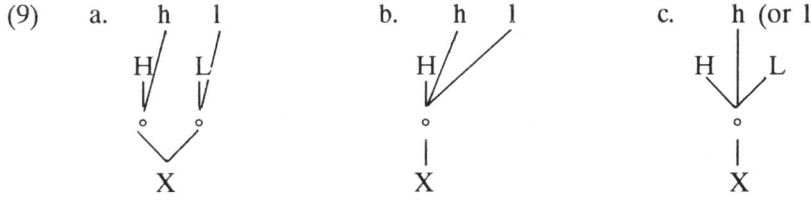

The dual representation of unitary contours forms a less secure aspect of this approach; perhaps contours never involve a register shift. Another question regards the composite contours. Formally, we could also have both parts sharing the same register feature. Such issues need attention, but we will not go into them here (cf. Yip, this vol. for some discussion).

2.3. The representation of register shifts

As stated in the introduction to this chapter, the tonal register of an utterance, i.e. the frequencies at which, say, the High tones and the Low tones are realized, can be shifted downwards, as well as upwards. In many African tone languages, the presence of a Low tone between two High tones triggers a downward shift in tonal register. This register shift then re-establishes at a lower level the phonetic pitch at which all following tones in the utterance are phonetically realized. Such phonetic sequences are frequently represented as in (10).

$$(10) \begin{bmatrix} - & & & & & & & & \\ & - & - & & & & & & \\ & & & - & - & & - & - & \\ & & & & & - & & & \\ H & L & H & H & L & L & H & L & H & H \end{bmatrix}$$

Observe that the lowering effect can take place an unlimited number of times, in principle, thereby allowing an indefinite number of pitch values for high and low tones. High tones later in the utterance may, in fact, have a lower pitch than low tones early on.

When register lowering occurs as in (10), the phenomenon is often called *downdrift*—not to be confused with *declination* which refers to the slight general decline in pitch which is found over most utterances in perhaps all languages (even when they consist of a span of like tones).

In some languages, register lowering occurs even when there is no overt indication of a Low tone, and this has most often been called *downstep*. In such cases, the presence is assumed of a Low tone which has lost its tone-bearing support. This is most usually due to either (a) the tone-bearing unit of the Low tone was lost historically (due, perhaps, to apocope) but the Low tone has survived, i.e. it is "floating"; or (b) the Low tone was displaced by another tone (due, perhaps, to the rightward spreading of the High tone immediately to its left) but, again, the Low tone has survived and has the effect of shifting the register ("key lowering") of the next H(s). In (11), below, the two sources of downstep are demonstrated. TBUs are represented by Xs:

(11) Register lowering   Register lowering
      due to "floating" Low   due to displaced Low

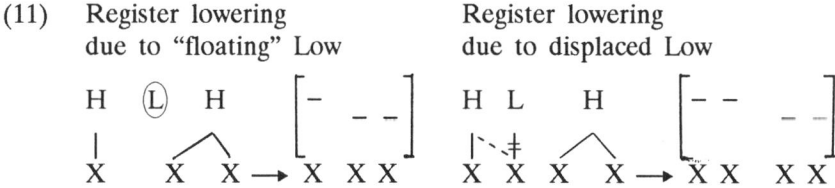

From the above description of downdrift and downstep, it is obvious that they are the same process, their differences merely mirroring their different derivations. In order to capture this fact, but at the same time to differentiate the two, Stewart (1965) proposed the terms *automatic downstep* to refer to the former (i.e. downdrift) and *nonautomatic downstep* to refer to the latter. Throughout this article we shall use the term *downstep* to refer to the phenomenon as a whole.

In Llogoori, a Bantu language, downstep occurs at the new occurrence of a H tone (cf. Clements 1990:66ff), i.e., there is no need for a preceding low tone. This looks like automatic downstep even though there are no overt Ls to trigger the process.

There are a number of problems associated with all these forms of downstep. Should shifts in register be accounted for in the phonological component or the phonetic component? Should a downstepped High tone be formally equated with a Mid tone in those languages where phonetic equivalence is demonstrated? Perhaps the most difficult problem concerns the cumulative nature of the shifts, i.e. the fact that successive occurrences of downstep result in ever lower levels of pitch. An additional problem comes up in Krachi, a Kwa language spoken in Ghana, where a register difference between two TBUs which are associated with one underlying tone is demonstrated to occur (Snider 1990). How should this be accounted for? These and other problems have prompted a number of proposals in the past including: Winston (1960), Schachter (1961), Pike (1966), Stewart (1971), Welmers (1973), Clements (1976, 1979, 1981, 1983), Hyman (1979, 1986), Pierrehumbert (1980), Yip (1980), Pulleyblank (1986), Inkelas (1987), and Snider (1988, 1990).

When one considers the cumulative nature of downstep, it becomes clear that any attempt to account for successive occurrences of downstep is doomed to failure with phonological rules which use binary features in the traditional manner. A number of linguists have therefore abandoned the idea that shifts in tonal register should be accounted for in the phonological component. They have, in turn, provided various accounts which assign gradient pitch values by means of left-to-right implementation rules in a phonetic component (cf. Johnson 1972; Peters 1973; Pulleyblank 1986; Pierrehumbert 1980; and Pierrehumbert and Beckman (1989).

Snider (1990) discusses some points which argue against handling register shifts in the phonetic component:

I.   In many African languages, downstep is phonemic; that is, its occurrence is the sole indicator that two utterances are distinct. "To account not only for the degree of downstep, but also for the fact of downstep in a nonphonological component would imply the claim that a native speaker's recognition of an emic distinction can be triggered *solely* by the implementation of a distinctive feature in the phonetic component. This would greatly increase the power of the phonetic component" (p. 469).

II. So far as is known, in languages in which downstep and upstep both play a role, the degree of register shift is the same in both cases. This should be coincidental in models that account for these phenomena with phonetic pitch implementation rules.

III. In many three-tone languages that also have downstep, a downstepped High tone is phonetically equivalent to a Mid tone. If downstep should indeed be accounted for in the phonetic component, any equivalence between a phonemic difference, on the one hand, and a "phonetic" difference, on the other hand, should be purely coincidental.

Not all linguists have abandoned the idea of handling register shifts in the phonological component. Huang (1980), Clements (1981, reprinted as Clements 1983), and Hyman (1986) are notable examples which have made use of hierarchical structures. In Clements (1983:155), for example, language-specific algorithms are used to construct tree-like structures above underlying tones.

(12)

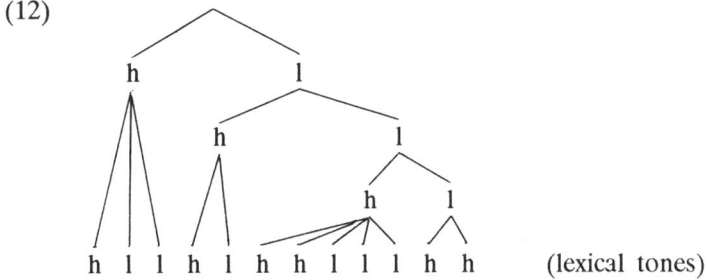

(lexical tones)

A structure like (12) is phonetically interpreted in such a manner that all features which dominate any given underlying tone are grouped into a "feature bundle" or matrix. Thus a Low tone dominated by, for instance, two l's would be phonetically realized at a lower pitch than one dominated by only one l.

Models which employ hierarchical structures like that of (12) are limited in that they are unable to account for changes in register which occur over two TBUs that are dominated by a single tone. Snider (1990:471) exemplifies this with data from Krachi, like (13).

(13)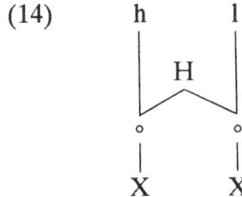
/alɪ kɔtona/ → [alɪ kɔtʊna] 'our mat'

In (13), the difference in pitch between the last and the penultimate TBU is demonstrated to be attributable to a difference in register, despite the fact that underlyingly, both TBUs are associated with the same High tone. The problem with hierarchical structures like that of (12) is that, regardless of how one constructs the tree, the pitch levels of the two final TBUs in (13) are going to be identical, which, of course, is incorrect. Such upsteps are non-local in effect since the final TBU is realized on the same pitch as the second and the third, instead of being lower. This prevents a treatment of such cases in terms of the local F0 adjustments (cf. Clements 1990:66).

Snider (1988, 1990) proposed a model incorporating the geometry in (8) which we will briefly discuss here as a contribution to the issues raised in the present volume. In this model (hereafter called the register tier model) upper case letters designate features on a Modal, or Tonal Tier, and lower case letters designate features on a Register Tier. Features from both tiers are associated with structural nodes on a Tonal Node Tier. The two feature tiers form different geometric planes with respect to the Tonal Node Tier.

(14)   h   l
         | |
         └─H─┐ |
           ╲ ╱ |
            o   o
            | |
            X   X

The structure in (14), then, forms an adequate representation of the final two TBUs in (13). In (14), both TBUs are associated with a single High tone and the second TBU is downstepped in relation to the first, since it is (indirectly) associated with a lower register feature on the Register Tier.

A similar proposal occurs in Inkelas (1987, 1989), but the unique aspect of the register tier model is how the cumulative nature of register shifts is handled. In this model, features on the Register Tier "are represented by **l** (one step lower than the preceding register) and **h** (one step higher than the preceding register)" (Snider 1990:461). This contrasts with other models which make use of the same geometry in that h and l are given a "relative" interpretation (i.e. lower and higher), as opposed to the more conventional "static" interpretation of features. The Modal Tier also contrasts with the Register Tier in this respect. By using this relative interpretation of the register features, the cumulative nature of register shifts can receive satisfactory treatment. Thus while two consecutive Ls on the Modal Tier would not indicate any phonetic difference, two consecutive l's on the Register Tier would indicate that the TBU (indirectly) associated with the second l would be realized at a lower pitch level than a TBU associated with the first (assuming, of course, that the OCP did not collapse the two l's).

In environments in which downstepping typically occurs, what happens is that a High tone which follows a Low tone shares the lower register of the preceding Low tone. In the register tier model, this is represented by the spreading of the lower register of the preceding Low tone to the tonal node associated with the following High tone. In this process, the higher register of the High tone is delinked. This rule of "l-Spread" can thus be represented as in (15).

(15)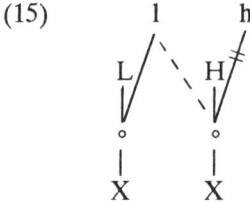

The operation of (15) may be seen in sequences like (16). In the utterance of (16) there are two occurrences of downstep, and these are discussed below.

(16)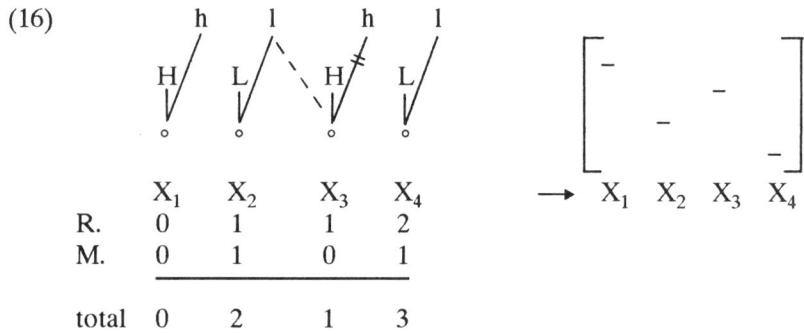

	X_1	X_2	X_3	X_4
R.	0	1	1	2
M.	0	1	0	1
total	0	2	1	3

In (16), X2 is realized on both a lower mode and a lower register than X1. Let us assume that the phonetic difference attributable to the difference between l and h is equivalent to that between L and H. This is true for some languages, but not for all. Let us further assume that this difference has a phonetic value of 1 degree. With these assumptions, X2 is realized 2 degrees lower than X1. X3 is realized 1 degree higher than X2 since, while it shares the lower register of X2, it is realized on the high mode, which is 1 degree higher than the low mode of X2. X3 is also realized 1 degree lower than X1. In this case X3 is realized on the high mode, the same as X1; it is 1 degree lower, however, since it is associated with l, which is "one step lower than the preceding register" (i.e. 1 degree). This is the first instance of downstep in this sequence. The phonetic value of X4 is 2 degrees lower than the value for X3. One degree of this difference is accounted for in that X4 is realized on the low mode, which is 1 degree lower than the high mode of X3. The second degree of difference is accounted for in that, while both TBUs are associated with an l, the l of X4 is interpreted as "one step lower than the preceding register" (i.e. 1 degree). The presence of the floating h from X3 blocks the OCP from collapsing the l's from X2 and X4, and downstep (the second instance of downstep) is effected between these TBUs.

To make these calculations explicit, we have added three rows of integers. The row labeled R gives integers from zero going up by 1 with every occurrence of l (and down with every occurrence of h). The row labeled M gives 0 for H and 1 for L. The row called *total* adds up the integers on the M and R row.

We turn our attention at this point to the matter of upstep. As pointed out by different linguists, upstep is related to downstep in that both seem to have their origin in floating Low tones. It is also often the case that languages with upstep also have downstep, albeit the two are in complementary distribution. Consider upstep in Zulu, as described in Cope (1970), and also discussed in Clements (1981, 1983).

Zulu has a highly productive rule of High tone spread in which a High tone spreads rightward onto, and displaces a following Low tone from, a following syllable. This only happens, however, when the Low tone syllable is nonfinal and does not begin with a "depressor" consonant. Thus when High-Spread occurs, a floating Low is created. If the tone that follows the now floating Low is High, one of two things happens. If this High tone is associated with the penultimate syllable of the utterance, downstep occurs. If it is associated elsewhere, upstep occurs. In (17), the underlying tones are placed below each utterance, and the surface realizations are indicated above. The symbols $^!$ and $_¡$ indicate downstep and upstep, respectively.

(17) a. *Downstep* b. *Upstep*

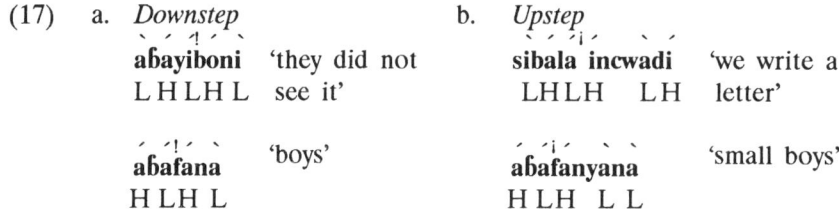

aɓayiboni 'they did not   sibala incwadi 'we write a
L H LH L see it'   LHLH   LH   letter'

aɓafana 'boys'   aɓafanyana   'small boys'
H LH L   H LH L L

The fact that these two (seemingly opposite) phenomena are conditioned by almost identical environments receives a straightforward explanation in the register tier model.

(18) a. *Downstep* b. *Upstep*

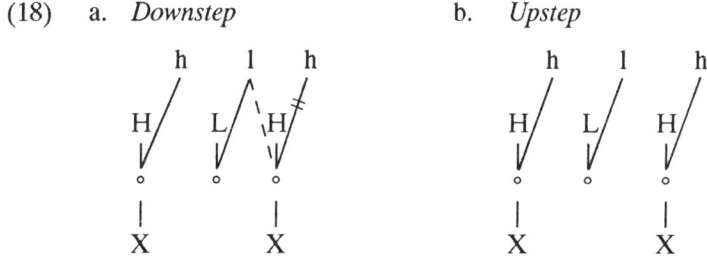

In both (18a) and (18b), the Low tone is unassociated, i.e., it is floating. In (18a), l-Spread has occurred and so the second High tone is downstepped in relation to the first High tone since it shares the lower register of the floating Low tone. In (18b), l-Spread has failed to occur and so the second High tone is upstepped in relation to the first High tone. This is due to the fact that the second TBU is associated with the higher register of the second High tone and so is "one step higher than the preceding register". Because the Low tone is floating, it is unable to have any direct influence on the surface realization. What its presence does do, however, is block the application of the OCP on the Register Tier, thereby preventing the two h's from collapsing into one. The model therefore reduces the difference between upstep and downstep in this type of environment to a single parameter choice; l-Spread, yes or no.

Like Yip (1980), Snider (1990) considers languages with more than four underlying levels of tone height (extremely rare) to be somehow special. The problem is important, however, and dealing with it is a matter of current investigation. The feature system of the register tier model therefore accommodates up to four underlying levels of tone. The different possibilities are set out in (19).

(19)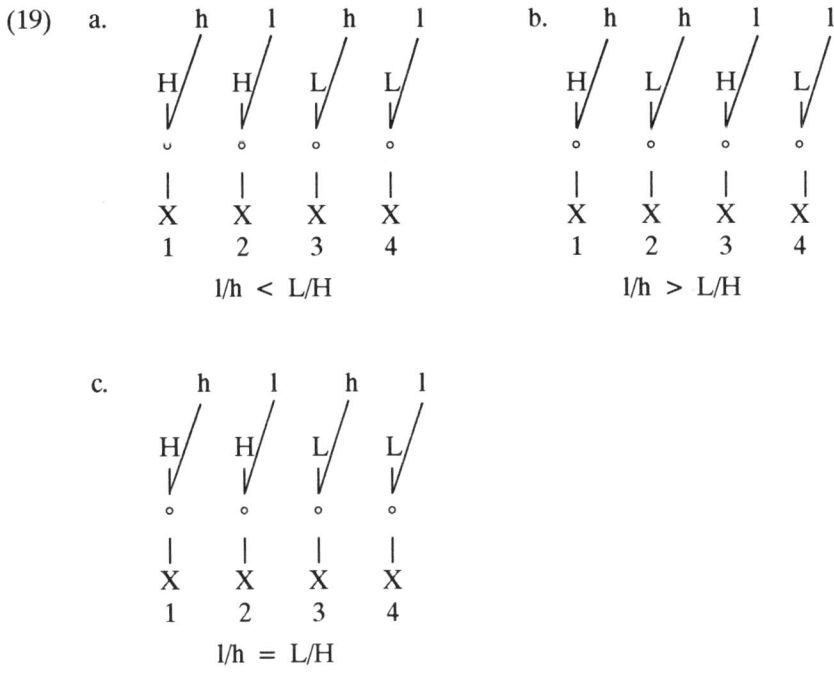

Let us assume that the phonetic difference attributable to the difference between l and h (register) is less than that attributable to the difference between L and H (mode). A language with these phonological characteristics could have up to four discrete levels of height, and its underlying tones would have the representations of (19a). A language with these same phonological characteristics reversed could also have up to four discrete levels of height, and its underlying tones would have the representations of (19b). A number of languages also have the phonological characteristics of (19c), in which the phonetic differences attributable to register are equivalent to those attributable to mode. Kagwe, mentioned above as having four underlying levels but only three surface levels (cf. Koopman and Sportiche 1982) would fit into this category. Many two-tone languages in Africa, including Krachi (discussed above), also have the phonological characteristics of (19c).

One thing which the register tier model has in common with other models that handle shifts of register in the phonological component concerns the relationship between downstepped High tones and underlying Mid tones. If upstep and downstep are dealt with in the phonological component, then it follows that an underlying High tone that has been downstepped will be phonologically nondistinct from one of the (potentially two) middle tones. This is because the same feature representation is being used for both.

Given the discussion immediately above, the Mid tone of a three tone system could have one of two feature characterizations: either (a) H mode and l register, or (b) L mode and h register. For those languages with three discrete levels of tone in which the Mid tone has the characterization of (a), this Mid tone will be phonologically and phonetically nondistinct from a downstepped High tone. And in a language with four underlying levels of tone, one of the two middle tones will be nondistinct from a downstepped High tone.

Two recent studies of tone provide overviews and critical discussions of both traditional and geometrical proposals for the representation of tonal phenomena (Bao 1990; Duanmu 1990). These proposals take up earlier ideas presented in Halle and Stevens (1971), in which a set of features is developed which generalize over tone and (most of the) phonation distinctions that seem relevant in natural languages. A similar undertaking can be found in Van der Hulst (1990/1991). All three proposals rigorously locate tonal distinctions under the laryngeal group of features in the following way:

(20)

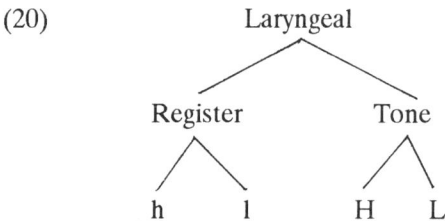

Bao (1990) and Duanmu (1990) use different feature names and there are a number of other differences that we will not discuss here. The importance of these proposals lies in the fact that an explicit connection is made between the tonal interpretation of the laryngeal features and the phonatory, especially voice (quality) interpretation of h and l. In her contribution to this volume, Yip also deals with such relations.

We feel that such proposals are compatible with the relative interpretation for register features proposed in the model of Snider (1990) but here we will not explore this point nor discuss how phonatory constriction features such as [Constricted] and [Spread] relate to the features in (20).

3. THE CONTRIBUTIONS TO THIS VOLUME

In this section we will briefly outline the content and essential claims of the contributions to this volume.

3.1. Mary Clark: Representation of downstep in Dschang Bamileke

This paper is a follow-up to Clark (1990), in which it is argued that register-lowering (downstep/downdrift) can be predicted from the tonal representation alone, with no need for a special "register" tier or metrical tree. In languages like Igbo, which have downstep between adjacent high tones and downdrift between high and low, register lowering can be accounted for by a phonetic-interpretation rule which lowers the pitch standard for high (and low) tones at the boundary between a high ([+UPPER]) tone and any following tone (T):

(21) $X^i \rightarrow X^{i+1}$ / [+UPPER] ___ T

(where X^n is the pitch standard for [+UPPER] tones at point n in the phonological representation; see Liberman and Pierrehumbert 1984 and Beckman and Pierrehumbert 1986).

Rule (21) applies, for example, at the points indicated by a raised exclamation point in the Igbo words below:

(22)   a!kàbó 'hedgehog'   é!gó 'coin' (cf. ewu 'goat')
         | | | | | \/
         H L H   H H   H

This analysis closely follows the proposals of Odden (1982) for Ki-Shambaa and Carlson (1983) for Supyire; in these analyses, the OCP is regarded not as a universal convention, but as a markedness condition which must be implemented by language-specific rules. Thus sequences of identical tonal features do occur, under some circumstances, and are realized with an intervening downstep, as in é!gó 'coin'.

In her article, Clark shows that an analysis along these lines can be applied, with good results, to Dschang Bamileke, which has downstep between high and low tones, but no downdrift:

(23)   a. tóŋó   [¯ ¯]   vs. tó!ŋó   [¯ _]
           'call (imperative)'   'reimburse (imperative)'
        b. èfɔ̀ màndzwì [_ _ _ _] 'chief of leopards'
           vs. àzɔ̀bɔ̀ màn!dzwì [_ _ _ _] 'song of leopards'

Languages of this sort have a register-lowering rule which applies at the boundary between identical tonal features, as follows:

(24) $X^i \rightarrow X^{i+1} / [\alpha T]$ ___ $[\alpha T]$, where 'T' is a tonal feature.

The "downstepped high" tone which follows a low tone, as in **mǝm¹bhʉ** 'dogs', must be treated as a mid tone, as proposed by Hyman (1985), with the features [+UPPER,−RAISED]. In other words, both tonal features—[UPPER] and [RAISED]—are employed in Dschang. This has interesting consequences for the downstep rule, in that the downstep environment (24) may occur on either tonal tier (the [UPPER] tier or the [RAISED] tier), or on both tiers at once, creating a double downstep, as in the form **à kè ¹kóŋó ‼ mó** 'He liked a child (yesterday)', whose representation is given below, with the feature [+UPPER] abbreviated as H/L, and the feature [+RAISED] as h/l:

(25)
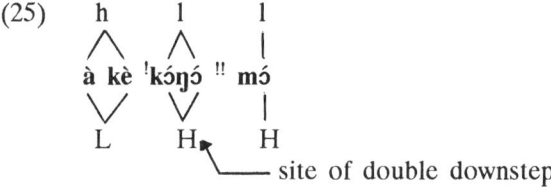
       site of double downstep

The discussion of Dschang downstep is couched within a complete analysis of the associative construction, which improves on previous treatments of this construction, in that it avoids the metathesis rule of Pulleyblank (1986), and the "tier-hopping" and re-structuring rules of Hyman (1985).

3.2. Larry Hyman: Register tones and tonal geometry

In this volume, Hyman proposes a geometry for tonal features which recognizes two structural nodes, a tonal node (TN) and a tonal root node (TRN). There are two features, privative H and L which may associate to the tonal node or to the tonal root node. In the former case these features characterize tone levels, whereas in the latter case they characterize register distinctions. If H and L both associate to the tonal node, a mid tone is the result.

(25)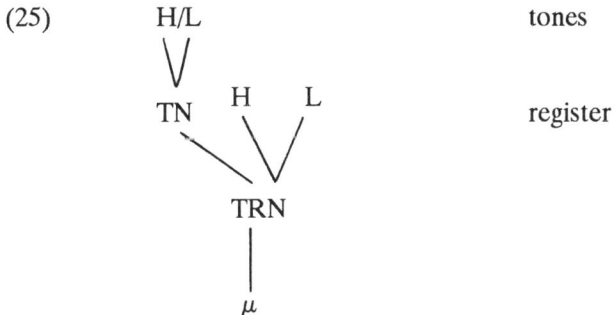

There are nine distinct representations:

(26)   (a)   (b)   (c)   (d)   (e)   (f)   (g)   (h)   (i)

T-plane: H   L   LH   H   L   LH   H   L   LH

R-plane: ∅   ∅   ∅   L   L   L   H   H   H

TONE: H   L   M   ↓H   ↓L   ↓M   ↑H   ↑L   ↑M

Note that in the model discussed in the previous section, the occurrence of both H and L (or h and l) does not produce a mid tone but rather a contour tone.

Hyman's model allows a wider variety of tonal assimilation processes than most other current proposals and Hyman briefly refers to suitable candidates for most of the logical possibilities. His system makes available a number of raised tones (↑L, ↑M and ↑H). The use of the first two is less obvious, but raised H can be identified as an upstepped H tone. Hyman then offers a discussion of upstep in three languages: Engenni, Mankon and Kirimi. In all cases we find an upstepping process by which a H tone is raised before a L. Hyman proposes that high tone raising results from assigning a floating L as a register specification to a following H or sequence of Hs. Then a single H is raised (this is accomplished by a H register specification which is inserted for this purpose) before a L, provided that this H tone is itself not associated to a L register feature by the first-mentioned rule. Hyman argues that the need for a register H feature can be demonstrated independently.

3.3. Bob Ladd: In defense of a metrical theory of intonational downstep

This paper defends the proposal in Ladd (1990) that register shifts in English and other intonation languages are controlled by "register trees" —abstract prosodic structures in which the relative height of prosodic constituents is specified—rather than being the result of a phonetic realization rule affecting sequences of abstract tones (as proposed by Pierrehumbert 1980, Clark this volume, and others). The motivation for this proposal is that it allows a common phonological representation for all downstepping contours without running into the difficulties of the "feature" notation proposed by Ladd (1983). An equally important advantage is that it provides a natural representation for the widely observed "nesting" of downstep (accent-to-accent, phrase-to-phrase) in utterances with fairly deep surface syntactic structure.

Ladd argues that the apparent attractiveness of Pierrehumbert's proposal depends crucially on doubtful assumptions about (a) the distinction between linguistic and paralinguistic functions of pitch phenomena, (b) the phonetic modelling of pitch range, and (c) prosodic structure.

Specifically, he claims that:

(a) Pierrehumbert is forced to treat phrase-level downstep as "paralinguistic", though the independent motivation for this is not convincing; conversely, she is forced to ignore the fact that overall modification of pitch range ("raising the voice") seems to work independently of phrase level downstep, though the two are treated identically in their model.

(b) Pierrehumbert is led, by the distinction between accent-level and phrase-level downstep, to treat the former as a narrowing of pitch range and the latter as a lowering, though this will make it impossible to model downstep in true tone languages (like Yoruba) in a unified way.

(c) She is forced to treat list intonation (in the Liberman and Pierrehumbert experiment on the quantitative invariance of downstep) as *not* involving phrase boundaries between the elements of the list, since those would block downstep in their model.

A discussion of Ladd's model is found in Clements (1990).

3.4. Victor Manfredi: Spreading and downstep: prosodic government in tone languages

Manfredi expresses a critical view on many influential studies of Benue-Kwa tone systems in the 1970's and 1980's.

He adopts and extends Bamba's (1984) proposal regarding the relationship between tone and metrical structure. This proposal replaces the "register tone" theory propounded by Manfredi (1979), Huang (1980), Clements (1981), Inkelas et al. (1987). He accepts and follows Kaye, Lowenstamm and Vergnaud (1987) and Charette (1988) with respect to phonological licensing in a constraint-and-principles based framework. His approach accounts for a wide range of tone systems in the typological space of the Benue-Kwa languages. The position of true mid tones in this typology is problematic, but Manfredi suggests that there is evidence that three-tone systems respect the same basic principles as two-tone systems. The fact that both H and L spread in Yorùbá (a three-tone system) suggests that both H and L can be strong only if there is a third possibility which is always weak (cf. Láníràn 1991).

Contrary to Clark (this vol.), Manfredi supports a strong version of the OCP and provides analyses of the major nominal and verbal constructions of Igbo which account for the same facts which Clark (1990) analyzes in a model that suspends the OCP.

In both Igbo and ɣɔmálá?-Yamba, the reanalyses proposed in the article rely on specific syntactic analyses—information not directly accessed by the respective rule-based analyses of Clark (1990) and Hyman (1985). It is argued that this tight interface between syntax and prosody is desirable, within a cognitively based generative grammar. Most of the alternative "floating tone" analyses are claimed to require extremely abstract underlying forms, which are based mainly on historically reconstructed forms.

3.5. John Stewart: Dschang and Ebrié as Akan-type tonal downstep languages

Dschang, a language with overt downstep, but without the overt automatic downstep of the classic downstep languages, and Ebrié, a discrete level language with three discrete levels, the mid tones of which are analyzable as downstepped high tones (Kutsch Lojenga 1985), display remarkable resemblances. Stewart analyses both as having, on a separate tonal tier, not only the same two binary tone features [high] and [stepping] but also the same four tonal autosegments, namely the two [−stepping], or linking, tones L̲, H̲, which may be linked or unlinked but which are not realized unless they are linked, and the two [+stepping] tones l, h, which are never linked and which are realized as downstep and upstep respectively. Downstep, as in Stewart's (1983) analysis of Adioukrou and Akan, is total in the sense that it consists of a downward stepping of the tone level frame to the point at which a following H̱ would be level with a preceding Ḻ; upstep is similarly an upward stepping of the frame to the point at which a following Ḻ would be level with a preceding H̱.

Dschang and Ebrié differ from Akan in a way that has not been recognized in any previous analysis of either language: they have a tonal autosegment that Akan lacks, namely the [+high, +stepping] segment h which is realized as upstep.

Dschang and Ebrié also resemble Akan in a way that has not been recognized in any previous analysis of either language: they have automatic downstep in the sense that they have H̱lḺ to the exclusion of H̱Ḻ. They further resemble Akan in that they eliminate inadmissible H̱Ḻ sequences, arising at word boundaries for instance, mainly by means of a low tone stepping rule which changes Ḻ to l after H̱.

Dschang and Ebrié have not only automatic downstep but also automatic upstep, or ḺhH̱ to the exclusion of ḺH̱. In Ebrié, moreover, though not in Dschang, upstep, whether automatic or non-automatic, is balanced against downstep in such a way that the linking tones are realized on three discrete levels.

Now Akan, with its infinite number of surface levels, and Ebrié, with its three surface levels, are representative of the two most common types of tone language found among the Niger-Congo languages of West Africa. Stewart tentatively suggests that, historically, systems like that of Ebrié develop from systems like that of Akan by bringing in upstep to reduce the number of surface levels from infinity to three. This is particularly plausible if it is correct, as is commonly supposed, that systems like that of Akan themselves develop from simple two-tone systems by the introduction of downstep: the introduction of downstep creates a gap, and that gap is sometimes subsequently filled by the introduction of upstep.

3.6. Moria Yip: Tonal register in East Asian Languages

Yip distinguishes between three different uses of the term register:

1. tonal register, dividing the pitch of the voice into two ranges, called [+upper] and [−upper]

2. phonation register, giving laryngeal characteristics such as murmur and creaky voice
3. intonation register, determining the level on which a lexical tone is actually realized in an utterance

1. Tonal register

Four level tones are distinguished by two binary features, [upper] and [raised]. Contour tones hold the register feature [upper] constant, and have sequences of values for [raised]: for example, a high rising tone is [+upper], [−raised, +raised]. Yip offers two types of evidence for this representation. First, there are rules which delete the [raised] value(s), but leave [upper] intact, as in Taiwanese and Suzhou. Second, there are rules which spread register, but leave [raised] unaffected (e.g. Fuzhou).

2. Phonation register

In Shanghai and Tibetan, there is a close connection between phonation and pitch, such that [−upper] syllables have voiced murmured onsets, and low pitch. In certain contexts, all tonal contrasts and murmur disappear in Shanghai, suggesting that the feature responsible for murmur is a tonal feature. In Tibetan, on the other hand, all laryngeal contrasts and murmur disappear together, suggesting that the feature responsible for murmur is a laryngeal feature. It is suggested that the feature [murmur] requires domination by both laryngeal and tonal nodes, and that deletion of either of these nodes causes loss of murmur. This special behavior, Yip suggests, shows that [murmur] cannot be identified with the purely tonal register feature, [−upper].

3a. Intonation register

The interaction between tone and intonation in Hausa and Mandarin shows that intonation register is to be distinguished from tonal register and is instead a way of realizing a particular tone (with all its features) phonetically. Inkelas, Leben and Cobler's (1987) use of "register" for Hausa intonation differs from tonal register in Chinese in two striking ways. First, their register effects a permanent resetting of the pitch range for the remainder of the utterance, not just that syllable. Second, there is a close connection between lexical Ls and L register, and lexical Hs and H register, unlike the four possible combinations found within lexical tone in Chinese.

3b. Chinese intonation

In Mandarin, contrastive stress raises high tones, and leaves alone or lowers low ones. It is argued that the phonetic scaling operation (Shih 1988) must include as its input not just tonal register [upper], but also the other tonal feature, [raised].

REFERENCES

Anderson, Stephen R. 1978. "Tone Features." In *Tone: a Linguistic Survey*, edited by Victoria A. Fromkin, 133–75. New York: Academic Press.
Archangeli, Diana and Douglas Pulleyblank. 1986. *The Content and Structure of Phonological Representations*. Ms. To appear, Cambridge, Mass.: MIT Press.
Bamba, Moussa. 1984. *Etudes phonologiques du Mahou*. Master's thesis, Université du Québec à Montreal.
Bao, Zhiming. 1990. "On the Nature of Tone." Ph.D. dissertation, Massachusetts Institute of Technology, Cambridge.
Bearth, Thomas and Hugo Zemp. 1967. "The Phonology of Dan (Santa)." *Journal of African Languages* 6, 9–29.
Beckman, Mary E. and Janet E. Pierrehumbert. 1986. "Intonational Structure in Japanese and English." *Phonology Yearbook* 3, 255–309.
Carlson, Robert. 1983. "Downstep in Supyira." *Studies in African Linguistics* 14, 35–45.
Chan, Marjorie K. M. forthcoming. "Contour-tone Spreading and Tone Sandhi in Danyang Chinese." To appear in *Phonology* 8.
Chang, Kun. 1953. "On the Tone System of the Miao-Yao Languages." *Language* 29, 374–78.
Charette, Monik. 1988. "Some Constraints on Governing Relation in Phonology." Ph.D. dissertation, McGill University, Montreal.
Chomsky, Noam and Morris Halle. 1968. *The Sound Pattern of English*. New York: Harper and Row.
Clark, Mary. 1990. *The Tonal System of Igbo*. Dordrecht: Foris Publications.
Clements, George N. 1976. "Tone as Speech Melody: a New Theory of Terracing." In *Proceedings of NELS 6*, 49–66.
———. 1979. "The Description of Terraced-Level Tone Languages." *Language* 55, 536–58.
———. 1981. "The Hierarchical Representation of Tone." In *Harvard Studies in Phonology*. Vol. 2, ed. by George N. Clements, 108–77. Cambridge, Mass.: Harvard University Linguistics Department.
———. 1983. "The Hierarchical Representation of Tone Features." In *Current Approaches to African Linguistics*. Vol. 1, ed. by Ivan R. Dihoff, 145–76. Dordrecht: Foris Publications.
———. 1985. "The Geometry of Phonological Features." *Phonology Yearbook* 2, 225–52.
———. 1990. "The Status of Register in Intonation Theory: Comments on the Papers by Ladd and by Inkelas and Leben." In *Papers in Laboratory Phonology I: between Grammar and Physics of Speech*, edited by Mary E. Beckman and J. Kingston, 58–72. Cambridge: Mass.: Cambridge University Press.
Cope, A.T. 1970. "Zulu Tonal Morphology." *Journal of African Languages* 9, 111–52.
Dikken, Marcel den, and Harry van der Hulst. 1988. "Segmental Hierarchitecture." In *Features, Segmental Structure and Harmony Processes*. Part I, edited by Harry van der Hulst and Norval Smith, 1–79. Dordrecht: Foris Publications.
Duanmu, San. 1990. "A Formal Study of Syllable, Tone, Stress and Domain in Chinese Languages." Ph.D. dissertation, Massachusetts Institute of Technology, Cambridge.
Flik, Eva. 1977. "Tone Glides and Registers in five Dan Dialects." *Linguistics* 201, 5–59.
Goldsmith, John. 1976. "Autosegmental Phonology." Ph.D. dissertation, Massachusetts Institute of Technology, Cambridge. [Reproduced by the Indiana University Linguistics Club.]
Gruber, Jeffrey. 1964. "The Distinctive Features of Tone. Ms. Massachusetts Institute of Technology, Cambridge.
Halle, Morris and K. Stevens. 1971. "A Note on Laryngeal Features." *MIT Research Laboratory of Electronics Quarterly Report* 101, 198–213.

Hollenbach, Barbara E. 1984. "The Phonology and Morphology of Tone and Laryngeals in Copala Trique." Ph.D. dissertation, University of Arizona, Tempeh.
———. 1988. "The Asymetrical Distribution of Tone in Copala Trique." In *Autosegmental Studies on Pitch Accent*, edited by Harry Van der Hulst and Norval Smith, 167–82. Dordrecht:Foris Publications.
Huang, Cheng-Teh James. 1980. "The Metrical Structure of Terraced-Level Tones." In *Proceedings of NELS 10*. Cahiers Linguistiques d"Ottawa 9, 257–70.
Hulst, Harry van der. 1988. "The Geometry of Vocalic Features." In *Features, Segmental Structure and Harmony Processes*. Part II, edited by Harry van der Hulst and Norval Smith, 77–125. Dordrecht: Foris Publications.
———. 1991. *On the Nature of Phonological Primes*. Ms., Leiden University. [2nd version of "The Book of Segments: the Molecular Structure of Phonological Segments", 1990.]
Hyman, Larry M. 1979. "A Reanalysis of Tonal Downstep." *Journal of African Languages and Linguistics* 1, 9–29.
———. 1985. "Word Domains and Downstep in Bamiléké-Dschang." *Phonology Yearbook* 2, 47–83.
———. 1986. "The Representation of Multiple Tone Heights." In *The Phonological Representation of Suprasegmentals*, edited by Koen Bogers, Harry van der Hulst and Maarten Mous, 109–52. Dordrecht: Foris Publications.
Hyman, Larry M., and Daniel Magaji. 1970. "Elements of Gwari Grammar." *Occasional Publication No. 27, Institute of African Studies*, University of Ibadan.
Hyman, Larry M., and Douglas Pulleyblank. 1988. "On Feature Copying: Parameters of Tone rules." In *Language, Speech and Mind: Studies in Honour of Victoria A. Fromkin*, edited by Larry M. Hyman and Charles N. Li, 30–48. London: Routledge.
Inkelas, Sharon. 1987. "Tone Feature Geometry." In *Proceedings of NELS 18*, edited by James Blevins and Juli Carter, 223–37. Amherst, Mass.: GLSA.
———. 1989. "Register Tone and the Phonological Representation of Downstep." In *Current Approaches to African Linguistics*. Vol. 6, ed. by Isabelle Haïk and Laurice Tuller, 65–82. Dordrecht: Foris.
Inkelas, Sharon, and William R. Leben. 1990. "Where Phonology and Phonetics Intersect. the Case of Hausa Intonation." In *Papers in Laboratory Phonology I: between the Grammar and Physics of Speech*, ed. by Mary E. Beckman and J. Kingston, 17–35. Cambridge, Mass.: Cambridge University Press.
Inkelas, Sharon, William R. Leben, and Mark Cobler. 1987. "The Phonology of Intonation in Hausa." In *Proceedings of NELS 18*, ed. by James Blevins and Juli Carter, 327–42, Amherst, Mass.: GLSA.
Johnson, C. Douglas. 1972. *Formal Aspects of Phonological Description*. The Hague: Mouton.
Kaye, Jonathan, Jean Lowenstamm, and Jean-Roger Vergnaud. 1987. "Constituent Structure and Government in Phonology." *Phonology* 7, 193–232.
Koopman, Hilda and Dominique Sportiche. 1982. "Le ton abstrait du kagwe." In *Projet sur les Langues Kru*, edited by Jonathan Kaye et al., 46–59.
Kutsch Lojenga, Constance. 1985. "The Tones of the Ebrié Associative Construction." *Journal of African Languages and Linguistics* 7, 1–22.
Ladd, D.R. 1983. "Phonological Features of Intonational Peaks." *Language* 59, 721–59.
———. 1990. "Metrical Representations of Pitch Register." In *Papers in Laboratory Phonology I: between the Grammar and Physics of Speech*, edited by John Kingston and Mary E. Beckman, 35–58. Cambridge, Mass.: Cambridge University Press.
Lánírán, Yétundé. 1991. "Intonation in Tone Languages: the Yoruba Example." Ph.D. dissertation, Cornell University, Ithaca, NY.
Leben, William R. 1971. "Suprasegmental and Segmental Representation of Tone." In *Studies in African Linguistics, Supplement 2*, 183–200.
———. 1973. *Suprasegmental Phonology*. Ph.D. dissertation, Massachusetts Institute of Technology, Cambridge. [Published, New York: Garland, 1979.]

Liberman, Mark and Janet Pierrehumbert. 1984. "Intonational Invariance under Changes in Pitch Range and Length." In *Language Sound Structure*, edited by Mark Aronoff and Richard T. Oehrle, 157–233. Cambridge, Mass.: MIT Press.

Longacre, Robert E. 1952. "Five Phonemic Pitch Levels in Trique." *Acta Linguistica* 7, 62–82.

Maddieson, Ian. 1978. "Universals of Tone." In *Universals of Human Language*, edited by Joseph H. Greenberg, 335–67. Stanford, Cal.: Stanford University Press.

Manfredi, Victor. 1979. *Morphologization of Downstep in Igbo Dialects.* Bachelor's thesis, Cambridge, Mass.: Harvard University.

McCarthy, John. 1988. "Feature Geometry and Dependency: a Review." *Phonetica* 43, 84–108.

Newman, Roxana Ma. 1971. "Downstep in Ga'anda." *Journal of African Languages* 10, 15–27.

Odden, David. 1982. "Tonal Phenomena in KiShambaa." *Studies in African Linguistics* 13, 177–208.

Peters, Ann M. 1973. "A New Formalization of Downdrift." *Studies in African Linguistics* 4, 139–54.

Pierrehumbert, Janet B. 1980. "The Phonology and Phonetics of English Intonation." Ph.D. dissertation, Massachusetts Institute of Technology, Cambridge.

Pierrehumbert, Janet B. and Mary E. Beckman. 1989. *Japanese Tone Structure.* Cambridge, Mass.: MIT Press.

Pike, Kenneth L. 1948. *Tone Languages.* Ann Arbor: University of Michigan Press.

———. 1966. *Tagmemic and Matrix Linguistics Applied to Selected African Languages.* [Reprinted 1970 by the Summer Institute of Linguistics of the University of Oklahoma, Norman.]

Pulleyblank, Douglas. 1983. "Tone in Lexical Phonology". Ph.D. dissertation, Massachusetts Institute of Technology, Cambridge. [Published 1986, Reidel.]

Russell, Jann M. 1986. *Some Tone Perturbation Rules in Moba.* Ms., Summer Institute in Linguistics, Togo.

Sagey, E. 1986. "The Representation of Features and Relations in Non-linear Phonology." Ph.D. dissertation, Massachusetts Institute of Technology, Cambridge.

Schachter, Paul. 1961. "Phonetic Similarity in Tonemic Analysis." *Language* 37, 231–38.

Shih, Chi-Lin. 1988. "The Prosodic Domain of Tone Sandhi in Chinese." Ph.D. dissertation, University of California at San Diego.

Snider, Keith L. 1988. "Towards the Representation of Tone: a Three-Dimensional Approach." In *Features, Segmental Structure and Harmony Processes.* Vol. 1, ed. by Harry van der Hulst and Norval Smith, 237–69. Dordrecht: Foris Publications.

———. 1990. "Tonal Upstep in Krachi: Evidence for a Register Tier." *Language* 66, 453–74.

Stahlke, Herbert. 1977. "Some Problems with Binary Features for Tones." *International Journal of American Linguistics* 35, 62–66.

Stewart, John M. 1965. "The Typology of the Twi Tone System." *Bulletin of the Institute of African Studies 1.* Legon, Ghana: Institute of African Studies, University of Ghana.

———. 1971. "Niger-Congo, Kwa." In *Current Trends in Linguistics.* Vol. 7: *Linguistics in Sub-Saharan Africa*, edited by Thomas Sebeok, 179–212. The Hague: Mouton.

———. 1983. "Downstep and Floating Low Tones in Adioukrou." *Journal of African Languages and Linguistics* 5, 57–78.

Wang, W. 1967. "Phonological Features of Tone." *International Journal of American Linguistics* 33, 93–105.

Wedekind, Klaus. 1983. "A Six-tone Language in Ethiopia." *Journal of Ethiopian Studies* 16, 129–56.

Welmers, William E. 1973. *African Language Structures.* Berkeley: University of California Press.

Williams, Edwin S. 1976. "Underlying Tone in Margi and Igbo." *Linguistic Inquiry* 7, 463–84.
Winston, Denis. 1960. "The 'mid tone' in Efik." *African Language Studies* 1, 85–192.
Woo, Nancy. 1969. "Prosody and Phonology." Ph.D. dissertation, Massachusetts Institute of Technology, Cambridge. [Reproduced by the Indiana University Linguistics Club.]
Yip, Moira J. 1980. "The Tonal Phonology of Chinese." Ph.D. dissertation, Massachusetts Institute of Technology, Cambridge. [Reproduced by the Indiana University Linguistics Club.]
———. 1989. "Contour Tones." *Phonology* 6, 149–74.

Representation of Downstep in Dschang Bamileke

Mary M. Clark

1. DOWNSTEP AND TONAL REGISTER

This paper will be concerned with the phonological representation of downstep, with particular application to Dschang Bamileke. This question has implications for the representation of tonal register in the following way:

It has been proposed by Hyman (1985), Inkelas, Leben, and Cobler (1988, henceforth: ILC), and others, that register lowering (downdrift and downstep) should be represented on a special tier called the "register tier", which also contains intonational information such as the rise in pitch at the end of a question. For example, under ILC's proposal, the Hausa statement **Yáa áikàa wà Máanú làabárìn wánnàn yáaròn álàrámmá** 'He sent Manu news of this boy of the alaramma' is represented as follows, where the brackets represent intonational phrases, and the L tones on the register tier represent points of register lowering. (In ILC's proposal, downdrift is a result of the spreading of the register L tones onto the following H):

(1)
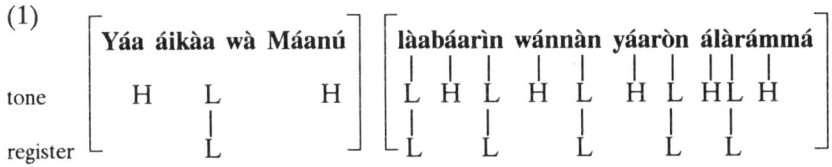

Notice, however, that since downdrift is phonologically predictable (it occurs whenever a low tone is followed by high), the information on the register tier in (1) is redundant. Thus this tier can be dispensed with, as shown in (2), with a register-lowering rule that reads directly off the tonal tier:

(2)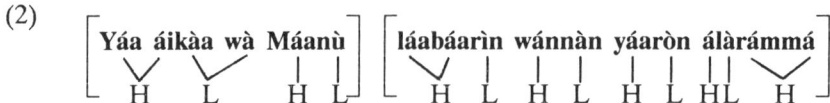

How should the register-lowering rule be stated? Liberman and Pierrehumbert (1984) and Beckman and Pierrehumbert (1986) have argued that tones are interpreted in terms of a pitch standard, X, which is adjusted upward or downward at particular points in the utterance; for example, the value of X is adjusted upward at the beginning of an intonational phrase, and downward at points of register lowering (downdrift or downstep). In English and Japanese, the degree of lowering at each register lowering point is proportional to the height of X at that point above a reference pitch r, which is constant for a given speaker. In other words,

(3) $X_{i+1} - r = s \cdot (X_i - r)$

(where s is the register-lowering constant, and X_i and X_{i+1} are the values of X before and after register lowering)

I suggest, then, that the Downdrift rule is simply an instruction to apply rule (3) in a particular phonological position; in other words, the Downdrift rule for Hausa is stated as follows:

(4) $X_i \rightarrow X_{i+1}$ (by the formula of (3)) / L __ H

Since the environment for this rule is provided by the tonal representation itself, there is no need for a register tier.[1]

---

1 Inkelas, Leben, and Cobler do not argue that the register tier is needed to account for Downdrift itself—obviously, it is not. Rather they argue that this tier is needed to account for the interaction between Downdrift and Final Raising at the end of a question. What needs to be explained is the fact that although Final Raising itself is confined to the last syllable or two, Downdrift is suspended throughout the entire final intonational phrase. In ILC's proposal, Final Raising consists of two processes: (i) a phonetic-interpretation rule that raises the realization for H at the end of a question, and (ii) a rule that assigns a register H tone to every high tone within the final intonational phrase:

(i)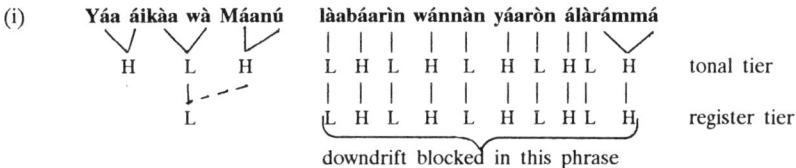

While this solution works well for down*drift*, it is not immediately clear that it can be extended to down*step*. The problem is that sequences of high (or low) tones may be found either with or without an intervening downstep, as illustrated by the following examples from Dschang, taken from Hyman (1985):

(5) a. tóŋɔ́   [⁻ ⁻]   vs. tó¹ŋɔ́   [⁻ _]

      'call (imperative)'   'reimburse (imperative)'

b. èfɔ̀ màndzwì [_ _ _ _ ┐] 'chief of leopards'

vs. àzɔ̀bɔ̀ màn¹dzwì [_ _ _ _ ┐] 'song of leopards'

Despite contrasts like these, which suggest that downstep is not predictable from the phonological representation proper, I will argue in this paper that downstep *is* phonologically predictable, and therefore no independent representation is needed for register phenomena.[2]

The register H tones block the application of Downdrift in the final phrase (cf. the statement version of this sentence in (1)).

Notice, however, that if the phonetic-interpretation portion of the Final Raising rule is stated correctly, then this rule, by itself, can account for both Final Raising effects. What is needed is a rule that raises the value of x at an accelerating pace throughout the final intonational phrase—something like the following:

(ii) $X_t - r = k \cdot \dfrac{l(X_n - r)}{l - t}$

where t is a point within the final intonational phrase (measured from the beginning of the phrase), l is the length of the final intonation phrase, k is the Final Raising constant, and X_n is the value that X would have without the effects of Final Raising)

By this rule, the value of X rises gradually at the beginning of the phrase, enough to counterbalance the effects of Downdrift; however, at the end of the phrase there is a very sharp rise in pitch. (Note that, as stated, rule (ii) creates an *infinite* rise in pitch at the end of the phrase. In an actual utterance, of course, X rises only to the top of the pitch range of the speaker's voice).

2 My argument has been stated here in terms of the register-tier proposal of Inkelas, Leben, and Cobler. However, the argument holds equally well against metrical representations of Downdrift, like that of Clements (1981) and Huang (1980). As far as I can see, there is no need for a special representation of any sort for register-lowering phenomena.

2. A PHONOLOGICAL REPRESENTATION FOR DOWNSTEP: THE FLOATING-TONE APPROACH

A number of linguists, especially Clements and Ford (1979) and Pulleyblank (1986), have argued that downstep is conditioned, phonologically, by a floating low tone. In this view, the contrasts of (5) are represented as follows:

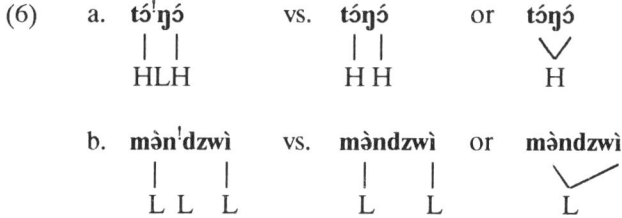

Pulleyblank (1986) argues for this approach on the grounds that it allows a very simple account of the downstep that sometimes appears at the site of a deleted low, as in the example below, from Dschang:

(7) ɲɲi e səŋ → ɲɲi e səŋ → ɲɲǐ ! śəŋ   'machete of bird
     | | | | | | | | |⌐| |
     L H L H   L H L H   L H LH

Under this analysis, the low tone is, of course, not actually deleted, but remains in the representation as a floating tone, and serves as a downstep operator. However, the nice results in this case must be balanced against several serious *dis*advantages of this approach, as follows: first, this framework requires a radical suspension of the Obligatory Contour Principle in Dschang, in that floating low tones must be maintained in the representation even when surrounded by low tones, as in (6b).[3] Secondly, this framework creates an unprincipled distinction between tonal and non-tonal features, in that it requires (some) floating tonal features to be retained in the phonological representation, and even to receive a phonetic interpretation, a power which has never, to my

---

3 This objection could be avoided, in this case, by re-analyzing the floating low tone in (6b) as a floating *high*. However, this solution would not help with the downstep that occurs between low and high, as in the word ǹ'dóŋ 'horn':

(i)   ǹ'dóŋ   'horn'
      | |
      LLH

knowledge, been claimed for *non*-tonal features. Thirdly, this approach makes an unprincipled distinction between floating and non-floating tones, in that, in languages like Dschang, which do not exhibit down*drift*, the register lowering rule must apply only in the environment of a *floating* low tone, thereby raising the question of why a *floating* low tone should affect the pitch register when a linked low does not. Finally, this approach is *empirically* problematical for many languages. For example in Dschang, contrary to what is suggested by the example of (5), the downstep in the surface form usually does not occupy the site of the deleted low. For example, consider the phrase àzɔ̀bɔ̀ ¹mə́tsɔ́ŋ 'tail of thieves', which Pulleyblank derives as follows:

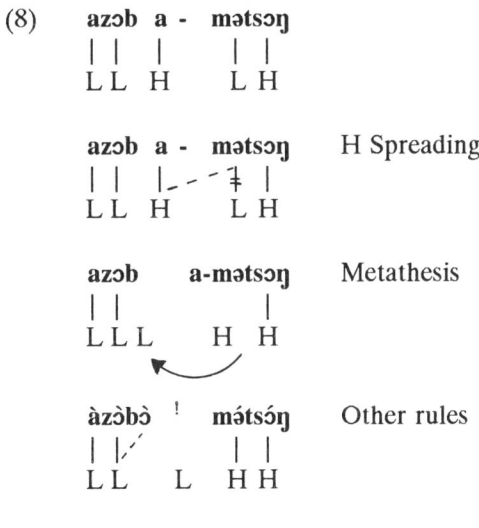

To move the downstep to the correct position in (8), Pulleyblank requires a metathesis rule, which he states as follows (1986:50):

(9)   L H L'   {H /]}

        1 2 3   4   → 1 3 2 4

Condition: No word boundary intervenes between 2 and 4.

The complex environmental restrictions on this rule are necessary to prevent the rule from applying to forms like (7), as well as other sorts of of cases which meet its structural description, but do not undergo the rule.

Hyman (1985) suggests that the environmental restrictions on rule (9) can be eliminated by introducing a postlexical re-structuring rule, which converts the *lexical* words (GWs) into *phonological* words (PWs), by removing the associative and gender prefixes and re-attaching them to the preceding word, if any:

(10) Original Word Division   Word Division after Re-structuring
      (GWs)   (PWs)

a. $\begin{bmatrix} \text{ɲ-ɲi} \\ | \ | \\ \text{L H} \end{bmatrix} \begin{bmatrix} \text{e-sǝŋ} \\ | \ | \\ \text{L H} \end{bmatrix} \rightarrow \begin{bmatrix} \text{ɲ} \\ | \\ \text{L} \end{bmatrix} \begin{bmatrix} \text{ɲi-e} \\ | \ | \\ \text{HL} \end{bmatrix} \begin{bmatrix} \text{sǝŋ} \\ | \\ \text{H} \end{bmatrix}$

(for (7) above)

b. $\begin{bmatrix} \text{azɔb} \\ | \ | \\ \text{L L} \end{bmatrix} \begin{bmatrix} \text{a-mǝtsɔŋ} \\ | \ | \ | \\ \text{H L H} \end{bmatrix} \rightarrow \begin{bmatrix} \text{a} \\ | \\ \text{L} \end{bmatrix} \begin{bmatrix} \text{zɔb-a-mǝ} \\ | \ | \ | \\ \text{L H L} \end{bmatrix} \begin{bmatrix} \text{tsɔŋ} \\ | \\ \text{H} \end{bmatrix}$

(for (8) above)

If (postlexical) H Spreading and Metathesis are defined on the domain PW, then Metathesis can be stated simply as follows, and it will apply, correctly, in (b) but not in (a):

(11) X   X
      | |
      L   H   L

As Hyman points out, however, this proposal does not completely solve the problems of the floating-tone analysis, since even "simple" metathesis rules like (11) have generally been regarded as theoretically undesirable. I would suggest, in addition, that the re-structuring rule itself is theoretically suspect, in that it rips apart a lexically-constructed word, in violation of the usual assumptions about lexical integrity.[4] To make

---

[4] Notice that Hyman's restructuring rule requires information about the location of the boundary between the prefixes and the stem, in contradiction to the Bracket Erasure Convention of Mohanan (1982). In fact, I agree with Hyman that there are postlexical rules in Dschang which are sensitive to the boundary between the prefix and the stem (see the

matters worse, there is an empirical problem with Hyman's word divisions, in that neither of his divisions (neither the GWs nor the PWs) provides the grouping that is needed for the rule of Contour Formation, which converts underlying forms like /ɲɲí/ 'machete' and /mə̀tsɔ́ŋ/ 'horn' to ɲɲĭ and mə̀tsɔ̌ŋ. This rule applies to a noun in phrase-final position, and also to the head noun of an associative phrase, if that noun ends with a vowel, as in (12a) below; however, the rule does not apply in examples like (12b), where the head noun ends underlyingly with a consonant.

(12) a. /ɲɲí + è + mə̀tsɔ́ŋ/ → ɲɲĭ mə̀tsɔ̌ŋ
'machete of thieves'
b. /àsáŋ + á + mə̀tsɔ́ŋ/ → àsáŋ-á mə̀¹tsɔ́ŋ (*àsăŋ á mə́¹tsɔ́ŋ)
'tail of thieves'

What needs to be said, it seems, is that Contour Formation applies *at the end of a word*, after the rule that merges the particle with the preceding vowel in (a). But this requires still a *third* word division, different from either the GWs or the PWs, in which the associative particle, but not the noun prefix, is suffixed to the first member of the phrase; in other words, there must be two re-structuring rules, as shown below:

(13) a. b.
[ɲɲí] [è-mə̀-tsɔ́ŋ]   [àsáŋ] [á-mə̀-tsɔ́ŋ]   Lexical grouping (GW's)
[ɲɲí-è-mə̀] [tsɔ́ŋ]   [àsáŋ-á-mə̀] [tsɔ́ŋ]   RESTRUCTURING #1
[ɲɲí-é-mə̀] [tsɔ́ŋ]   [àsáŋ-á-mə́] [tsɔ́ŋ]   H Spreading
[ɲɲí-é] [mə̀-tsɔ́ŋ]   [àsáŋ-á] [mə́`-tsɔ́ŋ]   RE-STRUCTURING #2
[ɲɲí] [è-mə̀tsɔ́ŋ]   ———   Assimilation and merger of particle vowel

[ɲɲĭ] [mə̀tsɔ̌ŋ]   ———   Contour Formation
[ɲɲĭ] [mə̀tsɔ̌ŋ]   [àsáŋá] [mə́¹tsɔ́ŋ]   OUTPUT

Clearly, there are serious unsolved *empirical* problems in the floating tone analysis, in addition to the theoretical problems which were pointed out above.

---

discussion of the rule of Contour Formation I in section 4.2 below). Apparently, the first syllable of the stem has some special phonological property—I assume stress—which distinguishes it from the other syllable(s). (Stewart 1981 makes a similar proposal, using the term "solid", rather than "stressed", for the special phonological property that distinguishes the first syllable of the stem. For empirical evidence that what is involved here is stress, see the derivations of (68) and (69) below, and the accompanying discussion.)

3. THE TONAL-FEATURE APPROACH

Carrell (1970), Goldsmith (1976), and Hyman (1985) have proposed a different representation of downstep, using a secondary tonal feature. In the most recent version of this proposal (that of Hyman 1985), downstep is created by the same tonal feature which, in other languages, creates mid and extra-low tones. For the sake of consistency with later discussion in this paper, I will state this proposal in terms of the feature system of Yip (1982) (with terminological revisions by Pulleyblank 1986).[5] In this system, mid and extra-low tones are created by the feature [−RAISED], as shown below:

(14) H (high)   = [+UPPER, +RAISED]
      L (low)   = [−UPPER, +RAISED]
      M̱ (mid)   = [+UPPER, −RAISED]
      Ḻ (extra low) = [−UPPER, −RAISED]

Stated in these terms, Hyman's proposal, as I understand it, is as follows: In some languages, such as Cantonese or Yala Ikom, the [−RAISED] tones M̱ and Ḻ are interpreted as distinct tone levels, and sequences of the form HM̱H or ḺḺḺ are realized as shown below:

(15)   HM̱H = [⁻ ₋ ⁻]   ḺḺḺ = [₋ ₋ ₋]

However, in languages such as Dschang Bamileke, where the feature [−RAISED] serves as an environment for downstep, these tonal sequences are realized as follows:

(16)   HM̱H = [⁻ ₋ ₋]   ḺḺḺ = [₋ ₋ ₋]

Sample representations for Dschang are given in (17) below, where, using the abbreviational system that I will follow throughout this paper, the feature [±UPPER] is represented with a (small) upper-case H and L, and the feature [±RAISED] with a lower-case h and l:

---

[5] It is not clear to me whether Hyman means to interpret the Dschang downstep feature as an instance of the same feature that creates a mid tone in other languages (that is, the feature "raised"), or whether he believes that this feature has been reanalyzed in Dschang as a "register" feature of the sort employed by Inkelas, Leben, and Cobler (section 1). For expository convenience, I will assume here that the downstep feature is the feature [-raised].

(17) a. 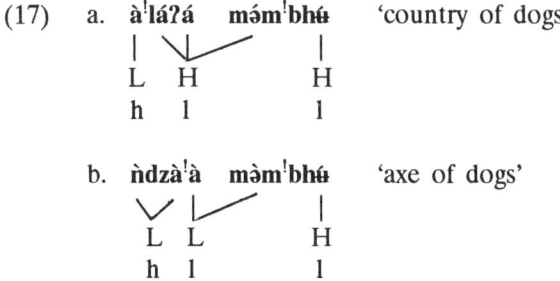 'country of dogs'

b. ǹdzà'à mə̀m'bhʉ 'axe of dogs'

Note that the first ^{'!'} in these representations is not a true downstep, but rather a transition from [+RAISED] to [−RAISED]. Hyman uses the raised exclamation point to indicate a transition from [+RAISED] to [−RAISED], as well as for true downstep, which occurs after [−RAISED].

While I believe Hyman's analysis is on the right track, it has some serious problems, as I will show. First, although Hyman succeeds in eliminating Pulleyblank's metathesis rule ((9),(11)), the "downstep creation" rules which he substitutes are, if anything, even more dubious, since they move a feature from one tier to another, a rule type which, to my knowledge, has never been proposed for any other phonological feature:

(18) a. X X   X X   (Hyman's rule (44b))
         | | = | |
         L H l   L H
                     !

(applies lexically, within the domain *GW*, and postlexically, within the domain *PW*)

b. X   X   X X   (Hyman's rule (44g))
    | | = | |
    H L H   H H
                   !

(applies postlexically within the domain *intonational phrase*)

Furthermore, Hyman's analysis requires the same restructuring rules that we saw above in the floating tone analysis. Some rules require the domain GW, in which the noun prefix is grouped with its own stem. For example, this is the grouping that is required for rule (18a) when it applies in the lexicon, to create the surface form à¹lá? 'country', from underlying /àlá?`/:

(19)   a-la?   (18a)   à-¹lá?
       | | ⟶ | |
       L H L   L H
                                  |

Other rules must be defined on the domain PW, in which the associative particle and the noun prefix are grouped with the preceding noun. This is the domain for rule (18a) when it applies *post*lexically, as in the example below:

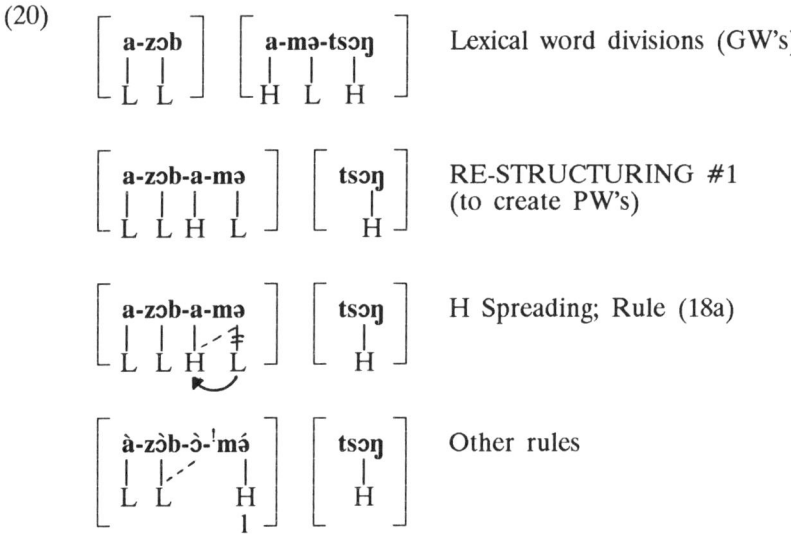

'song of thieves'

Furthermore, as we saw in (13) above, there must be a *second* restructuring rule, as well, to create the word division that is needed for the rule of Contour Formation. In the following section, I will propose a revision of Hyman's analysis which eliminates these restructuring rules and provides a simpler statement of the tone rules. After making this revision, I will return to the Downstep rule itself, and suggest a different statement of this rule than Hyman assumes.

4. REVISION OF HYMAN'S ANALYSIS

4.1. Lexical tone and the tonal representation

I assume here, as argued in Clark (1989), that the tonal features [UPPER] and [RAISED] are linked to a *tonal node* which branches from the laryngeal node, as shown in (21). Contrary to Hyman (1985) and Yip (1989), I assume that the two features are linked independently to the tonal node; this assumption will be justified in section 4.2 below.

(21)

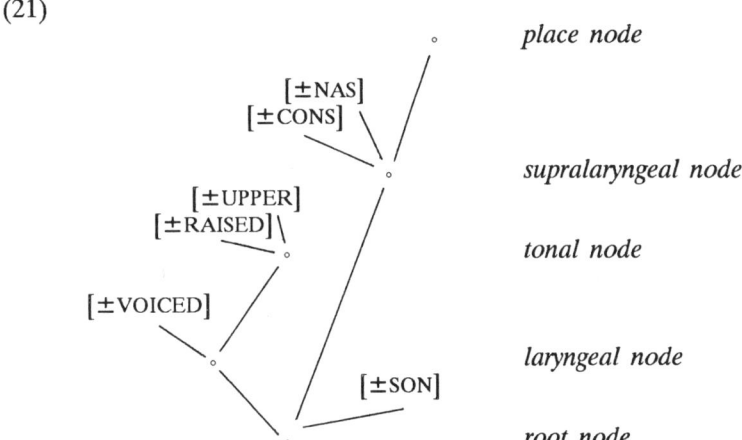

According to Hyman and Tadadjeu (1976), Bamileke noun stems fall into four tonal classes, as illustrated below:

(22) a. Downgliding low: è-fɔ̀ [_ _] nà [_]
                             'chief'   'animal'

     b. Non-downgliding low: ǹ-dzà° [_ _] kàŋ° [_]
                               'axe'   'squirrel'

     c. Mid (or downstepped high): ǹ!-dɔ́ŋ [_ —] !mɔ́ [—]
                                         'horn'   'child'

     d. High: ɲ-ɲǐ [_ ⌐] sə́ŋ [⁻]
                 'machete'   'bird'

If we ignore, for a moment, the class of non-downgliding low-toned nouns (22b), then the noun roots of Dschang fall into three tonal classes—a low-toned class (è-fɔ̀ 'chief'), a mid-toned class (ǹ¹-dɔ́ŋ 'horn'), and a high-toned class (ɲ̀-ɲí 'machete'). The surface tonal representations of these roots are set out below, using the feature system of (14) above. As earlier in this paper, the feature [±UPPER] is abbreviated with an uppercase H and L, while the feature [±RAISED] is abbreviated with a lower-case h and l:

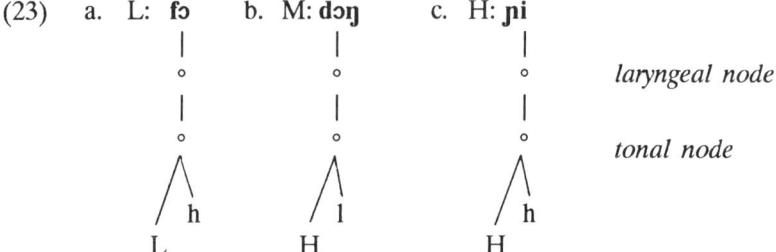

(23)   a. L: fɔ   b. M: dɔŋ   c. H: ɲi
                                                        laryngeal node

                                                        tonal node

To avoid clutter in the representation, I will generally employ a further abbreviation, in which the string of tonal nodes is replaced by the string of phonemes, as shown below:

(24)   a. h   b. l   c. h
            | | |
            fɔ   dɔŋ   ɲi
            | | |
            L   H   H

This representation is only an abbreviation, and should be interpreted as exactly equivalent to the more accurate representation of (23).

Following Pulleyblank (1986), I assume the (universal) default values [−UPPER] and [+RAISED]. The removal of these features, along with the redundant feature [+UPPER] for the mid tone, yields the following lexical tone representations for the roots of (24):

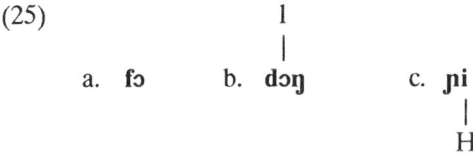

(25)   l
                            |
         a. fɔ   b. dɔŋ   c. ɲi
                                        |
                                        H

The isolation forms of these nouns are then derived by the following set of rules:

(26) LEXICAL COMPONENT
Stem Level: [UPPER] Assignment (27a,b)
Identical Tone Merger (27c)
Word Level: [UPPER] Assignment (27a,b)
Identical Tone Merger (27c)

POSTLEXICAL COMPONENT
Level I: [+RAISED] Assignment (27d)
Level II: Contour Formation II (27f)
Spreading (27e)

Statements of the rules are given below:

(27) a. [+UPPER] Assignment: $\circ \rightarrow H \ / \ \underline{}^{|}$

b. [−UPPER] Assignment: $\circ \rightarrow L$

c. Identical Tone Merger: SD $T_i \ T_j$
SC Merge T_i with T_j.
(where T is a feature on the [UPPER] tier)

d. [+RAISED] Assignment: $\circ \rightarrow h \ / \ [\underline{}_I$

(where I = intonation phrase)

e. Spreading: $\begin{array}{c} T \\ | \\ | \\ \circ \end{array}$ (where T = any tonal feature)

f. Contour Formation II: $\begin{bmatrix} \circ \\ \acute{\circ} \ \circ \\ | \ | \\ L \ H \end{bmatrix} \begin{array}{l} \textit{laryngeal} \\ \textit{tonal} \end{array}$

Rules (a), (b), and (d) are the default and redundancy rules for the tonal features. By the Strict Cycle Condition, these rules serve only to fill in unspecified features; they do not change already *existing* features.⁶ Identical Tone Merger (27c) enforces the Obligatory Contour Principle on the [UPPER] tier, by merging identical features on this tier.⁷ The condition that the merged features must be identical is not stated in the rule itself, but follows from a universal condition on merger rules —namely, that merged elements must be non-distinct. Spreading (27e) spreads a tonal feature onto an unspecified tonal node to its right. The directionality of this rule (that is, the fact that the target node links to the tone to its left, rather than the tone to its right) follows from the principle of Left-Right Application, cf. fn. 12 below, which states that a rule must apply *first* to the leftmost string that meets its structural description. The fact that the target node must be unspecified follows from the No Association Convention (Clark 1990:164), which forbids the association of a feature to a tonal node that already carries a specification for that feature. In Dschang, this convention goes into effect at the Word Level and remains in effect throughout the remainder of the phonology. Contour Formation (27f) creates a rising contour on the final syllable of nouns like ɲɲǐ 'machete'. The bracket at the end of the structural description indicates that this rule applies only at the end of a word (see (13) above).⁸ I assume here that "short" contours like that of ɲɲǐ have a structure like the following, with two tonal nodes linked to a single laryngeal node:

---

6 In the formulation of Kiparsky (1982a,b), the Strict Cycle Condition prevents the structure-changing application of a rule in a non-derived environment. Since default and redundancy rules, by their nature, apply in non-derived environments, they can never apply in a structure-changing way; that is, they cannot change a feature that was already present in the representation of a segment.
7 I assume here that the Obligatory Contour Principle is not a universal convention, but a markedness condition which must be implemented by language-specific rules. In Dschang, the Obligatory Contour Principle is maintained, on the [UPPER] tier, throughout most of the phonology, but it is not maintained on the [RAISED] tier.
8 Contour Formation II does not apply to the melody LM; for example, it does not apply to the noun ǹ'dóŋ 'horn'. I suggest that this is the result of a universal convention which prevents the formation of contour tones like the following, in which there is a change of feature on both tonal tiers:

(i)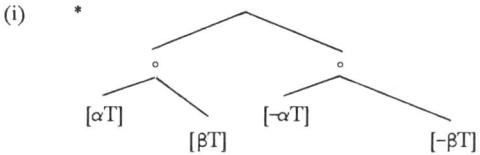

See Yip (1982, 1989) for discussion of a similar constraint on contour tones in Chinese.

(28)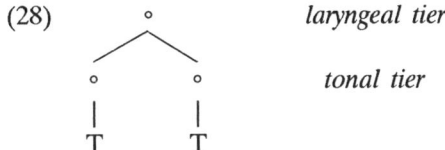

As for the organization of the phonology, I assume the version of lexical phonology that I argued for in Clark (1990), based on previous proposals by Kiparsky (1982a,b), Mohanan (1982), and others. In particular, I assume (i) that the rules are organized into "levels" or "strata" (justification for the level ordering of (26) will be given in section 4.6 below), (ii) that there is no extrinsic rule ordering except for the level ordering; within their levels, the rules apply whenever their structural descriptions are met, (iii) that all lexical levels are cyclical, in that the phonological rules apply alternately with the rules of word formation, and (iv) that the entire lexical phonology, along with the first phrasal level, Phrase Level I, is subject to the Strict Cycle Condition (Kiparsky 1982a,b).

Derivations for the three major tonal classes are given below:

(29)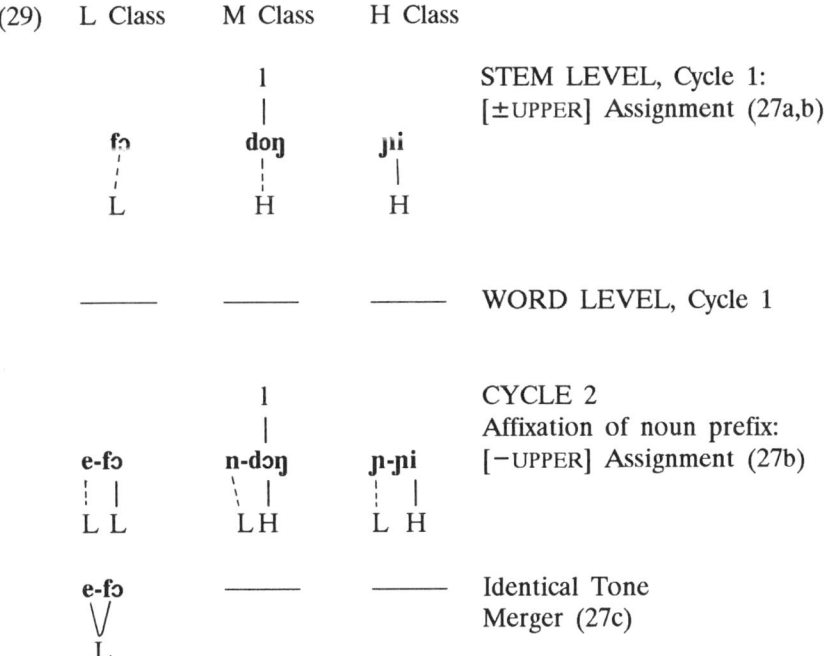

```
    h           h  l          h          PHRASE LEVEL I:
    ┆           ┆  ┆          ┆          [+RAISED] Assignment (27d)
    efɔ         ndɔŋ          ɲɲi
    \/          | |           | |
    L           L H           L H

    h                         h          PHRASE LEVEL II:
    |\                        |\         Spreading (27e);
    efɔ         ———           ɲɲi        Contour Formation II
    \/                        |/‾|       (27f)
    L                         L H

    èfɔ̂        n̂ˈdɔ́ŋ        ɲɲǐ        OUTPUT

    'chief'     'horn'        'machete'
```

Note that the raised exclamation point in n̂ˈdɔ́ŋ represents a drop from [+RAISED] to [−RAISED]. Like Hyman (1985), I use the raised exclamation point to indicate a drop from [+RAISED] to [−RAISED], as well as for a true downstep.

4.2. The class 1/9 associative

The Dschang associative construction is formed with either a high-toned or a low-toned particle, depending on whether the head noun belongs to gender class 1 or 9, or to one of the other classes. The examples below, from Hyman (1985:50-1), illustrate the Class 1/9 associative, in which the associative particle is the low-toned vowel è; note that, at normal conversational speed, the particle undergoes assimilation to the preceding segment, and its segmental portion disappears:

(30) a. /èfɔ̀   + è + màndzwì/ → èfɔ̂ màndzwì   'chief of leopards'
     b. /èfɔ̀   + è + nà/   → èfɔ̂ nà   'chief of animal'
     c. /èfɔ̀   + è + màmˈbhʉ̀/ → èfɔ̂ màmˈbhʉ̀   'chief of dogs'
     d. /èfɔ̀   + è + màtsɔ́ŋ/ → efɔ́ màtsɔ̀ŋ   'chief of thieves'
     e. /èfɔ̀   + è + sə́ŋ/   → èfɔ́ sə́ŋ   'chief of bird'
     f. /n̂ˈdɔ́ŋ + è + màndzwì/ → n̂ˈdɔ̀ŋ màndzwì 'horn of leopards'
     g. /n̂ˈdɔ́ŋ + è + nà/   → n̂ˈdɔ̀ŋ nà   'horn of animal'
     h. /n̂ˈdɔ́ŋ + è + màmˈbhʉ̀/ → n̂ˈdɔ̀ŋ màmˈbhʉ̀ 'horn of dogs'
     i. /n̂ˈdɔ̀ŋ + è + màtsɔ́ŋ/ → n̂ˈdɔ̀ŋ màtsɔ̀ŋ   'horn of thieves'
     j. /n̂ˈdɔ́ŋ + è + sə́ŋ/   → n̂ˈdɔ̀ŋ sə́ŋ   'horn of bird'
     k. /ɲɲí   + è + màndzwì/ → ɲɲǐ màndzwì   'machete of leopards'

l. /ɲɲí	+ è + nà/	→ ɲɲĭ nà	'machete of animal'
m./ɲɲí	+ è + màm'bhú/	→ ɲɲĭ màm'bhú	'machete of dogs'
n. /ɲɲí	+ è + màtsóŋ/	→ ɲɲĭ màtsɔ̌ŋ	'machete of thieves'
o. /ɲɲí	+ è + sə́ŋ/	→ ɲɲĭ ¹ sə́ŋ	'machete of bird'

I assume that the associative particle is, syntactically, a clitic, in the sense of Clark (1990); that is, it starts out as an independent lexical item (a preposition), and passes through the lexical phonology, where it receives its [−UPPER] tone. It then undergoes suffixation, in the syntax, to the preceding word, and the word that is created in this way re-enters the Word Level phonology, as shown below:[9]

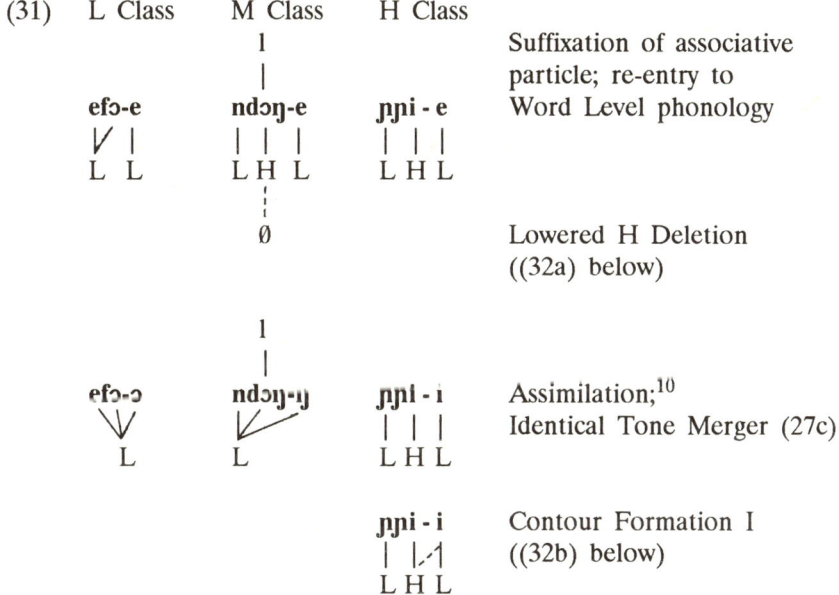

(31) L Class   M Class   H Class

Suffixation of associative particle; re-entry to Word Level phonology

Lowered H Deletion ((32a) below)

Assimilation;[10] Identical Tone Merger (27c)

Contour Formation I ((32b) below)

---

9 Within a given phonological level, the rules apply whenever their structural description is met. Thus, for example, in the derivation of (31), the rules of Lowered H Deletion, Assimilation, and Contour Formation apply simultaneously, as soon as the form enters the Word Level. When the ordering is unimportant, as in (31), I will allow considerations of expository clarity to determine the order in which the rules are actually set out. When the ordering is important, I will try to be more accurate, and will identify sets of rules that apply simultaneously.
10 The vowel e assimilates to a previous vowel, or to a postvocalic sonorant consonant. See Tadadjeu (1974) for a more detailed statement of the assimilation rules.

46 *The representation of tonal register*

In the analysis I am proposing, the noun prefix retains its prefixal status throughout the derivation, and, as shown in (31), the particle is treated as a suffix from the beginning; thus there is no need for the restructuring rules that were necessary in Hyman's analysis.

The new rules that appear in the derivation of (31) are stated below:

(32) a. Lowered H Deletion: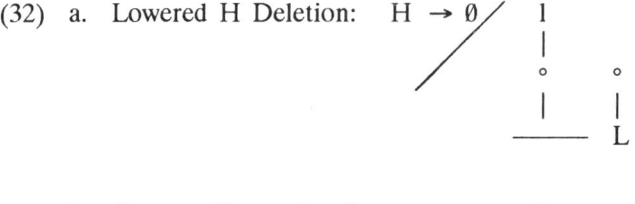

b. Contour Formation I: $°_j$ laryngeal

                    ____⎤
                   o   o   tonal

Condition: $°_j$ is not stressed.

Lowered H Deletion (32a) deletes the feature H when it shares a tonal node with the feature l, and is followed by L. Contour Formation I (32b) creates a short contour by spreading a tonal node onto the following laryngeal node. This rule is responsible for the fact that when the associative particle is *retained* in the surface output, as it may be in careful speech, it carries the tone of the stem, rather than its underlying low tone; for example, Hyman (1985:78) gives the careful-speech form sə́ŋŋ́ ¹ sə́ŋ 'bird of bird', from underlying /sə́ŋ-è sə́ŋ/). The condition that the target node must be unstressed prevents the formation of a contour tone on the first syllable of the noun stem (which I assume is stressed);[11] this condition is necessary at the Word Level to prevent the spreading of the prefix tone onto the stem in forms like ǹ'dɔ́ŋ 'horn', and it is also necessary at Phrase Level I, to prevent the tone of the head noun from spreading onto the following noun stem in forms like àsáŋá nà 'tail of animal' ((38l) below).

Phrases with head nouns like èfɔ́ and ǹ'dɔ́ŋ now follow automatically, as shown below:

---

11 See fn. 4 above.

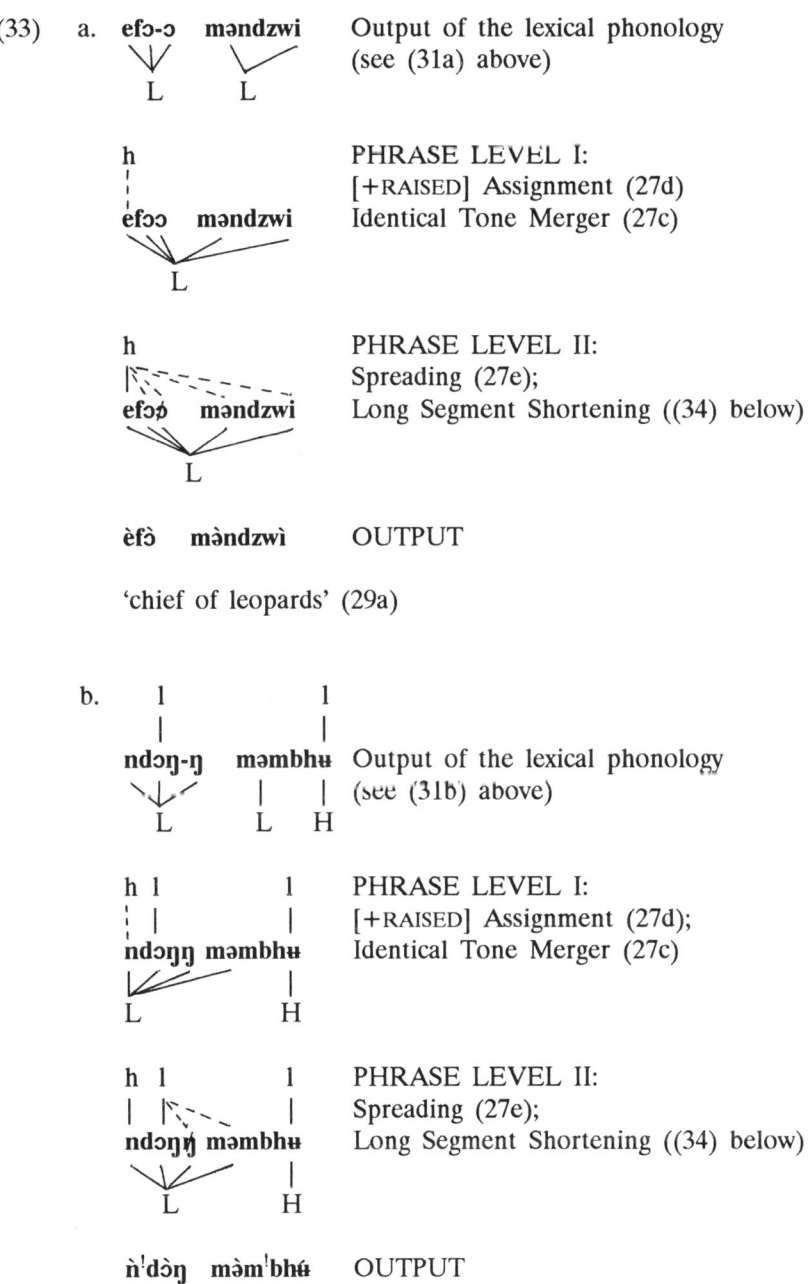

Note that Identical Tone Merger (27c) applies at Phrase Level I, as well as at the Word Level. The rule of Long Segment Shortening, which applies at Phrase Level II, is stated as follows:

(34)   Long Segment Shortening: SD
       (optional)

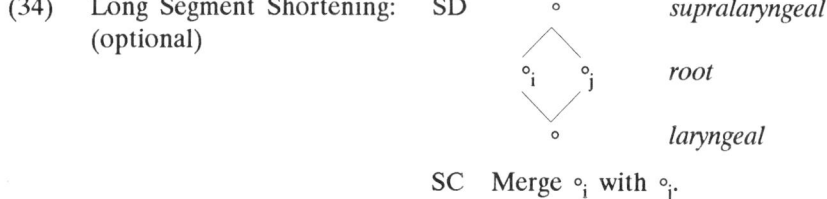

       SC   Merge $°_i$ with $°_j$.

This rule merges the associative particle with the segment that precedes it, provided that the two segments share all their laryngeal and supralaryngeal features.

Notice, incidentally, that the features [UPPER] and [RAISED] must be linked independently to the tonal node, as in (35a) below:

(35)   a.   b.   c.
           °   °   °
       [UPPER]   [UPPER]   [RAISED]
                                     | |
           [RAISED]   [RAISED]   [UPPER]

A geometry like (b), in which the feature [RAISED] is subordinated to the feature [UPPER], is precluded by forms like ǹ'dɔ̀ŋ màm'bhɵ̀ 'horn of dogs' (33b), in which the [RAISED] tier contains two features (h and l) corresponding to a single continuous feature (L) on the [UPPER] tier. The geometry of (c), in which the feature [UPPER] is subordinated to the feature [RAISED], is precluded by forms like ɲɲǐ màtsɔ́ŋ 'machete of thieves' ((37a) below), in which the [UPPER] tier contains a sequence of four features, LHLH, corresponding to a single, continuous feature (h) on the [RAISED] tier.

1/9 associative phrases in which the head noun ends with a high tone require two additional rules, as shown below:

(36)   PHRASE LEVEL I:
       a.   Contour Simplification:

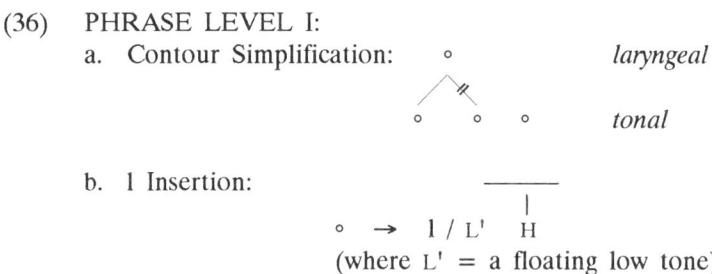

       b.   l Insertion:
                                                  ___
                                                   |
                        $° \rightarrow 1 / L'\ H$
                        (where L' = a floating low tone)

These rules are illustrated in the following derivations of the phrases ɲɲǐ mə̀tsɔ́ŋ /ɲɲí + è + mə̀tsɔ́ŋ/ 'machete of thieves' and ɲɲǐ ˈsɔ́ŋ /ɲ̀ɲí + è + sə́ŋ/ 'machete of bird':

(37) a.
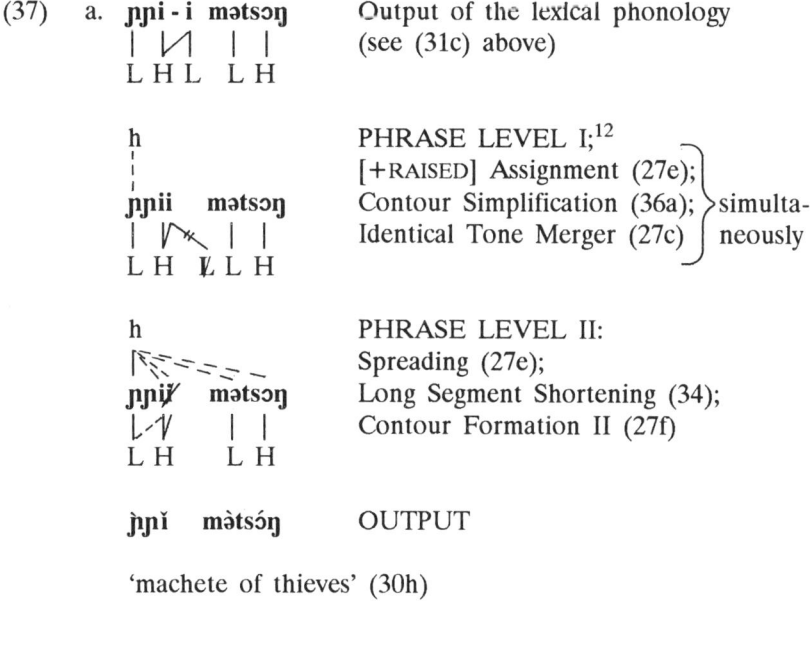

ɲɲǐ mə̀tsɔ́ŋ   OUTPUT

'machete of thieves' (30h)

b. ɲɲi - i sə̀ŋ   Output of the lexical phonology
   | M | | (see (31c) above)
   L H L H

---

12 The Level I output in (37a) still meets the structural description of Contour Formation; however, the reapplication of the rule is blocked by the principle of Left-Right Application, which is stated as follows (Clark 1990:304):

(i)   Given a phonological rule R of the form A → B / C ——— D, and a phonological string Γ of the form ... α ... β ..., where α is to the left of β, then
   a. R must apply with A = α, if it can, before it applies with A = β.
   b. Once R has applied with A = β, it cannot reapply on the same cycle with A = α.

In (37a), the rule of Contour Formation I has already applied to the L tone at the end of ɲɲí. By the principle of Left-Right Application, it cannot, then, reapply to the preceding H tone.

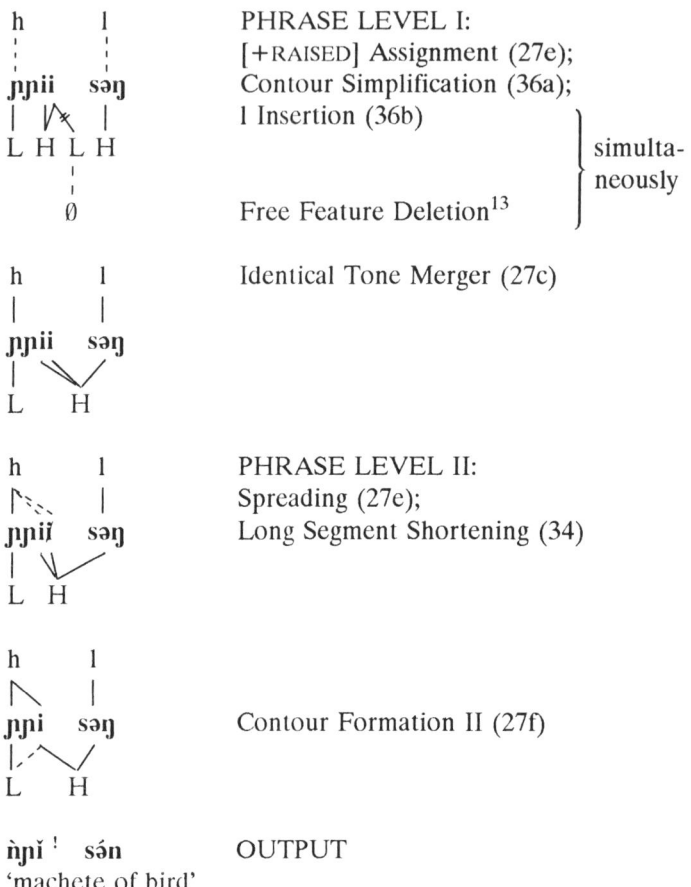

4.3 The general associative construction

When the head noun of the associative construction belongs to a gender class other than 1/9, the phrase is formed with a high-toned particle—á for class 7; é for the other classes—. The following paradigm, from

---

13 I assume here, as argued in Clark (1989, 1990), that "floating" features which cannot be associated, immediately, to a phonological segment are deleted, by a universal rule of Free Feature Deletion:

(i)   Free Feature Deletion: F' → ∅

Hyman (1985:50-1) illustrates the effects of the particle á, which is used when the head noun belongs to gender class 7:

(38) a. /àzɔ̀b + á + mə̀ndzwì/ → àzɔ̀bɔ́ mə̀n⁻dzwì 'song of leopards'
   b. /àzɔ̀b + á + nà/ ▸ àzɔ̀bɔ́ nà 'song of animal'
   c. /àzɔ̀b + á + mə̀m⁻bhʉ́/ → àzɔ̀bɔ́ ⁻mə́mbhʉ 'song of dogs'
   d. /àzɔ̀b + á + mə̀tsɔ́ŋ/ → àzɔ̀bɔ́ ⁻mə́tsɔ́ŋ 'song of thieves'
   e. /àzɔ̀b + á + sə́ŋ/ → àzɔ̀bɔ́ sə́ŋ 'song of bird'
   f. /à⁻lá? + á + mə̀ndzwì/ → à⁻lá?á mə́ndzwì 'country of leopards'
   g. /à⁻lá? + á + nà/ → à⁻lá?á nà 'country of animal'
   h. /à⁻lá? + á + mə̀m⁻bhʉ́/ → à⁻lá?á mə́m⁻bhʉ 'country of dogs'
   i. /à⁻lá? + á + mə̀tsɔ́ŋ/ → à⁻lá?á mə́⁻tsɔ́ŋ 'country of thieves'
   j. /à⁻lá? + á + sə́ŋ/ → à⁻lá?á sə́ŋ 'country of bird'
   k. /àsáŋ + á + mə̀ndzwì/ → àsáŋá mə́ndzwì 'tail of leopards'
   l. /àsáŋ + á + nà/ → àsáŋá nà 'tail of animal'
   m. /àsáŋ + á + mə̀m⁻bhʉ́/ → àsáŋá mə́m⁻bhʉ 'tail of dogs'
   n. /àsáŋ + á + mə̀tsɔ́ŋ/ → àsáŋá mə́⁻tsɔ́ŋ 'tail of thieves'
   o. /àsáŋ + á + sə́ŋ/ → àsáŋá sə́ŋ 'tail of bird'

Like its class 1/9 counterpart ((30) above), the class 7 associative particle cliticizes to the left, and the newly-formed word reenters the Word Level phonology, as shown below:

(39) a. **asaŋ-a**   b. **azɔb-a**   Underlying representation after cliti-
       | | | |╱ | cization of the associative particle;
       L H H   L H   re-entry to Word Level phonology

       asaŋ-a   **azɔb-ɔ**   WORD LEVEL:
       | ∨ |╱--⎤   Assimilation;[14]
       L H   L H   Identical Tone Merger (27c);
                                      Contour Formation I (32b)

Phrases like **àsáŋá mə́ndzwì** 'tail of leopards' and **àsáŋá mə́⁻tsɔ́ŋ** 'tail of thieves' then follow straightforwardly, as shown below:

---

[14] Unlike the vowel [e], which we saw in the Class 1/9 associative, the vowel [a] does not assimilate to a preceding sonorant segment, but takes on the qualities of the preceding vowel.

52 *The representation of tonal register*

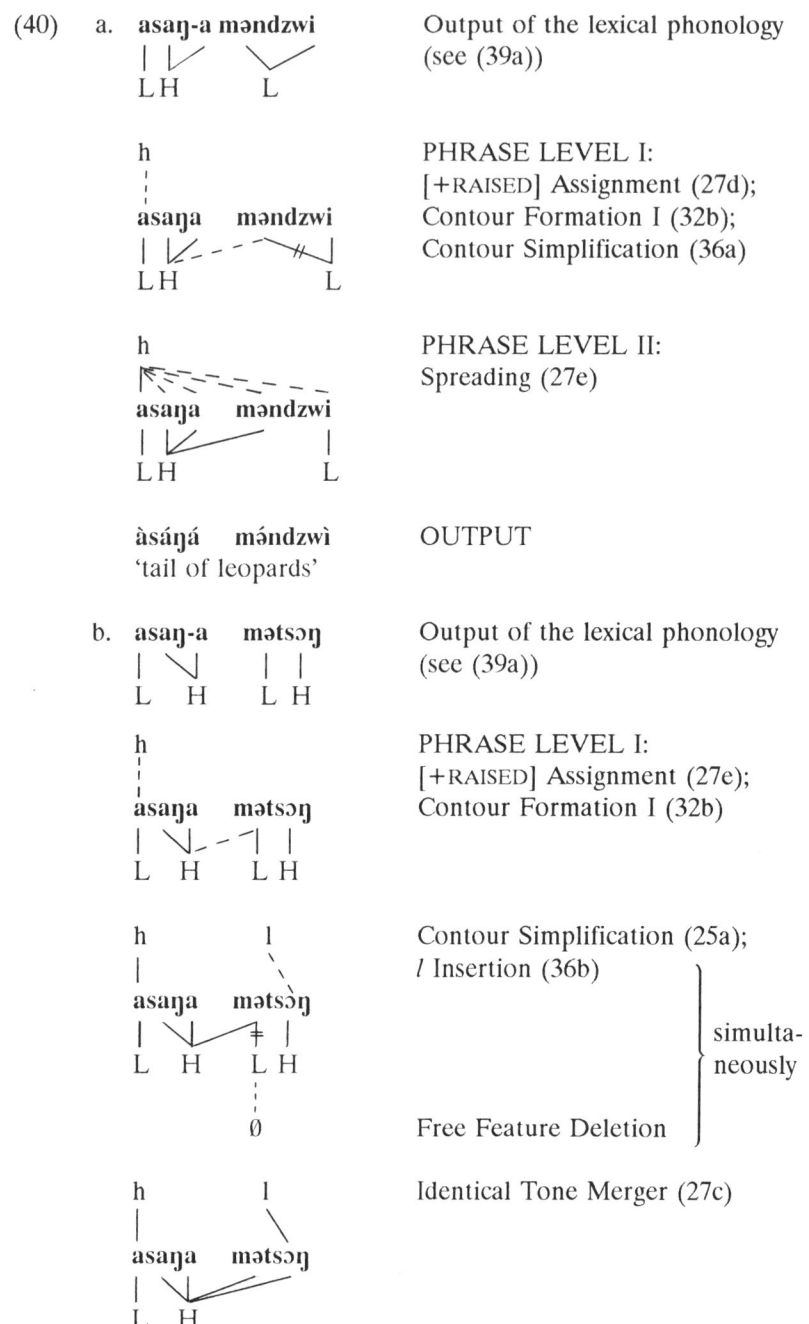

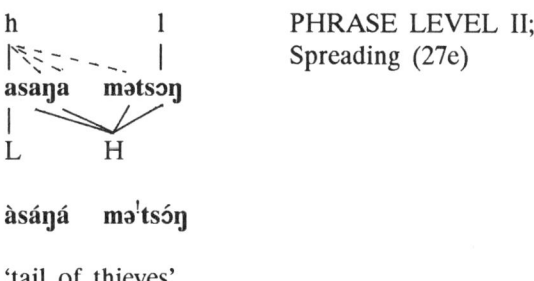

PHRASE LEVEL II;
Spreading (27e)

àsáŋá məˈtsɔ́ŋ

'tail of thieves'

Phrases like àzɔ̀bɔ̌ ˈmátsɔ́ŋ /àzɔ̀b + á + mə̀tsɔ́ŋ/ 'song of thieves', in which the head noun ends with a low tone, require a second *l* Insertion rule, which affects the high tone of a rising tone that is followed by low:

(41)   Mid Tone Formation: ∘ → l   /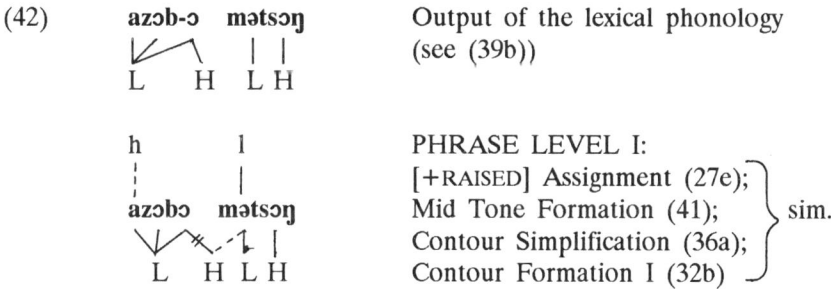

This rule applies in the second line of the derivation below:[15]

(42)   azɔb-ɔ mətsɔŋ   Output of the lexical phonology
       ⌐⌐\ | | (see (39b))
       L H   L H

       h   l   PHRASE LEVEL I:
       | | [+RAISED] Assignment (27e);
       azɔbɔ mətsɔŋ   Mid Tone Formation (41);   sim.
       \/×·↑ | Contour Simplification (36a);
       L   H L H   Contour Formation I (32b)

---

15 The rule of Mid Tone Formation places the feature l on the tonal node of the first H tone of (42), while this tone is, simultaneously, being shifted to the right by the rules of Contour Simplification and Contour Formation I. In this and future derivations, I have simplified the representation by placing the l tone in its final resting place (in (42), on the first syllable of mə̀tsɔ́ŋ) rather than in the position in which it is actually inserted.

54   *The representation of tonal register*

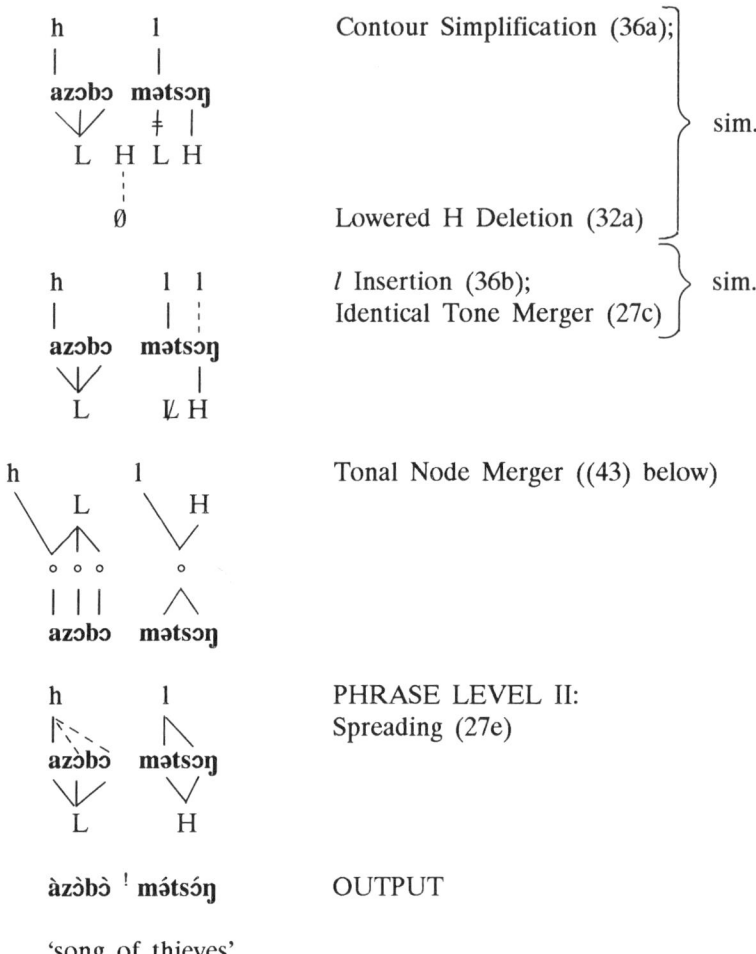

'song of thieves'

The rule of Tonal Node Merger, which applies in the fifth line of this derivation, is stated as follows:

(43)   Tonal Node Merger: SD   [−RAISED]
                                  |
                                  $°_i$ $°_j$, where $°_i$ is unstressed.

                            SC   Merge $°_i$ with $°_j$.

Like other merger rules, rule (43) applies only to elements which are nondistinct; thus tonal nodes which carry non-identical tonal features cannot undergo this rule.

Phrases like àzɔ̀bɔ̀ màn'dzwì 'song of leopards', in which the associative noun has level low tone, require an additional rule of L Dissociation, which is stated as follows:

(44) L Dissociation:

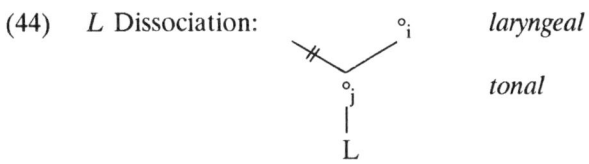

Condition: $°_i$ is stressed.

This rule applies in the last line of the derivation below:

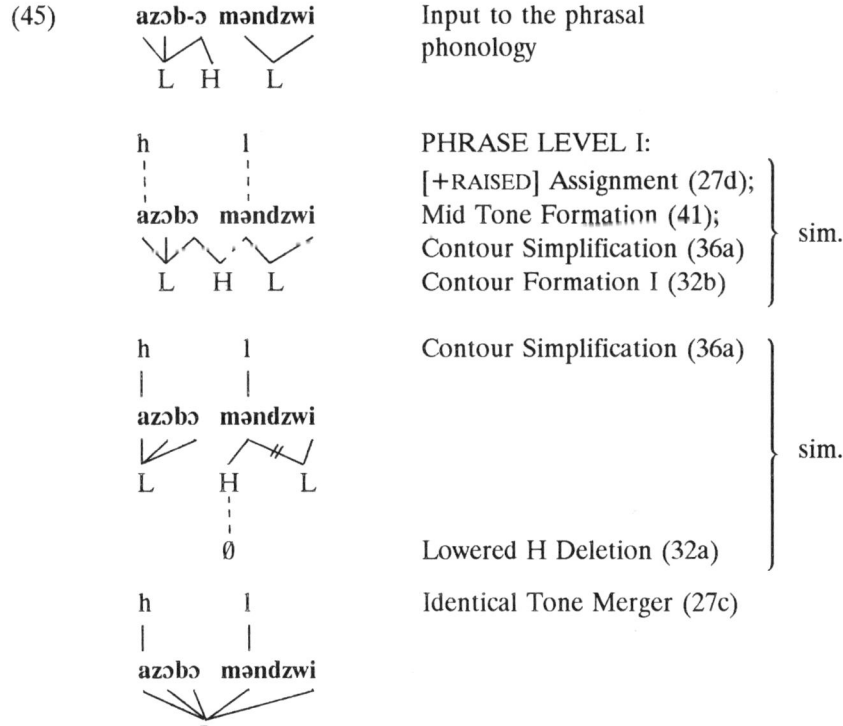

56   *The representation of tonal register*

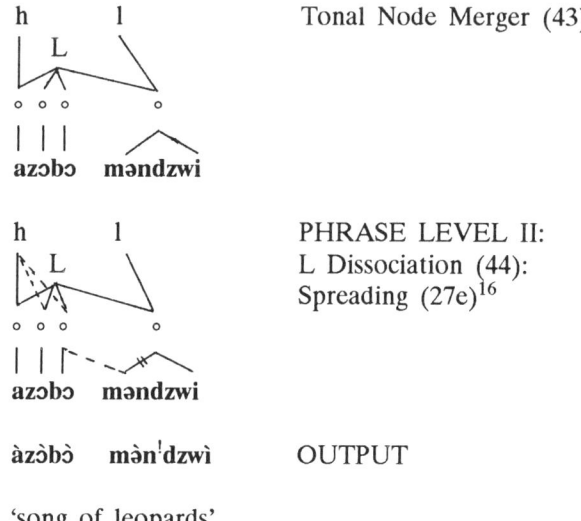

Tonal Node Merger (43)

PHRASE LEVEL II:
L Dissociation (44):
Spreading (27e)[16]

OUTPUT

'song of leopards'

The rule of L Dissociation (44) is needed, independently, to account for the position of the downstep in forms like ǹdzà ˈnà 'axe of animal', from underlying /ǹdzàˈà nà/. (See the discussion of nouns like ǹdzà˳ in section 4.4 below.)

4.4. *Nouns with rising-tone stems*

In my discussion so far, I have ignored the class of non-downgliding low-toned nouns. These nouns contrast with ordinary low-stemmed nouns, as shown below:

---

16 This derivation assumes a more general statement of the rule (schema) of Spreading, as follows:

(i)   Spreading: $\underset{\overset{|}{Y}}{X}$,   where X and Y are elements of any kind which can properly be associated.

In the derivation of (45), rule (i) links the de-toned laryngeal node of the vowel **e** to the tonal node to its left.

(46) Non-downgliding low-stemmed nouns:
ǹ-dzà° [_ _]   à-lə̀ŋ° [_ _]
'axe'   'stool'

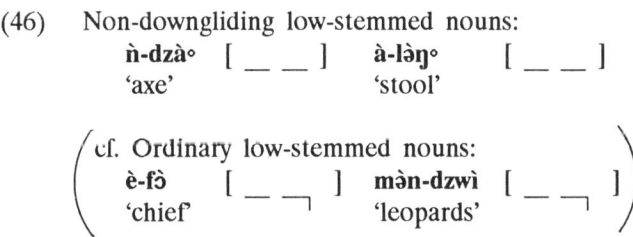

Hyman and Tadadjeu (1976) argue that the non-downgliding nouns end with a floating high tone, which protects them from final downgliding. In the framework I am assuming, floating tones are not allowed to remain in the representation (see fn. 13); thus the high tone at the end of the non-downgliding nouns cannot be a floating tone, but must be part of a contour, as shown below:

(47) a. **n-dza**   b. **kaŋ**
          \/\   /\
          L H   L H

Nouns of this type behave differently from ordinary low-toned nouns in the 1/9 associative. This is because the 1/9 particle sets up the environment for Mid Tone Formation and Lowered h Deletion, as shown below:

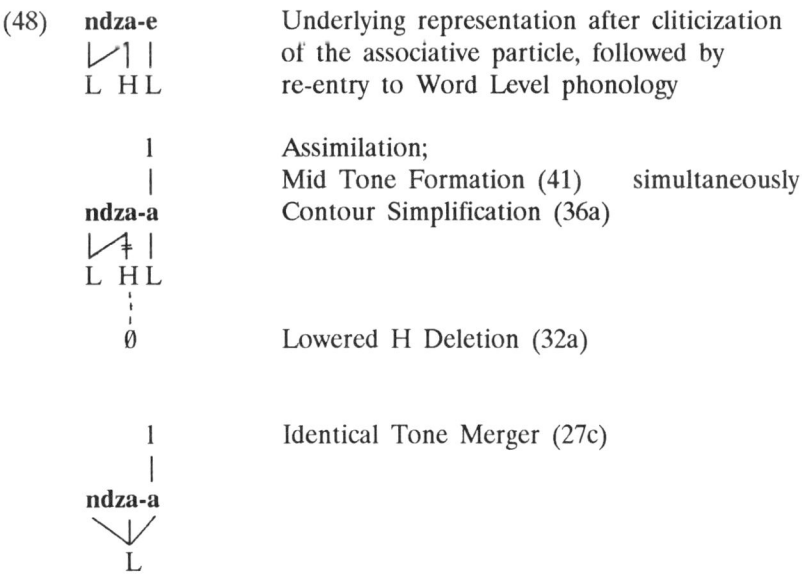

58   *The representation of tonal register*

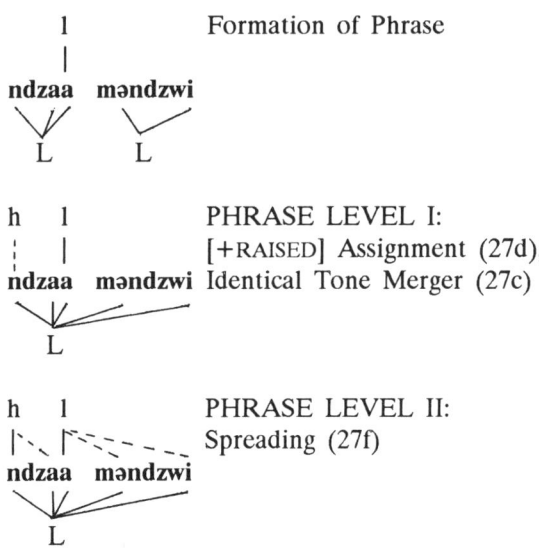

ǹdzà!à màndzwì OUTPUT

'axe of leopards'

(cf. èfɔ́ mǝ̀ndzwì 'chief of leopards', with an ordinary low-toned noun)

In the general associative construction, rising-tone nouns are indistinguishable from low-toned nouns. That is because the high-toned associative particle merges with the final tone of the rising contour, as illustrated below with the rising-tone noun àlǝ̌ŋ° 'stool':

(49)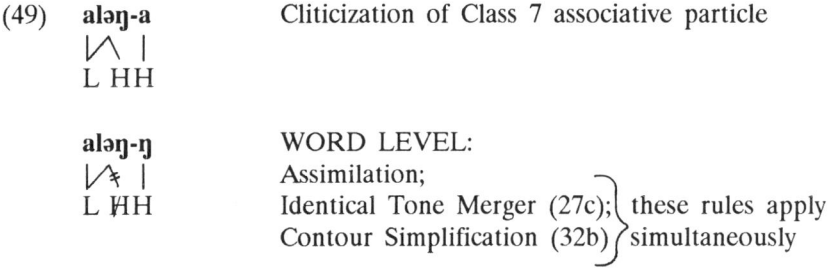

(cf. the combination of the low-toned noun àzɔ̀b with the particle á in (39b) above).

4.5 The verbs

According to Hyman and Tadadjeu (1976), Dschang verbs fall into two tonal classes—the "high-toned" class, which includes the root tɔ́ŋ 'call' and the low-toned (in our terms, toneless) class, which includes the root kɔŋ 'like'. A representative sampling of verb forms is given below:

(50)
	H Class	L Class
Infinitive	là¹-tɔ́ŋ	à-kɔ̀ŋ
Imperative	tɔ́ŋ-ɔ́	kɔ̀¹ŋ-ɔ́
Consecutive	ń-tɔ́ŋ	ǹ¹-kɔ́ŋ
Yesterday Conditional	tɔ́ŋ	¹kɔ́ŋ
Past Tense Indicative	tɔ́ŋ	¹kɔ́ŋ[17]

The forms of (50) are derivable by previously-motivated rules, plus two additional rules, as follows: first, a rule of Verbal *l* Insertion, which is stated below:

(51) Verbal *l* Insertion: $\circ \rightarrow 1 \;/\; \left[\begin{array}{c} \underline{} \cdots \\ | \\ \text{L} \quad \text{H} \end{array} \right]_V$

This rule assigns the feature [−RAISED] to a high-toned node which is preceded by a low tone within a verb. The rule accounts for the fact that, as can be seen in the examples of (50), *L* is never followed by a full *H* within the verb. This rule is illustrated below for the Imperative form:

(52)
```
tɔŋ      kɔŋ          STEM LEVEL, Cycle 1:
 |        |           [−UPPER] Assignment (27b)
 H        L


tɔŋ-a    kɔŋ-a        CYCLE 2: Affixation of suffix -á;
| |      | |
H H      L H
```

---

17 The indicative form contains an underlying falling contour which does not show up in the isolation form (see (66)-(67) below).

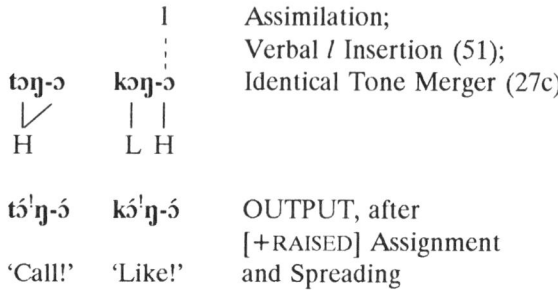

Assimilation;
Verbal *l* Insertion (51);
Identical Tone Merger (27c)

tɔ́'ŋ-ɔ́   kɔ́'ŋ-ɔ́   OUTPUT, after
                    [+RAISED] Assignment
'Call!' 'Like!'   and Spreading

The Consecutive and Yesterday-Past-Tense Conditional forms contain a tonal suffix, -*H*, which links to the final tonal node of the word, by the following rule:

(53) Docking: $\begin{bmatrix} \circ \\ \vdots \\ H \end{bmatrix}$ (Stem Level)

This rule applies at the Stem Level, before the No-Bumping Convention goes into effect; thus it "bumps" the tone which was underlyingly associated to the target node. The derivations for the Conditional forms tɔ́ŋ and ˈkɔ́ŋ are given below:

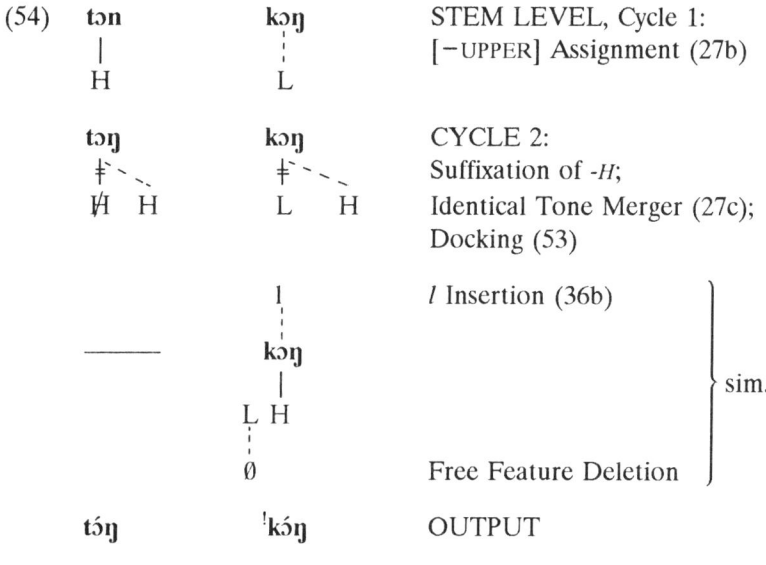

'called (cond.)' 'liked (cond.)'

The Consecutive is formed from these same stems, by the addition of the prefix ń-.

4.6 Summary

The tone rules of Dschang are listed below, within their levels, in alphabetical order:

(55) STEM LEVEL: Docking (53)
Identical Tone Merger (27c)
[±UPPER] Assignment (27a,b)
Verbal *I* Insertion (51)

WORD LEVEL: Contour Formation I (32b)
Contour Simplification (36a)
Identical Tone Merger (27c)
Lowered *H* Deletion (32a)
Mid Tone Formation (41)
[±UPPER] Assignment (27a,b)
Verbal *I* Insertion (51)

PHRASE LEVEL I: Contour Formation I (32b)
Contour Simplification (36a)
Identical Tone Merger (27c)
I Insertion (36b)
Lowered *H* Deletion (32a)
Mid Tone Formation (41)
[+RAISED] Assignment (27d)
Tonal Node Merger (43)

PHRASE LEVEL II: Contour Formation II (27f)
L Dissociation (44)
Spreading (27e)

The divisions among the levels are justified as follows: The first lexical level—the Stem Level—is motivated by the observation that the rule of Docking, alone among the association rules of Dschang, is able to "bump" a tone from its target node. I account for this exceptional property by assigning this rule to the Stem Level, and allowing the "No-Bumping" Convention to go into effect at the Word Level. In the postlexical phonology, the second level, Phrase Level II, is motivated primarily on grounds of ordering. The rule of Spreading (which spreads the feature [±RAISED] onto a following unspecified node) must be ordered at Phrase Level II, after the rules of [−RAISED] assignment. Similarly, the rule of Contour Formation II must be assigned to Phrase Level II, so that the contour it creates will not undergo the Phrase Level I rule of Contour Simplification. Finally, the rule of *L* Dissociation must be assigned to Phrase Level II, because it is a structure-changing rule that applies inside a lexical item, contrary to the Strict Cycle Condition; thus it must be ordered at Phrase Level II, after the Strict Cycle Condition has gone out of operation.

The grammar of (55) contains the same number of tone rules as that of Hyman (1985).[18] However, this grammar is simpler than Hyman's, in two important ways: first, this analysis does not require the complex restructuring rules that were necessary in Hyman's analysis (see sections 2 and 3 above). Secondly, it does not employ unusual rule types such as metathesis (9/11) or tier hopping (18). Except for *I* Insertion (36b), which I will return to below, these are garden-variety tone rules, common to many African tone languages.

5. THE DOWNSTEP RULE, RE-VISITED

Throughout the previous section, I have assumed, following the spirit of Hyman (1985), that the Dschang Downstep rule consists of a downward adjustment of the pitch standard X in the environment of the tonal feature [−RAISED]; that is,

(56) $X_i \rightarrow X_{i+1}$ (by the formula of (3)) / [-RAISED] ──────

However, this formulation of the rule must now be called into question, for two reasons: first, and most importantly, it is observationally inadequate, in that it provides no representation for the *double* downsteps which, according to Hyman and Tadadjeu (1976), are found in phrases such as the following:

---

18 If we ignore the default rules and the rule of Spreading, which will be needed in any analysis, then both my analysis and Hyman's require eleven tone rules. Hyman needs ten rules to account for the nouns (Hyman:72-4), and he will also need a rule of Docking, for the verbs. There are three rules in my analysis which have no correlate in Hyman's analysis: Identical Tone Merger (27c), Verbal I Insertion (51), and Contour Simplification (36a). Rules which are needed in Hyman's analysis, but not mine, are his two rules of Stem-L Spreading (Hyman:73, (44.e.i),(44e.ii)) and his rule of Free H Deletion (Hyman:74).

(57) à kè ˈkɔ́ŋɔ́ ˈˈ mɔ́   'He liked a child (yesterday).'

   (cf. the Conditional form à kè ˈkɔ́ŋɔ́ ˈmɔ́
   'if he liked a child (yest.)')

Secondly, rule (56) looks suspiciously different from the Downstep rule that we find in other languages. In many languages, including KiShambaa (Odden 1982), Supyire (Carlson 1983), Kikuyu (Clark 1989) and Igbo (Clark 1989), downstep can be shown to occur between adjacent identical tonal features, as shown below:

(58) a. Downstep: CV́ˈCV́
                       | |
                       H   H

      b. No Downstep: CV́ CV́
                        \ /
                         H

For example, downstep may be created simply by the concatenation of high tones:

(59) KiShambaa (examples from Odden 1982:187)

   a. nwana   du   nwáná ˈdù
       \/   + | →   \/ |
        H   H   H   H

      'child'   'only'   'only a child'

   b. ngoto   izafa   ngóˈtó ˈízàfá
      | | + | | | → | | | | |
      H H   H L H   H H   H L H

      'sheep' 'died'   'The sheep died.'

   c. ni   kui   níˈ kúí
       | +   \/   → | \/
       H   H   H   H

      'assert.' 'dog'   'It's a dog.'

64 *The representation of tonal register*

    d. u   wa   lol   e   ú'wálólè
         | + | +   + | → | \/ |
         H   H   L   H H L

    'you' 'them' 'look at' final 'You look at them.'
                                  vowel

(60)   Supyire (examples from Carlson (1983:36))

    a. kà ū ú kú ˈ wíí   b. yyéré ˈ sí ˈ wíí ˈ sá?áŋkì
        | | \/   \/   \/ | \/ \/ |
        LM H   H   H H H H L

    and he SEQ it look-at   stop FUT look again

    'and he looked at it'   'stop and look again'

(61)   Ìgbo (examples from Clark 1990)

    a. i   ga   →   í'gá
        | + | | |
        H   H   H H

    aff. inf. go   'to go'

    b. a   gaɣį   →   á'gáɣį
        | + \/ | \/
        H   H   H H

    non-   go-neg.   'didn't go'
    consecutive

    c. ǫ   tųbhara →   ǫ́'tų́bhàrà
        | + | \/ | | \/
        H   H L   H H L

    he/she threw in   'he/she threw in'

d. V   ji   V́-ˈjí
    | + | → | |
    H   H   H   H

    assoc. yam   'of yams'

⎛ e.g., mkpa   V-ji   m̀kpà   áˈ-jí ⎞
⎜   \/ + | | →   \/ | | ⎟
⎝   L   H H   L   H H ⎠

       'stick' 'of yams'   'a stick of yams'

Downsteps of this type do not receive a natural account in either the floating-tone or the tonal-feature analysis; for example, under the tonal-feature analysis, the Igbo infinitive íˈgá (62a) would require an additional, otherwise unmotivated rule to change the second high tone to [−RAISED].[19] Under the approach I wish to propose, no rule is necessary —the downstep follows from the independently-motivated phonological representation, by a register-lowering rule that lowers the value of X at the boundary between identical tones:[20]

(62) X_i → X_{x+1} / [+UPPER] ──── [+UPPER]

Returning now to Dschang, I would like to suggest that the Dschang downstep rule is of the same form as (62), except that it is more general,

---

19 It has been suggested to me by otherwise intelligent linguists that this extra rule is justified on the grounds that it removes the OCP violation. Notice that this is not true. For example, after the application of this rule, the Igbo verb ọ́ˈtụ́ˈbhá 'which he/she threw in' would be represented as follows:

(i)   h l   l
         | | |
         ọ́ˈtụ́ˈbhá
         | | |
         H H   H

Rather than removing the OCP violation, the assignment of the feature [−RAISED] to the second and third H tones creates an *additional* OCP violation on the [RAISED] tier.

20 Because some phonological levels have "OCP" rules that eliminate sequences of identical tonal features, the concatenation of identical tones does not *always* create a downstep in KiShambaa, Supyire, and Igbo. However, at phonological levels which *lack* such rules, identical-tone sequences are created both by the concatenation of high tones, as in (59)-(61), and by the deletion of a low tone between H's as in the Igbo sentence Àdhá ˈ gáfèr úl 'Adha passed the house', from underlying Àdhá-à gáfèrè úl.

in that it lowers the pitch standard (X) between *any* pair of identical features:

(63) $X_i \rightarrow X_{x+1} / [\alpha T] \underline{\quad} [\alpha T]$

For the data we have looked at so far, this formulation yields the same results as (56). For example, in the phrases below, both (56) and (63) will, correctly, lower the pitch register before the final syllable of màm'bhʉ:[21]

(64) a.   h   l   l
           ala?a məmbhʉ   =   à'lá?á mə́m'bhʉ
           L   H

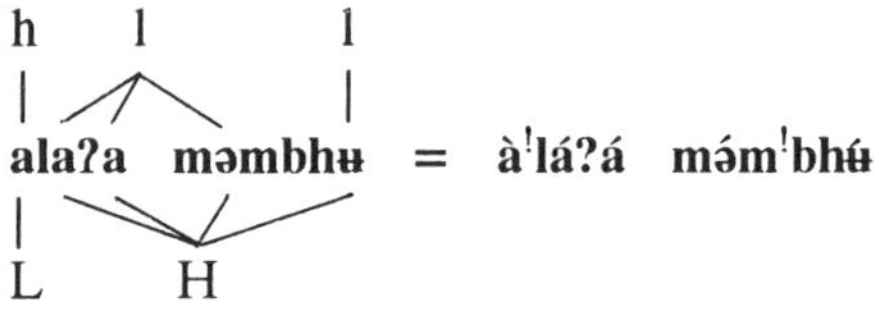

'country of dogs'

b.   h   l   l
     ndzaa məmbhʉ   =   ǹdzà'à mə̀m'bhʉ
     L   H

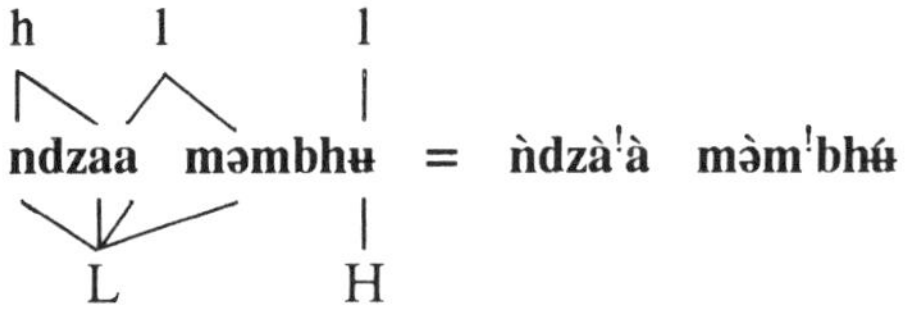

'axe of dogs'

The statement of (63) has an advantage, however, in that it allows for a downstep on the [UPPER] tier, as well as the [RAISED] tier; thus *double* downsteps like that of (57) can be treated as the result of a simultaneous occurrence of the downstep environment *on both tonal tiers,* as shown below:

(65)   h   l   l
       a ke kɔŋɔ mɔ   =   à kè 'kɔ́ŋɔ́ ''mɔ́
       L   H   H

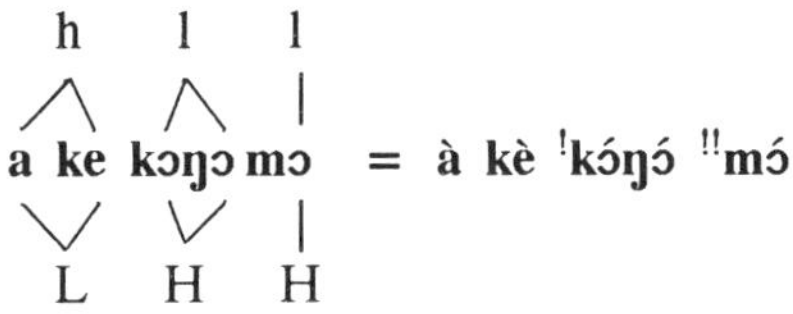

'He liked a child (yesterday).'

---

21 The reader will recall that only the second raised exclamation point in these examples is actually a downstep; the first "!" represents a drop from [+RAISED] to [−RAISED].

How does this representation come about? Let me begin with the observation that the yesterday-past-tense Indicative form carries a tonal suffix -V̀, which creates a falling contour at the end of the verb: /tɔ́ŋŷ/ 'called'; /'kɔ́ŋŷ/ 'liked'. This contour is simplified, in the isolation form, by the following rule:

(66) Falling Contour Simplification: L ⟶ ∅ / ∘ ∘   laryngeal
    (Phrase Level II) | |
                                                 H ——— tonal

However, the contour makes its presence felt when the verb is followed by a complement, as in the example below:

(67) à kè ˈkɔ́ŋ màmˈbhʉ   'He liked dogs (yesterday).'   (Indicative)

    (cf. the Conditional form à kè ˈkɔ́ŋ mámˈbhʉ
                              'if he liked dogs (yest.)')

Notice that the Indicative form behaves like a Class 1/9 associative, showing that the verb ends (underlyingly) with a low tone, while the Conditional behaves like the General Associative, showing that the verb ends with a *high* tone.

According to Hyman and Tadadjeu, when the complement of the verb belongs to gender class 1a, it carries a prefix á-, which shows up overtly when the object noun is emphasized: à kè ˈkɔ́ŋɔ́ ˈɔ́ˈmɔ́ 'He liked a child (yesterday)'. (Notice that the verb, also, carries the affix -á, as an agreement suffix; both [a]'s are changed to [ɔ] to agree with the vowel of the verb root.) If we assume that emphasis on the object noun includes stressing of the prefix á-, then the derivation proceeds straightforwardly, as shown below:

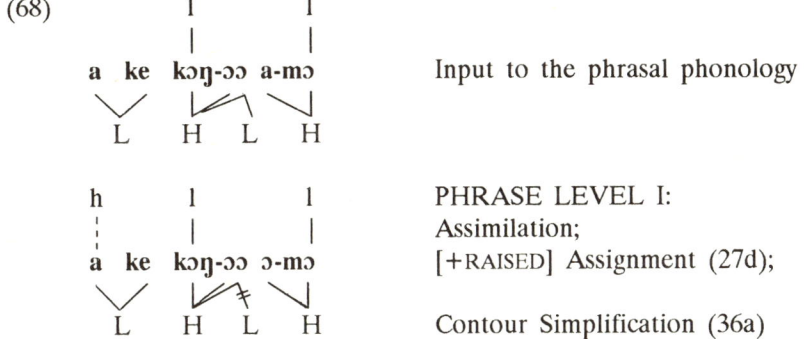

(68)

Input to the phrasal phonology

PHRASE LEVEL I:
Assimilation;
[+RAISED] Assignment (27d);

Contour Simplification (36a)

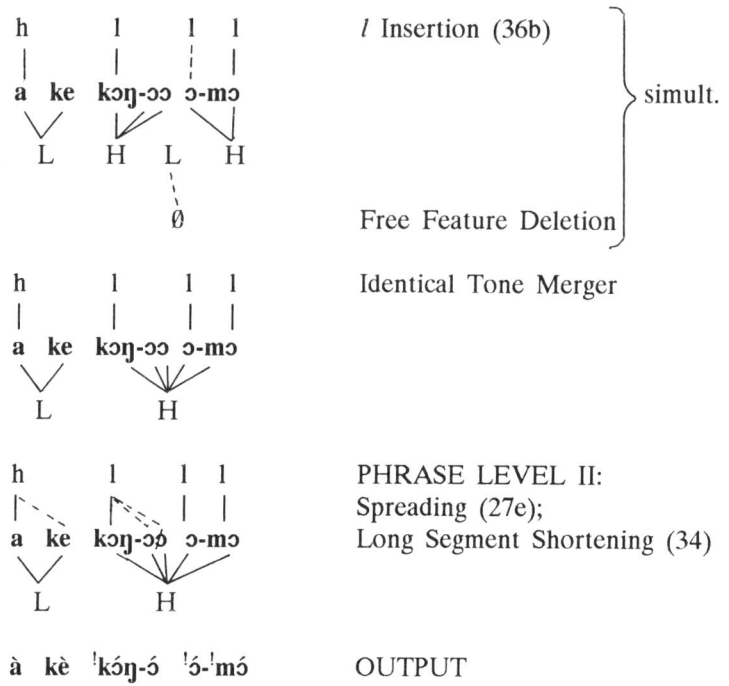

à kè ˈkɔ́ŋ-ɔ́ ˈɔ́-ˈmɔ́   OUTPUT

'He liked a *child* (yesterday).'

Because the noun prefix is stressed in (68), Contour Formation I (32b) cannot apply—that is, the L tone at the end of the verb does not spread onto the object noun. However, when the complement noun is *not* emphasized (that is, when the noun prefix is *not* stressed), Contour Formation does apply, with the following results:

(69)

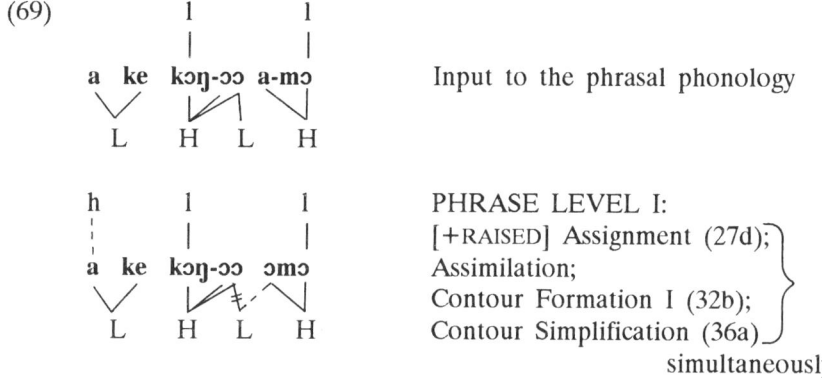

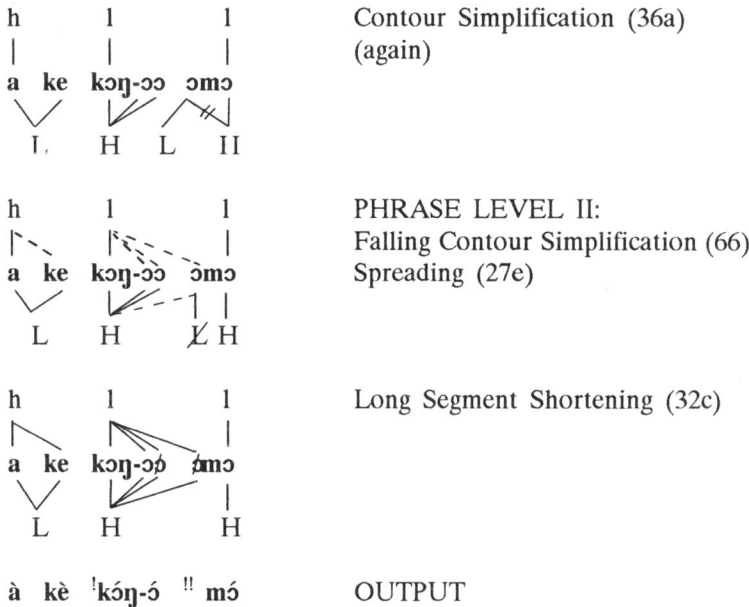

'He liked a *child* (yesterday).'

In this case, the output melody contains an identical-tone sequence on *both* tonal tiers—both the [UPPER] tier and the [RAISED] tier—and the result is a *double* downstep, as shown. The ability to account for the double downstep in forms of this type is a strong advantage of the identical-tone analysis.

In closing, let me make two other general observations about the analysis. First, this analysis helps to explain the occurrence of the otherwise mysterious rule of *l* Insertion (36b), which inserts an *l* tone on the tonal node that follows a floating low, as in the second line below:

(70) səŋ-ŋ səŋ   Input to phrasal phonology

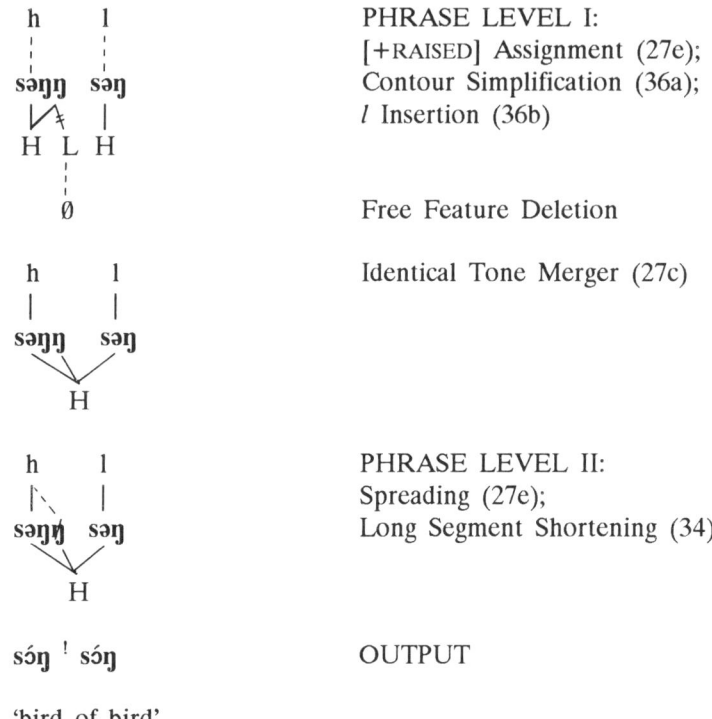

'bird of bird'

Notice that the *l* tone which is inserted by this rule appears at a point which, without the rule of Identical Tone Merger, would be a boundary between H tones. I suggest, then, that at an earlier stage of the language, Contour Simplification applied at Phrase Level II, when Identical Tone Merger is no longer in operation. At that time, forms like (70) surfaced with a HH sequence on the [UPPER] tier, and received a downstep by rule (63). However, because of the availability of the feature *l* to represent lowered pitch in Dschang, the downstep of (70) was re-interpreted as an instance of this feature, introduced by a rule of *l* Insertion.

Secondly, consider Hyman's question about the relationship of Dschang, in which the feature *l* is a signal for downstep, to other closely related languages, in which the feature *l* signifies an ordinary mid tone. In the framework I am proposing, these two sorts of languages differ in two ways: In languages with an ordinary mid tone, the feature [+RAISED] is introduced in the lexical phonology, and the rule of Identical Tone Merger applies on the [RAISED] tier, as well as the [UPPER] tier. This produces an alternating pattern of *h*'s and *l*'s, just as we find on the

[UPPER] tier in Dschang. In languages like Dschang, in contrast, the rule of [+RAISED] Assignment applies at the phrasal level, and the rule of Identical Tone Merger is confined to the [UPPER] tier only. In languages of this sort, every *l* after the first is preceded by *l*, and hence serves as an environment for downstep.

6. CONCLUSION

In conclusion, I have argued in this paper that downstep is phonologically predictable: it is the response of the phonetic-interpretation mechanism to a sequence of identical tonal features. If this argument is correct, then downstep can be accounted for by a phonetic-interpretation rule like (63), which reads directly off the phonological representation; it is neither necessary nor desirable to provide a special representation such as the register tier of Inkelas, Leben, and Cobler, or the metrical trees of Clements (1981) and Huang (1980).

I should also say something about the relationship between down*step* and down*drift*. It has usually been assumed that, in the many languages which exhibit both down*step* (between [+UPPER] tones) and down*drift* (between [+UPPER] and [−UPPER]), these two phenomena should be collapsed into a single phonetic interpretation rule. This assumption has recently been called into question by Dolphyne (1987), who shows that, in Akan, the degree of lowering for down*step* is significantly greater than for down*drift*. However, should it prove desirable to collapse these two phenomena in some languages, that can easily be done in this framework, by a rule of the following form:

(71) $X_i \rightarrow X_{i+1}$ / T ——— [+UPPER] or [+UPPER] ——— T

(where T = any tonal feature on the [UPPER] tier)

Which of the two environments is chosen in (71) depends on whether a high tone is lowered after *l* at the beginning of an intonational phrase. The environment on the left is appropriate for languages like KiShambaa, where high tone is lowered after low, even in first position in the phrase (Odden 1982); the environment on the right is appropriate for languages like Igbo, in which the *first* high tone is not lowered even when it is preceded by low.

References

Archangeli, Diana. 1984. "Underspecification in Yawelmani Phonology and Morphology." Ph.D. dissertation, Massachusetts Institute of Technology.
Beckman, Mary E. and Janet B. Pierrehumbert. 1986. "Intonational Structure in Japanese and English." *Phonology Yearbook* 3, 255–309.
Carlson, Robert. 1983. "Downstep in Supyire." *Studies in African Linguistics* 14, 35-45.
Carrell, Patricia L. 1970. *A Transformational Grammar of Igbo*. West African Language Monographs, no. 8. Cambridge: Cambridge University Press.
Clark, Mary. 1989. "Downstep without Floating Tones." Ms., Department of English, University of New Hampshire, Durham, N.H.
———. 1990. *The Tonal System of Igbo*. Dordrecht: Foris Publications.
Clements, George N. 1981. "The Hierarchical Representation of Tone." In *Harvard Studies in Phonology* 2, edited by G.N. Clements, 50–108.
Clements, George N. and Kevin C. Ford. 1979. "Kikuyu Tone Shift and its Synchronic Consequences." *Linguistic Inquiry* 10, 179–210.
Dolphyne, Florence A. 1987. "The Phonetics and Phonology of Downstepped High Tones." Paper delivered to the 18th Annual Meeting of the African Linguistics Society, UQAM, Montreal.
Goldsmith, John. 1976. "Autosegmental Phonology." Ph.D. dissertation, Massachusetts Institute of Technology, Cambridge. [Published by New York: Garland Publishing Corp., 1979.]
Huang, James. 1980. "The Metrical Structure of Terrace-level Tones." In *Proceedings of NELS 10*, edited by John T. Jensen, 257–70. Amherst, Mass.: GLSA.
Hyman, Larry M. 1985. "Word Domains and Downstep in Bamileke-Dschang." *Phonology Yearbook* 2, 47–83.
Hyman, Larry and Maurice Tadadjeu. 1976. "Floating Tones in Mbam-Nkam." In *Southern California Occasional Papers in Linguistics* 3, edited by Larry M. Hyman, 57–111. Los Angeles: Department of Linguistics, University of Southern California.
Inkelas, Sharon, William R. Leben, and Mark Cobler. 1988. "The Phonology of Intonation." In *Proceedings of NELS 17*, edited by Joyce McDonough and Bernadette Plunkett, 327–41. Amherst, Mass.: GLSA.
Kiparsky, Paul. 1982a. "Lexical Morphology and Phonology." In *Linguistics in the Morning Calm*, edited by I.-S. Yang, 3–91. Seoul: Hanshin.
———. 1982b. "From Cyclic to Lexical Phonology. In *The Structure of Phonological Representations*. Part 1, edited by Harry van der Hulst and Norval Smith, 131–75. Dordrecht: Foris Publications.
Liberman, Mark and Janet Pierrehumbert. 1984. "Intonational Invariance under Changes in Pitch Range and Length." In *Language Sound Structure*, edited by Mark Aronoff and Richard T. Oehrle, 157–233. Cambridge, Mass.: MIT Press.
Mohanan, K. P. 1982. "Lexical Phonology. Ph.D. dissertation, Massachusetts Institute of Technology. [Distributed by the Indiana University Linguistics Club, Bloomington, Indiana.]
Odden, David. 1982. "Tonal Phenomena in KiShambaa." *Studies in African Linguistics* 13, 177–214.
Pulleyblank, Douglas. 1986. *Tone in Lexical Phonology*. Dordrecht: Reidel Publishing Co.
Stewart, John M. 1981. "Key Lowering (Downstep/Downglide) in Dschang." *Journal of African Languages and Linguistics* 3, 113–38.
Tadadjeu, Maurice. 1974. "Floating Tones, Shifting Rules, and Downstep in Dschang-Bamileke," *Studies in African Linguistics, Supplement* 5, 283–90.

Yip, Moira. 1982. "The Tonal Phonology of Chinese. Ph.D. dissertation, Massachusetts Institute of Technology. [Distributed by the Indiana University Linguistics Club, Bloomington, Indiana.]
———. 1989. "Contour Tones." *Phonology* 6, 149–74.

Register Tones and Tonal Geometry

Larry M. Hyman

1. INTRODUCTION*

From the very beginning of the study of African tone systems, it was recognized that tonal oppositions are relative in nature: a tone is H(igh) not because it is realized on a particular pitch (as measured by absolute fundamental frequency), but rather because it stands in opposition to L(ow) tone, realized in the same environment with relatively lower pitch. This recognition has been particular critical to the study of so-called terrace-level systems (Welmers 1959, 1973) in which "downdrift" and "downstep" produce iterative register-lowering that reportedly can result in a L tone having the same or higher pitch than a H tone occurring later in the same phrasal span. The literature on this subject is quite extensive (see Clements 1979; Hyman 1979, 1986 and references cited therein) and has generated a number of proposals for the formal treatment of these phenomena. My own work, for instance, has been characterized by three concerns: First, how does one determine whether a system is a terrace-level one (e.g. whether a tone intermediate between H and L is a downstepped high tone ($^!$H) or a mid tone (M))? Second, how does one formalize downdrift and downstep (this concern being shared by a number of researchers). Third and finally, how does one reveal the phonetic and historical relationships that exist between downstepped and lowered tones, e.g. between $^!$H and M?

Despite the tentative answers that have been provided, these questions still remain open and their answers subject to revision. Both developments in theory and the constantly expanding data base have kept register-lowering in the forefront of research on African tone systems. In this paper I would like to expand the discussion to include the issue of register-*raising*. By studying the process or processes by which tones are raised, as opposed to lowered, I hope to gain further insight into the three questions posed at the end of the preceding paragraph. As we

---

* I would like to thank Sharon Inkelas and Keith Snider for their thoughtful comments on an almost identical earlier form of this paper, as well as Will Leben for discussions of these issues on a number of occasions.

shall see, the same questions arise in this new context. Thus, we must first ask how we know whether a raised H tone is an "upstepped" H, i.e. a H preceded by some kind of upstepping operator ($^{\uparrow}$H) or constitutes a new discrete level tone, e.g. a superhigh tone (S). Second, how does one formalize upstep (or tone raising in general)? Third and finally, assuming that both exist, how does one reveal the relationship between $^{\uparrow}$H and S?

In this paper I shall be interested in recurrent properties of tonal upstep, by which I mean a raising of H tone by a register feature.[1] In section 2 I shall present the tonal geometry and tone features that I assume in this study. In the following three sections I shall describe upstepping of H tone in three African languages: Engenni (section 3), Mankon (section 4) and Kirimi (section 5). A brief conclusion is presented in section 6.

2. THE PROPOSAL

In this section I shall present a model of tone feature geometry that accounts for a number of recurrent tonal phenomena found in African languages. Such a model must meet the two requirements of providing i) a set of tone features and ii) a geometry specifying how these features relate to each other and to non-tonal features. Concerning the first requirement, I propose to retain the tonal features of Hyman (1986), which are here defined as in (1).

(1)   Tone features: H = at or above a neutral reference tone height
                     L = at or below a neutral reference tone height

One can think of the "neutral reference tone height" as being a M pitch. The reason that I have not defined H as necessarily "above" and L as necessarily "below" the reference tone height is that the two features may cooccur (see below). In this system, a tone-bearing unit (TBU) which has only a H feature will normally be a H tone, and a TBU which has only a L feature will be a L tone. Combinations of these features allow for additional tone heights as well as tonal contours, as we shall see.

Concerning the second requirement, I shall argue for the representation of tone in (2).

---

1 I therefore will not go into the issue of whether there is a distinct entity "raised H" that is not equatable with upstep.

(2)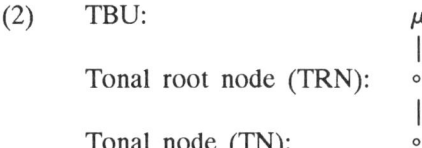

The structure in (2), which has been proposed by Yip (1989) to capture properties of contour tones in East Asian languages, embodies two essential claims. First, tone features link up to a tonal node (TN). Second, these TNs link to a tonal root node (TRN). As in other proposals (Archangeli and Pulleyblank 1986; Hyman and Pulleyblank 1988; Inkelas 1987, 1989; Snider 1988, 1990; Yip 1988, 1989, this volume), the TRN links directly to the TBU, which is indicated as a mora (μ) in (2).[2]

I shall claim that the proposals in (1) and (2) combine to produce all of the relevant tonal distinctions found in African languages. For example, the three tone heights L, H and M can be indicated, respectively, as in (3).

(3)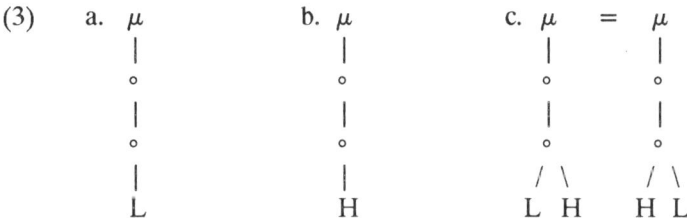

As seen in (3c), a M tone is obtained when the features L and H both link to the TN. Rather than saying that the L and H cancel each other out, as was assumed in my earlier study, I shall here assume that the "co-unification" of the two features is permitted because the definitions in (1) are not mutually exclusive. Specifically, when they combine, the resulting tone can only be "at the neutral reference height". Thus, both representations in (3c) would represent a tone that is M.

In this framework, I assume that sub-nodal ordering of features is not possible, i.e. that features may either combine (because they do not have

---

2 There are occasional claims in the literature that tone may link directly to a syllable—e.g. see Clements (1984) for Kikuyu. My claim is that tone, like other features, always targets the same landing site, the mora. In cases where the TBU appears to be the syllable, there is a restriction that tone can link only to the *head* (i.e. first) mora of a syllable. In other words, there may be non-tonal moras, but not tonal non-moras (depressor consonants notwithstanding).

conflicting values or definitions) or they cannot. Hence the two representations in (3c) cannot be contrastive. On the other hand, nodes are ordered, as we see in the representations of LH (rising) and HL (falling) tones in (4).³

(4)

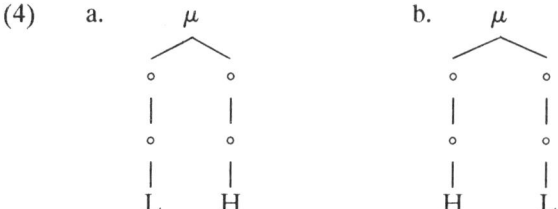

Rising-falling (LHL) and falling-rising (HLH) contours can be represented as three TNs linking to the TBU. Other contours such as LM and ML etc. are obtained by manipulating the features of (1) and the structures of (2), as seen in (5).

(5)

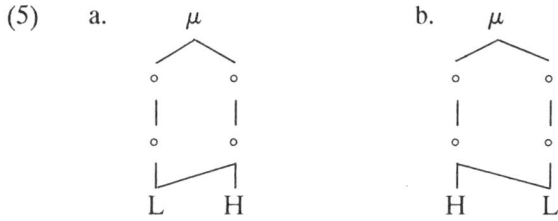

We thus see how the features H and L define three tone heights—as well as a number of tonal contours, when their TRNs are sequenced. The crucial question that now arises is how one can represent more than three tone heights. It is this question that motivates a distinction between the TRN and the TN in (2). Before elaborating the actual proposal, let us consider the range of phenomena that should or might be represented. It seems that there are three separate types of phenomena we might consider:

First, there are languages that have more than three discrete tone heights, e.g. Jukun (Welmers 1973), various Kru languages (see Kaye et al 1982) and Igede (Bergman 1971), the latter receiving considerable

---

3 This approach would seem to have problems capturing some of the properties of contour tones in East Asian languages (Yip 1989; Chan 1989). However, Yip makes an interesting case in favor of distinguishing between tonal contours (as in East Asian languages) vs. tonal clusters (as in African languages). The former have more than one TN reporting to a single TRN, while the latter have a separate TRN for each TN (see Yip 1989).

theoretical attention (Stahlke 1977; Clements 1983). By "discrete" is meant that the language allows a maximum of four tone heights. Particularly troublesome would be a case where there were four such levels and no particular redundancies or restrictions on their distribution. If the four heights are symmetric in this way, i.e. no one of them is derived from one of the other three, then this would require revision of the tone features in (1), perhaps along the lines of the features [upper] and [raised] adopted by Yip (1980) and Pulleyblank (1986).

Second, there are languages that have raising or lowering processes that must be represented by an adequate model of tonal geometry. These processes may be discrete in the sense that a non-iterating additional level is derived (e.g. a raised L, a lower M, etc.). They may also be non-discrete or "terracing" by allowing iteration of the process. The most well-known such case is the downstepping of H tones, where there can, in principle, be a sequence H-$^!$H-$^!$H... that iterates indefinitely, with each $^!$H lower than the last (but still not reaching L tone). However, there are also cases of $^!$L, e.g. Bamileke-Dschang (see Hyman 1985 and references cited therein) and $^!$M, e.g. Ngamambo (Hyman 1986). There also are cases of tone raising, e.g. so-called upstepped H tones, though an iterating upstepping process is unknown in Africa.

Third, there are numerous intonational phenomena that alter the pitch height of tones, creating superhighs, superlows and so forth. Intonational downdrift is a well-known example. The tendency has been to treat such intonational raising and lowering with the same tone features used for other purposes (Hyman 1986; Inkelas 1989, Leben, Inkelas and Cobler 1989; Snider 1988).

The proposal that is made in these works is that there are two different tonal planes: one consisting of the features needed to capture basic tonal oppositions, the other consisting of the features needed for so-called register effects—i.e. raising and lowering for allophonic, phonemic or intonational purposes. Two binary oppositions, one per tier, do not suffice, however, to capture the reality of a downstepped M tone ($^!$M) such as in Ngamambo (Hyman 1986), since if two features are required to get the M (cf. (3c)), what feature can give us the downstep—and where is it in the tonal geometry?

The solution I would like to propose rejects the notion that one tone feature defines tone level and the other tone register. Instead, *both* features can define basic tone levels, as in (3), but in addition, one or both of these features is available to define register shifts up and down. If we assume with the above scholars that there is a second tonal "plane" for register, but accept our view of the tonal geometry in (3), this produces at least the following tonal representations:

(6)		(a)	(b)	(c)	(d)	(e)	(f)	(g)	(h)	(i)
T-plane:	H	L	LH	H	L	LH	H	L	LH
R-plane:	∅	∅	∅	L	L	L	H	H	H
TONE:	H	L	M	ˡH	ˡL	ˡM	ˢH	ˢL	ˢM

In (6) the three-way opposition of (3) is represented on what is identified as the tonal (T-) plane, which links to the tonal node. The register (R-) plane that links to the tonal root node has also been represented with three possibilities: no feature (∅), L, and H. (A LH representation, if allowed, would have been equivalent to ∅ and is thus not given.) The resulting tones are given in the third row: first, the basic H, L and M in (6a–c), then downstepped and upstepped variants of H, M and L in (6d–f) and (6g–i), respectively.

The table in (6) is much more complex than the possibilities considered by Africanists who, working on register, generally side-step the question of M tones. Inkelas (1989), for instance, proposes a system where ˡH and ˢH have the representation as in (6d) and (6g) in Chaga. However, in her system (6e) stands for a regular L tone, while (6h) represents a prepausal level or non-falling L, symbolized as L°. It is not clear how downstepped Ls would be treated in her system, since she has already used (6e) for regular Ls. The representation in (6h) stands for L° for Inkelas, which should mean that you cannot get a downstepped non-falling L. As shown by Hyman and Tadadjeu (1976) and Hyman (1985), however, Bamileke-Dschang has all of the oppositions in (7).

(7) a. L-L, L-L°
    b. L-ˡL, L-ˡL°

Perhaps the same features would be defined differently for Bamileke-Dschang than for Chaga. Since there are four different L tones (L, L°, ˡL, ˡL°), it is not clear how this could be possible, given that the system is restricted to two features. In any case, it should be preferable to establish a single set of features that can apply universally to define equivalent oppositions across languages.

With this proposal, tonal geometry provides for four types of structure, as seen in (8).

(8)   a.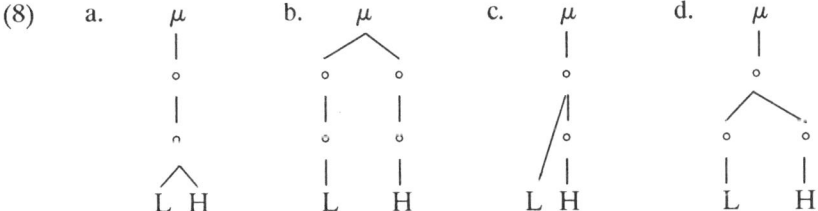

In (8a) the L and H features link to the TN and thus combine to define a M tone. In (8b) the L and H each has its own TN and TRN. Since the TBU is linked to two TRNs, (8b) defines a LH rising tone. In (8c) we see that while the H links first to a TN and then to the TRN, the preceding L links directly to the TRN. The interpretation of a tonal feature linking directly to the TRN is that it is a register feature, in this case a downstep. (8c) thus unambiguously stands for a $^{!}$H tone.[4] Finally, (8d) is the representation that Yip (1989) proposes for a LH rising tone that functions as a unit (as seen from its one root node). While apparently attested in Southeast Asian languages, I have not seen (8d) to be needed in the African languages I am familiar with.[5]

The structural distinctions in (8) also allow for the corresponding four types of assimilation by spreading shown in (9).

(9)   a.

---

4   This account is very similar to Yip's (this volume) proposal that the feature [raised] links to the feature [upper], the latter serving as a register feature. I differ only in considering the L in (8c) and other examples to be on a separate tier, and hence available for spreading independently of the TN, while in Yip's proposal, the spreading of [upper] will automatically take the dependent feature [raised] with it. Note that while it is crucial for the representation of $^{!}$H that the H have a TN and the L not have one, the order of the L and the H is of no consequence. This follows from the position I have taken that only tonal nodes are linearly ordered. The register L could thus have been placed after the H in (8c) with the same result.
5   If attested in Africa, however, I would expect (8d) to likely appear in the Kru family, where contours have occasionally be interpreted other than as sequences (see for example Newman 1986).

In each case we start with a representation of L-H realized on two moras. In (9a) the L spreads onto the following TN, thereby modifying L-H to L-M, as required in both Ngamambo and Kom (Hyman 1986; Hyman and Pulleyblank 1988). In (9b), where a TRN spreads onto the following TBU, we effect the familiar change from L-H to L-LH, as in Yoruba (Akinlabi 1984; Pulleyblank 1986). In (9c), where the L spreads directly onto the following TRN (without its intervening TN), the following H undergoes a register lowering. The output of this process is thus L-$^!$H, i.e. the familiar downdrift phenomenon (if to be expressed as part of the phonology). Finally, (9d) is the form the L-spreading rule would take if a unitary LH contour is produced by the process. With the above structural distinctions we are thus able to account for all three tonal assimilations as cases of spreading. We also are able to keep the outputs of (9a) and (9c) distinct—something which was a problem in Hyman (1986), where emphasis was on the superficial resemblance between H tone lowering to M and H tone lowering to $^!$H.[6]

We also are able to improve on the formulation of tone level and tone register assimilations in complicated tone systems such as are found in Bamileke-Dschang and Ngamambo. In Bamileke-Dschang, a word domain with a linked L-H followed by a floating L is realized as L-$^!$H, e.g. /ǹ-dóŋˋ/ 'horn' is realized [ǹ$^!$dóŋ]. Within the proposed framework, this change is expressed as in (10a).

(10)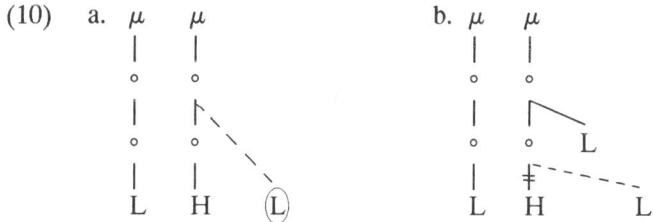

The unlinked L links to the TRN and becomes a register feature, as desired. Although one writes L-$^!$H, with the downstep operator $^!$ preceding the affected tone, it does not matter that the register L follows the H in (10a), since only nodes are linearly ordered with respect to one another. A second rule in Bamileke-Dschang results in this L-$^!$H being

---

6 Allowance was and should be made for M tone not to be phonetically identical to $^!$H, as in Yala Ikom (Armstrong 1968) and Ga'anda (Newman 1971). I have also noted that $^!$H is much lower in some languages (e.g. Dagbani; Aboh dialect of Igbo) than is normally expected. These variations can be accounted for if we assume that the features, especially in their register function, provide different instructions to the phonetic implementation rules in different languages.

realized as L-¹L when the sequence is followed by another L. This rule is formalized in (10b), where the register L now spreads onto the TN, delinking the H. The binodal representation is thus well equipped to account for the unusual source of L-¹H and the ¹L phenomenon of Bamileke-Dschang. It also is well suited to derive M and ¹M in Ngamambo. The first rule needed in this language is identical to (10a) in Bamileke-Dschang, except that it requires that the first L be unlinked, as seen in (11a).

(11)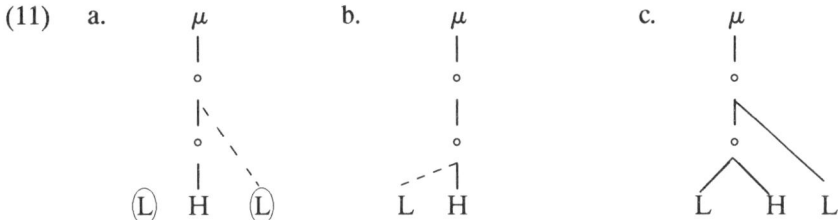

This is followed by a second rule that spreads any L (linked or unlinked) onto a following H TN, as seen in (11b). The result is that those sequences undergoing both (11a) and (11b) will come to be realized with a ¹M tone, i.e. as in (11c). Or, to take another source of ¹M, the derivation is given in (12) for the surface H-¹M of Ngamambo [fɨ-¹kìŋ] 'pot' in:

(12)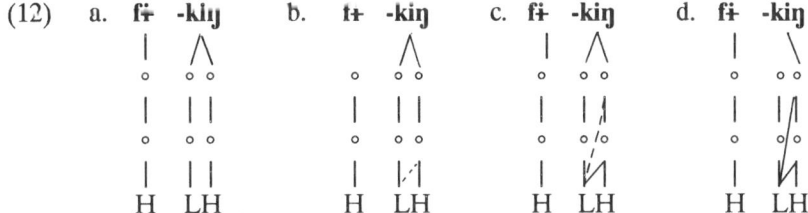

In (12a) we start with a H linked to the prefix fɨ- and a LH linked to the stem -kiŋ. In (12b) rule (11b) has applied, spreading the L to the following TN, deriving M tone. In (12c) a special rule applies lowering the M of the -LM rising contour. Since this lowering affects subsequent M tones, we identify this rule as register lowering and provide for the L to spread to the TN of the following H. The final step in (12d) delinks the L TN from the stem, thereby modifying intermediate H-L¹M to surface H-¹M.

Other cases of tone- and register-lowering can be accounted for without event. What is less clear is whether this (or any other) system can account for apparent cases of register-*raising* or *upstep*. The table in (6) allows for the register of H, L and M to be raised to ⁺H, ⁺L and ⁺M in (6g–i). Perhaps ⁺L can be identified as the raised, non-falling L of Bamileke-Fe'fe', which does not reach the level of M (Hyman 1972). This ⁺L tone contrasts with the lower, falling L only before pause, however. It in fact seems doubtful that a distinction between the two will ever be required, since as has been shown in a number of Grassfields Bantu languages (Bamileke, Ngemba, Babanki, Kom, Aghem, Ngamambo etc.), in Eastern Bantu languages such as Kikuyu (Clements 1984) and Chaga (McHugh 1985; Inkelas 1989), the Chadic language Tangale (Kenstowicz and Kidda 1987) and others, ⁺L (or L°) results from a following floating H that prevents "downgliding" (Stewart 1971) from applying prepausally.[7]

If a ⁺L tone is doubtful, the identity of a ⁺M tone is even less clear. There are two interpretations of ⁺M that come to mind. First, a tone that is derived from M, but is intermediate in pitch between M and H, i.e. a raised M. Second, a tone that is phonetically identical to H but which functions as M, i.e. an upstepped M. I know of no need for either type of tone.[8]

This leaves ⁺H as the only viable candidate for a register H tone. The literature abounds with reports of raised, upstepped, or super-H tones (henceforth, ⁺H). ⁺H seems rarely (never?) to be part of the underlying system, except maybe for sporadic grammatical morphemes that require exceptional listing. Instead, it is produced by a wide range of conditions, which can involve dissimilation, accent and intonation. If a register H feature does exist, there is no formal reason why it shouldn't have the same properties as register L, i.e. producing raised variants of L, H and M. Since ⁺H is the most clearly attested tone that can be said to have undergone register raising, it behooves us to take a closer look at systems which have this property. For this purpose I propose to consider three languages in the following sections: Engenni (section 3), Mankon (section 4) and Kirimi (section 5). Each of these languages has an

---

7 Kenstowicz and Kidda (1987) don't actually make the connection between the facts they have in Tangale and what has been reported in the other languages cited. However, by proposing that L-H becomes prepausal L-L° via L tone spreading + delinking of the H, Tangale fits in with what is known about other African tone languages: First, L° is accounted for as in Bamileke etc., and second, with the proper rule formulation, Tangale ceases to be the only example reported in the literature where tone appears to exhibit geminate blockage.

8 The case of the raised H (R) tone which Clements (1978) analyzes as a raised variant of M hopefully can be analyzed with H tone spreading creating a H Ⓛ H sequence, where the H TBU before the Ⓛ goes up to ⁺H, as in the languages discussed in the following sections, and then spreads as proposed by Clements.

upstepping process by which a H tone is raised before a L, which we shall now attempt to describe.

3. H TONE RAISING IN ENGENNI

The first language under consideration is Engenni, as described by Thomas (1974, 1978). In contrast with the other two languages to be considered, Engenni has a so-called discrete-level tone system, allowing for only three tone heights: H, L and ꜛH. The ꜛH tone is derived from a H that is followed by L, as seen in (13):

(13) a. mì móní wó   'I saw you.'
         mì móní ꜛwó bhèè   'I did see you'
     b. ìꜛkpílàmá nú   'as for snail'
         ìꜛkpílàꜛmá nà   'the snail'

The forms in (13) show alternation between H and ꜛH, the latter being obtained when there is a following L tone. The word ìꜛkpílàmá 'snail' also shows that ꜛH may be derived internally to a morpheme which has an underlying H-L sequence, as seen also in (14).

(14) a. /ómù/   →   ꜛómù   'house'
         /ónù/   →   ꜛónù   'mother'
     b. /únwónì/ →   úꜛnwónì   'mouth'
         /ávúvò/ →   áꜛvúvò   'bat'

In cases where the L tone vowel is elided, the ꜛH tone is still retained on the surface:

(15) a. /únwónì ólíló/   →   úꜛnwón' ólíló   'mouth of a bottle'
     b. /ó vúmù ópílópó/ →   ó ꜛvúm' ópílópó 'she will dry the
                                                pig meat.'

One way to account for the ꜛH realizations in (15) is to order H tone raising (or "upstep" as Thomas refers to it) to precede vowel elision. The alternative is to let vowel elision apply first, but allow H tone raising to be sensitive to a floating L (which by the familiar stability effect would not be affected by vowel elision). Thomas points out that unpredictable upstepping occurs in various parts of the grammar, e.g. before a serialized verb, as in (16):

(16) a. ò dó í⁺gbó̱ dhẹ́mésè 'He wove the net bigger.'
(lit. he wove net made big)⁹
b. ọ̀ dú ópíló⁺pó̱ gbêì 'he bought a pig (and) killed it'

As Thomas herself hypothesizes (1974:15, note 1), this can be due to a "lost L which occurred with the pronominal prefix to the second verb". In synchronic Engenni we can let H tone raising be sensitive to a floating L.

We now turn to the two constraints on S within the "phonological clause" in Engenni: the sequences *⁺H-H-⁺H (non-raised H wedged between upstepped Hs) and *⁺H⁺H (two upstepped Hs in sequence) are disallowed. This accounts for why upstepping does not occur on dhẹ́mésè in (16a), nor on gbẹ́ì in (16b). The generalization is that, going from left to right, one cannot obtain subsequent ⁺H tones in a phonological clause unless each ⁺H is separated from the preceding ⁺H by a *surface* L tone (i.e. not a floating L). Additional examples are seen in (17).

(17) a. /ó díre ẹ́dà/ → ó ⁺dír' ẹ́dà
'She will cook beans.'   (*⁺ẹ́dà)
b. /ágbà íkùlélè/ → ⁺ágb' íkù⁺lélè
'railing of iron'   (*⁺íkù⁺lélè)

The question is why these constraints should be in effect?

The solution I propose involves the following rule ordering: first, a floating L is assigned as a register tone on the following H or sequence of Hs; second, a single H TBU is raised to ⁺H before L. If the TBU in question has a register L assigned by the first rule, ⁺H tone is not obtained. The relevant structures are shown in (18).¹⁰

(18) a. H-(L)-H-L → ⁺H-H-L (*⁺H-⁺H-L)
b. H-(L)-H-H-L → ⁺H-H-H-L (*⁺H-H-⁺H-L)

After application of the first rule, (18a,b) have the representations in (19a,b).

---

9 The failure of H tone raising to apply in **dhẹ́mésè** or **gbêì** is principled and discussed below.
10 In all of the Engenni discussion, a transcribed H is not realized on a raised level unless it is itself preceded by a ⁺ operator. This differs from Mankon (section 3), where the ⁺ potentially affects a sequence of Hs.

(19)

In (19a) register L affects a single TBU, since there is only one H that follows. In (19b), on the other hand, two H TBUs are affected which are shown with a single H feature, assuming that successive H features have by this point in the derivation been fused into one. Crucial in this account is the claim that there is an asymmetry between downstep and downdrift: the former interacts with the creation of ꜛH, while the latter does not. We shall see that the same holds true in Mankon and Kirimi in subsequent sections.[11]

This then leaves us with the question of how to derive the ꜛH tone itself. Two possibilities suggest themselves. The first is that there is a register H feature that in combination with level H defines the ꜛH tone. The second is to attribute the ꜛH level to the phonetic implementation rules. In this case, any H would be interpreted as ꜛH if it (a) is followed by L; and (b) does not have a register L. In other words, the difference between Engenni with its ꜛH, H and L system, and a comparable H, M, L system (such as in Kom, for instance, where M is derived from H after L) is one of phonetic interpretation of phonological features. At stake is the question of whether there is a phonological H register tone in Engenni—or ultimately in any language. There is Engenni-specific evidence that a register H tone simplifies the tonology in rather significant ways. Thomas (1978:12—13) lists a number of grammatical contexts where an "upstep phoneme" is needed in Engenni. While some of these reduce to the presence of a L tonal morpheme, as was suggested to precede the serialized verbs in (16), others are not as amenable to such an analysis. For example, "the genitival relationship between two

---

[11] Inkelas (1987a) is the only person who has addressed the question of how constraints such as *ꜛH-ꜛH and *ꜛH-H-ꜛH might be accounted for in some principled way. However, her OCP account does not seem to extend in a natural way to the cases I discuss in this paper. Since Ⓛ may condition raising on the preceding H, it should be clear that this H and a H that might follow Ⓛ the cannot have coalesced into an OCP-driven single feature representation, as Inkelas suggests. It is equally important to note that not all languages having H tone raising obey the *ꜛH-ꜛH and *ꜛH-H-ꜛH constraints. In Bamileke-Fe'fe', for instance, it is possible to get both of these sequences (Hyman 1976). I would claim that this is because the source of ꜛH has nothing to do in synchronic Fe'fe' with a following L or Ⓛ tone. (In Hyman 1976 I arbitrarily identify ꜛH as a H tone. Its marked status, e.g. near non-presence in underlying representations, suggests an analysis along the lines of Thomas' ꜛH tone in Engenni.)

nouns is marked by an initial upstepped high tone on the second noun" (Thomas 1974:15), as seen in (20):

(20) a. /ògà/ + /ígbó/ → òg' ⁺ígbó 'edge of the net'
b. /àdhù/ + /ópílópó/ → àdhw' ⁺ópílópó 'eye of a pig'
c. /àdhù/ + /òkò/ → àdhw' ⁺ọ̀kò 'front of the canoe'

(20a,b) show the first H of the second noun going up to ⁺H, while (20c) shows the initial L of /òkò/ 'canoe' becoming a ⁺HL falling tone. It is quite clear that a (L) tone will not give us these alternations. The most straightforward analysis is to posit a (H) tone. This will (H) link to a following L TBU to create a HL contour which then may become ⁺HL (if this does not produce *⁺H-⁺H or *⁺H-H-⁺H) as in (20c). If the second noun begins with a H TBU, then the (H) links to this TBU as a register H, and we obtain the S tone we require (again, assuming that the constraints are not broken—cf. (17b), where the initial H of /íkùlélè/ 'iron' cannot become ⁺H either from the genitive upstepping process *or* from the L of the following TBU [kù]).

This analysis is rather unusual, in that one is not accustomed to finding cases where a H tone causes another H tone to go up in pitch.¹² One alternative might be that the floating tone in the genitive is not H, but rather ⁺H, whatever its feature representation might be. Another is to have (H) as before, but a morphologized upstepping rule that simply says: raise the initial H of a genitive noun (which automatically will apply to (20c), if the (H) links to the following L TBU before upstepping). Finally, we could apply Clark's (1989) Igbo analysis to Engenni: the genitive tonal morpheme would be a (H) (L) sequence. The (H) would raise to ⁺H because of the following (L) and then link to the following vowel in all cases (except perhaps where this would violate the constraints on ⁺H). I take as self-evident that all of these analyses are more complex than the simple floating H analysis with its register effects.¹³

---

12 Remarkably, however, the situation in Bamileke-Fe'fe' is identical but mirror-image: a (H) genitive marker is always assigned to the previous syllable. If this syllable is L, a LH contour is obtained on the surface. If it is H, the syllable becomes ⁺H (cf. Hyman 1976—though I spoke of M becoming H, not H becoming ⁺H). In this language we must say that the (H) is assigned leftwards to the TN unless the TN already has a H feature, in which case (H) is assigned to the TRN as an upstepping register feature.
13 Note that this partially addresses a concern expressed to me by Douglas Pulleyblank (personal communication) that this highly articulated view of tonal geometry allows more possibilities than are attested, e.g. floating H level tone, floating H register tone, floating H level + H register tone etc. It would be desirable to demand that floating tones be totally without structure, but that their effects can be either on the tone level or the tone

I therefore conclude that register H is needed in Engenni in addition to register L. The final statement is that H tones that have not gotten either register L from the linking of (L) or register H from the upstepping process, will merge with the former category. Whether this is to be done by phonetic implementation or by assignment of a default L register tone (cf. Inkelas' 1989 account of Chaga) is something I will leave open, as we turn now to consider two other cases of H tone raising.[14]

4. H TONE RAISING IN MANKON

The related processes of H tone raising in Mankon have been documented by Hyman and Tadadjeu (1976) and Leroy (1977, 1979). Mankon belongs to the Ngemba dialect cluster within Eastern Grassfields Bantu, which makes it closely related to Bamileke-Dschang. While the above cited works see ⁺H tones resulting from the simplification of HL contour tones, in this study I shall instead refer to the role of floating L tones in conditioning H tone raising and/or tonal downstep. As seen in (21), floating L may condition the raising of a *following* H in Mankon:

(21)   L   H   (L)   H   →   L   H   ⁺H

This rule states that if a floating L tone is wedged between H tones, the first of which is itself preceded by a L tone, the second H tone goes up to S, as in (22).[15]

---

register, as we have just seen. The other desire would be to insist that floating tones all become incorporated into the tonal geometry or be stray erased (see below). Both of these 'desires' raise issues that need further investigation, e.g. how to order floating (structureless) tones with respect to other tones, how to get floating tone effects that have nothing to do with register, and so forth.

14 Since the tone system of Engenni is relatively simple in inventory, it is worth mentioning the following underspecification account: underlying tones are either L or ∅. A toneless vowel acquires H before L. As before, the genitive morpheme is a floating H which either goes onto a following ∅ vowel or combines with a following L to create a HL contour tone. H tone is interpreted as raised H or Thomas' "top" tone; all remaining toneless vowels are interpreted with default M (=non-raised H) tone. In order to see if this goes through, one would have to look carefully at the tone rules in the language—i.e. does one need regular H tone to be there for tone mapping and tone rules early in the derivation?

15 These and other examples show that word-final schwa frequently deletes in Mankon (see Warnier [Leroy] and Voorhoeve 1975; Leroy 1977).

(22)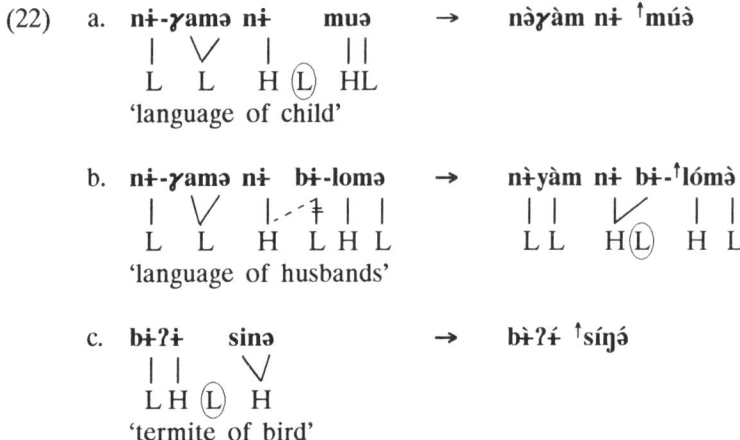

In (22a), the floating L is a segmentless class 1 prefix on the noun 'child', whose H goes up to ⁺H. (22b) shows that (21) is also triggered by Ⓛ that comes to be unlinked by virtue of a H tone spreading rule. As also seen, the doubly linked H still counts as one H tone in satisfying the structural description of (21). Note also that unlike Engenni, the ⁺ upstepper in (22c) affects all successive H TBUs in Mankon, not just the one TBU that follows the (here the class 9 genitive marker). Finally, we see in (23) that pause counts as a L tone for the purpose of H tone raising:

(23)   bɨ   yiŋə   →   bɨ́ ⁺yíŋə̀   'they have come'
         | ||
     ∥ Ⓛ H   Ⓛ HL

In (23), the initial floating L is a pause-initial boundary tone. Since it is always present to mark pause, (21) will apply in this environment. It should thus not be possible to start an utterance with a ⁺H-⁺H sequence.[16]

If, on the other hand, the H Ⓛ H sequence is not preceded by L, the Ⓛ is interpreted as a downstep operator as per our normal expectations. However, in examples such as (24), the downstep interval

---

16 This is consistent with the materials available to me, which consist in part of paradigms transcribed with the help of Jacqueline Leroy in which there are no post-pause S-H sequences. It should be noted, as Dr. Leroy once cautioned me, that the situation is somewhat more complex overall than the brief presentation I am giving it here: Mankon appears to have a domain sensitivity like that of its relative Bamileke-Dschang (Hyman 1985), but this requires further investigation.

is produced not by lowering the second H, but by raising the pitch level of the *preceding* H TBU:

(24) a. bɨ-sinə   bɨ   muə   →   bɨsíŋ ꜛbɨ́ ꜜmúə̀
        | \/ | ||
        L H   H   Ⓛ   H L
        'birds of child'

   b. bɨ-siŋə bɨ   bɨ-lomə   →   bɨsíŋ bɨ́ ꜛbɨ́ꜜlómə̀
      | \/ |.--‡ | | | | | | |
      L H   H L H L   L H   H Ⓛ H L
      'birds of husbands'

In (24a) upstepping is caused by the floating L prefix on 'child', while in (24b) H upstepping is conditioned by the L that is delinked as a result of H tone spreading from the genitive bɨ onto the L tone prefix bɨ of 'husbands'.

It can be seen from these examples that a second raising process is needed that affects only a single H TBU, as in (25).

(25)   H Ⓛ H   →   ꜛH ꜜH

As a result of this second upstepping process, the H of the H-L stem in (26a) is noticeably lower than the raised H tone on the same TBU in (26b).

(26) a. à-ɣáɣə̀   'distance'
     b. à-ꜛɣá́ꜜɣə́ káŋə̀   'distance of squirrel'[17]

Rule (25) is however not completely general. Consider the sentences in (27):

(27) a. bɨ   zuŋə a   bɨʔe   →   bɨ́ꜛzúŋə̀ ꜛbɨ́ʔꜜə́
        | | | |.--‡ |
        H Ⓛ   H L   H   L H
        'they are buying a termite'

---

17 (26b) derives from /a-ɣaɣə + a + kaŋə/ through loss of the final ə of -ɣaɣə, producing a H Ⓛ H sequence which later become S H, as transcribed.

b. bɨ lo n-dzuŋə a   muə →   bɨ ꜛló ń-ˈdzúŋə́ ˈmúə̀
    | |ˏ-⸽   ⋁ | || *[ˈŋə́]
    H H L   H H Ⓛ   HL
    'they brought a child'

In (27a) ꜛH is first derived on [zú] by (21), recalling that the utterance begins with a boundary L marking pause. As also seen, ꜛH is again derived on [bɨʔ], this time by rule (25). Thus, Mankon does allow more than one ꜛH tone within a phrase or clause. In (27b), however, ꜛH is derived only on [ló ǹ] by (25). Although a later H Ⓛ H sequence occurs between the verb -dzúŋə́ and the object ˈmúə̀, (25) fails to apply and we do not obtain *[-dzúꜛŋə́].

I would like to propose that the reason for this is exactly as in Engenni: in Mankon, if a ꜛH has been created in an utterance, one cannot create a subsequent ꜛH unless there is a surface L that intervenes. There is a surface L in (27a) on [ˈzúŋə̀], and thus a second ꜛH can be derived. Since there is no such surface L in (27b), instead of H tone raising, we obtain standard downstepping (marked by ˈ).

We conclude that similar processes of upstep (H tone raising) can occur in either a discrete-level language such as Engenni, which is limited to three tone levels, or in a terrace-level language such as Mankon, which exhibits the standard recursive downstepping phenomenon. Upstepping in both languages has also been seen to be sensitive to the same surface L condition. We can account for this condition if we assume for both languages: 1) that upstepping is in fact a register phenomenon and 2) that only H tones can receive a register specification. In Engenni this is clear, since only H changes its level (to ꜛH), while L remains L in all environments. In Mankon, we have both upstepping and downstepping—but, crucially, I would like to claim, these processes can only target H tones.

Looking at the outputs in (27) we thus see that the same downstep relation obtains whether the sequence is H-ˈH without upstep or ꜛH-ˈH with upstep. As I pointed out in Hyman (1979), there is a general tendency to raise a H in anticipation of a downstep, to which we can attribute this second upstepping process.[18] Thus, we need only modify

---

18 As an example of this, contrast the following Luganda sentences:

(i)   àbásíbá kígùndú   'the ones who tie up Kigundu'
(ii) tèbásíbá ˈkígùndú   'they don't tie up Kigundu'

In isolation, both verb forms have the same tones, i.e. àbásíbâ 'the ones who tie', tèbásíbâ 'they don't tie up'. The L of the final HL is subject to the rule of L tone deletion (Hyman, Katamba and Walusimbi 1987) in the affirmative sentence (i), but not in the negative

(25) to reflect the constraint that it not apply if there is an earlier ↑H within the same "phonological clause" unless there is an intervening surface L.

There are several ways we might implement these findings. In (28) I summarize what I think is a straightforward proposal:

(28) a. Concerning L-H Ⓛ H (where pause also = L):
          i.   link Ⓛ to preceding TRN (=register L tone)
          ii. assign Ⓗ to following TRN (=register H tone)

      b. Concerning other H Ⓛ H sequences:
          i.   link Ⓛ to following TRN (=register L tone)
          ii. spread register H and L to following contiguous TRNs
          iii. assign Ⓗ to TRN preceding register L

      c. Constraints:
          i.   *Register L + Register H
          ii. *Register L or H + Tonal L

We begin by singling out in (28a) the special environment needed for (21). (28a.i) links the Ⓛ to the preceding TRN, while (28a.ii) introduces a H on the following TRN to account for upstepping. Ideally the change in (21) would be stated as a single change. This could be done if we simply suppress (28a.i.) and leave the floating Ⓛ with nowhere to go. I have kept (28a.i.) in part because this would unify the first procedure in both (28a) and (28b) to be the association of all Ⓛs as register tones. Though not an argument directly, I adhere to this view also because of the comparative evidence that shows that the Ⓛ of L-H Ⓛ lowers the preceding H tone in much of Grassfields Bantu (see Hyman 1985, 1986).

Concerning other H Ⓛ H sequences, the Ⓛ links to the following TRN (to cause downstepping). This is followed by spreading of both register tones. Finally, a H register tone is linked to a TRN that precedes a TRN with a register L. Because of the constraint in (28c.i), a register H will not be assigned to a TRN that already has a register L (by (28b.i)). I have included register spread (28b.ii) as a rule, though I a priori share the desire implicit in Snider (1988) to make the register tone link only to the first affected TRN (with subsequent featureless

---

sentence (ii). Consequently, the L merely delinks to simplify the contour and becomes a downstep operator in (ii). It is this downstep that causes the whole sequence of Hs to be higher in (ii) than they are in (i), as is particularly clear from the difference in the intervals L-H vs. L-↑H in the two sentences (cf. the Amo examples in Hyman 1979:25, note 5).

TRNs automatically realized at the same register). If we followed this suggestion here, the failure to get sequences of $*^{\uparrow}$H $^{!}$H^{n} $^{\uparrow}$H would be unaccounted for, other than to say that an upstep cannot occur within the "scope" of a downstep. Of course, by keeping L tones out of the register system entirely by the constraint in (28c.ii) we have been able to account for why a new upstep is possible in utterances such as (28a). This decision has interesting consequences for the conceptualization of downstep in general. In orthodox downstepping languages, where one finds $^{!}$H but not $^{!}$L (or $^{!}$M), register lowering is a property of H tones, and the lowering of Ls is a biproduct. In languages such as Bamileke-Dschang, where there is an opposition between L-L and L-$^{!}$L, it is of course necessary to allow register L to combine with tonal L. Finally, in Ngamambo, where there is an opposition between M-M and M-$^{!}$M, register L may in fact only combine with tonal M (Hyman 1986). The parameters thus consist of stating, first, which tone or tones in a language may accept a register feature, and second, under what conditions. In the next section we see that the Cahi dialect of Kirimi chooses to incorporate aspects both of Engenni and of Mankon.

5. UPSTEP IN KIRIMI (CAHI DIALECT)

Previous work on the tonology of Kirimi, a Bantu language spoken in Tanzania, consists of an unpublished Ph.D. dissertation (Olson 1964) which was reworked and interpreted by Schadeberg (1978, 1979). These descriptions are based on the Qirwana dialect, which we have found to diverge tonally from the more conservative Cahi dialect which I shall describe in this section.[19] Since this dialect has not been described, I provide limited paradigms in Table 1.[20]

---

19 Research on the Cahi dialect of Kirimi was carried out in a field methods course in 1985. I am grateful to Ms. Grace Puja, our informant, as well as to the members of this course for their participation in the analysis of this tone system. The Cahi tonal system is not only of interest for its registers, but also sheds light on how a tone may "shift" from one syllable to the next. Olson (and hence Schadeberg) describes Qirwana with a rule that spreads a H to the next vowel and and a rule that lowers all Hs to L before another H (which Goldsmith 1984 has termed "anti-Meeussen's Rule"). The combined effect is that the last of a sequence of phonological Hs will surface, but on the next vowel. Cahi has the same H tone spreading rule, but instead of lowering Hs to L, the lowering is only to M, as we shall see. Thus, we have a distinction between L-H and M-H that Olson does not describe for Qirwana. We note that the distinction between L and M was not immediately obvious and was in many contexts hard to hear. It thus is no surprise that it would be lost in another dialect (assuming that Olson's transcriptions are correct).
20 Which may also serve as a good data analysis problem on tone.

Table 1. Cahi Verb Forms

1. INFINITIVES

   a. *Examples showing stems with L vs. H verb roots:*

ùrèkà	ùtūmā̀
'to leave'	'to send'
ùyànjà	ùtēmā̀
'to love'	'to send'
ùrìmì	ùtūngā̀
'to cultivate'	'to tie'

   b. *Examples showing 'to leave' and 'to send' with an object:*

ùrèkà mùrìmì	ùtúm⁺á mùrìmì
'to leave a farmer'	'to send a farmer'
ùmùrèkà	ùmùtūmā̀
'to leave him/her'	'to send him/her'
ùvá⁺rékà	ùvātūmā̀
'to leave them'	'to send them'

   c. *Infinitives occurring with applied suffix meaning 'to/for'*

ùrèkèyà	ùtú⁺míyà
'to leave for'	'to send to'
ùrèkèyà mùrìmì	ùtú⁺míyà mùrìmì
'to leave for a farmer'	'to send to a farmer'
ùmùrèkèyà	ùmùtú⁺míyà
'to leave for him/her'	'to send to him/her'
ùvá⁺rékèyà	ùvátú⁺míyà
'to leave for them'	'to send to them'

   d. *Reduplications meaning 'here' and 'there'*

ùrèkàrèkà	ùtú⁺mátùmà
'to leave here and there'	'to send here and there'
ùmùrèkàrèkà	ùmùtú⁺miyà
'... him/her ...'	'... him/her ...'
ùvá⁺rékàrèkà	ùvátú⁺mátùmà
'... them ...'	'... them...'

2. PRESENT TENSE

   a. *Examples showing present tense prefix -ku- (variant -u-):*[21]

   ùkùrèkà   ùkùtūmā̀
   'he/she is leaving'   'he/she is sending'
   ùkùrèkà mùrìmì   ùkùtú⁺má mùrìmì
   '... a farmer ...'   '... a farmer ...'
   ví⁺úrèkà   ví⁺útùmà
   'they are leaving'   'they are sending'
   ví⁺úrèkà mùrìmì   ví⁺úꜜtúmá mùrìmì
   '... a farmer ...'   '... a farmer ...'

   b. *Forms with object prefix:*

   ùkùmùrèkà   ùkùtūmā̀
   'he his leaving him'   'he is sending them'
   ùkùvá⁺rékà   ùkùvātūmā̀
   'he is leaving them'   'he is sending them'
   ví⁺úmùrèkà   ví⁺úmùtūmā̀
   'they are leaving them'   'they are sending them'
   ví⁺úꜜvàrékà   ví⁺úvàtùmà
   'they are leaving them'   'they are sending them'

   c. *Forms with applied suffix*

   ùkùrèkèyà   ùkùtú⁺míyà
   'he is leaving for'   'he is sending to'
   ùkùrèkèyà mùrìmì   ùkùtú⁺míyà mùrìmì
   '... a farmer ...'   '... a farmer ...'
   ùkùmùrèkèyà   ùkùmùtú⁺míyà
   '... for him/her ...'   '... to him/her ...'
   ùkùvá⁺rékèyà   ùkùvátú⁺míyà
   '... for them ...'   '... to them ...'

   ví⁺úrèkèyà   ví⁺úꜜtúmíyà
   'they are leaving for'   'they are sending to'
   ví⁺úrèkèyà mùrìmì   ví⁺úꜜtúmíyà mùrìmì
   '... a farmer ...'   '... a farmer ...'
   ví⁺úmùrèkèyà   ví⁺úmùtú⁺míyà
   '... for him/her ...'   '... to him/her ...'
   ví⁺úꜜvárékàrèkà   ví⁺úꜜvátúmátùmà

---

21 Neither **u-** prefix in these examples is the same morpheme as the infinitive **u-**.

d. *Reduplications*

ùkùrèkàrèkà	ùkùtú⁺mátùmà
'he leaves here and there'	'he sends here and there'
ùkùrèkàrèkà mùrìmì	ùkùtú⁺mátùmà mùrìmì
'... a farmer ...'	'... a farmer ...'
ùkùmùrèkàrèkà	ùkùmùtú⁺mátùmà
'... him/her ...'	'... him/her ...'
ùkùvá⁺rékàrèkà	ùkùvátú⁺mátùmà
'... them ...'	'... them ...'
ví⁺úrèkàrèkà	ví⁺úˈtúmátùmà
'they leave here and there'	'they send here and there'
ví⁺úmùrèkàrèkà	ví⁺úmùtú⁺mátùmà
'... him/her ...'	'... him/her ...'
ví⁺úˈvárékàrèkà	ví⁺úˈvátúmátùmà
'... them ...'	'... them ...'

3. REMOTE PAST

   a. *Forms with 3rd singular subject*:

wàrèkīèè	wàtūmīèè
'he left'	'he sent'
wàrèkíéé ⁺múrìmì	wàtúmíéé ⁺múrìmì
'he left a farmer'	'he sent a farmer'
wàmùrèkīèè	wàmùtūmīèè
'he left him/her'	'he sent him/her'
wàvá⁺rékìèè	wàvātūmīèè
'he left them'	'he sent them'

   b. *Forms with 3rd plural subject*:

⁺várèkīèè	⁺vátùmìèè
'they left'	'they sent'
⁺vàrèkíéé ⁺múrìmì	⁺vá⁺túmíéé múrìmì
'they left a farmer'	'they sent a farmer'
⁺vámùrèkīèè	⁺vámùtūmīèè
'they left him/her'	'they sent him/her'
⁺váˈvárékìèè	⁺vávàtùmìèè
'they left them'	'they sent them'

c. *Reduplications*:

wàrèkīerēkīeè
'he left here and there'
wàrèkíérékíéé ᵀmúrìmì
'... a farmer ...'
wàmùrèkīerēkīeè
'... him/her ...'
wàváᵀrékìèrèkìeè
'... them ...'

wàtūmīetūmīeè
'they sent here and there'
wàtúmíétúmíéé ᵀmúrìmì
'... a farmer ...'
wàmùtūmīetūmīeè
'... him/her ...'
wàvātūmīetūmīeè
'... them ...'

ᵀvárèkīerēkīeè
'they left here and there'
ᵀvárèkíérékíéé ᵀmúrìmì
'... a farmer ...'
ᵀvámùrèkīerēkīeè
'... him/her ...'
ᵀváᵀvárékìèrèkìeè
'... them ...'

ᵀvátùmìetùmìeè
'they sent here and there'
ᵀváᵀtúmíétúmíéé múrìmì
'... a farmer ...'
ᵀvámùtūmīetūmīeè
'... him/her ...'
ᵀvávàtùmìetùmìeè
'... them ...'

4. UNDERLYING REPRESENTATIONS

a. *Verb roots/noun stem*:

/-rèk-/, /-yànj-/, /-rìm-/	'leave, love, cultivate'
/-túm-/, /-tém-/, /-túng-/	'send, cut, tie'
/-rìm-i̯/	'farmer' (< -rìm- 'cultivate' + 'agentive')

b. *Prefixes*:

/ù-/	'infinitive'	/-mù-/	'him/her'
/mù-/	'noun class 1'	/-vá-/	'them'
/ù-/	'he/she'	/-kù-, -ù-/	'present tense'
/ví-/	'they'	/-à-/	'remote past tense'

c. *Suffixes*:

| /-à/ | 'infinitive, present tense' | /-iy-/ | 'applied' |
| /-i̯eé/ | 'remote past |

In Table 1, upstepped H is again symbolized as ⁺H. In order to obtain the representations that are needed prior to the assignment of register, we need to recognize the following two rules: a) a rule spreading the suffixal tone (e.g. L of the infinitive and present tense or H of the remote past /-ieé/²²) to all preceding toneless vowels (including toneless vowels of reduplicated stem); b) a rule of H tone spreading to the right (which delinks a following L).²³ This having been said, we now note the following generalizations concerning tonal registers:

I. A H tone is raised to ⁺H before a L tone, whether linked, as in (29a), or unlinked, as in (29b).

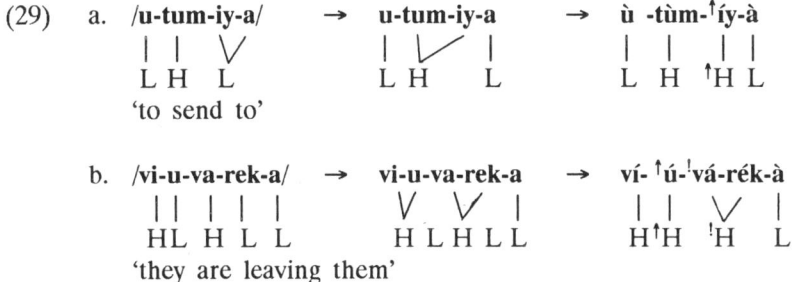

(29)   a. /u-tum-iy-a/   →   u-tum-iy-a   →   ù -tùm-⁺íy-à
          | | \/ | \/ | | | | |
          L H L   L H   L   L H ⁺H L
       'to send to'

       b. /vi-u-va-rek-a/   →   vi-u-va-rek-a   →   ví- ⁺ú-!vá-rék-à
          | | | | | \/ \/ | | | \/ |
          HL H L L   H L H L L   H⁺H !H L
       'they are leaving them'

In (29a) the H of the verb root -túm- spreads onto and delinks the L of the applied suffix -iy-. This is followed by the raising -íy- to -⁺íy- conditioned by the L of the following tense suffix -à. In (29b) H tone spreading applies twice, delinking the L of the present tense prefix -ù- and the L of the verb root -rék-. This is followed by raising the derived

---

22 The transcription /ḭbee/ is intended to indicate that these forms always involve a long [e:] on the surface, which may ultimately be more insightfully captured by setting up a bisyllabic /ḭ.e/ sequence, from which length would be predicted by rule.
23 It will be observed that almost all forms are given with either underlying H or L tone. The exceptions are the applied extension -iy- and the -i- part of the -ieé remote past suffix, which are toneless. Unlike many other Bantu languages, little is gained by trying to suppress L tones in underlying representations, since in this case "default L" would have to be inserted quite early, e.g. in time to delink them to create the register L features needed for downstep. An analysis where one H feature causes the next to downstep, as in Kishambaa (Odden 1982) was attempted, but rejected. Finally, note that there are exceptional H tones that do not spread by H tone spreading, e.g. ùhúrà 'to hate', ùsúcà 'to bring back'. As pointed out by Schadeberg (1978), these reconstruct with an extra TBU. The second form thus reconstructs as *u-suk-i-a, where the -i- suffix is a causative (cf. ù-sùuk-à 'to return', which transparently undergoes H tone spreading). What happens in these exceptional cases is that the form acts as though there were an extra mora to spread the H onto, which however cannot surface. The upstepping in 'to hate' and 'to bring back' is of course completely regular.

H of the present tense suffix to ⁺H, conditioned by the unlinked L. As also seen, although followed by L, the derived H of **-rék-** does not become ⁺H, since there is no *surface* L between it and the ⁺H of **-⁺ú-**. The same constraint observed in Engenni and Mankon is thus applicable in Cahi (cf. below).

II. A sequence of Hs is lowered to M before pause. This can either be from one underlying H, as in (30a), or a sequence of Hs, as in (30b):

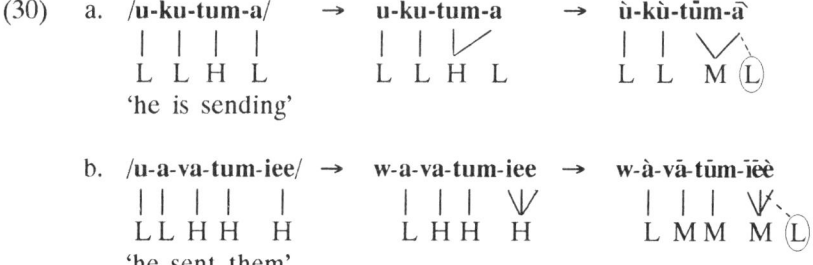

(30) a. /u-ku-tum-a/ → u-ku-tum-a → ù-kù-tŭm-a᷄
 | | | | | | |/ | | \/
 L L H L   L L H L   L L M (L)
 'he is sending'

 b. /u-a-va-tum-iee/ → w-a-va-tum-iee → w-à-vā-tūm-īèè
 | | | | | | | | \/ | | | \/
 L L H H H   L H H H   L M M M (L)
 'he sent them'

In (30a) H tone spreading first applies, delinking the final L. This is followed by lowering of the one H (now linked to two TBUs) to M before pause. A prepausal M vowel will on the surface become a ML falling tone. This has nothing to do with the unlinked L, since the latter is not available to create the fall in (30b). In this latter example we first glide the 3rd sg. subject prefix /u-/ to [w-] and assign the suffixal H to both vowels of the **-iee** remote past suffix. Each of the three Hs in sequence go down to M before pause. The prepausal boundary (L) will accomplish this effect by associating as a *tonal* feature to the last TN of the utterance.²⁴ Below, I suggest that the fall of M before pause should be accomplished by a phonetic implementation rule.

III. One or more TBUs on a ⁺H level becomes L before pause, as seen in (31).

(31) a. /vi-u-tum-a/ → vi-u-tum-a → ví-⁺ú-⁺túm-á → ví-⁺ú-tùm-à
 | | | | \/ \/ | | \| | | \/
 HL H L   HL H L   H⁺H L H   H⁺H L
 'they are sending'

---

²⁴ Note that this boundary L comes in late so as not to cause upstepping of a preceding H.

b.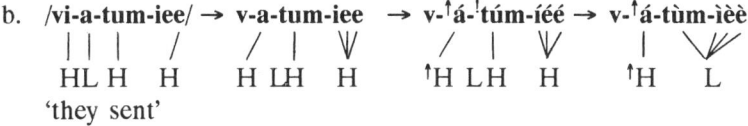
'they sent'

The underlying form in (31a) first undergoes two applications of H tone spreading. This is followed by the creation of the conversion of H Ⓛ H into a ꜛH-ꜜH sequence, by means yet to be discussed. Finally, as seen, the ꜜH-H sequence becomes L-L before pause. In (31b) the derivation is similar: The suffixal H is first spreads to all the suffixal vowels, then H tone spreading takes place (along with vowel coalescence). Again, a ꜛH-ꜜH is created, but this time it is two H features and three syllables that undergo the change from ꜜH to L before pause.

The reader can verify from the paradigms in Table 1 that the above characterization is quite general in the language. What remains to be seen is how we are to state the register effects. For this I propose the following to take place after the non-registral tone rules have applied:

(32)   a. Processes:
         i. Fuse sequences of Hs into a single H feature (as per OCP)
         ii. Link Ⓛ to following TRN (=register L, i.e. downstep)
         iii. Spread to following TRNs (with H TN)
         iv. Assign Ⓗ to any TRN followed by L (i.e. L can link either to TRN or TN)
         v. Assign prepausal boundary to last TN of utterance

       b. Constraints:
         i. *Register L + Register H
         ii. *Register L or H + Tonal L

       c. Phonetic implementation:
         i. Final TBU with L falls in pitch before pause
         ii. ꜜM = L
         iii. 'Downdrift'

The process of fusion in (32a.i) is generally assumed to be in effect, given that register is a late phenomenon. In languages such as Kishambaa (Odden 1982), Supyire (Carlson 1983), Temne (Nemers and Mountford 1984) etc., where one H feature is downstepped by another, presumably register L is assigned before fusion. (32a.ii) creates the expected downstepping, while (32a.iii) spreads it to all successive TNs—which, given the constraint in (32b.ii), will automatically mean TRNs with a H TN. The upstepping process is stated in (32a.iv) to affect a TRN that is followed by a L, whether this L links to the TN (i.e. is a surface L) or to the TRN (i.e. is a downstepper). Finally, the prepausal boundary (L) is assigned to the last TN of the utterance. Where this TN is L, there will be no effect. Where it is (non-downstepped) H, the result will be a M tone, as in (33a).

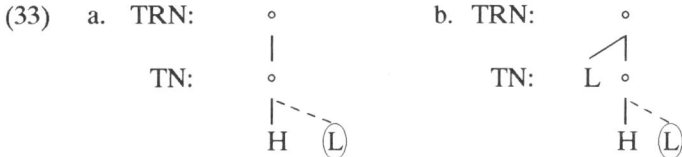

Since all successive Hs will have been gathered up into a single TN with one H feature, this means that we will obtain a sequence of M tones before pause, as desired. In (33b), on the other hand, where the final sequence of Hs is qualified by a register L (a downstepper), we see that when the prepausal L links to the tonal node, we obtain what on the surface should be downstepped mid (ˈM). However, there is no such entity in Cahi. Instead, the configuration in (33b) is realized with L tone. We can propose a rule to modify the structure in (33b) to get this output or, as I prefer, we can let the phonetic implementation rules interpret ˈM the same as L. In other words, a H that has been lowered twice is equivalent in pitch to a L tone.

The constraints in (32b) are the same as we saw in Mankon. The phonetic implementation rule in (32c.i) says that any tone with a L feature falls before pause. This will automatically mean M (which consists of the features H and L linked to the TN) as well as L (and ˈM, which is equivalent to it, as per (33c.ii)). Finally, downdrift (33c.iii) will be left to phonetic implementation.[25]

With (32) we are thus able to account for a range of register effects on tone in Cahi. Unfortunately there are still some aspects that I would like to see streamlined. For example, it would be desirable to get the

---

25 I might mention that the most difficult phonetic distinction to perceive in Cahi was that between a final L and a single final phonological H, as contrasted in (i) and (ii):

(i) /ìnù/ 'mortar' (ii) /ìrú/ 'knee' [ìrū̂]
/ìgwè/ 'stone' /ìtwé/ 'head' [ìtwē̂]
/ìlà/ 'intestines' /ìbì/ 'excrement' [ìbī̂]

The rise of the final ML falling tone in (ii) may be very slight, though the two tonal patterns have definitely not merged (as have L and ˈH before pause).

spreading of a register tone to following likes tones to be automatic. For the time being this will have to stipulated by rule.[26]

6. CONCLUSION

In the preceding sections we have established a view of tonal registers that has broad application in the statement of downstep and upstep in African languages. I started with the assumption that the same tone features are involved in basic tonal oppositions as in secondary or register tonal contrasts. To capture the different effects of the like features, I proposed that features having a register function link directly to the tonal root node (TRN), while (the same) features having a discrete tonal function link to the tonal node (TN), which in turn links to the TRN. The geometrical structure one obtains converges with that proposed by Yip (1989, this volume) and Chan (1989), whose concerns are to account for properties of contour tones as well as register. Among the implications of this approach to African languages is that still another representation for canonical tonal downstep has been proposed: a L feature linking to the TRN (usually, but not always, with a H linked to the TN). The question is whether this representation might have benefits beyond those we have already seen.[27] In (10a) we saw that a sequence L-H (L) can become L-!H in Bamileke-Dschang by directly linking the (L) to the TRN of the preceding H. In an approach that treated the downstep trigger as an unlinked L (Clements and Ford 1979),

---

[26] As was pointed out in the section on Mankon, the alternative would be to say that only the first TBU affected by a register tone is indicate, with all subsequent tones affected (save those which for language-specific reasons cannot accept a register tone). Since this does not (and I don't think can) follow from the geometry alone, it is not clear how to make this an intrinsic property of the analysis. The basic idea is that registral effects can be quite global in nature, i.e. raising or lowering long stretches of tones. Ultimately we have intonational effects, as when all tones are raised to express a question or surprise. It is not clear that this should be seen as the same as the downstepping and upstepping processes dealt with in this paper.

[27] One additional benefit is that it, like previous "register tier" proposals, attempts to rid the output of unlinked tonal features which, unlike their segmental counterparts, were not stray-erased prior to phonetic implementation. If registers can be encoded not by floating tones, but rather by tonal features linked to the appropriate place in the tonal geometry, this anomalous behavior of tonal features is no longer with us. Of course this presupposes that we can do away with all uses of floating tones before phonetic implementation, whether they have a register effect or not. I have in mind the very useful function of a final floating H that blocks downgliding before pause, creating the L° tone famous in Grassfields Bantu and elsewhere. Recall with respect to (7) that Bamileke-Dschang has an opposition between L-L, L-L°, L-!L and L-!L°. The final (H) cannot link as a register H because of the contradiction that would be obtained in the case of !L°. So where does it link, if it does?

it would be necessary to have a rule metathesizing the Ⓛ, as proposed by Pulleyblank (1983) or the ! itself. A somewhat less impressive but possible additional result is that we now can incorporate unpredictable downstep, e.g. within a morpheme, by having a L lexically linked to a TRN. This might be the solution for the OCP problem posed from Kishambaa by Odden (1982, 1986). In this language a H will cause a following H to downstep. Odden argues that there is no reason to put in unlinked Ls just to trigger these downsteps. In fact, he shows that there are monomorphemic noun stems such as (34a) that must be entered with two H features in violation of the OCP:

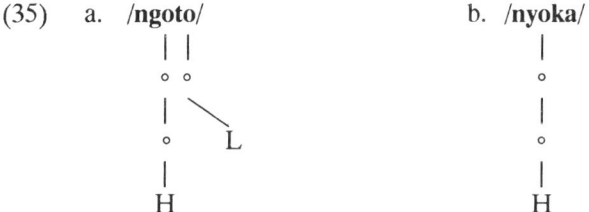

(34)   a. /ngoto/ → ngó!tó 'sheep'   b. /nyoko/ → nyókó 'snake'

As seen in (34b), a noun stem with a single H on the first of two TBUs would first spread that H to the second TBU, but would be realized with two syllables on a single H pitch level. In this framework it would be possible to enter these nouns as in (35).

(35)   a. /ngoto/   b. /nyoka/

Lexical downstep is indicated by having a L prelinked to the second TRN in (35a). Both forms will undergo spreading of the H TN to the second vowel, but this vowel will be realized as !H in (35a) because of the lexical register L. This solution is more satisfying than one with a lexical Ⓛ since, as pointed out by Odden, Ⓛ is not generally motivated as a downstep trigger in this language—and is at best redundant. The lexical register L in (35a), on the other hand, represents an exceptional downstep using exactly the representation that will be acquired from the general rule that assigns register L (=downstep) to a H that follows another H. Perhaps this approach is applicable to other OCP problems with tone.[28]

---

28 Of course, it remains to be seen what argument would be logically available against the OCP, if we have as many devices available as current theory provides.

I would like to conclude by asking whether the results obtained here cannot be transferred to other problematic phonological features. The binary treatment of vowel height, for instance, has been an area of considerable controversy (see Hyman 1988 and references therein). Superficially it seems as though the same exact issues arise as I have raised for tone. Thus, corresponding to the synchronic and diachronic relatedness of M vs. ¹H are the vowels [e, o] vs. [i̧, u̧]. The mid vowels [e, o] might be treated as having H and L vowel features linking to a vowel height node parallel to our TN, while the so-called [−ATR] vowels [i̧, u̧] would have a H vowel feature linking to the vowel height node, but a L feature linking directly to the "vowel root node" (dorsal?) as a register feature. In this way we would capture the relationship between low vowel and [−ATR], the latter specification being replaced by the register vowel feature L. This would account for the apparent phonetic non-distinctness of these two sets of vowels in a number of languages (see Hyman 1988). Correspondingly, where needed, H could function as a register vowel feature replacing [+ATR], capturing its relation to high vowels, e.g. as in Kinande (Mutaka 1986; Schlindwein 1987). In this way we can capture with feature geometry the relationship between vowel height and features known variously as [ATR], [RTR], [tense] and so forth. Of course, there are frameworks such as dependency phonology (Anderson and Ewen 1987) in which the same features may enter into different head-dependent relations to get precisely these effects. Given that the present paper is concerned only with tonal registers, I no more than note the issue of vowel height and ATR as an intriguing parallel to what I hope has been successfully demonstrated for tone.[29]

REFERENCES

Akinlabi, Akinbiyi. 1984. "Tonal Underspecification and Yoruba Tone." Ph.D. dissertation, University of Ibadan.

Anderson, John M. and Colin Ewen. 1987. *Principles of Dependency Phonology.* Cambridge: Cambridge University Press.

Archangeli, Diana and Douglas Pulleyblank. 1986. "The Content and Structure of Phonological Representations." Ms. To appear, Cambridge, Mass.: MIT Press.

Armstrong, Robert G. 1968. "Yala (Ikom): a Terraced-level Language with Three Tones." *Journal of West African Languages* 5, 41–50.

---

[29] There virtually is no end to the quest for parallels. It thus has occurred to me that so-called secondary place features needed to express palatalization, labialization etc. may be to the corresponding primary places (palatal, labial etc.) as register tones are to discrete tones (and perhaps as ATR is to vowel height).

Bergman, Richard. 1971. "Vowel Sandhi and Word Division in Igede." *Journal of West African Languages* 8, 13–25.
Carlson, Robert. 1983. "Downstep in Supyire." *Studies in African Linguistics* 14, 35–45.
Chan, Marjorie K. M. 1989. "Contour-Tone Spreading and Tone Sandhi in Danyang." Paper presented at the First Northeast Conference on Chinese Linguistics. Ohio State University, May 5–7.
Clark, Mary. 1985. "Downstep without Floating Tones. Ms., University of New Hampshire.
———. 1989. *The Tonal System of Igbo*. Dordrecht: Foris Publications.
Clements, George N. 1978. "Tone and Syntax in Ewe." In *Elements of Tone, Stress and Intonation*, edited by Donna Jo Napoli, 21–99. Washington, D.C.: Georgetown University Press.
———. 1979. "The Description of Terraced-Level Tone Languages." *Language* 55, 536–58.
———. 1983. "The Hierarchical Representation of Tone Features." In *Current Approaches to African Linguistics*. Vol. 1, edited by Ivan R. Dihoff, 145–76. Dordrecht: Foris Publications.
———. 1984. "Principles of Tone Assignment in Kikuyu." In *Autosegmental Studies in Bantu Tone*, edited by George N. Clements and John Goldsmith, 281–339. Dordrecht: Foris Publications.
Clements, George N. and Kevin Ford. 1979. "Kikuyu Tone Shift and its Synchronic Consequences." *Linquistic Inquiry* 10, 179–210.
Goldsmith, John. 1984. "Meeussen's Rule." In *Language Sound Structure*, edited by Mark Aronoff and Richard T. Oehrle, 245–59. Cambridge, Mass.: MIT Press.
Hyman, Larry M. 1972. *A Phonological Study of Fe'fe'-Bamileke*. Supplement 4 to *Studies in African Linguistics*.
———. 1976. "D'où vient le ton haut du Fe'Fe'-Bamileke?" In *Papers in African Linguistics in Honor of Wm. E. Welmers*. Supplement 6 to *Studies in African Linguistics*, edited by Larry M. Hyman, Leon C. Jacobson and Russell G. Schuh, 123–34.
———. 1979. "A Reanalysis of Tonal Downstep." *Journal of African Languages and Linguistics* 1, 9–29.
———. 1985. "Word Domains and Downstep in Bamileke-Dschang." *Phonology Yearbook* 2, 47–83.
———. 1986. "The Representation of Multiple Tone Heights." In *The Phonological Representation of Suprasegmentals*, edited by Koen Bogers, Harry van der Hulst and Maarten Mous, 109–52. Dordrecht: Foris Publications.
———. 1988. "Underspecification and Vowel Height Transfer in Esimbi." *Phonology* 5, 255–73.
Hyman, Larry M., Francis Katamba, and Livingstone Walusimbi. 1987. "Luganda and the Strict Layer Hypothesis." *Phonology Yearbook* 4, 87–108.
Hyman, Larry M. and Douglas Pulleyblank. 1988. "On Feature Copying: Parameters of Tone Rules." In *Language, Speech and Mind: Studies in Honour of Victoria A. Fromkin*, edited by Larry M. Hyman and Charles N. Li, 30–48. London: Routledge.
Hyman, Larry M. and Maurice Tadadjeu. 1976. "Floating Tones in Mbam-Nkam." In *Studies in Bantu Tonology*, edited by Larry M. Hyman, 57–111. Southern California Occasional Paper in Linguistics 3. Los Angeles: University of Southern California.
Inkelas, Sharon. 1987. "Tone Feature Geometry" In *Proceedings of NELS 18*, edited by James Blevin and Juli Carter, 223–37. Amherst, Mass.: GLSA.
———. 1989. "Register Tone and the Phonological Representation of Downstep." In *Current Approaches to African Linguistics*. Vol. 6, edited by L. Tuller and I. Haik, 65–82. Dordrecht: Foris Publications.
Kaye, Jonathan, Hilda Koopman and Dominique Sportiche. 1982. *Projet surles langues Kru. Premier rapport*. Université du Québec à Montréal.

Kenstowicz, Michael and Mairo Kidda. 1987. "The Obligatory Contour Principle and Tangale Phonology." In *Current Approaches to African Linguistics.* Vol. 4, edited by David Odden, 223–38. Dordrecht: Foris Publications.

Leben, William R., Sharon Inkelas and Mark Cobler. 1989. "Phrases and Phrase Tones in Hausa." In *Current Approaches to African Linguistics.* Vol. 5, edited by P. Newman and Robert D. Botne, 45–61. Dordrecht: Foris Publications.

Leroy, Jacqueline. 1977. *Morphologie et classes nominales en mankon.* Paris: Société d'Etudes Linguistiques et Anthropologiques de France. [Distributed by Peeters.]

———. 1979. "A la recherche de tons perdus: structure tonale du nom en ngemba." *Journal of African Languages and Linguistiques* 1, 31–54.

McHugh, Brian. 1985. "Phrasal Tone Rules in Kirua (Vunjo) Chaga." Master's thesis, University of California, Los Angeles.

Mutaka, Ngessimo. 1986. "Vowel Harmony in Kinande." Ms., University of Southern California, Los Angeles.

Nemers, Julie and Keith W. Mountford. 1984. "Interaction of Segmental and Tonal Levels: the Case of [ɯ] in Temne." *Studies in African Linguistics* 15, 107–61.

Newman, Paul. 1986. "Contour Tones as Phonemic Primes in Grebo." In *The Phonological Representation of Suprasegmentals,* edited by Koen Bogers, Harry van der Hulst and Maarten Mous, 175–93. Dordrecht: Foris Publications.

Newman, Roxana Ma. 1971. "Downstep in Ga'anda." *Journal of African Languages* 10, 15–27.

Odden, David. 1982. "Tonal Phenomena in KiShambaa." *Studies in African Linguistics* 13, 177–208.

———. 1986. "On the Role of the Obligatory Contour Principle in Phonological Theory." *Language* 62, 353–83.

Olson, Howard Stanley. 1964. "The Phonology and Morphology of Ribmi." Ph.D. dissertation, Hartford Seminary Foundation.

Pulleyblank, Douglas. 1983. "Tone in Lexical Phonology." Ph.D. Dissertation, Massachusetts Institute of Technology, Cambridge.

———. 1986. *Tone in Lexical Phonology.* Dordrecht: Reidel.

Schadeberg, Thilo C. 1978. "Über die Töne der nominalen und pronominalen Formen im Rimi." *Afrika und Übersee* 61, 189–209.

———. 1979. "Über die Töne der verbalen Formen im Rimi." *Afrika und Übersee* 62, 288–313.

Schlindwein, Deborah. 1987. "P-bearing Units: a Study in Kinande Vowel Harmony." In *Proceedings of NELS 17,* edited by Joyce McDonough and Bernadette Plunkett. Amherst, Mass.: GLSA.

Snider, Keith L. 1988. "Towards the Representation of Tone: a 3-Dimensional Approach." In *Features, Segmental Structure and Harmony Processes (Part I),* edited by Harry van der Hulst and Norval Smith, 237–65. Dordrecht: Foris Publications.

———. 1990. "Tonal Upstep in Krachi: Evidence for a Register Tier." *Language* 66, 453–74.

Stahlke, Herbert. 1977. "Some Problems with Binary Features for Tones." *International Journal of American Linguistics* 35, 62–66.

Stewart, John. 1971. "Niger-Congo, Kwa." In *Current Trends in linguistics.* Vol. 7, *Sub-saharan Africa,* edited by T. Sebeok, 179–212. The Hague: Mouton.

———. 1981. "Key Lowering (Downstep/Ddownglide) in Dschang." *Journal of African Languages and Linguistics* 3, 113–38.

Thomas, Elaine. 1974. "Engenni." In *Ten Nigerian Tone Systems. Studies in Nigerian Languages.* Vol. 4, edited by John Bendor-Samuel, 13–26. Dallas and Arlington: Summer Institute of Linguistics and University of Texas.

———. 1978. *A Grammatical Description of the Engenni Language.* Dallas and Arlington: Summer Institute of Linguistics and University of Texas.

Warnier, Jacqueline [Leroy] and Jan Voorhoeve. 1975. "Vowel Contraction and Vowel Reduction in Mankon." *Studies in African Linguistics* 6, 125–49.
Welmers, Wm. E. 1959. "Tonemics, Morphotonemics and Tonal Morphemes." *General Linguistics* 4, 1–9.
———. 1973. *African Language Structures*. Berkeley: University of California Press.
Yip, Moira. 1980. *The Tonal Phonology of Chinese*. Ph.D. dissertation, Massachusetts Institute of Technology. [Distributed by the Indiana University Linguistics Club, Bloomington.]
———. 1988. "Tone Contours as Melodic Units: Tonal Affricates." In *Proceedings of WCCFL* 7, 347–62. Stanford University.
———. 1989. "Contour Tones." *Phonology* 6, 149–74.
———. this volume. "Tonal Register in East Asian Languages."

In Defense of a Metrical Theory of Intonational Downstep

Robert Ladd

1. INTRODUCTION*

The underlying subject of this paper, as the title suggests, is the phonological nature of downstep in languages without lexical tone. In particular, I will be defending my proposal (Ladd 1988, 1990) that register shifts in English and other intonation languages are controlled by "register trees"—abstract prosodic structures in which the relative height of prosodic constituents is specified. After a brief introduction to the proposal, however, most of the paper will be about the distinction between linguistic and paralinguistic features in intonation, and about the phonetic modelling of pitch range. By the end of the paper the reason for all the digressions will, I hope, have become clear.

I presuppose without comment the view that intonational phonology, like tonal phonology in lexical tone languages, operates (at some level of description) in terms of a small number of primitive "tones" such as H(igh) and L(ow). Intonation contours, like fundamental frequency (F_0) contours in tone languages, are thus to be seen as the manifestation of an abstract string of phonological elements. The theoretical and empirical foundations of this view were laid by Bruce (1977) and Pierrehumbert (1980), and much useful work on pitch phonology in a variety of languages has followed in the decade since. This paper is intended as a contribution to that tradition.

2. BACKGROUND

In making the case that intonational structure is basically linear, Pierrehumbert (1980) proposed that much of what had previously been

---

* Some of the ideas in this paper—and even a few of the sentences—are taken more or less directly from three other works, namely Ladd (1989), Ladd (1991), and Connell and Ladd (1990). I thank Bruce Connell for acceding to this self-plagiarism. I alone am responsible for the content of the paper, and in particular for any misrepresentation of the work of Pierrehumbert and her colleagues that may be contained herein.

discussed as "declination" in English intonation is actually the result of phonological "downstep". Downstep applies to certain individual pitch accents, lowering the accentual F_0 peak relative to the preceding peak; a sequence of such accents will yield the downward F_0 slope of "declination". This proposal was backed up by instrumental studies showing the constancy of the quantitative F_0 relation between pairs of adjacent accents in a downstep series (Liberman and Pierrehumbert 1984). Since then the existence of downstep in non-tonal languages, like the linear approach generally, has been widely accepted (cf. Ladd 1983 and Gussenhoven 1984 on English; van den Berg et al. 1991 on Dutch; and Poser 1984, Pierrehumbert and Beckman 1988; and Kubozono 1989 on Japanese).

However, Pierrehumbert's descriptive insight was embedded in an analysis of English intonational phonology that I have elsewhere criticised (Ladd 1983; cf. also Gussenhoven 1984; Gussenhoven and Rietveld forthcoming) as both excessively abstract and functionally unrevealing. Specifically, Pierrehumbert's analysis treats downstep as the consequence of a phonetic realisation rule that affects the scaling of the second H tone in certain H-L-H sequences. For example, she analyses the difference between downstepping and non-downstepping sequences of prenuclear high accents as follows:

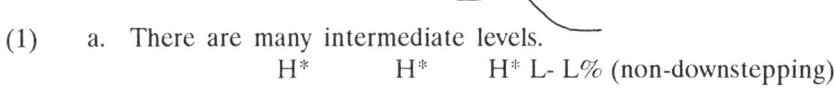

(1)   a. There are many intermediate levels.
            H*   H*   H* L- L% (non-downstepping)

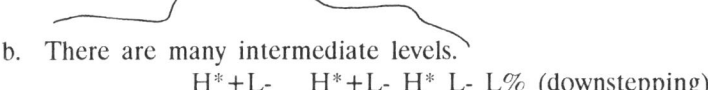

      b. There are many intermediate levels.
          H*+L-   H*+L- H* L- L% (downstepping)

whereas downstepping and non-downstepping series of falling accents would apparently be analysed as

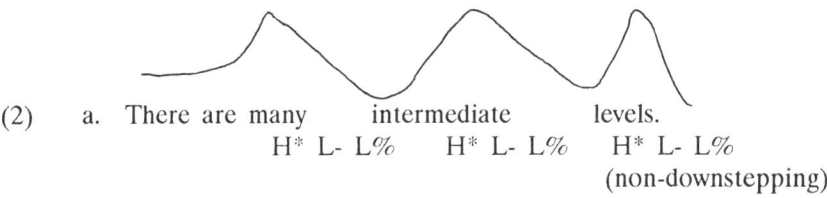

(2)   a. There are many   intermediate   levels.
           H* L- L%   H* L- L%   H* L- L%
                                                      (non-downstepping)

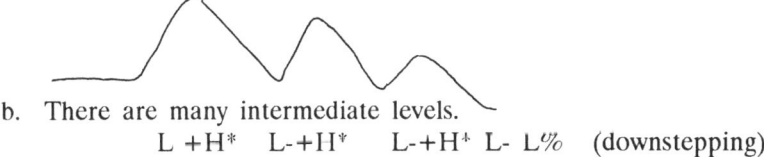

b. There are many intermediate levels.
L +H*   L-+H*   L-+H* L- L%   (downstepping)

That is, the underlying phonological distinction between a downstepping and a non-downstepping sequence of accent peaks is analysed as a difference between certain sequences of tones and certain others; the downstepping is, as it were, epiphenomenal on a more basic difference of tonal sequence.

In Ladd (1983), I pointed out that this analysis obscures the functional similarity between a downstepping contour and an otherwise similar series of non-downstepping pitch accents; at the same time it obscures the functional similarity shared by all downstepping contours as against all non-downstepping contours. In effect, I argued, downstep *means* something; it is an independent intonational choice orthogonal to the choice of pitch accent type. This makes it necessary, I suggested, to represent the presence or absence of downstep as such, independently of the representation of the pitch accents involved. For example, one might (as I proposed in Ladd 1983) use a "downstep feature":

(3)   H*   H*   or   H*L   H*L
               | |
              [d.s.]   [d.s.]

or, more or less equivalently, a link to a register tone:

(4)   H*   H*   or   H*L   H*L
               | |
               L   L

Either of these analyses will make it possible to treat downstep and pitch accent type as two independent variables in a phonological description of intonation contours.

In response to criticisms of the downstep feature idea by Beckman and Pierrehumbert (1986), and following earlier proposals for treating downstep in African languages by Huang (1980) and Clements (1983), I have more recently (Ladd 1987, 1988, 1990) proposed a different way of achieving the same goal of making downstep orthogonal to pitch accent type. This is to treat English downstep in terms of metrical trees that encode the relative height of prosodic constituents. The downstep relation between two tones (T), for example, can be represented as

(5)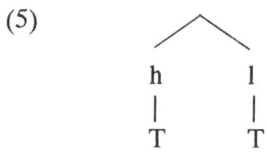

The borrowing of the relational tree formalism from metrical phonology is intentional: the mapping of abstract height relations onto actual F_0 values is conceptually quite like the mapping of abstract prominence relations onto actual phonetic properties of syllables.[1]

Crucially for later sections of this paper, relations of relative height can hold not only between terminal elements (tones or pitch accents), but also between higher constituents such as phrases. That is, we might have a "register tree" like the following:

(6)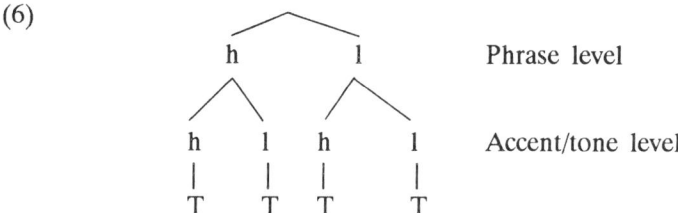

The simplest case in which this kind of higher-level downstep is apparent is what we might call "declination within declination" (e.g. Cooper and Sorensen 1981; Thorsen 1985, 1986), in which there is a downward trend within each phrase of an utterance and a similar downward trend from one phrase to the next across the utterance (Fig. 1). As I suggest in Ladd (1987, 1988), register trees like the one in (6) may be used not only for such simple nesting of downstep, but can also represent the way in which fine details of F_0 closely reflect constituent structure (Ladd 1988; Kubozono 1989). These phrase-level register phenomena are, in my view, the most important motivation for using register trees.

---

[1] For reasons that cannot be discussed here, the opposite relation

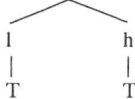

is non-downstepping, but not necessarily upstepping; that is, I assume a basic two-way distinction of the possible register relations between prosodic constituents. For further discussion of how these abstract relations may be mapped onto actual register shifts, see Ladd (1990).

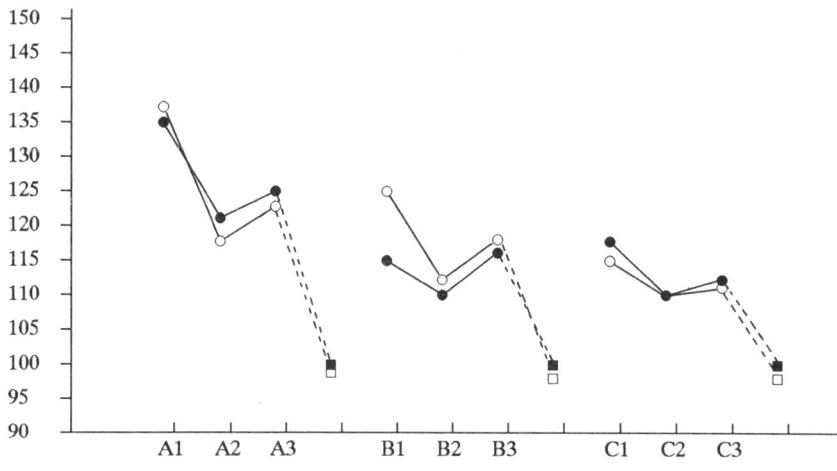

Figure 1
F_0 data from two different types of three-clause sentences, showing F_0 downtrends across each clause and from one clause to the next (from Ladd 1988)

Pierrehumbert and Beckman, however, stand by Pierrehumbert's linear analysis of English downstep, and indeed, they comment on the "tenacity" of the idea that downstep might involve structured phonological relations (1988:169). I think their arguments against the metrical view are largely faulty, but too influential—and as I shall show, too attractive—simply to ignore. In the third part of the paper I will try to show where I think they go wrong, but in order to unpack their premises and conclusions I must first take the reader on a couple of long digressions.

2.1. First digression—defining *paralinguistic*

In the analysis of intonation it has long been apparent that "pitch range"—the vertical scale of F_0—can vary from speaker to speaker, from situation to situation, or even from one part of an utterance to another, without in some sense affecting the phonological identity of a given contour. It is entirely possible, for example, for a fall in pitch from 120 Hz to 80 Hz to be phonologically equivalent to a fall in pitch from 300 Hz to 150 Hz. This is not to say that the factors that bring about the differences are well understood or even widely agreed upon, but the existence of phonological equivalence despite differences of vertical scale is universally taken for granted.

Some of the factors that influence vertical scale are, of course, fairly uncontroversial. Some, for example, are clearly extralinguistic, the most obvious being the differences in overall F_0 level brought about by differences between male and female larynx size. Others, like downstep, are clearly linguistic.[2] But many lie somewhere in between, in the shadowy realm commonly referred to as "paralinguistic", and in order to shed light on Pierrehumbert and Beckman's rejection of register trees it will be necessary to come to some deeper understanding of this term and how it has been used in the linguistic description of intonation.

To the extent that *paralinguistic* means anything, it would appear to have to do with expressive meaning—meaning overlaid on the linguistic message and conveyed in ways that are, like the facial expression of emotion, widely shared by speakers of different languages and cultures. Along with voice quality, one of the most important dimensions of paralinguistic expression is pitch range; it is well established that certain "active" emotions (anger, joy, etc.) are consistently expressed by raising and widening the overall pitch range, while for other less active emotions (boredom, sadness, etc.) the pitch range is lowered and narrowed (e.g. Williams and Stevens 1972; Bezooijen 1984). This makes it meaningful to describe two different F_0 contours spoken by the same person as phonologically identical but with a paralinguistically modified vertical scale. The case of a sentence in a tone language spoken gently or with the voice raised in anger illustrates the distinction clearly and presents no conceptual problems.

When we are dealing with intonation in a language like English, however, it is seldom so easy to distinguish linguistic and paralinguistic effects. Many features of intonation, not just the expressive uses of pitch range, are widely shared by languages around the world, and many of the functions of intonation seem to involve the expression of non-propositional attitudes and presuppositions. This means that almost anything to do with intonation might be (and at various times probably has been) considered paralinguistic—"around the edge of language", in Bolinger's phrase. And therein lies the problem for the analyst. The implicit job of any analysis of intonation is to identify just those aspects of intonation that are "linguistic" and include them in our phonological analysis, while leaving out the paralinguistic features that merely modify the realisation of a given intonation contour without affecting its

---

2 It may seem uncontroversial to class downstep as a vertical scale effect that does not affect the underlying phonological identity of the downstepped tone, but in fact this represents hard-won theoretical understanding during the middle part of this century. Because downstep is clearly linguistic, it was common in older accounts of African languages to treat downstepped High tones as separate Mid tone phonemes.

underlying phonological identity. Since there are no clear independent criteria for distinguishing linguistic and paralinguistic *a priori* however, the distinction has normally been drawn wherever it is required to support a given linguistic analysis. That is, once an analyst has come up with a set of linguistic distinctions that cover a certain range of intonational data, any data that do not fit are thereupon declared paralinguistic, thus providing an ostensibly principled basis for excluding them from the linguistic analysis in the first place.

I do not mean to suggest that this circularity has been practiced deliberately. There is clearly good reason to believe in a distinction between linguistic and paralinguistic, and yet in a non-tone language the distinction is genuinely difficult to draw. Nevertheless, it is a fact that many of the unresolved debates over intonational phonology over the past fifty years or so have hinged precisely on the question of which phenomena to exclude as paralinguistic (cf. Ladd 1980, chapter 5).

For example, the British "nuclear tone" tradition has been dogged since its inception (Palmer 1922) with uncertainty over the distinctions between "high rise" and "low rise" or "high fall" and "low fall". Palmer, for example, treated the high/low distinction as basic to the rises but paralinguistic (in the terms being used here) in the falls, a decision apparently echoed by Halliday (1967) and Kingdon (1958). O'Connor and Arnold (1973), on the other hand, treat the distinction as basic to both (i.e., high fall and low fall are atomically different tone types, as different as e.g. high fall and fall-rise), while Crystal (1969) explicitly treats the distinction as paralinguistic in both cases, so that the only linguistic distinction is fall vs. rise.

Similarly, in the American "pitch level" approach pioneered by Pike (1945) and widely adopted during the 1950s (e.g. Trager and Smith 1957), it was never quite possible to agree on the number of pitch levels needed for an adequate description. The usual number was four, but Gage (1958) cautiously presented evidence for a fifth level between levels 2 and 3, and even the convinced four-level analysts conceded that there was some special relationship between the top two levels (viz. that the top level was essentially only an emphatic version of the next level down). More generally, the "levels-vs.-configurations" debate (Bolinger 1951)—the long-running dispute between the pitch-level theory and any analysis (like the nuclear tone tradition) based on atomic pitch movements—was itself an instance of the same problem: for Trager and Smith, falls 21, 31, and 41 were linguistically distinct, while for Bolinger or Crystal they were paralinguistic variants of the same linguistic category Fall.

The details of these theoretical impasses are perhaps of primarily historical interest today, but the general point they illustrate is highly relevant to the issue at hand: in the absence of an independent definition of paralinguistic, such disagreements in the analysis of intonation are both inevitable and all but undecidable.

2.2. Second digression: phonetic models of vertical scale

The theoretical impasses just described are not, however, exclusively due to the absence of good definitions of the paralinguistic. An equally important problem is the difficulty, given the existence of pitch range variability, of providing appropriate *phonetic* descriptions of pitch distinctions, linguistic or otherwise. If we observe that in a particular contour type one peak is consistently higher than another, how are we to describe the difference in height? It is clear that any description in terms of one speaker's actual F_0 values cannot readily be generalised to other speakers, but it is not at all clear how else one might refer to such effects on pitch level in any but impressionistic ways.

In many traditional descriptions, this problem has been dealt with by effectively ignoring it. The phonological identity of intonational primitives is characterised in terms of *pitch movements*—rise, fall, fall-rise, etc. —which do not necessarily require any specification of level. Once we accept the view that the primitives of the phonological description are discrete tones, however, the problem of tonal scaling—providing a phonetic interpretation of the tones—becomes very much more salient, as both Bruce and Pierrehumbert acknowledged in their early work. That is, by making explicit reference to pitch level (in the form of a distinction between High and Low tones), descriptions in the tradition of Bruce and Pierrehumbert incur an obligation to give an account of the factors that bring about the variation in the height of Highs and the depth of Lows.

A good deal of work has been done to discharge this obligation over the last 10 or 15 years, as numerous investigators have formulated more or less explicit models of F_0 to accompany more or less explicit phonological analyses of intonation. Without oversimplifying unduly,[3] it can be

---

[3] The work summarised in what follows includes that of Bruce and Gårding (Bruce and Gårding 1978; Bruce 1982; Gårding 1983), 't Hart and his colleagues ('t Hart and Collier 1975, 1979; Cohen, Collier, and 't Hart 1982), Pierrehumbert and her colleagues (Pierrehumbert 1980; Liberman and Pierrehumbert 1984; Pierrehumbert and Beckman 1988), Clements (1979, 1990), Ladd and his colleagues (Ladd 1990; Ladd et al. 1985; Connell and Ladd 1990), and van den Berg et al. (1991). This summary clearly ignores many differences of mathematical detail between competing models, but it is an attempt to state what all the models have in common. Note that, as I use the term here, "baseline" is not necessarily

said that these phonetic models are built around the notion of *baseline*, a speaker-specific reference value at or near the bottom of the speaking range, and *tonal space*, a subset of the overall range, relative to which phonological target levels can be defined. The tonal space is somewhat above the baseline and is defined relative to it; its width and its location relation to the baseline are determined, at least in part, by speaker-specific factors. More relevantly for the problem of downstep, the quantitative properties of the tonal space can change during the course of an utterance for linguistic and paralinguistic reasons. For example, suppose we have a pitch accent analysed phonologically as a sequence of H tone and L tone and modelled phonetically as a fall from the top of the tonal space to the bottom: two given occurrences of this pitch accent at different points in an utterance could be phonetically different, even though both were modelled as a fall from the top of the tonal space to the bottom, because the tonal space itself could be higher or lower, wider or narrower. This is shown in figure 2.

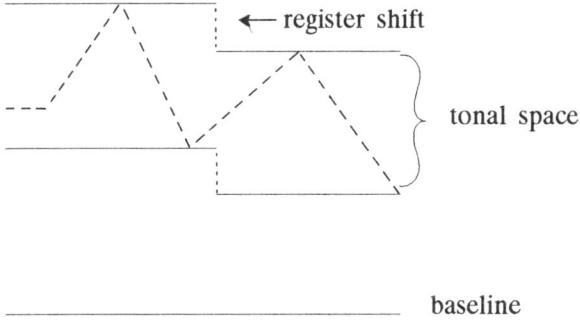

Figure 2
Basic elements of the type of phonetic F_0 model described in the text. The idealised F_0 contour shown consists of two HL (falling) accents followed by a fall to baseline at the end of the contour.

---

a declining line (as in e.g. the model of Maeda 1976 or Pierrehumbert 1980) but can simply be a fixed value. Also, "tonal space" is an ad hoc term. In various contexts the same general abstraction has been referred to as *tone level frame* (Clements 1979), *grid* (Gårding and her coworkers, e.g. Gårding 1983), *transform space* (Pierrehumbert and Beckman 1988, but note that this is not really intended as a technical term), and *register* (e.g. Connell and Ladd 1990). The lack of any accepted term for this concept is indicative of uncertainty about whether it is really a construct in its own right or simply a consequence of the interaction of various model parameters; only for Gårding does the "grid" clearly have a life of its own.

Given this conception, a phonetically explicit description of intonation will involve:

I.   a description of the phonologically distinct tone or accent types and how they are scaled relative to the tonal space;   *and*

II. a description of how the tonal space evolves over the course of an utterance (it could be subject to linguistic, paralinguistic, and even extralinguistic modifications).

In order to characterise the tonal space at any given point in the utterance, we will need to specify:

I.   the speaker-specific baseline;

II. the location of the tonal space relative to the baseline;

III. the width of the tonal space.

Some of the factors that influence these three parameters will be relatively fixed settings for a given speaker (e.g. male-female differences); some will vary from situation to situation (e.g. bored vs. excited); and some—as in the case of downstep—may vary from one tone to the next.

It should be clear that, even if it turns out to be wrong in some fundamental way, this approach to pitch range represents a considerable advance over the vagueness of descriptions like "low rise". For example, given the three parameters needed to describe the location of the tonal space, one might be tempted to equate specific parameters with specific types of influences on vertical scale—say, to treat the reference level as extralinguistic, the location of the tonal space as paralinguistic, and the width of the tonal space as linguistic. It strikes me as unlikely that life is that simple, but the very existence of such an explicit hypothesis about vertical scale is a thoroughgoing novelty in intonation research.

2.2.1. Phonetic models of downstep

One of the problems to which these phonetic models of F_0 have been applied is that of downstep, and register shifts generally. Given the baseline-plus-tonal-space approach, the most obvious way to model downstep is to modify the properties of the tonal space. In particular, one might either shift the tonal space downwards or make the tonal space narrower (see Fig. 3). Both approaches have been tried in recent work.

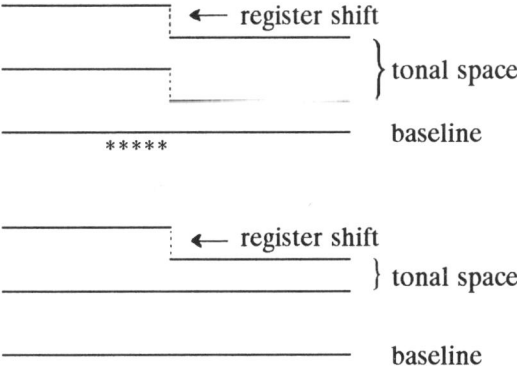

Figure 3
Two ways of characterising downstep in a phonetic F_0 model using the notion of "tonal space". In the model shown in the top part of the figure, the tonal space is lowered (brought closer to the baseline); in the model shown in the bottom part of the figure the tonal space is narrowed (i.e. only the top of the tonal space is lowered.

In my own model (Ladd 1987, 1990), downstep affects the height of the tonal space above the baseline, and its width which I treat as a fairly constant speaker characteristic—is unaffected.[4] Downstep takes as its input a given parameter value for the height of the tonal space and reduces it by a fixed proportion. (The existence of a fixed proportion in the phonetics of downstep was discovered by Pierrehumbert 1980.) The particular value of the parameter that is input to a given application of downstep depends on a number of factors, including the long-term characteristics of the individual speaker's voice, the speaker's emotional state, and of course the pattern of previous register shifts in the utterance.

In the model proposed by Pierrehumbert and Beckman, by contrast, downstep leaves the height of the tonal space unaffected, and operates to narrow the tonal space by a fixed proportion. Specifically, in their terms,

---

[4] Strictly speaking, what is unaffected is the model parameter that controls the width of the tonal space; because of the way the parameters interact in the model, the tonal space does narrow slightly as it is lowered and widens slightly as it is raised, even though the width parameter remains constant.

terms, the height of the "reference line" (the neutral mid-point of the tonal space) above the baseline is affected only by paralinguistic and speaker-specific factors, and what downstep does is to lower the "High tone line" that determines where High tones are scaled relative to the reference line. Strictly speaking, in other words, what is being narrowed by downstep is the *upper half* of the tonal space. Pierrehumbert and Beckman say very little about the lower half, which they do not need for Japanese; "Low" tones in Japanese—which are only boundary tones and "unstarred" trailing tones in the accentual configuration H*+L—are scaled within the upper half of the tonal space. (Scaling Low tones in the upper half of the tonal space is not as implausible as it might seem; my own model scales "unstarred" tones on the midline, which given the current state of data and models, is effectively indistiguishable from Pierrehumbert and Beckman's approach. In both models, the lower half of the tonal space is reserved for accented Low tones, which do not occur in Japanese.)

3. THE CASE AGAINST REGISTER TONES

3.1. Pierrehumbert and Beckman's arguments

We are now ready to consider the Pierrehumbert/Beckman case against register trees. The first part of the case (Beckman and Pierrehumbert 1986:298–300) is not actually directed at the register tree proposal, but more generally at the implicit threat posed to Pierrehumbert's linear analysis by the phenomenon of nested downstep (Fig. 1 and example (6) above). Obviously, if downstep is a phonetic realisation rule affecting certain phrase-internal sequences of tones, then downstep from one phrase to the next should not occur. Since nested downstep, or something looking very much like it, manifestly does occur, it must be handled in a different way if the linear analysis is to be rescued.

What Beckman and Pierrehumbert propose is that nested downstep has nothing to do with phrase-internal downstep (their "catathesis"). Instead, they say, "the relative pitch range of [downtrending] phrases can be accounted for independently by principles proposed in Brown et al. (1980). [Brown et al.] suggest that the pitch range is raised when initiating a new topic, and lowered when concluding one. For discourse segments consisting of only one topic, a downtrend is accordingly predicted." In other words, the pitch range for each "intermediate phrase"[5] is selected independently according to discourse principles, and these "phrasal manipulations of overall pitch range mimic catathesis" (299f.). Later in the same context, Beckman and Pierrehumbert suggest that certain other vertical scale effects related to discourse organisation may be "truly paralinguistic" (305).

This line of argument is virtually unanswerable. By conceding that phrase-to-phrase downtrends "mimic" phrase-internal downstep, they acknowledge the phonetic similarity, but the fact that the similarity extends to quantitative detail (cf. Ladd 1987; van den Berg et al. 1991) they leave as an unexplained coincidence. (There is, after all, no obvious reason why the downtrend created by a sequence of independent paralinguistic choices should duplicate the effect of a phonologically conditioned phonetic realisation rule.) Moreover, the paralinguistic explanation does not really have the independent support they claim for it. The "independent principles" of Brown et al. (1980) are in fact rather informal and decidedly non-quantitative statements of rough tendencies in conversational interaction.[6] Beckman and Pierrehumbert's decision to exclude nested downstep from consideration can thus scarcely be said to be motivated as rigorously as much of the rest of their work.

The second part of the case against register trees is presented in Pierrehumbert and Beckman (1988). They demonstrate very clearly that the presence or absence of downstep (which is triggered in Japanese by the occurrence of word-accent) can be detected phonetically in a two-word phrase even when speakers are instructed to place emphasis on one word or the other. That is, downstep and emphasis involve independent manipulations of the vertical scale. Since Pierrehumbert and Beckman assume that, in a register tree proposal, the difference in emphasis would be represented on the tree as either h-l or l-h, and since that distinction is obviously pre-empted for downstep, they conclude that the register tree proposal is incapable of expressing the phonetic distinctions that demonstrably occur. In their words, "tonal prominence

---

5 Beckman and Pierrehumbert (1986; also Pierrehumbert and Beckman 1988) argue, convincingly in my view, for a distinction between "intermediate phrases" and "intonational phrases", the latter being made up of one or more of the former. True phonological downstep, in this analysis, occurs only *within* intermediate phrases. See further sec. 3.2.4 below.

6 What Brown et al. (1980:127) actually say is the following: "It seems that participants in a conversation co-operate by signalling when they are about to embark on a new topic by raising pitch and a second speaker will then accept this new topic by, to begin with, also marking it by raising pitch—'I realise you have broached a new topic and I am following your lead.'— On the other hand, when both participants assume that what they are talking about is contained within an ongoing topic, they will both mark their assumption of this by remaining low in tessitura."

and catathesis cannot be treated by a uniform phonological mechanism in Japanese" (173).

As I pointed out in my review (Ladd 1989) of their book, however, this cannot be taken as an argument against the register tree proposal, because it is based on the false assumption that the only relations expressible between prosodic elements under such a proposal would be h-l and l-h. But the metrical representation of register is not intended to supplant the metrical representation of relative prominence. That is, I assume that it is possible for s-w or w-s relations to coexist in a metrical tree with h-l and l-h relations. Indeed, the whole point of recognising downstep in English, as Pierrehumbert (1980) first observed, is that a downstepped accent may be "nuclear" or otherwise more prominent than the preceding accent, even though it is scaled lower. Relative strength or prominence and relative intonational (register) height are two distinct phenomena, but that separateness is clearly representable in a metrical analysis.

While neither of Pierrehumbert and Beckman's two arguments unambiguously knock out the register tree proposal, it cannot be said that in parrying them I have struck the final blow in the proposal's favour, either. In fact, down to this point the disagreement between the Pierrehumbert/Beckman view and the register tree analysis has all the elements of a classic Paralinguistic Stalemate. The details of the debate are specific to the data at hand, but the form of the argument is entirely traditional.

First, Pierrehumbert and Beckman say that a metrical representation of downstep is not necessary, because one of the main phenomena that motivates it—nested downstep—is paralinguistic anyway. Second, they argue that the metrical representation is not sufficient, because it is too impoverished to deal with linguistic distinctions of F_0 scaling that interact within the intermediate phrase (the Japanese downstep and emphasis data). In other words, they argue for the superiority of their analysis on the grounds that it is capable of handling a linguistic distinction (downstep vs. emphasis) supposedly not treatable in a competing analysis; they defend their system against the charge that it is unable to deal with a given phenomenon (nested downstep) on the grounds that the phenomenon is paralinguistic and hence irrelevant to evaluating the phonological analysis. In the absence of an independent definition of paralinguistic, this stalemate would be exactly as unresolvable as comparable disagreements in the 1950s.

Pierrehumbert and Beckman, however, have taken an important step forward, because unlike traditional practitioners of paralinguistic arguments, they do have an independent (if implicit) diagnostic for distinguishing between linguistic and paralinguistic. This is based on their analysis of prosodic domain types:

> Linguistic effects on F_0 scaling apply to prosodic domains *smaller than the intermediate phrase*; paralinguistic effects on F_0 scaling apply to prosodic domains *of intermediate phrase size or larger*.

Moreover, this distinction is correlated with a distinction in their phonetic model:

> Linguistic effects—those that apply within the intermediate phrase—affect the *width* of the tonal space; paralinguistic effects—applying to phrase-size domains or larger—affect the *height* of the tonal space above the baseline.

Far from leaving the argument in a stalemate, in other words, Pierrehumbert and Beckman have put together some testable (or at least independently assessable) definitions in a very elegant descriptive package. They are able to define paralinguistic in terms of independently motivated definitions of prosodic domains and their independently motivated phonetic model of F_0 scaling. All the elements of their analysis support all the others. The distinction between linguistic and paralinguistic, the definitions of prosodic domains, the phonetic modelling of F_0, and—let us not lose sight of the issue at hand—the linear phonological analysis of downstep: all dovetail together so nicely that the overall structure, one might think, must be right.

But the undoubted elegance of the account is very delicate. If the balance of any of the individual elements is disturbed, the validity of the whole construct is compromised. Since the individual elements have the virtue of being relatively explicit, it is possible, by evaluating them on their own merits, to assess the plausibility of the analysis as a whole. This is the task undertaken in the next section.

3.2. Problems with Pierrehumbert and Beckman's arguments

3.2.1. Problems with the phonetic model of downstep

First of all, there are potential problems with their phonetic model of downstep as a narrowing of the upper half of the tonal space. If Low tones downstep along with High tones—and in at least some languages there is clear evidence that they do—then there are only two ways that Pierrehumbert and Beckman could model this. First, they could scale Low tones proportionally to High tones in the upper half of the tonal space. This, as we saw, is what they do for Japanese; as we noted, this is by no means so implausible as it might seem, since in Japanese all

Low tones are either boundary tones or the "unstarred" trailing tone in the bitonal accent configuration H*+L. However, for Low tones in a true tone languages (i.e. Low tones unrelated to accentual configurations) this is not a theoretically defensible option, since there is no natural dependence of Low on High. Moreover, if all Low tones were scaled in the upper half of the tonal space there would then be no use at all for the lower half. The second possibility for downstepping Low tones would be to scale them (as would seem natural) in the lower half of the tonal space, and downstep the Low tone line in the same way the High tone line is downstepped in their Japanese model. The problem here is that in a given downstep sequence the lower half of the tonal space becomes wider as the top half becomes narrower. More generally, in such a model the downstepping of Lows is mathematically entirely independent of the downstepping of Highs, so that nothing would suggest that they were even part of the same phenomenon.

Obviously, these problems could easily be dealt with in a revised model. The phonetic models proposed by Ladd (1990) and Clements (1990), for example, both treat downstep by shifting the entire tonal space downwards, which automatically downsteps Low tones and thus does not encounter the difficulty just outlined. If Pierrehumbert and Beckman were to adopt such a model, however, they would lose the *phonetic* basis of their distinction between linguistic (narrowing) and paralinguistic (lowering), because in such a model the height of the tonal space can be affected by both linguistic and paralinguistic effects (that, indeed, is why they are so hard to tell apart). That is, an independently motivated change to their phonetic model would eliminate one of the elegant internal consistencies of their overall description of downstep.

3.2.2. Problems with the function of paralinguistic effects

Another difficulty with Pierrehumbert and Beckman's account is the functional incoherence of what they define as paralinguistic. Their phonological and phonetic characterisations of the linguistic/paralinguistic distinction are, as we have seen, both clear and simple. Functionally, however, the phenomena that they group together as paralinguistic are rather heterogeneous, and conversely some of the phenomena that end up on opposite sides of their linguistic/paralinguistic divide seem actually quite closely related.

Specifically, the connection they posit between the discourse-related uses of pitch range (nested downstep, signalling of new topics, etc.) and the interpersonal or emotion-related uses (raising the voice in noise or to express interest or arousal) is either not very plausible, or else too plausible. That is, the relationship between newness of topic and interest or arousal does make metaphorical sense (cf. Bolinger 1986, passim), but can scarcely be said to be susceptible to rigorous evaluation. Nevertheless, if we accept the Pierrehumbert/Beckman account of downtrends across phrases, is seems necessary to acknowledge that it applies equally well to the downtrends that Pierrehumbert and Beckman wish to treat as linguistic. That is, the meaning difference between a downstepping intermediate phrase and a non-downstepping one arguably involves the same difference as that between a downtrending sequence of phrases and a non-downtrending one: single topic throughout (downtrend or downstep) vs. new or important topic in mid-domain (reversal of downtrend or non-downstep). I remain agnostic about the value of such metaphorical explanations of intonational contrasts; my point here is that Pierrehumbert and Beckman's functional explanation for phrase-to-phrase downstep, if it works at all, will work for accent-to-accent downstep as well.

Once again, then, the elegant meshing of apparently independent elements of the analysis breaks down when one of the elements is called into question. In Pierrehumbert and Beckman's analysis, the supposed paralinguistic motivation of phrase-to-phrase downtrends and the definition of linguistic and paralinguistic in terms of prosodic domain size complement each other nicely. If the paralinguistic account of downtrends applies to domains of any size, this complementarity is lost.

3.2.3. Problems with experimental results on range expansion

The third (and in my view most telling) problem with Pierrehumbert and Beckman's overall picture is that it requires them to explain away a striking regularity seen in all published experimental data on expansion of overall range. Pierrehumbert (1980), Bruce (1982), Liberman and Pierrehumbert (1984), and Pierrehumbert and Beckman (1988) all report experiments in which specific intonation contours were uttered in varying overall ranges. In all of these experiments, two types of intonation-related variables were manipulated: first, the test utterances involved differences of emphasis, discourse structure, phrasing, length, etc.; second, each of the test utterances was pronounced in two or more overall pitch ranges.[7]

---

[7] In some of these experiments speakers were given explicit instructions about the intonational features under investigation—e.g. in the experiment first reported in Pierrehumbert (1980), speakers had to pronounce the sentence *Anna came with Manny* so that it answered either *Who came with Manny?* or *Who did Anna come with?* In other experiments, the texts were constructed in such a way as to bring about these distinctions

In every case, the two manipulations of the contour can be distinguished quite clearly in the experimental results. The patterns of relative F_0 within contours—the patterns that signal relative prominence, discourse status, etc.—remain extraordinarily constant, while the overall range varies from just a few semitones to (in some cases) a few octaves. The discovery of this constancy was one of the many important contributions of Pierrehumbert's thesis, and its role in establishing the significance of discrete target levels in intonational phonology should not be underestimated.

Yet to Pierrehumbert and Beckman these results pose a problem. For the pattern of constant F_0 relationships is found not only within intermediate phrases—where, according to Pierrehumbert and Beckman, the F_0 relations reflect linguistically determined modifications of the tonal space—but also from one intermediate phrase to the next. According to Pierrehumbert and Beckman, there can be no phonological relations of pitch range between intermediate phrases; rather, the pitch range is independently set for each phrase, on paralinguistic principles. That means that it is formally impossible in Pierrehumbert and Beckman's theory to distinguish the overall pitch range setting for the utterance from the pitch range settings for the individual phrases: the constant patterns in the latter are merely the consequence of consecutive choices within an utterance, choices that by remarkable coincidence all bear the same relation to one another whether the voice is lowered or raised.

Pierrehumbert and Beckman's explanation for this coincidence invokes a sketchily defined "speaker strategy":

> The design of [Pierrehumbert's Anna/Manny experiment] is typical in that it encouraged the subjects to zero in on a certain fixed pragmatic relationship—in that case, the relationship of an answer focus to a background focus. The constant relationship between the nuclear peak heights for these two foci *may well reflect the subjects' uniform strategy* for realizing this constant pragmatic relationship.
> (Beckman and Pierrehumbert 1991, emphasis supplied)

No independent evidence of such a strategy is provided, nor is any explanation given for why all the subjects adopted the same strategy. Moreover, it is not true that the Anna/Manny experiment is typical in drawing subjects" attention to an intonational distinction; in both Bruce's

---

automatically—e.g. one set of experiments reported in Pierrehumbert and Beckman (1988), which systematically varied the location of accented and unaccented words, prosodic boundaries, etc. The instructions to vary the overall pitch range varied from explicitly emotional ("involved" vs. "detached", Bruce 1982) to more pragmatic ("degrees of overall emphasis", Pierrehumbert 1980) to clearly situational (speaking as if to someone in a quiet room, across a busy street, etc., Pierrehumbert and Beckman 1988).

experiment and some of Pierrehumbert and Beckman's experiments the intonational variables (accentuation, phrasing, etc.) were manipulated in the preparation of the speech materials by the experimenter. In fact, Beckman and Pierrehumbert (1991) go on to say that it is *more* typical in these experiments

> to present the subject with a randomized list of sentences to read without providing explicit cues to the desired pragmatic and intonational interpretation. In this case, the subject will surely invent an appropriate pragmatic context, which may vary from experiment to experiment or from utterance to utterance in uncontrolled ways.

This being the case, it seems all the more remarkable that constant pitch relations are found in the results of all these different experiments in three different languages. Unless Pierrehumbert and Beckman can state more explicitly what they mean by "strategy", and tell how such a uniformly applied "strategy" can be distinguished from the effect of a phonological relationship, and present some independent evidence that we are dealing with the former rather than the latter, it is at best difficult to evaluate their claim.

3.2.4. Problems with the definition of prosodic domains

Finally, even if one accepts the idea of a speaker strategy for realising paralinguistic choices in an experimental situation, there remains still a further difficulty with Pierrehumbert and Beckman's view, namely the definition of "intermediate phrase". Since apparent pitch range relations between intermediate phrases are to be regarded only as evidence for the speaker strategy, it is crucial that *genuine* pitch range relations, such as downstep, must operate within a single intermediate phrase. Now, in the experiment that established the quantitative regularity of downstep, Liberman and Pierrehumbert (1984) had their speakers produce the downstepping contours on lists of names of berries—texts such as *Blueberries, bayberries, raspberries, mulberries, and brambleberries.* By what criteria do the individual items of such a list *not* constitute separate intermediate phrases?

All traditional descriptions of intonation (e.g. Hockett 1958:45, exx. 100–102; O'Connor and Arnold 1973:3) show at least the possibility of boundaries of some sort between the elements of a list. Yet Liberman and Pierrehumbert ask us—implicitly, as the matter is never raised—to consider the entire list a single intermediate phrase. Since the absence of boundaries is crucial to the Pierrehumbert analysis, it would seem appropriate for the authors to present some independent evidence that no such boundaries occur.

I hasten to add that, in my view, one of the valuable features of the theory of tonal structure presented in Beckman and Pierrehumbert (1986) and Pierrehumbert and Beckman (1988) is that it points the way to some independent definitions of various prosodic domain types. As noted above, I find the distinction between "intermediate" and "intonational" phrase convincing and useful (though I agree with Hayes and Lahiri forthcoming that the terminology is unhelpful and accept their identification of the "intermediate" phrase with the "phonological" phrase of other work). I have elsewhere (Ladd 1986, forthcoming) discussed the inadequacies of traditional definitions of prosodic boundaries, and I have no doubt that independent phonetic definitions of prosodic domain types will soon be possible. My only point here is to draw attention to the delicately balanced interdependence of Pierrehumbert and Beckman's phonological definition of paralinguistic, their definition of intermediate phrase as applied to the elements of a list, and their linear analysis of downstep. Adjustments to any of these elements seem likely to bring the whole structure down.

Note, incidentally, that the prosodic status of the list elements is critical only for Pierrehumbert's linear theory of downstep. In a metrical theory like the one being defended here, it is of no consequence whether the lists are considered to be one phrase or many. In fact, one can imagine two different renditions of a downstepping list—renditions that might reasonably be called a single phrase and a sequence of phrases—with identical pitch relations between the accentual High tones in each case. Pierrehumbert and Beckman would have to give two completely separate and unrelated accounts of these patterns: the single-phrase version would manifest true linearly-conditioned downstep, while the multi-phrase version would exhibit independent paralinguistic settings of pitch range on each item that merely mimic the true downstep on the version spoken in a single phrase.

4. REASSEMBLING THE PIECES

How else might we put the pieces of the register puzzle together, if not in the way proposed by Pierrehumbert and Beckman? Centrally, of course, I assume the existence of phonologically specified register relations, of the sort that can be appropriately represented by a metrical tree, and I assume that this is the basis of downstep in English and other European languages. This approach, as noted at the beginning of the paper, provides a natural account of the existence of nested downstep. However, given the explicitness of Pierrehumbert and Beckman's theory with respect to phonetic modelling, prosodic domains, and the definition of paralinguistic, it is insufficient simply to restate the register tree proposal and leave it at that. In this brief final section I discuss how we might incorporate robust accounts of these other areas into a metrical phonology of register.

On prosodic domains I have nothing to add to what I said above, namely that independent phonetic definitions of prosodic domain types seem both desirable and attainable, and that Pierrehumbert and Beckman's work seems to be a step in this direction. I have elsewhere (Ladd 1986, forthcoming) proposed a theory of prosodic structure that may help in the attainment of this goal, but the details are not relevant to the issues raised in this paper.

On phonetic modelling, I reiterate my claim that it is empirically more viable to model register shifts in terms of the height of the tonal space rather than the width. This has a couple of interesting consequences. Most importantly, it means that *several independent factors* contribute to the *same* model parameter (height of tonal space above baseline). Tonal space height reflects not only register effects, but also such factors as long-term characteristics of the speaker's voice and emotional effects on pitch range. It is thus not possible to distinguish linguistic and paralinguistic phenomena strictly according to which model parameters they affect—which is in effect what Pierrehumbert and Beckman attempt to do. Indeed, as I suggested earlier, one of the reasons that paralinguistic and linguistic pitch range effects are so difficult to tell apart is precisely that they affect the same parameters.

There may, however, be a difference worth exploring, and this brings us to the differences between linguistic and paralinguistic. When the tonal space is raised or lowered by register effects, it is raised or lowered *relationally*: a given register setting is determined with reference to a previous one. Downstep is both categorical and intrinsically relational: at a given point in the utterance, either the tonal space is downstepped or it is not, and if it is, it is downstepped with reference to a previous level. Emotional effects on pitch range, by contrast, do not refer to earlier values of the height parameter, and do not come in steps. They simply raise and lower the tonal space gradually according to the degree of emotional arousal, interest, etc. This suggests that an alternative definition of the linguistic/paralinguistic distinction may rest on whether a given vertical scale effect is relational or simply involves an "extra-structural" property of a prosodic domain (for more on the notion of extrastructural properties of prosodic domains see Pierrehumbert and Beckman 1988, chapter 6). *Paralinguistic* effects modify vertical scale *without regard to structure; linguistic* effects, being relational, cannot help respecting structure in one way or another. This, rather than domain size, may be the most appropriate basis of the distinction between linguistic and paralinguistic.[8]

Finally, it is worth mentioning that metrical relations are not necessarily the only way of controlling register shifts. I believe that all *intonational* downstep phenomena—in English and other European languages—are satisfactorily accounted for in this way, but it is obvious that in some languages downstep is indeed triggered by a specific tonal sequence, such as H-L-H. There is no particular reason to try to force this linear phenomenon into the metrical mold (that is, I believe Pierrehumbert may be correct in rejecting e.g. Huang's use of trees for downstep in African tone languages); in fact, there is plenty of reason not to, since it seems likely that both types of phonological register effects can coexist. Coexisting types of downstep, I believe, provide the explanation for the subtle phonetic effects discovered by Kubozono (1989), which he analyses as involving "metrical boost". Possibly a consideration of structural effects on tone sandhi (e.g. Hung 1989) might shed some light on how the coexistence is managed. In any case it seems likely that downstep must ultimately be acknowledged as having interacting metrical and linear sources.

REFERENCES

Beckman, Mary E. and Janet B. Pierrehumbert. 1986. "Intonational Structure in English and Japanese." *Phonology Yearbook* 3, 255–310.

———. 1991. "Tactics and Strategies for Thinking about F_0 Variation." In *Gesture, Segment, Prosody: Papers in Laboratory Phonology II*, edited by G.J. Docherty and D.R. Ladd. Cambridge: Cambridge University Press.

Berg, Rob van den, Carlos Gussenhoven, and Toni Rietveld. 1991. "Downstep in Dutch: Implications for a Model." In *Gesture, Segment, Prosody: Papers in Laboratory Phonology II*, edited by G.J. Docherty and D.R. Ladd. Cambridge: Cambridge University Press.

Bezooijen, Renée. 1984. *Characteristics and Recognizability of Vocal Expressions of Emotion.* Dordrecht: Foris Publications.

Bolinger, Dwight. 1951. "Intonation: Levels vs. Configurations." *Word* 7, 199–210.

———. 1986. *Intonation and its Parts*. Stanford: University Press.

Brown, Gillian, Karen Currie and Joanne Kenworthy. 1980. *Questions of Intonation*. London: Croom Helm.

Bruce, Gösta 1977. *Swedish Word Accents in Sentence Perspective.* Lund: Gleerup.

---

8 Naturally, if paralinguistic effects are gradient and non-relational, one might expect them to apply mostly to larger domains, because too many non-relational modifications of small domains could interfere with linguistic relational effects. On the other hand, nothing in principle would seem to rule out paralinguistic modification of pitch range in a short domain, and I suggest that "emphasis"—as distinct from focus or prominence—is paralinguistic raising of the tonal space for a domain as short as a single word.

———. 1982. "Developing the Swedish Intonation Model." *Working Papers*, 1–116. University of Lund, Department of Linguistics.
Bruce, Gösta and Eva Gårding 1978. "A Prosodic Typology for Swedish Dialects." In *Nordic Prosody*, edited by E. Gårding, G. Bruce and R. Bannert, 219–28. Lund: Gleerup.
Clements, G. N. 1979. "The Description of Terrace-level Tone Languages." *Language* 55, 536–58.
———. 1983. "The Hierarchical Representation of Tone Features." In *Current Approaches to African Linguistics*. Vol. 1, edited by I. Dihoff, 145–76. Dordrecht: Foris Publications.
———. 1990. "The Status of Register in Intonation Theory." In *Between the Grammar and the Physics of Speech: Papers in Laboratory Phonology I*, edited by John Kingston and Mary E. Beckman, 58–72. Cambridge: Cambridge University Press.
Cohen, A., René Collier and Johan 't Hart. 1982. "Declination: Construct or Intrinsic Feature of Speech Pitch?" *Phonetica* 39, 254–73.
Connell, Bruce and D.R. Ladd. 1990. "Aspects of Pitch Realisation in Yoruba." *Phonology* 7, 1–29.
Cooper, William and John Sorensen. 1981. *Fundamental Frequency in Sentence Production*. Heidelberg: Springer-Verlag.
Crystal, David. 1969. *Prosodic Systems and Intonation in English*. Cambridge: Cambridge University Press.
Gage, William. 1958. "Grammatical Structures in American English Intonation." Ph.D. Dissertation, Cornell University, Ithaka.
Gårding, Eva. 1983. "A Generative Model of Intonation." In *Prosody: Models and Measurements*, edited by A. Cutler, D.R. Ladd, 11–25. Heidelberg: Springer.
Gussenhoven, Carlos 1984. *On the Grammar and Semantics of Sentence Accents*. Dordrecht: Foris Publications.
Gussenhoven, Carlos and Toni Rietveld. forthcoming. "Two Theories of the Nuclear Tones of English." *Linguistics*.
Halliday, M.A.K. 1967. *Intonation and Grammar in British English*. The Hague: Mouton.
't Hart, Johan. 1979. *Naar automatisch genereren van toonhoogte-contouren voor tamelijk lange stukken spraak*. IPO Technical Report No. 353, Eindhoven.
't Hart, Johan and René Collier. 1975. "Integrating Different Levels of Intonation Analysis. *Journal of Phonetics* 3, 235–55.
Hayes, Bruce and Additi Lahiri. forthcoming. "Bengali Intonational Phonology." *Natural Language and Linguistic Theory*.
Hockett, Charles F. 1958. *A Course in Modern Linguistics*. New York: Macmillan.
Huang, C.-T. James. 1980. "The Metrical Structure of Terraced-level Tones." In *Proceedings of NELS 11*, edited by J. Jensen, 257–70. Cahiers Linguistiques d'Ottawa, vol. 9. University of Ottawa, Department of Linguistics.
Hung, Tony T.N. 1989. *Syntactic and Semantic Aspects of Chinese Tone Sandhi*. Bloomington: Indiana University Linguistics Club Publications.
Kingdon, Roger 1958. *The Groundwork of English Intonation*. London: Longman.
Kubozono, Haruo. 1989. "Syntactic and Rhythmic Effects on Downstep in Japanese. *Phonology* 6, 39–67.
Ladd, D.R. 1980. *The Structure of Intonational Meaning: Evidence from English*. Bloomington: Indiana University Press.
———. 1983. "Phonological Features of Intonational Peaks." *Language* 59, 721–59.
———. 1986. "Intonational Phrasing: The Case for Recursive Prosodic Structure." *Phonology Yearbook* 3, 311–40.
———. 1987. "A Phonological Model of Intonation for Use in Speech Synthesis by Rule." In *Proceedings of the European Conference on Speech Technology*, edited by J. Laver and M. Jack, 21–24. Edinburgh.

———. 1988. "Declination 'Reset' and the Hierarchical Organization of Utterances." *Journal of the Acoustical Society of America* 84, 530–44.
———. 1989. "Review of Pierrehumbert and Beckman 1988". *Journal of Linguistics* 25, 519–26.
———. 1990. "Metrical Representation of Pitch Register." In *Between the Grammar and the Physics of Speech: Papers in Laboratory Phonology I*, edited by John Kingston and Mary E. Beckman, 35–58. Cambridge: Cambridge University Press.
———. 1991. "An Introduction to Intonational Phonology." In *Gesture, Segment, Prosody: Papers in Laboratory Phonology II*, edited by G.J. Docherty and D.R. Ladd. Cambridge: Cambridge University Press.
———. forthcoming. "Compound Prosodic Domains." Paper presented at the Scuola Normale Superiore, Pisa, March 1990.
Ladd, D.R., Kim Silverman, Frank Tolkmitt, Gunther Bergmann and K.R. Scherer. 1985. "Evidence for the Independent Function of Intonation Contour, Pitch Range, and Voice Quality." *Journal of the Acoustical Society of America* 78, 435–44.
Liberman, Mark and Janet Pierrehumbert. 1984. "Intonational Invariance under Changes in Pitch Range and Length." In *Language sound structure*, edited by M. Aronoff and R. Oerhle, 157–233. Cambridge, Mass.: MIT Press.
Maeda, Shinji. 1976. "A Characterization of American English Intonation." Ph.D. Dissertation, Massachusetts Institute of Technology, Cambridge.
O'Connor, J.D. and G.F. Arnold. 1973. *Intonation of Colloquial English*. 2nd ed. London: Longman.
Palmer, Harold. 1922. *English Intonation, with Systematic Exercises*. Cambridge: Heffers.
Pierrehumbert, Janet 1980. "The Phonology and Phonetics of English Intonation." Ph.D. Dissertation, Massachusetts Institute of Technology, Cambridge.
Pierrehumbert, Janet and Mary Beckman. 1988. *Japanese Tone Structure*. Cambridge, Mass.: MIT Press.
Pike, Kenneth L. 1945. *The Intonation of American English*. Ann Arbor: Univ. of Michigan Press.
Poser, William J. 1984. "The Phonetics and Phonology of Tone and Intonation in Japanese." Ph.D. Dissertation, Massachusetts Institute of Technology, Cambridge.
Thorsen, Nina. 1985. "Intonation and Text in Standard Danish." *Journal of the Acoustical Society of America* 77, 1205–16.
———. 1986. "Sentence Intonation in Textual Context–Supplementary Data." *Journal of the Acoustical Society of America* 80, 1041–47.
Trager, George L. and H.L. Smith. 1951. *An Outline of English Structure*. Battenburg Press, Norman OK. Reprinted in 1957 by the American Council of Learned Societies, Washington.
Williams, Carl E. and Kenneth N. Stevens. 1972. "Emotions and Speech: Some Acoustical Correlates." *Journal of the Acoustical Society of America* 52, 1238–50.

Spreading and Downstep: Prosodic Government in Tone Languages

Victor Manfredi

1. INTRODUCTION*

Since its origin in two studies of Ìgbo, autosegmental phonology has endured a conceptual tension between automatic and rule-governed spreading. Williams' (1971) Tone Mapping rule ensures that toneless morphemes receive tonal specifications, but skips over tonal morphemes and melody-final floating tones. Goldsmith's (1976) Well Formedness Condition (WFC) associates all tones automatically, left-to-right and one-to-one, spreading the melody-final tone onto toneless positions, or linking extra tones onto the final tone-bearing position. Halle and Vergnaud (1982) remark that the WFC does not exclude rules of tone spreading, so that the tone mapping framework, being thoroughly rule-governed, is mechanically simpler. Economy aside, automatic spreading has been challenged by two sorts of claims: nonmorphemic, surface floating tones (in so-called Grassfields Bantu languages, cf. Voorhoeve 1971; Hyman 1972; Tadadjeu 1974) and phonetic default tones on surface toneless elements (in Yorùbá, cf. Akinlabí 1982). To accommodate these cases, Pulleyblank (1983) does away with automatic spreading altogether.

Arguments against rule-governed spreading have, by comparison, been few. There are different views of what is at stake in giving up the WFC. Depending on the content attributed to association lines, their manipulation by phonological rules is a more or less significant departure from the original goals of the theory. If association lines simply encode "synchronization" (Halle and Vergnaud), crucial reference to linking is a straightforward way of stating phonotactic constraints (Hayes 1986). But if association lines denote constituency relations, i.e. predictable locality

---

* This paper was drafted during a summer 1988 visit to the Groupe de recherche en linguistique africaniste, Université du Québec à Montréal (Jean Lowenstamm, co-director), supported by CSRH grant 411–85–0012 and FCAR grant 87–EQ–2612. Some material was presented in talks at Ìlọrin (1980–81), Nsúká (1982–83), Port Harcourt (1984), Amherst (1988), the 14th Conference on African Linguistics (Madison 1983), and the 4th and 5th Conferences of the Linguistic Association of Nigeria (Benin-City 1983, Nsúká 1984). Thanks to M. Bamba, M.M. Clark, R.-M. Déchaine, E.'N. Émẹ́nanjọ, H. van der Hulst, Ú. Ìhìónú, Y. Lániran, P.A. Nwáchukwu, O.O. Oyèláràn and K.R.M. Williamson for discussion.

domains, it is inconceivable that they are formally autonomous of the features or elements they connect.

The status of association lines also has consequences for the Obligatory Contour Principle (Leben 1973). Odden (1986) restricts the OCP to underlying representations, so as not to force identical tones to "collapse into a single tone" across morpheme boundaries. Clark (1989) eliminates the OCP even in the lexicon, so that the relative pitch of sequential H tones is encoded in the number of underlying identical autosegments. On the other hand, if the OCP holds both in the lexicon and in phrasal phonology, then association lines reflect independently determined constituency relations. Kaye, Lowenstamm and Vergnaud (1985, 1987) theorize government among syllable constituents (rimes and onsets) and within the segment (heads and operators). In their framework, *rules* of spreading are not statable; the distribution of surface floating and default elements is constrained by structure preservation, minimality and proper government (Charette 1988; Nikiema 1988; Kaye 1989).

Section 2 critiques rule-based tone typology. While every logical combination of {H, L} tones spreads automatically in some Benue-Kwa language, tone spreading is nonrandomly parameterized. H-spreading excludes total downstep but does not conflict with partial downstep. L-spreading excludes partial downstep but is a prerequisite of total downstep. A language with two types of L tone, spreading and non-spreading, has both types of downstep. The spreading of both H and L tones contradicts downstep altogether. These implications are understandable if both spreading and downstep are represented in terms of prosodic government by tonal elements, following Bamba's (1984) claim that downstep is the effect of metrical constituency on the pitch realization of tone elements.[1]

Section 3 establishes prosodic government domains in two languages which have been analyzed in terms of rule-governed spreading: ɣɔmaláʔ-Yamba and Ìgbo. Prosodic government predicts the tonal effects of syntactic structure, effects which are handled in extant analyses by diacritic tones and association lines. These cases, together with the typology, constitute arguments against rule-governed spreading. Section 4 argues that metrical structure is encoded in the three lexical tone classes of Ìgbo. A concluding comment (section 5) draws the cases together in support of the hypothesis that prosodic phonology requires,

---

[1] Benue-Kwa is the largest genetic constituent of Niger-Congo. Greenberg (1963:39, fn. 13) observes a lack of evidence for an isogloss between Kwa (in which he tentatively includes Kru) and Benue-Congo. Williamson (1989), following the lexicostatistic analysis of Schadeberg (1986), suggests a division in between Gbè and Yoruboid (see Capo 1985 for a critique).

Manfredi: Spreading and downstep

not a level of representation intermediate between syntax and phonology, but a theory of the different subtypes (lexical, phrasal, metrical, tonal, syllabic ...) of the government relation.

2. TONE AND LOCALITY IN BENUE-KWA

Goldsmith's WFC predicts tone contours at the right margin of an association domain, just if the underlying tones exceed the available tone-bearing units in number. But, in some languages, phonetic tone contours occur in other positions, or are restricted to certain tone combinations:

(1)	Yorùbá (Awóbùlúyì 1964)	H spreads onto L L spreads onto H
	Èdó (Ámáyó 1976) western forms of Ìgbo	H spreads onto L
	"central" Ìgbo	
	ɣɔmalá?-Yamba (Hyman 1985)	some Ls spread onto H
	ɣekoyó (Clements 1984)	L spreads onto H

This range of options might suggest a parametrized association convention, according to which certain tones have the inherent property of spreading onto tone-bearing positions. Two of the cases could be handled this way. In Èdó and western Ìgbo, L never spreads. In ɣekoyó, what has been called "H-spreading" is actually a flop rule across word boundary, and never results in a falling tone contour.

Parametrized association has difficulty with Yorùbá's three tones {H, M, L} because, while H spreads onto L, and L onto H, neither H nor L spreads onto M. (M never spreads.) Akinlabí (1982) suggests that M is a default tone which arises after spreading applies, but this says nothing about ɣɔmalá?-Yamba, a language in which L tones divide into two classes, respectively spreading and non-spreading.

To account for ɣekoyó, Clements and Ford (1979) propose another kind of parametrized association, which they dub accentual. Dispensing with a L-spreading rule like (2a), they treat the formation of word-final LH contours as a WFC effect, by positing a pre-cyclic tone shift or initial tone association rule (ITAR). In (2b), the first tone links to the star [∗] diacritic, and the other linkings follow from the WFC:

(2) a. L H   L H
         | | →   ⋈
         x x   x x

   b. L H   L H   L H
                → | →   ⋀
         *   *   *
         x x   x x   x x

Maintaining (2b), Clements' (1984) account of ɣekoyó still requires a highly marked inventory of lexical tone melodies, as well as rules of leftward H tone association and falling tone simplification. And, the ITAR plus WFC can't handle Èdó and Yorùbá, languages with contour tones which are non-final in a monomorphemic association domain.

If spreading-induced contours are not tone association effects, two possiblities remain: they result from language-specific rules, or else they attest inherent properties of those elements which spread, as these properties are licensed by the phonological context. In comparing the alternatives, the relation between spreading and downstep is relevant.

For Stewart (1965, 1971, 1983) "downstep" describes the lowered phonetic register of a high tone preceded by a low tone. Lowering is cumulative and persists throughout the tone phrase, but is reversed at syntactic pauses. The triggering L need not surface; if it doesn't, the downstep is "non-automatic". If there is no synchronic evidence for a L tone, downstep is triggered diacritically. L-delinking, which yields non-automatic downstep (marked by a macron), can be expressed by one of the rules in (3). What varies is the direction of assimilation, and the survival vs. elision of the original L-bearing unit:

(3) a. H L H   H L H̄
         | | | →   ⋈ |
         x x x   x x x

    b. H L H   H L H̄
         | | | → | ⋀
         x x x   x x x

    c. H L H   H L H̄
         | | | → | |
         x x x   x   x

All the rules in (3) involve two assumptions: a tone automatically delinks from a timing unit which is affected by spreading or elision, and floating tones do not automatically reassociate. In Akan (Schachter and Fromkin 1968), L is delinked either by rightward or by leftward H-spreading (3a, 3b), or by TBU elision (3c). In "central" Ìgbo, elision is not found, and H-spreading is leftward (3b). Yorùbá, Èdó and western Ìgbo attest elision (3c) and—in other contexts—non-delinking, rightward H-spreading (4a). Amáyó observes that H-spreading is bled by elision: H does not spread across a floating L tone (4b).

(4) a.   H L   H L
         | | →   ⋈
         x x   x x

     b. H L L   H L L
         | | ⇸   ⌐⌐⌐⌐⌐
         x x   x x

Other combinations of spreading and delinking are more problematic. (4a) flatly contradicts (3a). L-delinking (3a–c) bleeds L-spreading (2a), but there is a conceivable feeding relationship by which spreading feeds delinking so as to mimic the effect of (3a) and (3c).[2] In (5), the "early" application of the L-spreading rule functions as a diacritic for subsequent delinking, i.e. for non-automatic downstep.

(5) a.   *L-spreading*   *H-spreading,*   *LH-simplification*
                                     L-delinking

     H L H   H L H   H L H   H L H̄
     | | | → | ⋈   →   ⋈⋈   →   ⋈ |
     x x x   x x x   x x x   x x x

     b.   *L-spreading*   *L-delinking via*   *LH-simplification*
                                        TBU-elision

     H L H   H L H   H L H   H L H̄
     | | | → | ⋈   → | ⋈   → | |
     x x x   x x x   x x   x   x

One can exclude the derivations in (5) by stipulating that L-spreading and L-delinking cannot cooccur in one grammar. However, this is falsified by ɔ̌malá?-Yamba and Yorùbá. In Yorùbá, the downstep which

---

2 Rightward L-spreading cannot trigger downstep of the type in (5b).

results from L-delinking ("the assimilated low tone") is limited in domain to one syllable: subsequent syllables with the same value as the downstepped tone can exceed its pitch level.³ In ɣɔmalá?-Yamba, automatic downstep is perseverative but not triggered by all surface L tones, and some non-automatic downsteps are total.

The phenomenon of total downstep, found in ɣekoyó and ɣɔmalá?-Yamba, challenges Stewart's claim that the downstep trigger is always a floating L tone. Total downstep lowers a H tone all the way to the level of a L tone in the same position. A following L tone is lower still. Thus the tonal sequence in (6), where total downstep is marked by a double macron, would have the phonetic interpretation shown.

(6) [H, H̿, L] $\begin{bmatrix} - & - & \\ & & _ \end{bmatrix}$

If an abstract L tone was responsible for total downstep, it would possess properties distinct from both kinds of concrete L tones which are found in ɣɔmalá?-Yamba: one kind spreads onto a following H without downdrifting it, as in (7a), while the other kind downdrifts a following H tone (by the interval of a partial downstep), but without spreading onto it, as in (7b).⁴

(7) a. [H, L, H] → [H, L, L̂H] $\begin{bmatrix} - & & / \\ & _ & \end{bmatrix}$

  b. [H, L, H] → [H, L, H̄] $\begin{bmatrix} - & & - \\ & _ & \end{bmatrix}$

Type (7a), and not (7b), is found in ɣekoyó; the total downstep trigger in that language is distinct from both. Accordingly, Clements and Ford propose that the trigger for ɣekoyó total downstep is not floating L but floating "super-L", a non-surfacing type of low tone. But they do not explain why total downstep is restricted to phrase-level phonology, although partial downstep (in other languages) can occur morpheme-internally. This distributional asymmetry suggests that the triggers of the two downstep types are not formally comparable; below, I will provide a straightforward account for this fact.

In two instances, Stewart (1965) recognized the arbitrariness of floating L tone as the trigger of partial downstep: lexical downsteps where no alternation occurs, and syntactic downsteps for which no low tonal morpheme is motivated (see also Fromkin 1976). Among generative

---

3 Láníran (1991) provides instrumental descriptions of several highly marked pitch phenomena in the Yorùbá terraced tone system, as compared to systems of the Ìgbo type.
4 Tadadjeu (1974:284, fn. 1) describes L-spread as optional and limited to utterance-final position.

Bantuists (Voorhoeve et al. 1969; Voorhoeve 1971; Williamson 1970, 1986; Hyman 1972, 1976), the main justification for nonmorphemic floating tones (many of which are diacritic downstep triggers) is historical reconstruction. Notwithstanding Kiparsky's (1974) caveats, some autosegmentalists imported this abstract notation wholesale. Pulleyblank (1983) treats Hyman and Tadadjeu's (1976) floating tones like observational data.

To summarize, it is impossible to account for downstep alone, or for the relation between spreading and downstep, across all the language types in (1) by means of rules, without using tones and/or rules diacritically. The remaining possibility is that every instance of spreading and downstep reflects inherent, parametric properties of tone elements, subject to universal prosodic constraints. I will now show that this alternative premise correctly predicts the co-occurrence of downstep, total and partial, with the full set of spreading phenomena, both intra- and cross-linguistically, for the languages in (1).

Spreading and downstep differ with respect to locality. In most languages, the lowering effect of a downstep (whether partial or total) persists over a potentially unbounded phonetic span. The downstep found in Yorùbá is "local" (nonperseverative). Spreading, by definition, is constrained by adjacency on the relevant tier. Stewart (1981) observes that partial downstep is in complementary distribution with the spreading of a low tone onto the domain of a following high tone. This is borne out for the five types in (1):

(8)	Yorùbá	local downstep H spreads onto L L spreads onto H
	Èdó/western Ìgbo	partial downstep H spreads onto L
	"central" Ìgbo	partial downstep
	ɣɔmalá?-Yamba	some partial downsteps some total downsteps some Ls spread onto H
	ɣekoyó	total downstep L spreads onto H

In the terminology of Hyman (1978), a L tone can affect a following H either "horizontally" (by spreading onto it) or "vertically" (by inducing partial downdrift). (8) suggests that both kinds of assimilation cannot be triggered by the same token of L tone. Further, total downstep correlates with L-spreading. In all, (8) has three sets of implications:

(9) a. Total downstep contradicts H-spreading and requires L-spreading.
b. Partial downstep contradicts L-spreading (but does not require H-spreading).
c. Perseverative, i.e. non-local, downstep contradicts the joint presence of H-spreading and L-spreading.

To express (9) in terms of tone rules minimally requires a distinction between tonal and register tiers of tonal autosegments (Manfredi 1979; Huang 1980; Clements 1981; Inkelas et al. 1987):

(10) 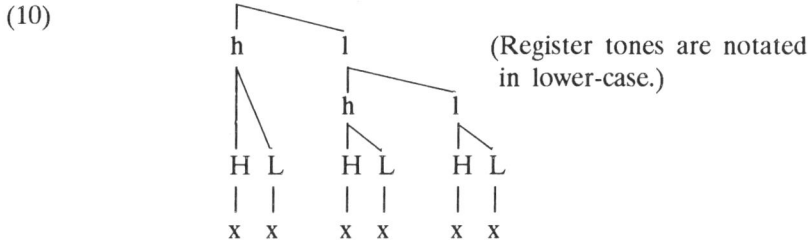 (Register tones are notated in lower-case.)

But the register tone hypothesis only restates the problem as feature geometry: it attributes two nonintersecting sets of properties to identically-named autosegments, depending on which tier they occupy. If (10) represents partial downstep, what prevents the spreading of tonal-L between "tonal feet" (register domains)? And how could a representation like (10) account for the two types of tonal-L (spreading and nonspreading) which cooccur in ɣɔmalá?-Yamba?

Alternatively, suppose that tones have a single set of properties, all local and invariant, while long distance, relational phenomena like downstep reflect the interaction of tone and metrical structure (Bamba 1984, 1988, 1989). In a kindred vein, Clements and Ford argue that, if the accentual character of ɣekoyó "tone shift" is accepted at face value,

> we would immediately want to take the further step of attributing underlying (or rule-inserted) accent to all lexical tone languages. This is because it would make no sense to argue that Kikuyu had fixed initial accent simply on the basis of the hindsight afforded by tone shift, while denying fixed accent to such typologically similar tone systems as those of Ewe, Igbo or Akan. (1979:198)

Accepting the logic of this statement, I will now show that the three generalizations in (9) can be restated as a single relationship between between tonal and metrical structure. Bamba proposes that the H element in a downstep system projects an [s] node which automatically entails a following [w] position, cf. (11a); i.e., it is a *metrical governor*. Correspondingly, a spreading H can be characterized as a *tonal governor*, projecting two positions on the tone-bearing level, as in (11b). In charm-and-government phonology, elements which create contours by spreading domain-internally are said to project two skeletal x-slots (Prunet 1986; Nikiema 1988). This double-projection property is analogous to syntactic government: the co-occurrence of metrical and tonal government in (11b) can be likened to a verb which both governs (θ-marks) and overtly Case-marks its internal argument, as in (11c).

(11) a. b. c.

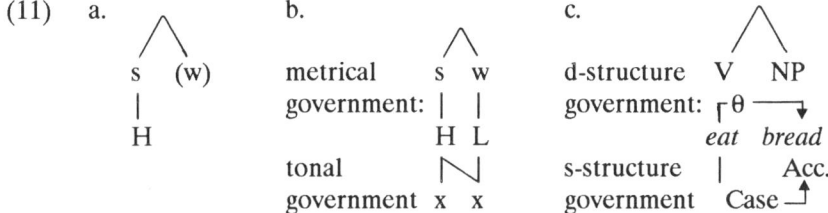

The OCP dictates that phonetically distinct H tones belong to different metrical feet, so that a [HH̄] sequence looks like (12a). An L tone intervening between H_1 and downstepped H_2 occupies the weak position of the first foot, as in (12b). But (12a) respects the OCP even if there is no intervening L tone (the weak position being optional), because the two H tones are not strictly adjacent. Conversely, adjacent H-bearing syllables in the same pitch register must belong to the same metrical constituent, as in (12c). The OCP rules out (12d), with distinct H tones sharing a single foot:

(12) a. b.

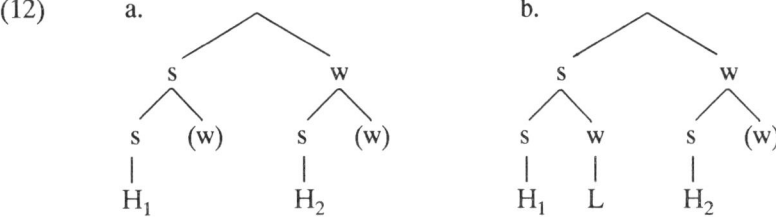

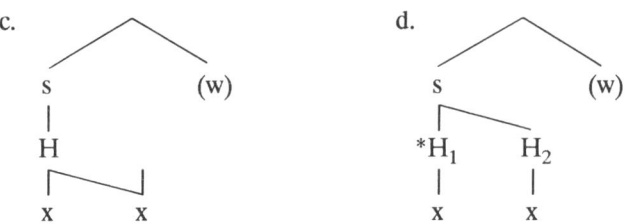

Assuming (11–12), the generalizations in (9b–c) follow from the definition in (13):

(13) *Minimality Condition*
      Each domain has a unique governor.

(13) explains why, across downstep systems, L-spreading is more restricted than H-spreading. In an automatic downstep configuration like (12b), (13) excludes the spreading of L onto H_2, since this would require L to govern (tonally) into the second foot—the metrical domain of H_2. Note that (13) does not exclude the co-occurrence of L-spreading and partial downstep in the same *language*, just in the same constituent. In other words, if H is the metrical governor, L-spreading (tonal government) can occur only within a sub-metrical domain, in which by definition H does not govern, as in (20a) below.

This government asymmetry between L and H, essential in all downstep systems, is most vivid with total downstep. Total downstep lowers a H tone to the pitch of a L tone. In (14), this is represented as $[_w \; H_2]$: a [w] metrical position directly dominating H2. For pitch interpretation, the timing unit bearing H_2 is equivalent to one bearing L. That is, the tonal content of a weak position is metrically "invisible".[5]

(14)

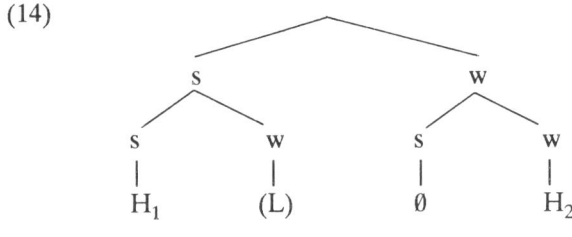

---

5 Cf. the process of vowel reduction in "stress" languages (languages in which metrical structure is a projection of syllable weight): a vowel in a weak metrical position gets the phonetic interpretation of a schwa. Metrically weak positions are invisible to projected features—a government-based constraint, analogous to syntactic visibility (Roberts 1985).

Manfredi: Spreading and downstep

(14) shows that a total downstep is immediately preceded by [$_s$ ∅]: an empty [s] position.[6] If the [s] position before a total downstep was occupied by a H tone, such as H_1 as in (15), a partial downstep (on H_3) could immediately follow a total downstep (on H_2):

(15)
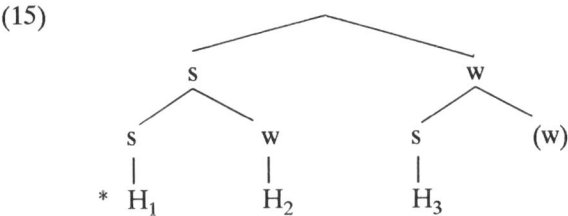

But (15) is ill-formed. The interpretion of (15) would require a greater pitch drop between metrical feet than occurs in (12a–b) and (14), making tones function as covert accents. To put the matter more simply: downstep, whether total or partial, is by definition a relationship between metrical feet, so the relation between H_1 and H_2 in (15) cannot be downstep of any kind. In ɣekoyó, all downsteps are total. Clements and Ford (1978, 1979) observe that the surface tone preceding the downstep is always H. Their downstep displacement rule (16a) is represented as in (16b):

(16) a. $[H^!L_Q] \rightarrow [H_Q^!]$ (X_Q = the maximal sequence of X elements)

b.
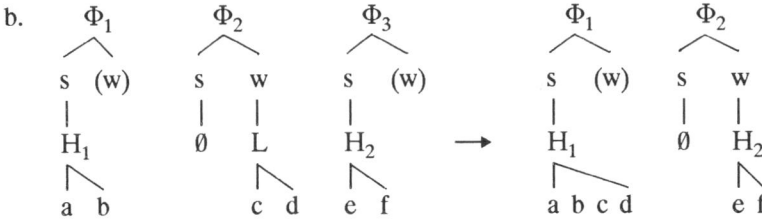

The change in (16b) is driven by well-formedness considerations. The left side of (16b), which arises in phrasal contexts, is phonetically uninterpretable. Unless there was a systematic possibility for a "super-low" L in this position, the [$_s$ L] in the second foot would require a zero pitch drop between Φ_1 and Φ_2—otherwise the pitch change between

---

6 [$_s$ ∅] (empty, strong position) is a marked type of constituent which occurs in a very restricted set of prosodic contexts. By contrast, weak positions are optional except phrase-finally, where the notation [$_w$ ∅] indicates a weak position that is both obligatory and empty, cf. (18b).

adjacent feet would be diacritically determined by the tones, robbing the metrical hypothesis of content.

(14) suggests that what permits total downstep is a parametric loosening of the bijective mapping between tones and metrical positions found in "pure" partial downstep languages (where H uniquely projects [s]). If either H or L can be immediately dominated by either [s] or [w], two new possibilities arise: [$_w$ ...H...] and [$_s$ ...L...]. This allows two different tone elements to share one (branching) metrical position. The four permutations are given in (17):

(17)

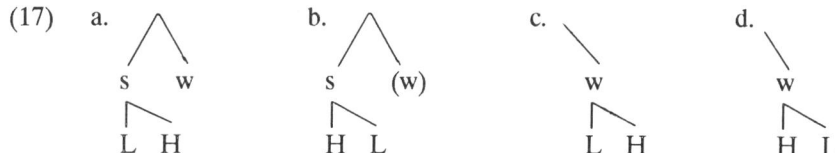

Most of these are independently ruled out. If only [s] can tonally branch, (17c–d) are excluded. This is quite natural since [$_w$ H] is phonetically identical to L, so that both [$_w$ LH] and [$_w$ HL] would be level in pitch. Two possibilities remain: [$_s$ LH] (17a) and [$_s$ HL] (17b). In fact, only (17a) ever occurs—another clue about the relationship of tonal and metrical government.

In ɣɔmaláʔ-Yamba, Tadadjeu (1974) and Hyman (1985) observe a contrast between two types of L tone: a phonetically raised L which spreads onto the following H (but doesn't downdrift it), and a nonraised L which induces partial downdrift on the following H (but never spreads onto it).[7] Two types of L also contrast in the context "L _ ##": one maintains a steady pitch level, the other drops off. Suppose that in both contexts, the former type of L is the left member of a branching [s] as in (18), and the latter type is immediately dominated by [w] as in (19).

(18)

---

[7] Contra Hyman (1985:79, fn. 20), I describe the phonetic lowering of an LH sequence in (24c) as downdrift (automatic downstep), so as to preserve a uniform cross-linguistic representation of phonetically and phonologically identical phenomena. The fact that downdrift does not occur after all surface L tones in all languages does not warrant its dismissal as an "old concept".

(19) a. 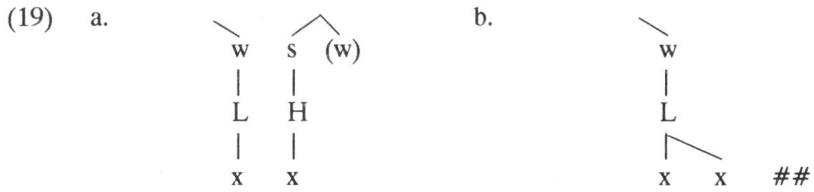 b.

A raised, potentially spreading L tone (a tonal governor) is immediately dominated by [s]; but an [s] position must also contain a H tone, since H is the metrical governor. Because the LH sequence shares the same foot, there is no downdrift between them, cf. (18a). A sentence-final L can be directly dominated by [s] if and only if the following weak metrical position is empty, cf. (18b): although H metrically governs L, [[$_s$ L] [$_w$ ∅]] is nevertheless well-formed because L is metrically stronger than ∅. This theorem gives a principled basis to the frequent observation that the {H~L} contrast is neutralized sentence-finally. In the same way, the fact that L-spreading is restricted to utterance-final position in ɣɔmalá?-Yamba (cf. footnote 4 above) seems to depend on the fact that there is no following constituent to be metrically governed by the H tone onto which L spreads. In ɣekoyó, too, LH tone contours are apparently restricted to phrase-final position. The parallel restrictions in the two languages follow from (13).[8]

There is no evidence, however, that a non-branching [s] can dominate a nonfinal L, as in (20a). There is also no phonetic distinction between two types of HL sequences, corresponding to the prosodically distinct LH sequences in (18–19). Such a distinction would require some HL sequences, but not others, to exhibit spreading.[9] In fact, no H-spreading occurs in ɣɔmalá?-Yamba or ɣekoyó, so [$_s$ HL] is excluded, cf. (20b).

(20) a. 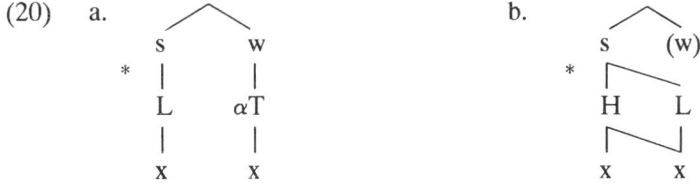 b.

---

8 Voorhoeve's idea (adopted by Hyman) is that L-dropoff is blocked by a word-final, floating H tone. My analysis in (18b) is not completely different. Condition (21a) below licenses nonbranching [s L] just in final position, since an L tone is metrically stronger than zero, but a non-final [$_s$ L] must be part of a branching [$_s$ LH] constituent. The difference is that Voorhoeve's floating H is totally abstract: it never surfaces.
9 Stewart's (1983) contrary claim concerns diacritic H-spreading that feeds L-delinking, cf. (3a).

The ill-formed representations in (20) have in common a L tone as the rightmost daughter of a [s] node, i.e. nonfinal L immediately preceding a weak position. Such a restriction is reminiscent of the exclusion of "super-heavy" CVVC syllables, in which both rime and nucleus branch (Kaye, Lowenstamm and Vergnaud 1987; Charette 1988). In both cases, a metrical governor is lacking, adjacent to a weak position.

Tonal elements are potentially both tonal and metrical governors; there is an asymmetry in the constraints on the respective levels. While metrical structure is never fully autonomous of submetrical domains, be these projections of tone or syllable weight (or both, for Kishambaa)[10], the correspondence of tonal and metrical domains can be more or less close. The proposal that metrical domains "extend" the properties of tonal elements as governors/governees recalls the extension of syntactic government to long-distance domains (Kayne 1984; Koster 1986).

(13) has the corollaries in (21). With respect to metrical structure, tonal elements universally respect the constraint in (22), cf. footnote 6 above. A bijective relation between metrical and tonal governors obtains parametrically, cf. (23).

(21) a. *Metrical Projection Theorem*
    A [s] position immediately dominates a metrical governor.
  b. *Metrical Locality Theorem*
    A [w] position is strictly adjacent to a metrical governor.

(22) *Tone Visibility Constraint*
  Tonal government is not possible from a [w] position.[11]

(23) *Prosodic Domain Parameter*
  A [s] position *uniquely* dominates a tonal governor: {yes}, {no}.

In pure partial downstep systems like Ìgbo and Èdó, the value for (23) is {yes}. In these systems, there are three formal possibilities for an initial L tone. The first, adjunction under a strong position as in (24a), is ruled out by (23). Instead, as proposed by Bamba (1988), an initial L can adjoin under a weak position, as in (24b). Alternatively, an initial L could belong to a unique foot projected by an initial [$_s$ ∅] con-

---

10 In Kishambaa there is downstep between all lexical and phrasal H tones, except if a H-bearing domain arises by spreading (Odden 1982). A metrical account, preserving the OCP, would make every [s] position a co-projection of an underlying H and its rime constituent.
11 (22) implies that both L and H are metrically strong in Yorùbá, a claim which is possible only in a three-way system with {H, M, L}. I cannot develop this claim in the present space, but see Lániran (1991) for striking evidence that L is strong in Yorùbá.

stituent, as in (24c). Initial L tone is phonetically raised in Ẹ̀dó (Elugbe 1977), Ìgbo and ɣɔmalá?-Yamba, but not in Kishambaa (Odden 1986:364, fn. 11). This systematic difference might correspond to the representational distinction between (24b) and (24c), both of which are well-formed in principle.

(24)

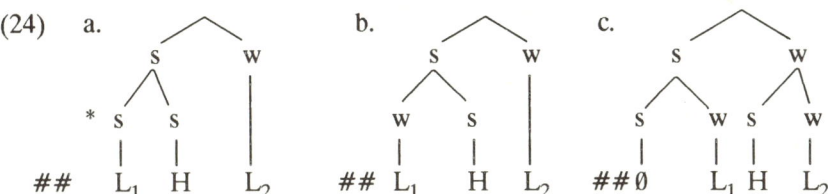

(23) also raises the question of what counts as a tonal governor. In pure partial downstep systems, the only candidate is H (the metrical governor). Two variants of partial downstep are distinguished by the presence/absence of tonal government. In Ẹ̀dó and western Ìgbo, H is the tonal governor, spreading onto [$_w$ L] as in (11b). A string of syllables linked to a single H tone has the phonetic tendency to rise in pitch. In "central" Ìgbo, no tone spreads (in the localistic sense: any tone contours involve the docking of a tonal morpheme): therefore, metrical government entirely supplants tonal government, making (23) vacuously true.[12] With the revised parametrization in (25) below, this indeterminacy of (23) is removed.

In Yorùbá, both H and L tones spread, apart from one context. Given (13), this shows that metrical domains are in general not formed. The exception arises via the elision of a L-bearing timing unit: the "floating L" becomes the weak branch of a metrical constituent, and a downstep is produced. This result is confirmed in both Yorùbá and Ẹ̀dó, as already observed in (4b): H-spreading fails to occur just across an "assimilated" (i.e. floating) low tone. This constraint is understandable as a minimality effect: spreading does not cross metrical constituents.

In total downstep systems, tonal and metrical domains are fully distinct: the metrical governor is H and the tonal governor is L. H does not project a strong metrical position: some H tones occur in weak positions, and some L tones occur in strong positions (both initially and non-initially). But total downstep systems still satisfy (21): a nonfinal [s] dominating a L tone must branch to [$_s$ LH], cf. (18a). Nonbranching [s] nodes need not contain H just in case the corresponding [w] position is weaker than L, cf. (18b), where [$_s$ L] governs an obligatorily empty,

---

12 The syntactic analogue is a language in which structural Case is completely abstract.

sentence final [w] position. (22) is also respected in total downstep systems: no spreading is possible from a weak metrical position.

The typological array in (8) attests the independently varying parameters in (25), subject to the constraints in (13), (21) and (22).

(25) a. *Metrical Government Parameter*[13]
 The metrical governor is {H}, {L}, {∅}.
 b. *Tonal Government Parameter*
 The set of tonal governors is {H}, {L}, {H, L}, {∅}.
 c. *Prosodic Domain Parameter* (revised)
 Tones freely occupy metrical positions: {yes} {no}.

(25a) selects the basic type of tonal licensing for metrical government domains. The value {H} selects downstep, {L} selects upstep and {∅} selects neither. (25b) accounts for the fact that local tone spreading varies cross-linguistically among four logical possibilities. Closely related languages/dialects differ with respect to (25b), and the learner can determine the setting from the simple, positive evidence of intramorphemic contour tones.

A "mixed" system such as ɣɔmalá?-Yamba, in which only some L tones exhibit spreading, is evidence for the independence of the tonal and metrical parameters. The tonal governor is {L}, but tonal government from a weak metrical position is ruled out by (22). Further, as attested by both ɣɔmalá?-Yamba and ɣekoyó, (13) prevents spreading in a nonfinal [$_s$ LH] constituent, so the actual cases of L-tone spreading are a subset of a subset of the total number of L tones: [[$_s$ LH] [$_w$ ∅]]. Stating this in the form of a spreading rule obscures the generalizations which hold for each of the sub-relations on which it is jointly based, and which have independent, highly valued empirical consequences in other contexts.

(25c) restates (23) more generally, with markedness reversed. A *yes* value for (25c) has three major consequences: H may be dominated by [w], L may be dominated by [s], and [s] may branch. The distinguishing phonetic alternation of a total downstep system, "H→L in weak position", can also be observed from simple, positive evidence. Total downstep intrudes marginally in many partial downstep systems: downstepped H in final position is phonetically low in Mbàisén (Ùwaláàka

---

13 As already noted, the possibility of both {H, L} as metrically strong is probably instantiated in the three-tone system of Yorùbá. The statement of (25a) remains valid for two-tone systems as it stands, for reasons which are intuitively clear: a two-tone system cannot have both tones metrically strong.

1982), Ìzîi (Meir et al. 1975) and Éhugbò (Manfredi 1979). The possibility of branching [s] can be induced from the contrast between two kinds of L tone: [_w L] which downdrifts but does not spread, and [_s L] which spreads but does not downdrift. This contrast, being supported by two concomitant phonetic cues, is also easily learnable.

A *yes* value for (25c) licenses total downstep. The fact that an [s] position may branch to LH implies the separation of tonal and metrical domains. Once the domains are separate, (13) requires the learner to identify a governor for each. H must remain the metrical governor, because all weak positions are phonetically nonhigh. This makes L the only candidate for tonal governor in a total downstep language.

A *no* value for (25c) makes a metrical foot a pure projection of H, as in (11a): every H is linked to [s], and every L to [w]. Nothing requires every [w] to link to a L tone however, so partial downstep is possible with either *yes* or *no* values of (25c); *no* excludes total downstep. *No* is the unmarked value since positive evidence for this setting is less straightforward.

The next section compares prosodic government domains in the associative constructions of a "Semi-Bantu" language and Ìgbo.

3. PROSODIC GOVERNMENT

ɣɔmalá?-Yamba ("Dschang-Bamiléké") is discussed by Tadadjeu (1974), Hyman and Tadadjeu (1976), Pulleyblank (1983), Hyman (1985). Their principal data are drawn from the "associative" construction, a complex nominal resembling the Semitic construct state. Although the associative construction is sometimes translated by an English DP like *the feather of the/an eagle*, restrictions in phrasal expansion and definiteness make it semantically closer to an English nominal compound like *eagle feather*. One difference from a compound is the presence of a morpheme between the two nouns. But unlike a possessive morpheme or other determiner, the associative morpheme does not imply definiteness. In other words, as in the construct state, the dependent noun in an associative construction is not independently referential.

The associative morpheme is an agreement prefix on the dependent noun, coindexed with the head noun. Welmers (1963) reconstructs the associative morphemes of proto Niger-Congo as à and ká. In many daughter languages, its phonetic shape has undergone reduction; some reflexes lost their segmental content but kept the tone. In some languages, agreement morphology has become entirely vestigial, so the question of abstractness arises. In ɣɔmalá?-Yamba, associative prefix agreement is productive.

For a prosodic account of this construction, the crux is its syntactic licensing. As a nominal clitic, the associative morpheme on the dependent noun spells out a relation between two nominal heads. The best-understood licensing relation is thematic, as defined in X-bar theory (Chomsky 1981), but it is not obvious that this is the appropriate one. For Borer (1983), the Hebrew construct state is a thematic, phrasal projection (but note that Borer 1987, 1989 cites it as an example of word formation in the syntax). Another possibility is that the licensing projection is not thematic but "functional": responding to proposals by Fassi-Fehri (1987), Ritter (1988) proposes that the construct state is a projection of the determiner, essentially as in (26):[14]

(26)
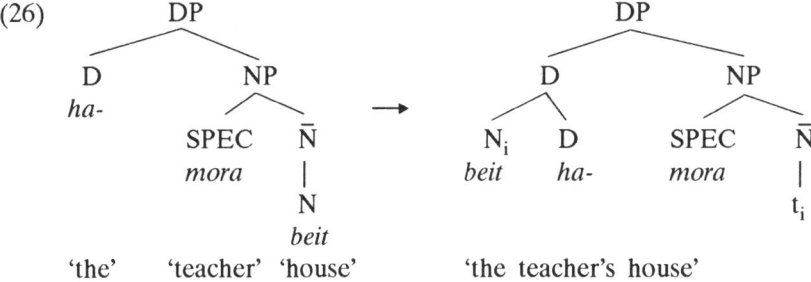

'the' 'teacher' 'house'   'the teacher's house'

Yet, Ritter must invoke more than head movement to account for the surface order; the unanswered question is why the head noun *beit* 'house' doesn't incorporate to the right of the proclitic *ha-* 'the', yielding an ungrammatical output **ha-beit mora*. My suggestion is that this indeterminacy cannot be resolved because head movement is the only re-ordering mechanism available within a phrasal (i.e. X-bar) schema. Higginbotham (1985) offers another model of licensing, neologistically called "autonomous" θ-marking, to handle the noncategorial (or syncategoremic) meaning of prenominal adjectives. Since *a big butterfly* may not be big in absolute terms, there are evidently two kinds of semantic composition between the adjective and the noun. The basic relation is θ-identification, as in all predicative constructs: one knows that the properties of bigness and of being a butterfly intersect in the same individual. The extra relation is independent of the head-complement configuration of X-bar theory, on which both Borer (1983)

---

14 On the categorial status of possessive morphemes as determiners, cf. Fukui (1986), Abney (1987).

and Ritter (1988) rely. Suppose that autonymous θ-marking is a local relationship between thematic heads: an X^0 category can θ-mark the head which governs it. Discussing the similarity of adjective and adverb licensing, Travis (1988) embeds this proposal in an incorporation structure, following Baker (1985): Y^0 autonymously θ-marks X^0 in the structure $[_{X^\circ} X^0 + Y^0]$, where X^0 governs Y^0. I adopt Travis' idea as follows. In (27), the (base-generated) incorporation of N_j is mediated by an agreement chain between N_i and the coindexed clitic. N_j autonymously θ-marks its governor N_i (perhaps via the intermediate governor agr_i). I assume that an affix governs its subcategorized complement (Lieber 1980). In this structure, unlike the noun incorporation structures discussed by Baker (1985), the referential index of 'eagle' cannot percolate.

(27)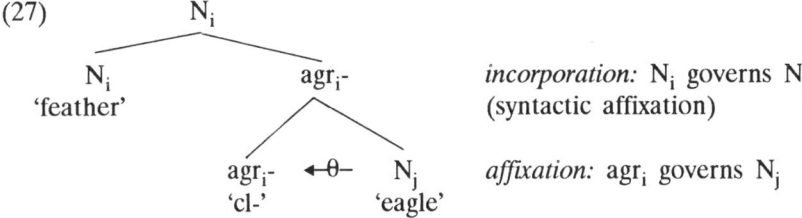

           incorporation: N_i governs N_j
           (syntactic affixation)

           affixation: agr_i governs N_j

Hyman states that, depending on the agreement class of the head noun, the associative clitic is lexicalized in ɣɔmálá?-Yamba as / è- /, / á / or / é- /. A propos the underlying form of these morphemes, he astonishingly remarks that "the segmental information is, as far as I have been able to determine, totally irrelevant for the study of tone" (1985:78, fn. 3). But, just as in Hyman's (1976) description of the Àbọ́ dialect of Ìgbo, this assertion obscures syllable-based generalizations about tone association domains (cf. Manfredi 1983a). Two important observations relate to the segmental form of these morphemes: / á- / always acquires the quality of the preceding vowel (whether or not a consonant intervenes), while the syllabic features of / è- / almost never surface (Hyman 1985:78, fnn. 4, 7). In accordance with the second observation, the two clitics can be represented as in (28):

(28)   class 1, 9 $\begin{bmatrix} L \end{bmatrix}$ class 7 $\begin{bmatrix} H \\ | \\ x \\ a \end{bmatrix}$
    agreement prefix: agreement prefix:

152 The representation of tonal register

The floating L in (28) is a morpheme, and as such is learnable, given appropriate alternations. The same cannot be said of the nonmorphemic floating tones posited by Voorhoeve and Hyman (and carried over without argument by Pulleyblank); to these I now turn. As noted, ɣɔmalá?-Yamba shows four distinct surface tone patterns on bisyllabic nouns. Tadadjeu and Hyman cite them on the segmental base [lətɔn]. The first tone in each pattern is L. Three of the four contrasts are manifested exclusively on the second syllable; in one word, the initial L is predictably raised. Tadadjeu distinguishes the four patterns by positing one morpheme-final, lexical floating tone, justified by appeal to historical reconstructions. The first observation about this tone quadruplet is that it is only near-minimal, because it is composed of two lexical nouns and two infinitives. The latter are unquestionably bimorphemic, presumably formed by syntactic affixation as in (29).

(29) a. $\begin{bmatrix} \begin{bmatrix} L \\ | \\ x \\ lə\text{-} \end{bmatrix} \begin{bmatrix} H \\ | \\ x \\ tɔŋ \\ v \end{bmatrix} \end{bmatrix}$ b. $\begin{bmatrix} \begin{bmatrix} L \\ | \\ x \\ lə\text{-} \end{bmatrix} \begin{bmatrix} L \\ | \\ x \\ tɔŋ \\ v \end{bmatrix} \end{bmatrix}$

The lexical nouns may also analyze as prefix+root, since there are no high tone-initial nouns.

Applying the metrical representations in (18–19), which are phonetically motivated as discussed in section 2, it turns out that the syntactic and lexical lə̀- prefixes differ prosodically:

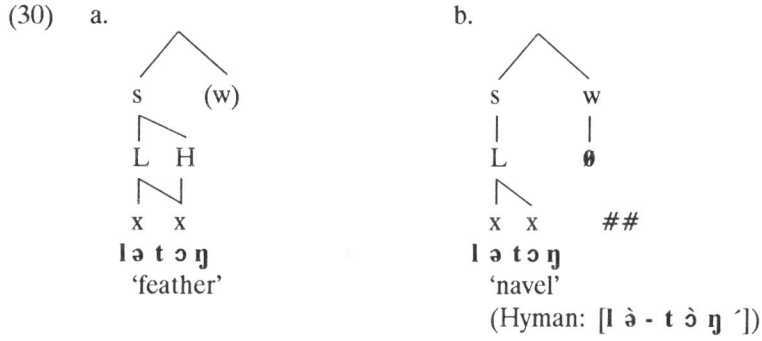

(Hyman: [l ə̀ - t ɔ̀ ŋ ´])

(31) a.

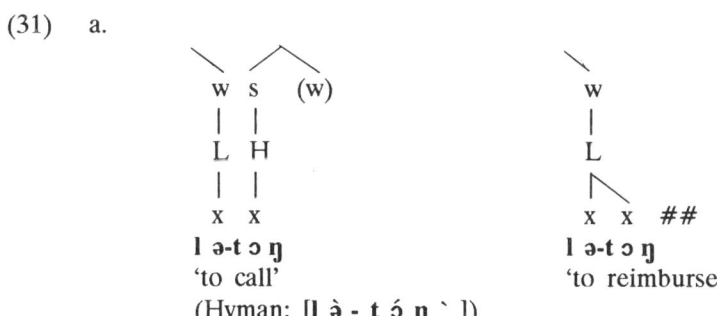
'to call'
(Hyman: [l à - t ó ŋ ˋ])

'to reimburse'

The two lexical nouns begin with a metrically strong position, but the infinitive prefix is metrically weak. The generalization in (32) does not translate into a floating tone framework.

(32) *Clitic Prosody Hypothesis*
Syntactic affixes are metrically weak.

Concerning the verb root 'call', Hyman does not indicate underlying tone consistently. At the end of his discussion, he cites the verb with lexical H tone (1985:64, data 28a), disregarding his initial hypothesis of a final, floating L tone (1985:48, data 1c). The floating L seems to be needed just to trigger his rules of "L-metathesis" and "ᶦH-lowering". In a footnote (1985:78, fn. 8), he justifies the floating L on morphological grounds, as an independent suffix which is present on a "nominal" infinitive [là-tóŋ-ˋ]. This form contrasts with a "verbal" infinitive, otherwise identical, that lacks the suffix. The two infinitives select different concord for their complements: Class 1 Genitive concord is [ˋ], while the corresponding Accusative concord is [á]. Disregarding the nominalizing suffix, the phrases are as in (33):

(33) a. 'to call me (Acc.)' [là-tóŋ [á-ɣá]] → [làtóŋówá]
     b. 'to call me (Gen.)' [là-tóŋ [ˋ-ɣá]] → [là-ˈtóŋ ɣǎ]

The phonetic output in (33a) is evidently straightforward, with rounding harmony spreading from the verb to its complement. In the output of (33b), the total downstep between L tones, and the spread of L onto the final syllable, must be accounted for. But an associative construction 'bird horn' lacks the L-spread:

(34) 'bird horn' [ǹ-dóŋ [ˋ-sáŋ]] → [ǹˈdòŋ sáŋ] *[ǹˈdòŋ sǎŋ]

The phonetic discrepancy between (33b) and (34) raises a descriptive problem for Hyman. He posits a final floating L tone equally on both [là-tɔ́ŋ-` ] and [ǹ-dɔ́ŋ`], in the latter case presumably not on morphological grounds. But the two floating L tones do not have consistent phonetic consequences: both cause the preceding H tone to be downstepped (in his account), yet only the former triggers a rising tone on a class I complement. Moreover, he cites no syntactic or semantic difference for the twin types of infinitives. In the framework developed in the preceding section, the difference between (33b) and (34) is not tonal but prosodic: a spreading L tone must occupy a [s] position. Given the generalization in (32), there is no way to preserve Hyman's "nominal infinitive" hypothesis. Rather, the phonetic difference reflects a property of the complement. There are a number of possible stories; for the present discussion, nothing much hinges on the choice, once it is clear that the "nominal infinitive" hypothesis does not justify a phonological floating tone suffix on a noun like 'horn'. The contrast between "strong" and "weak" pronouns is widespread in the Benua-Kwa family (cf. Oyèláràn 1970; Manfredi 1987), and the prosody of the object pronoun in (33b) makes it plausibly a strong metrical constituent. For concreteness, I will represent the strong pronoun as a Kase Phrase, headed by an X^0 category (n.b. not a syntaxtic affix) which is metrically strong:

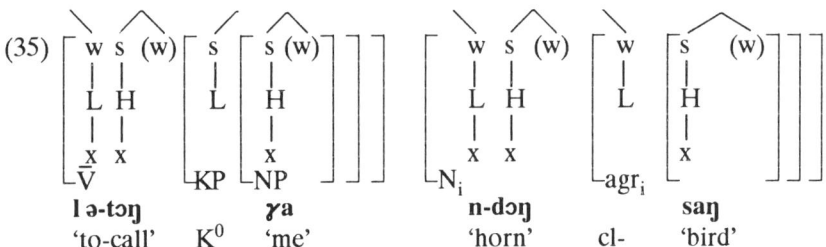

The representations in (74) yield the correct phonetic outputs with two additional assumptions. At the accentual level, the OCP merges $[_s$ L] $[_s$ H] → $[_s$ LH], because the output is a well-formed configuration in this language, and the input is not, cf. (18a, 25c) above. At the timing level, the tonal prefix of the dependent category flops onto the final timing unit of its governing category, causing the already associated H tone to delink, creating a total downstep (i.e. $[_s$ ∅]). The output is given in (36):

(36)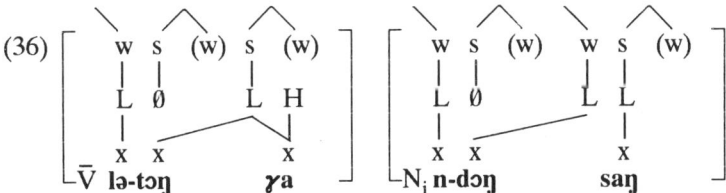

My claim is that the apparent leftward tone flop in (36) is the consequence of bringing the governee into the prosodic domain of its governing category. I will portray this process informally as in (37a). Other data exemplify the reassociation in (37b). The two domain changes are not contradictory.

(37)   *Prosodic Cliticization*
    a. *Domain Allocation* An unassociated element acquires as its association domain the adjacent timing unit of its governing category.
    b. *Domain Expansion* The association domain of the governing category expands to include one timing unit of the governee.

In the rest of this section, I show that (37) explains the phonetic alternations in the associative construction. The problem is to account for all possible tonal/metrical permutations of the structure in (27), where each noun ranges over the four patterns in (30–31), and the clitic is either of the elements in (28). Of the (4 x 4 x 2 =) 32 possibilities, 'bird horn' in (32) is one; I will consider four others. The example 'rooster song' combines a bisyllabic head noun of the prosodic shape [$_w$ L] with a bisyllabic [$_s$ L] dependent noun, linked by the class 7 (á-) prefix. Prosodic cliticization (38b) occurs in both cycles; in the outer cycle (38c), the reality of this process is attested not just by tone but by the forced spread of vowel features.

(38) 'rooster song'

a.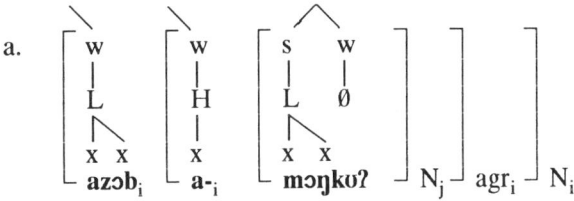

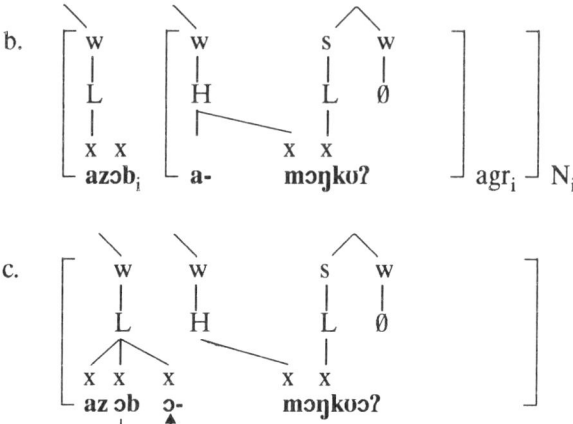

(38) shows three changes from UR: one on each level of representation, except on the tonal level: there are exactly zero tone rules involved, if *tone rule* means a stipulation which affects the tonal tier. On the metrical level, (38a) shows that the H tone prefix occupies a weak position, in accordance with (32). On the timing level, (38b) and (38c) show, in successive-cyclic fashion, the effect of prosodic cliticization (37b). The claim that this process is prosodically driven is supported by the fact that it is mirrored on the segmental level, by vowel assimilation. This parallelism of tonal and segmental reassociation under syntactic government is not accidental, as would be claimed by separate tone and vowel harmony rule. All other aspects of the representation, notably the tones, remain stable, subject to the OCP.

Phonetic interpretation requires that the three domains in (39a) are metrically connected. This yields the superstructure in (39b), equivalent to the pitch notated by Hyman as in (39c):

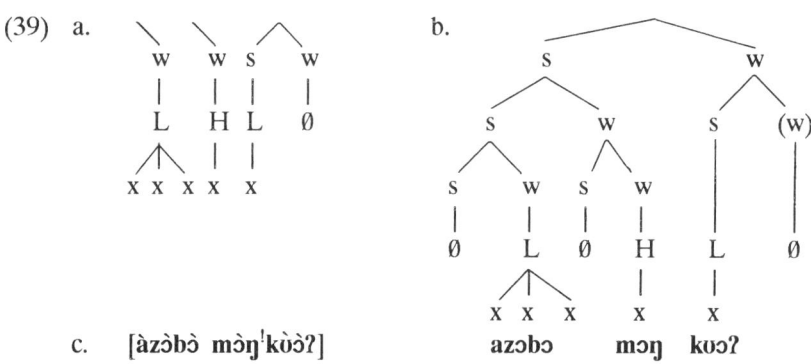

Manfredi: Spreading and downstep 157

In (39a), well-formedness (cf. 21b) requires the projection of empty strong positions. Since a [$_w$ L] position directly precedes [$_w$ H], a [$_s$ ∅] position is interpolated between them as in (53), yielding a total downstep in (39b). Empty metrical positions cannot occur in lexical items; their appearance in phrasal contexts is forced by the conjunction of (21) and (22). The rest of the Tadadjeu-Hyman data follow in the same way. The derivations in (81–83) are evidence for Bamba's (1984) proposal that the OCP respects prosodic structure. This can be formulated as in (40a), which can be viewed as a special case of (40b):

(40) a. The OCP requires both categorial identity and strict locality (metrical adjacency).
b. *Structure-preservation*:
Metrical governors are conserved.

In (42c), two L tones separated by a [$_w$ ∅] do not trigger the OCP. Identical tones in successive [s] positions are not metrically adjacent, but identical tones in adjacent branches of different feet are: [$_w$ L], [s L] → [$_s$ L] in (42d) and [$_w$ H], [$_s$ H] → [$_s$ H] in (44d). In (43c), [$_s$ H], [$_w$ H] → [$_s$ H]. (40) wrongly predicts the merger of [$_w$ L], [$_s$ L] in the first cycle of (42). This merger does in fact occur, but only after the docking of [$_w$ L] in (42c). My proposal is (41):

(41) The OCP affects only pronounceable elements (those with non-null association domain).

With these assumptions, the remaining derivations yield Hyman's cited phonetic outputs.

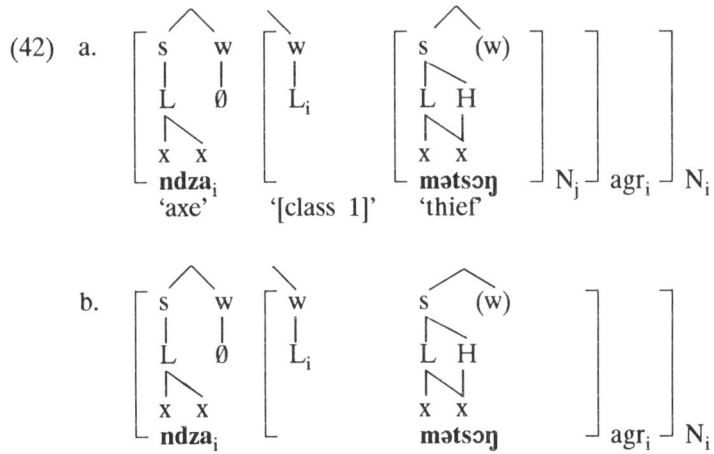

158 *The representation of tonal register*

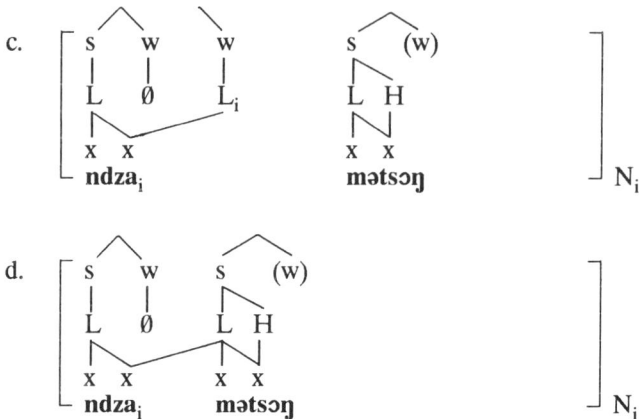

e. [ǹdzà!à mə̀tsɔ̌ŋ]   'thieves' axe'

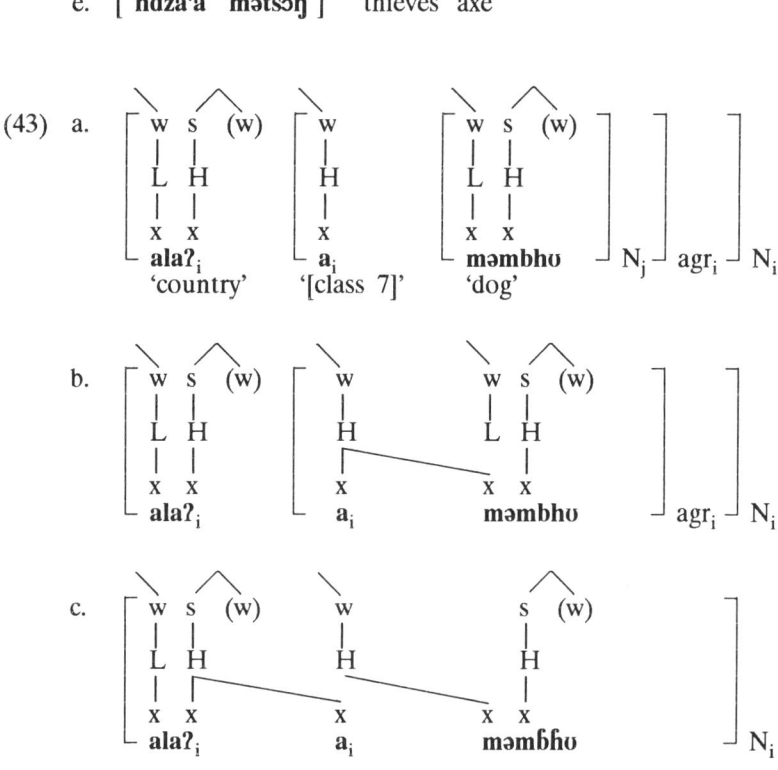

Manfredi: Spreading and downstep 159

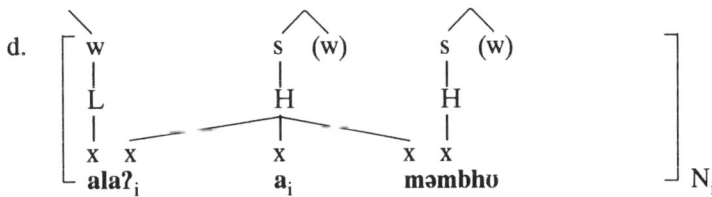

e. [àláʔámə́m¹bhó] 'dog country'

(44) a. 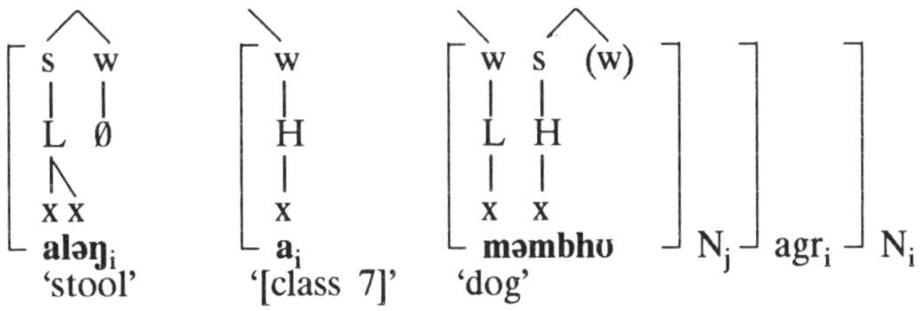 [stool 'aləŋᵢ'] [class 7 'aᵢ'] [dog 'məmbʊ']ₙⱼ agrᵢ]ₙᵢ

b. 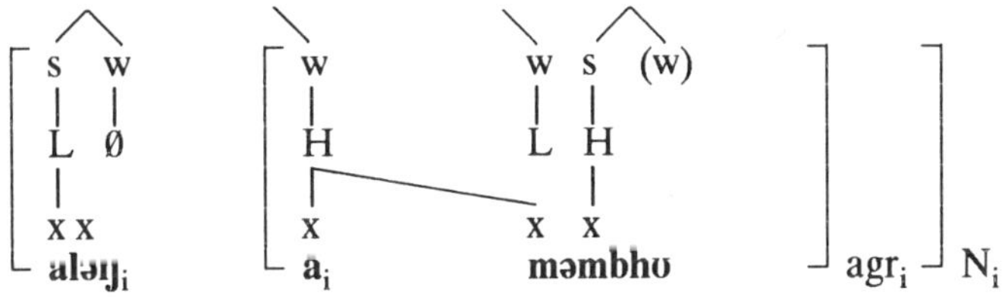 (similar structure) agrᵢ]ₙᵢ

c. 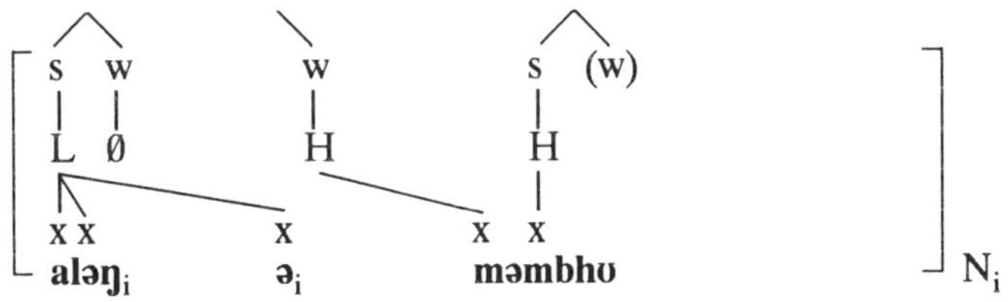 (similar structure)]ₙᵢ

d. 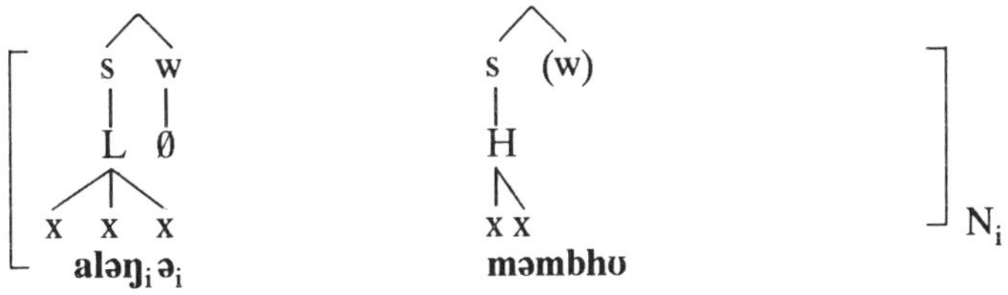 (similar structure)]ₙᵢ

e. [àlə̀ŋ ə̀ ᵢmə́mbhó]   'dog stool'

Ìgbo[15] has both an "associative" construction and a related form, first described in Green and Ígwè (1963), which has been dubbed "specific" insofar as the dependent noun bears the independent referential value of a specific entity. In the specific form, if the dependent noun is personal, its thematic relationship to the head noun is possessor. I represent the two constructions as in (45):

(45)a. *associative*   b. *specific/possessive*

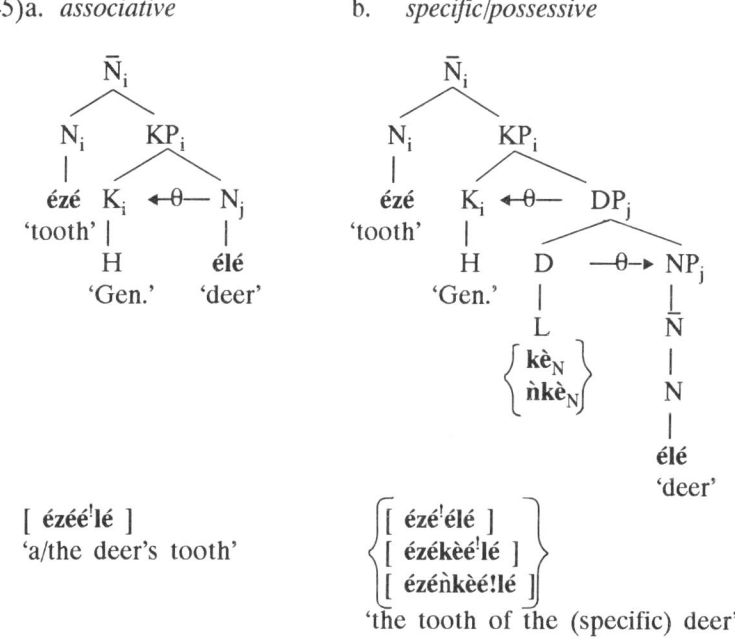

Over the past three decades, most analyses of Ìgbo attributing some autonomy to tonal representation (Welmers 1963, 1970; Voorhoeve et al. 1968; Williams 1971; Hyman 1976; Goldsmith 1976; Éménanjọ 1978; Clark 1982, 1989; Williamson 1986; Íhìọ́nú 1988) have held that the associative morpheme is a H tone. Two problems remain. First, there has yet no been non-arbitrary account of the tonal effects of this morpheme, which may occur on either noun, both or neither, depending on their inherent tonality and internal word-structure. Second, as is

---

15 Within the Ìgbo-speaking area, there is parametric varition with respect to (25b); as indicated in (8), H tone spreads automatically onto L tone in western dialects. There is also metrical variation, most evident in the extreme eastern forms of the language spoken in the Cross River basin. In this section, I will stick to the standard language. A reminder: in this section only, tone marking is not orthographic: every syllable bears a tone mark, either H or L, and downstep is indicated [!].

glaringly apparent in a licensing framework like government-binding theory, there is the fundamental question of how the H tone gets there in the first place.

Take the latter problem first. As with the associative construction in ɣɔmalá?-Yamba, it is not that the associative morpheme needs to be licensed; rather, how does this morpheme license the dependent noun? In other words, what is the syntactic category of the associative morpheme? The proposal given in (27) for ɣɔmalá?-Yamba cannot be maintained for Ìgbo, because Ìgbo noun class morphology is purely vestigial, and the Ìgbo associative morpheme does not display any agreement alternations—unlike the ɣɔmalá?-Yamba morpheme, cf. (28). An alternative proposal is given in (45a): the Ìgbo associative morpheme is a K^0 (Kase) element which governs its complement, the dependent noun, in a KP (Kase Phrase), cf. Fukui (1986). Recall from (25c) that every H tone in Ìgbo projects a strong metrical position, so that the syntactic representation of the K^0 morpheme is [$_s$ H]. The automatic nature of the relationship between H tone and [s] position means that, in a language for which the setting of the parameter in (25c) is {no}, there is no informational loss if a morpheme composed of a single H tone element has no metrical structure in the lexicon.

The KP hypothesis is contentful to the extent that it has consequences for the rest of the grammar. In fact, it captures an important syntactic generalization. As pointed out in different ways by Voorhoeve et al. (1969) and Williams (1971), the noun complement of a perfective verb is also licensed by a H tone morpheme. If Ìgbo perfective verbs are intransitive (a proposal which there is no space here to discuss), then every instance of the H tone morpheme spells out inherent (i.e. genitive) Kase. Although Williams (1971:481) explicitly discounts the idea of unifying the two morphemes, this conclusion is forced by Lieber's constraint that homophonous, distinct lexical entries, are possible in a morpheme-based framework just if they

> share only phonological representation, [and] have neither category, nor semantic representation, nor any argument structure or diacritics in common.   (1981:179)

The two H tone morphemes share the categorial property of selecting a noun complement, and are both right-branching; this forces the learner to assign them to an identical lexical entry.[16]

---

16 At a deeper level, the H tone, like English -*en* (Baker, Johnson and Roberts 1989), has the properties of a clitic: it spells out an internal argument position and absorbs structural Case. It may not be accidental that both English -*en* and Ìgbo [$_s$ H] are detransitivizing as well as aspectually perfective.

Thematically, there is no difference between the associative constructions of Ìgbo and ɣɔmalá?-Yamba—or, for that matter, with the Semitic construct state (Borer 1987, 1989). In all, the dependent noun has no independent referential value, and the semantic range of the construction accordingly includes idiosyncratic (i.e. lexical) compounds. I propose that the K^0, inherently nonreferential, inherits the referential index of its governor, so that the "autonomous" θ-marking of N_i by N_j, is mediated by K^0_i.

(45b) in turn differs from (45a) in the referential value of the dependent noun. The most straightforward way to represent this, following Abney (1987), is to say that the complement of K^0 is a DP, where the D is spelled out either as a tonal morpheme or as the possessional noun (ǹ)kè 'portion; the one of' (from the verb -kè 'allocate, divide'). Most determiners in the language follow the NP, but the prenominal position of (ǹ)kè is made more plausible by the fact that ǹkè is itself a noun, so that its complement is expected on the right.

Beginning with the associative construction, the tone alternations exhibit phenomena which are closely parallel to those seen in ɣɔmalá?-Yamba, in particular the effects of prosodic cliticization as in (37). The effects of one further constraint are notable in the data:

(46) *Metrical Projection Constraint*
A metrical constituent must be linked to (a) or (b):
a. a timing unit (i.e. via a nonzero tone);
b. a zero tone (if the language allows zero tones).

In a pure partial downstep language like Ìgbo, since zero tones are not licensed, cf. (25c), the relevant case is (46a). (46a) is vacuously satisfied by the representation of a purely tonal morpheme in the lexicon, since metrical structure is redundant for such a morpheme and no constituent can be said to exist. In a language such as ɣɔmalá?-Yamba, in which tones are freely distributed in metrical positions (subject to the various independent constraints discussed in section 1), (46) also rules out the presence in the lexicon of metrical structure on tonal morphemes composed of a single tone element. It is thus interesting to note the existence of a generalization such as (32), which permits the metrical structure of these elements to be determined post-lexically on a morphological basis in such a language.

Postlexically, (46) has consequences for the association domain of the K° morpheme. Contrast two examples. In (47), both nouns bear L tone throughout. KP is governed by N_i, and K^0 is not governed by N_j, so (37) predicts that the [$_s$ H] morpheme cliticizes to its left; this in fact occurs, cf. the outer cycle (47c). No tone association is required on the inner cycle (47b): the associative morpheme satisfies (46a) by linking through its [w] position to the already associated initial L tone of N_j.

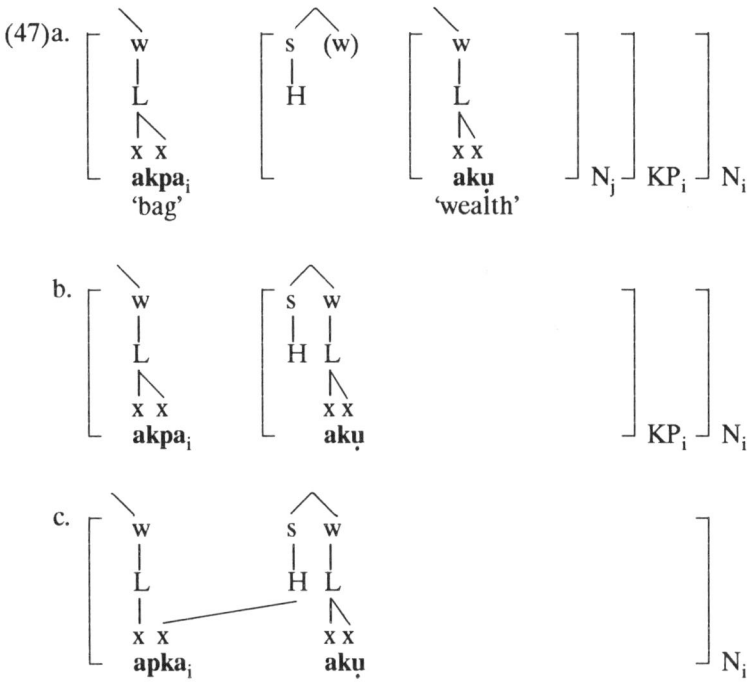

d. [àkpáákụ̀] 'bag of riches'

Now consider an example in which both nouns bear H tone throughout. In (48), cliticization occurs in the inner cycle (48b), causing a downstep between the two skeletal points. There is no other way for the associative morpheme to satisfy the metrical WFC (46a).[17]

---

[17] Unlike what occurs in ɣɔmalá?-Yamba, vowel assimilation in Ìgbo is regressive, so the flop of vowel features seen in (87c) says nothing about prosodic government: it does not indicate that N_j governs N_i. The cross-linguistic difference in assimilation is more plausibly related to the difference in syllable structure; there are essentially no closed syllables in Ìgbo.

164 *The representation of tonal register*

(48)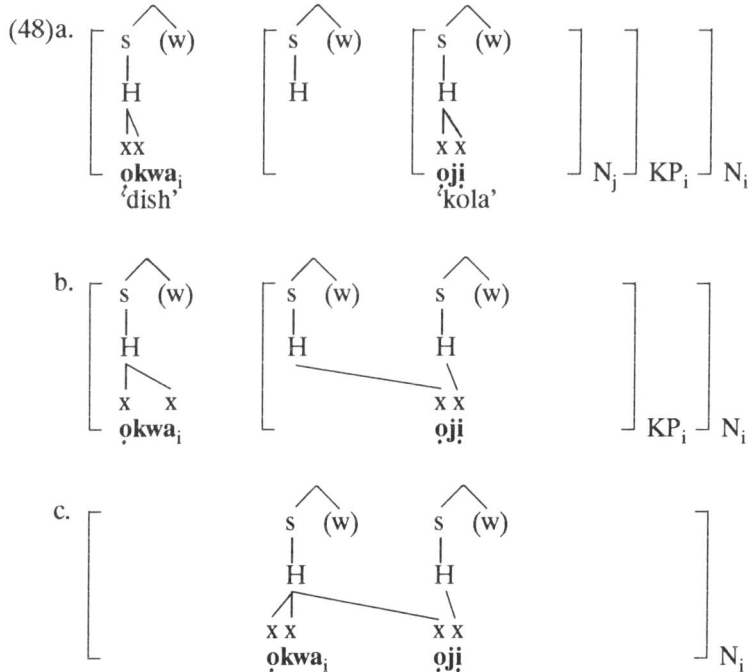

d. [ókwǫ́ǫ́ˈjí] 'kola dish'

The absence of downstep between N_i and KP is due to an independent fact about Ìgbo (and other pure partial downstep languages, but not, e.g., Kishambaa, cf. Odden 1982): consecutive words respectively ending and beginning with H tone are not in general separated by downstep. This can be formulated as a parametric condition on prosodic domains, cf. (49a). Its effect is sketched in (49b); examples are given in (49c); in (49d), no violation occurs.

(49) a. *Prosodic Rhythm Parameter*
Timing units immediately separated by a maximal projection (XP) can be metrically distinct iff they are tonally distinct: {on}, {off}

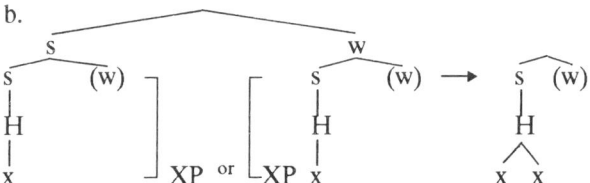

c. [_N ónyé [_AP ọ́má]]   [ónyọ́ọ́má]   *[ónyọ́¹ọ́má]
   person   good
   'good person'

   [_V í-¹tá [_NP ọ́jí]]   [í¹tọ́ọ́jí]   *[í¹tọ́¹ọ́jí]
   to-chew   kola
   'to chew cola'

   [_D [_NP ọ́jí] áhụ̀]   [ọ́jyááhụ̀]   *[ọ́jyá¹áhụ̀]
          kola Det
          'that kola'

d. [_N óbì [_AP ọ́má]]   [óbyọ̀ọ́ma]
   heart   good
   'good heart'

   [_V í-chè [_NP ọ́jí]]   [íchọ̀ọ́jí]
   to-present kola
   'to present cola'

   [_D [_NP óbì] áhụ̀]   [óbyàáhụ̀]
          heart Det
          'that heart'

The alternations in (47–48) are the tonal effects of the associative morpheme, but a number of independent phenomena also occur in associative constructions. Notable among these is a process which Clark (1978) calls "smoothing": the initial L tone of an LH nominal complement delinks, creating a [¹HH] contour, after H, cf. (50). The forms in (51) show that this change is unrelated to the associative morpheme. (51a) shows that no associative morpheme follows an infinitive, or else we would find a downstep before the second syllable of 'kola'; yet LH smoothing occurs in that context, cf. (51b):

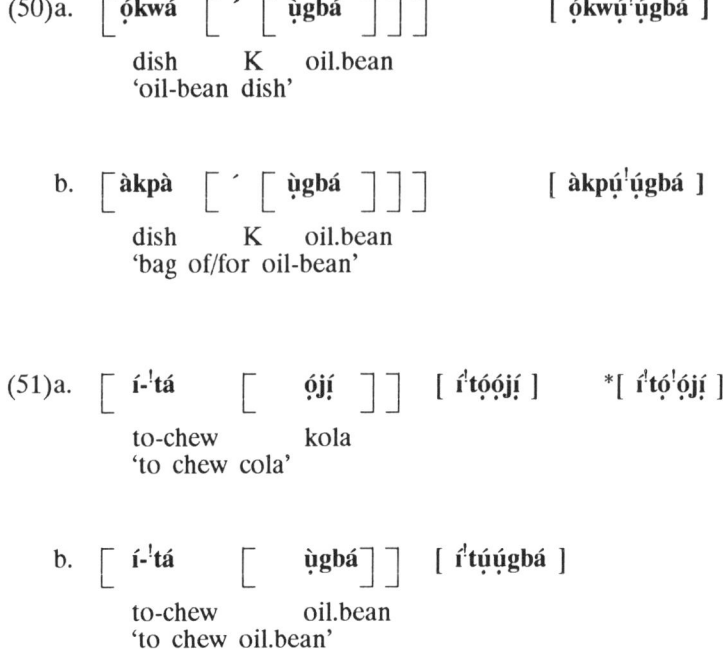

Finally, as Williamson succinctly observes, "[t]he tones of the Specific construction operate identically with the Associative if an initial H of N_2 is replaced by L" (1986:188). This replacement follows directly from the representation in (45b) with [$_w$ L] occupying the D position, given (46a). To satisfy metrical well-formedness, the L tone must take over the association domain of the initial tone of the dependent noun. (If the dependent noun is L-initial, the effect is vacuous, and the specific form is identical to the associative.)

4. METRICAL TONE CLASSES

A number of Ìgbo dialects attest a third underlying tone class of monosyllabic verbs, in addition to the two tone classes (H and L) found in other dialects and in standard Ìgbo. Williamson (1983b) shows that the lexical membership of the three classes is consistent across Igboid in all those dialects which have them; and in dialects with just two classes, all potential members of the third class belong to the H class. Although three classes can be derived mechanically with floating tones, this would imply at least four logical possibilities, but only three are ever attested. The metrical analysis developed above suggests a more constrained analysis. [$_s$ L] being ruled out independently by (25a), L cannot be a metrical governor. The three remaining possibilities are [$_w$ L] and [$_s$ H] and [$_w$ H]; the third of these, while possible, is marked and merges with one or the other of the first two, depending on the context. In this section, I will account for data from the literature on Mbàisén and Ọ̀gbakiri.[18]

In Mbàisén, as described by Swift et al. (1962), Nwáchukwu (1983a), the tonal behavior of the three verb classes combined with various derivational and inflectional morphemes is shown in (52). Each of the verbs 'fall', 'walk' and 'eat' represents a tone class. Although the phenomenon is inconsistently reflected in the literature, Mbàisén (among other dialects) has phonetic lowering of sentence-final downstepped H. In (52), the forms in square brackets give the lowered pronunciation.[19]

(52)   'fall'   'walk (to)'   'eat'

a.   *imperative*
     dhàá   jhèé   ríe
    indicative (3sg. subject)
     ọ́ dhàra   ó jhère   ó ríri   [ó rìrì # #]

b.   *participle*
     ádhà   èjhé   èrí
    infinitive
     ídhà   íjhé   [íjhé # #]   írí   [ìrì # #]
    negative imperative
     ádhàla   ejhéle   [éjhèlè # #]   érile   [érìlè # #]
    negative indicative (lexical subject)
     ádhàghị ejhéghi [éjhèlè # #] érighi [érìghì # #]
    negative indicative (3sg. subject)
     ọ̀ dhághị ò jhéghí [ò jhéghì # #] ò ríghí [ò ríghì # #]

c.   *gerund*
     ọ̀dhidha òjhighé   òríri

---

18 Éménanjo (1981) describes three tone classes of monosyllabic verbs in Òweré, whose tonal behavior is closely similar to, but not identical to, that found in Mbàisén.
19 Forms in square brackets have phonetic, not orthographic tone marking, i.e. every syllable bears either [´] or [`], and downstep is marked by [!]. For a part of Èzínàíhìte Mbàisén, P.A. Nwáchukwu (p.c.) notes the occurrence of tonal variation in the 'fall' class, which while important goes beyond the scope of the present discussion.

The first set of forms (52a) shows a two-way split in tonal behavior. In the imperative, which is formed with a H tone suffix, the root is pronounced low in both the 'fall' and 'walk' classes, but high in the 'eat' class. In the indicative, formed with the toneless -rV suffix, the same split is found.[20] Sentence-finally, where the downstepped H in the indicative of the 'eat' class is subject to phonetic lowering, the three classes are pronounced the same.

The second set of forms (52b) shows a different two-way split. Except for the 3sg indicative negative, the 'fall' class has L tone on the root, while in both the 'walk' class and the 'eat' class the root has H. In the 3sg indicative negative, the expected prefix H tone is displaced onto the root, and the expected root tone (L for 'fall', H for 'walk' and 'eat') is displaced onto the negative suffix. As in (52a), a sentence-final downstepped H is phonetically lowered, superficially merging the three classes in that context.

In the gerund (52c), which is formed by reduplicating the stem consonant plus a high vowel, the three classes are phonetically distinct. The tone of the gerund can be described as follows: the root in (52c) bears the same tone that the root has in (52b), while the high vowel infix of (52c) bears the same tone as the root in (52a).[21]

The analysis now proceeds. First consider the fact that, in sentence-final position in Mbàisén, a downstepped H tone is pronounced L. In metrical formalism, such a H tone would be represented as weak: $[_w$ H]. Weakened H, while not generally possible in a partial downstep system, is strictly speaking not ruled out by the parameters in (25). Rather, it is possible only in final contexts; nonfinally, it leads to ill-formedness as shown in (15).

Nevertheless, the weakening of H in final position is not found in all partial downstep systems. In keeping with the cognitive approach to phonology, it can be expressed as a parameter, where parametric formulation is constrained to be maximally concrete and general, and minimally stipulative and arbitrary. One way to account for the occurrence of H weakening effect is by a domain condition like (53):

(53) *Minimal Foot Parameter*
A minimal prosodic domain contains
both a governor and a governee: {on}, {off}

---

20 Indicative is Éménanjọ's term for the -rV verb-form, dubbed "factative" by Welmers and Welmers (1968). This suffix is discussed by Winston (1973) and Nwáchukwu (1976b).
21 Éménanjọ (1975b) and Williamson (1984) describe the gerund in detail.

The observation is that a sentence-final H, if metrically strong, thereby violates (53), since there is no subsequent tonal material for it to govern. A paraphrase of the parameter is therefore as follows: "You {can/can't} end a sentence with a [s] position."

To satisfy (53), a sentence-final H must be incorporated in the preceding [w] position. There are two possibilities. If the penultimate tone is also H (i.e. if the final H is downstepped), then there is an unoccupied, governed [w] position which is available for the final H. If the penultimate tone is L, then the sentence-final H must adjoin to it. These two possibilities are shown in (54), which represents the sentence-final pronunciation of the infinitive and participle of 'eat'. In each case, the left side of the arrow violates (53), while the right side satisfies it.

(54) *Final H incorporated into preceding [$_w$ ∅]*

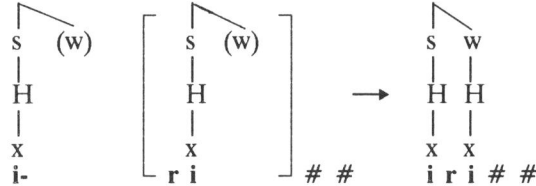

Final H adjoined to preceding [$_w$ L]

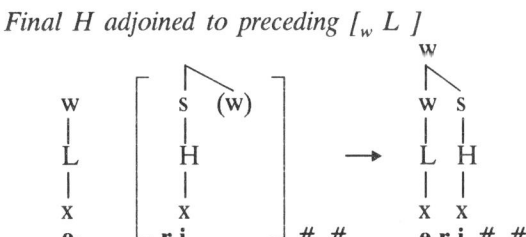

By definition, a nonfinal H tone cannot violate (53), because there is always a subsequent [w] position. In other words, the licensing of nonfinal empty [w] position is unexceptional in partial downstep systems. This can be seen in (55). In the example, parentheses indicate phonetic elision of a rime along with its L tone. Despite the loss of its immediate governee, the tone labeled H_1 does not violate (53), because its metrical government domain extends along the path indicated in boldface, to include a governee.

(55)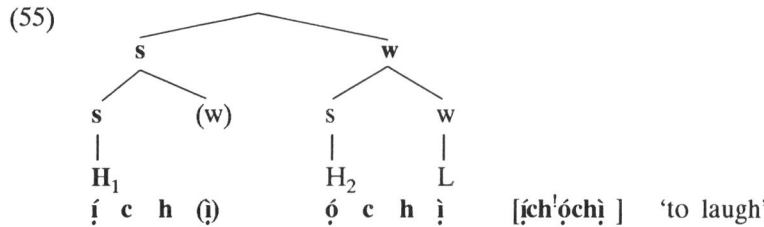

[íchⁱóchì] 'to laugh'

The above discussion of (53–54) shows that [$_w$ H] is possible in Mbàisén, in at least one (fairly restricted) context. [$_w$ L] and [$_s$ H], by contrast, are freely available in any partial downstep system, apart from the parametric occurrence of minor restrictions like (53). The fourth logical possibility, [$_s$ L], is ruled out absolutely for all partial downstep systems, including all dialects of Ìgbo, by the metrical government parameter (25a).

Since [$_w$ H], while marked, is not ruled out in principle in Mbàisén, one can ask if it arises anywhere else, other than in sentence-final position after H. Another potential instance of [w H] in Mbàisén is the third lexical tone class. Accordingly, a metrical analysis of the three lexical tone classes is as follows:

(56)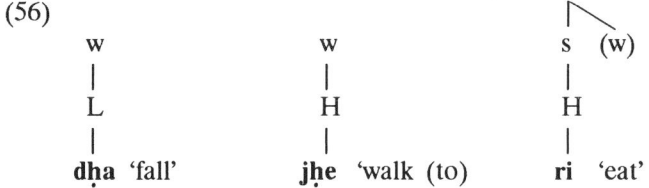

[$_w$ H] is formally possible for a monosyllabic lexical item, since prosodic domains are not defined in such a context; but, it is marked, because H is the metrical governor in a partial downstep language. This markedness explains why in dialects like Ònicha which have just two tone classes of monosyllabic verbs, the 'walk' class is merged with the 'eat' class, not with the 'fall' class. The metrical account of the third class treats it as a species of H rather than of L, and dialects which lack the third class show that this is the correct generalization.[22]

---

22 Nnééwi, which is geographically between Ònicha and Mbàisén, has a vestigial third tone class. In Igboid there are the three verbs 'to be', which in Nnééwi have the following shapes: nò 'be at', dú 'be describable as', wú '[copula]'. Éménanjo (1981:257) reports a three-way tonal contrast among these verbs in the 3sg indicative negative: ó nòhọ, ò dúhò, ó wúhọ (orthographic tonemarking).

Consider again the forms in (52a). In Mbàisén, with either a H tone suffix (as in the imperative) or no tonal suffix (as in the indicative) verbs of the 'fall' and 'eat' classes retain their inherent tone, respectively L and H. But in the same context, a verb of the 'walk' class is phonetically low. If 'walk' verbs are underlyingly [$_w$ H], this lowering can be compared to the sentence final lowering of [$_w$ H], characteristic of Mbàisén. In other words, the lowering of the 'walk' class verbs roots in the imperative and indicative might be viewed as a second consequence of the well-formedness parameter in (53), independent of the fact of phrase-final lowering which suggested it in the first place. To examine that possibility, consider the metrical representations of the indicative and imperative, given in (57).

(57) a. *Imperative*

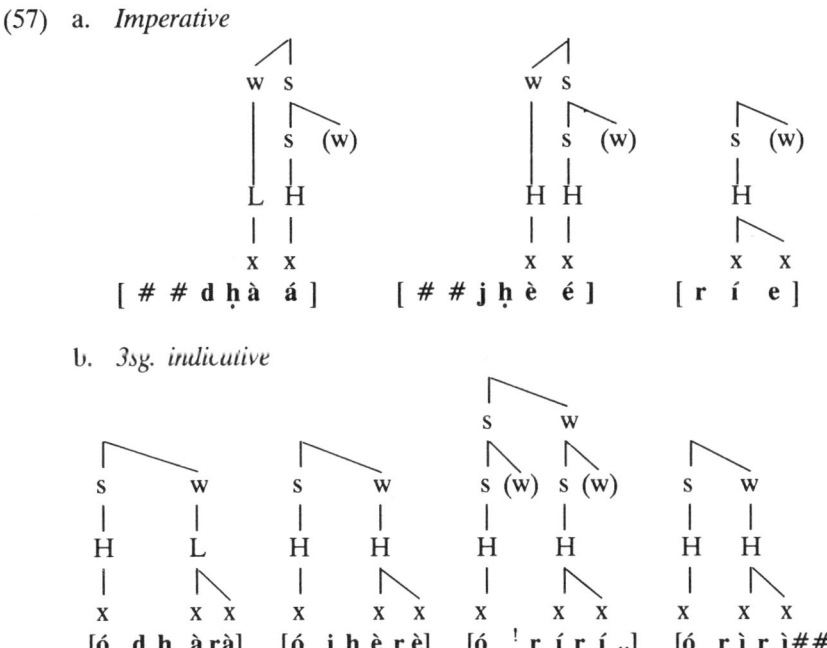

b. *3sg. indicative*

In the imperative (57a), both 'fall' and 'walk' begin with a [w] position, while 'eat' begins with a [s] position. But the parameter in (53) rules out a stray initial [w]. The simplest way for an initial [w] to satisfy (53) is for it to adjoin to the following [s]. In this way, the metrical representations in (56) and the independently motivated parameter in (53) account for the fact that the 'fall' and 'walk' classes pattern together in the imperative.

In the 3sg. indicative (57b), the clitic subject bears H tone, which metrically governs the prosodic domain of the verb. The tonal difference between the verb classes arises because the two classes which are metrically [w] (i.e. 'fall' and 'walk') form the immediate sister to the [s] position of the subject, while the class which is metrically [s] (i.e. 'eat') must thereby constitute a separate domain, i.e., a downstep intervenes between the clitic subject and the verb. As noted, this downstep is lost sentence-finally, as already discussed.

In the forms in (52b), 'walk' and 'eat' pattern tonally together, and it is 'fall' that is the odd one out. Given the representations in (56), this means that the metrical distinction between [$_w$ H] and [$_s$ H] is not crucial in these forms, although (57) shows that it is crucial in the forms in (52a). This difference can only be understood in terms of the different affixes involved in the two sets of forms. The forms in (52b) involve suffixes, one toneless and one composed of H tone. While some of the forms in (52b) involve toneless suffixes, all of them involve prefixes.

In the participle, the prefix tone is opposite (or 'polar') in category (H or L) to that of the root. (This statement excludes the 'obligative' participle, which Émenanjọ 1981 shows to be a true nominal.) The other forms in (52b) all involve a prefix which bears H tone; this is true even for the 3sg indicative negative, once it is seen that the prefix tone is displaced onto the root in this form. The negative forms all have a toneless suffix, either **ghị/ghi** or **-la/le**.

The participle, which roughly translates English **-ing**, is fully productive and regular. However, unlike the English V-**ing** and the Ìgbo infinitive and gerund, it is not a free form.[23] As observed by Green and Ígwè (1963:170f.), a participle is always the complement of an auxiliary verb (although, as Émenanjọ 1981 notes, in western dialects the main verb complement of some auxiliaries is prefixless). This observation offers a way to understand the polar tone of the participle prefix, in contrast to the inherent tone of the prefixes of the other derivatives (the infinitive prefix bears H tone, the gerund prefix bears L tone, etc.).

With a prosodic analysis of tone, as developed above, and on the hypothesis that the participle prefix is underlyingly toneless, then, given the fact that the participle is not a free form, it follows that the surface tone of the participle prefix is not determined in isolation. Rather, it must be determined in its minimal prosodic domain, which includes the

---

[23] Accordingly, Nwáchukwu (1976a) rightly rejects the term *participle*—which has acquired the force of tradition in Ìgbo grammar, possibly because the form often translates English *-ing*.

syntactic governor. This is so because a prosodic domain requires a syntactic constituent. Although the last statement is not universally subscribed to by phonological theorists (e.g. Nespor and Vogel 1986), it may be considered the null hypothesis, and is adopted as such by Giegerich (1985). This line of reasoning at any rate offers a reason why it is just the participle, i.e. the one verbal derivative which is not a free form, which exhibits the phenomenon of tone polarity.[24]

Accordingly, the tone polarity of the participle prefix can be understood as follows. It has been observed that the so-called participle always complements a finite auxiliary. And in Ìgbo, a finite auxiliary always appears in the factative form; this fact is important because, in Ìgbo, an auxiliary verb can have no tonal suffix.[25] And if, by hypothesis, the participle prefix is toneless, this means the root tone of the Aux is always adjacent to the root tone of the participle. Now the Aux syntactically governs its complement, the participle. It would seem reasonable, in this circumstance, to require that the Aux should prosodically govern the root of the participle. It remains to consider how such a requirement might be met, for the three verb classes, to explain why the participle prefix must bear the tone opposite to that of the root.

If the verb root of the participle is [$_w$ L], the prefix is H. If the prefix were L, then the OCP would merge the prefix and the root into the domain of a single tone. But this would prevent the Aux from prosodically governing the verb root of the participle, since the participle prefix now shares the prosodic constituent of the root. The only remaining possibility, which guarantees that the participle root has its own prosodic constituent, is that the participle prefix must bear H tone.

If the verb root of the participle is [$_w$ H], the prefix is L. If the prefix were H, it might be [$_w$ H] or [$_s$ H]. If the prefix were [$_w$ H], the OCP would merge its tone with that of the root, blocking prosodic government by the Aux as in the preceding paragraph. And if the prefix were [$_s$ H], this itself would prosodically govern the root, forming a minimality barrier to government by the Aux. The only remaining

---

24 In fact, the literature describes another verbal derivative which is not a free form: the bound verb complement (BVC). This terminology does not challenge the prosodic generalization just stated, however, since the BVC is homophonous with the participle, i.e. the BVC prefix also exhibits tone polarity. Indeed, as remarked in the previous footnote, Nwáchukwu (1976a) already described the Ìgbo "participle" as a bound verb. One reason that the participle and the BVC may have received different names is that they can cooccur in a single predicate; but in a syntactic framework which allows for head movement, the BVC can be thought of as a resumptive lexicalization of the verb trace.

25 Auxes are stative (i.e. non-eventive) verbs, and like some stative main verbs they do not require the -rV suffix unless they denote past time.

possibility, which guarantees that the participle root has its own prosodic constituent, is that the participle prefix must bear L tone.

If the verb root of the participle is [_s_ H], the prefix is L. If the prefix were H, it might be [_w_ H] or [_s_ H]. If the prefix were [_w_ H], the OCP would merge its tone with that of the root, blocking prosodic government by the Aux as before. If the prefix were [_s_ H], the OCP would also merge its tone with that of the root, blocking prosodic government by the Aux. The only remaining possibility, which guarantees that the participle root has its own prosodic constituent, is that the participle prefix must bear L tone.

The above reasoning is frankly speculative. If it is conceptually flawed, there is a phonological approach available in a system like Clark's (1989), which employs the mechanism of default H-tone insertion. However, a purely phonological approach can never explain why the phenomenon of tone polarity occurs just in a syntactically bound form. For the remaining forms in (52b), the H prefix directly licenses the lexical tone of the root, as in these infinitive forms, all of which satisfy (53) without further comment:

(58)

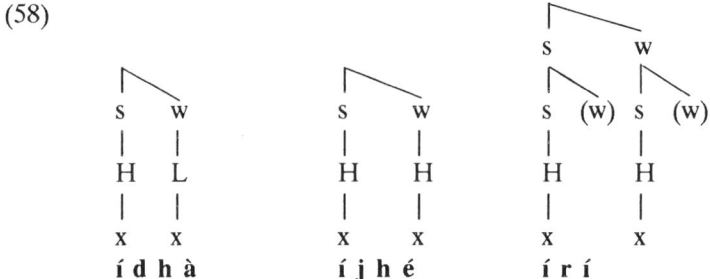

In sentence-final position, the phonetic effect of (53), as represented for 'to eat' in (54), is correctly predicted for 'to walk'. If, on the other hand, the infinitive is non-final, the pitch of the final syllable will remain downstepped H, for both 'to walk' and 'to eat'.

In the 3sg. negative indicative, a prefix H tone displaces the stem tone, which in turn surfaces on the suffix; this can be captured by any autosegmental analysis. As in other Kwa languages, this rightward tonal displacement is triggered by the clitic subject (cf. Amáyó 1981).

The three distinct tonal shapes of the gerunds in (52c) can be predicted if the reduplication process has a metrical formulation, viz: reduplication copies tonal material iff it is metrically strong; otherwise, the L tone of the prefix spreads onto the reduplicated syllable.

The lexical tonal classes in Ọgbakiri are similar to those of Mbàisén; what differs are the individual verb affixes and the phonetic outputs. In

Ògbakiri, the three classes are phonetically distinct in all contexts. Wórùkwó (1983) cites four forms of the infinitive: with null complement, with a bound verb complement that adds emphasis (hence the gloss 'really'), with a lexical complement (here the noun **wíri** 'food'), and with both kinds of complement.[26]

(59) Ògbakiri

ékèé	'to divide'
ékèé ekèé	'to really divide'
ékèé wíri	'to divide food'
ékèé wíri èkeé	'to really divide food'
èsîi	'to boil'
èsí esîi	'to really boil'
èsí wíri	'to boil food'
èsí wíri esìi	'to really boil food'
èrí	'to eat'
èrí èrí	'to really eat'
èrí wíri	'to eat food'
èrí wíri eri	'to really eat food'

The behavior of these three tone classes follows from the same underlying forms posited for Mbàisén in (56) above, assuming a domain condition something like (61):

(60)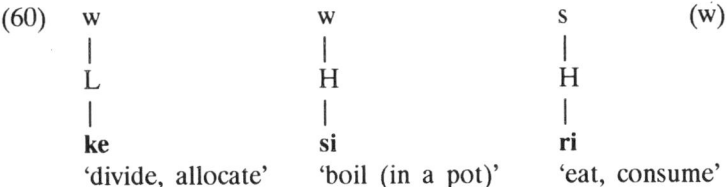

      'divide, allocate'   'boil (in a pot)'   'eat, consume'

(61) *Minimal Base Parameter*
    A derivational base prosodically governs its affixes: {on}, {off}

---

26 Any lexical complement must precede the bound verb complement if any. The same restriction holds in Mbàisén. Cf. Éménanjọ (1975a, 1984); Nwáchukwu (1985, 1987); Ihìónú (1989).

(61) requires that, in derived forms, the base contains a metrical governor. The 'eat' class of verbs, with an underlying [$_s$ H], satisfies (61) with no further comment. For the 'divide' class, with an underlying [$_w$ L], the minimal way to satisfy (61) is by suffixing a [$_s$ H], to which the root [$_w$ L] adjoins. The most interesting case is the 'boil' class, with its marked, underlying [$_w$ H]. The question is what additional structure will give a metrical governor.

If phonology respects structure preservation, there is no possibility of changing the tone or metrical strength of the root. This leaves two possibilities: suffix [$_s$ H] or [$_w$ L]. If [$_s$ H] is suffixed, the result is a sequence of [$_w$ H] [$_s$ H]. But this still does not satisfy (61), because this [$_s$ H] would not be adjacent to a prefix, and hence could not govern it. The other possibility is to suffix [$_w$ L]. Discussion of ɣɔmalá?-Yamba showed that [$_w$ L] is the only element which can be governed by [$_w$ H]. Accordingly, as metrical governor of [$_w$ L], [$_w$ H] can project a higher [s] position, satisfying (61). The lexical bases of the three tone classes are given in (62).

(62) *bases*

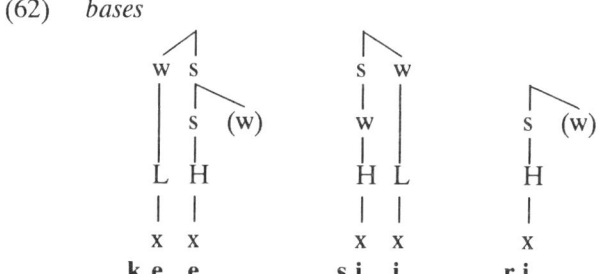

5. PROSODIC TYPOLOGY

How does the prosodic typology of Benue-Kwa, as sketched above, relate to other languages? Before Bamba proposed that tone was sensitive to metrical structure, metrical formalism was restricted to the analysis of stress languages. In autosegmental theory, pitch accent languages like Japanese and some Benue-Congo languages were represented by means of accentual diacritics on tone melodies (cf. Haraguchi 1975; Clements and Goldsmith 1983).

There is a typological fact about metrical structure which suggests that Bamba is correct. Informally, "tone languages" seem to have one of two typological properties: either their basic syllable structure is CV (as in the Kwa languages), or their basic word structure is monosyllabic (as in Chinese). In a functional sense, this means that tone languages do not "need" metrical structure to attach to syllabic constituents, either because all syllables have nonbranching rimes (i.e. are monomoraic) as in Kwa, or because all words are prosodically nonbranching (as in Chinese). In all these languages, metrical structure is "available" to attach to tones.

"Stress" languages, on the other hand, have both of the opposite properties: a wide variety of syllable types (e.g. CV, CVC, CVV, and possibly others) and polysyllabic words. In all these languages, that is, metrical structure is unavailable to attach to tones. But, as argued by Jibril (1984), there is no reason to suppose that "stress" languages lack tone features. It would be a strange world indeed if some human languages possessed phonological features (or elements) which were unknown in other human languages. It is more reasonable to suppose that "stress" languages have tone elements, but since these elements cannot attach to metrical structures, the result is what has been called intonation, i.e. "semantic" control of pitch. Conversely, it would be strange to think that "tone" languages were simply deprived of metrical structure. What would it mean to say that a speaker of a tone language did not "possess" metrical structure as part of her knowledge of language? How about those people who are bilingual in a "tone" language and a "stress" language?

The alternative to this conceptual nightmare is the position adopted by Kaye, Lowenstamm and Vergnaud (1985, 1987), among others, that there is a universal inventory of phonological elements, among which are numbered tones, and a universal "syntax" of these elements, including the principles underlying syllable structure and metrical structure. What differs from one language to another is not the inventory of these elements and principles, but the parameters which govern their interrelationship. Accordingly, I propose the following parameter to account for the difference between "stress" languages and "tone" languages, consistent with the metrical analysis of Benue-Kwa tone as presented in this chapter:

(63)   *Prosodic Linking Parameter*
       The units which project metrical structure attach are:
       {tones}, {rimes}

In the formulation of (63), the choice of "rimes" instead of "syllables" reflects the consensus that syllable onsets are metrically irrelevant.

Obviously, a parameter like (63) is only the beginning. A serious prosodic typology would have to account for the phenomena like pitch accent, stress timing vs. syllable timing etc. But the limitations of (63) should not obscure its basic claim: that phonological typology can be explanatory, i.e. cognitively based.

6. PROSODY AND SYNTAX

> *Wherever notions like the foot or the phonological phrase are of interest in the formalization of phonological processes, they turn out either to be relationally defined or to coincide with syntactic structure.*
>
> — Giegerich (1985:10)

The above analyses of a range of nominal and verbal constructions in Yɔmalá-Yamba and Ìgbo lack the arbitrariness of earlier proposals. In my analyses, rules are eliminated, representations are constrained by universal principles, and language particular phenomena are captured in a small handful of parameters with independent empirical content. In implementing these cognitive goals, it has been necessary to make a number of proposals concerning the relationship between tonal and metrical elements. The role of metrical structure is central in determining tone association domain, and syntax is clearly relevant in this connection. In retrospect, it is not surprising that tonologists could not explain the "associative construction", since they had never proposed a syntax for the "associative marker".

In recognition of the syntactic nature of tone domains, I have called the metrical effects of syntax on tone association *prosodic*. Many rule-based accounts of tone languages also posit prosodic domains, but here Occam's rasor comes in. An analysis with both rules and prosody is less explanatory than one with just prosody.

At another remove, there is the question of where prosody comes from. Nespor and Vogel (1986) claim that prosodic domains are a form of representation *sui generis*, while Clark (1989) has argued that prosodic domains are none other than syntactic phrases. I agree with Clark on this point. Where I differ with Clark is in the nature of the relationship between tone and syntax: for her, syntax directly triggers the application of tone rules, whereas I have shown that many tone rules express—in a completely stipulatory way—the mediating effect of metrical structure, which has a principled basis. However, Clark and I agree that there is no need to construct a special, prosodic level of representation, in the manner of Nespor and Vogel, to account for tone association. Surveying metrical phonology in stress languages, Giegerich also reaches a negative conclusion regarding the existence of prosodic structure as an autonomous derivational level.

The strands of the overall argument converge in the phenomenon of prosodic cliticization (37) and in the kind of prosodic OCP effect in

(49a). I have called the latter effect rhythmic in homage to Liberman and Prince; it requires a certain degree of prosodic contrast at a major constituent boundary. Since tone projects metrical structure, it is the metrical structure which adjusts. In both phenomena, it is necessary to state a direct relationship between syntax and metrical structure. Something would be lost in attributing prosodic effects like (37) and (49) to the mediation of a special prosodic constituent structure.

In postulating the *simultaneous* presence of different subtypes of the government relation (phrasal, metrical, tonal, syllabic...), phonology becomes an important source of syntactic information, just as syntax can be seen to condition phonological processes.

REFERENCES

Abney, Steven P. 1987. "The English Noun Phrase in its Sentential Aspect. Ph.D. dissertation, Massachusetts Institute of Technology, Cambridge.
Akinlabí, Akinbíyí. 1982. "The Phonological Nature of Yorùbá Tone." Paper presented at the 3rd Annual Conference of the Linguistic Association of Nigeria, Ilorin.
———. 1985. "Tonal Underspecification and Yorùbá Tone." Ph.D. dissertation, University of Ìbàdàn.
Akinlabí, Akinbíyí and Yétúndé Lánírán. 1988. "Tone and Intonation of Declarative Sentences in Yorùbá." Paper presented to 19th Conference on African Linguistics, 15–17 November, Boston University.
Ámáyó, Áírẹ́n. 1976. "A Generative Phonology of Ẹdo (Bini)." Ph.D. dissertation, University of Ìbàdàn.
———. 1981. "Tone Rules and Derivational History in Ẹdo Phonology." *Kìubàrà* 4, 81–96.
Armstrong, Robert G. 1968. "Yala (Ikom): a 'Terraced-Level' Language with Three Tones." *Journal of West African Languages* 5, 49–58.
Awóbùlúyì, Ọládélé. 1964. "The Phonology and Morphophonemics of Yorùbá." Ph.D. dissertation, Columbia University.
Baker, Mark C. 1985. "Incorporation: a Theory of Grammatical Function Changing." Ph.D. dissertation, Massachusetts Institute of Technology, Cambridge. Published, Chicago: University of Chicago Press, 1988.
Baker, Mark. C., Kyle Johnson and Ian Roberts. 1989. "Passive Arguments Raised." *Linguistic Inquiry* 20, 219–51.
Bamba, Moussa. 1984. "Etudes phonologiques du Mahou." Master's thesis, Université du Québec à Montréal.
———. 1988. "A Theory of Tone-Accent Interaction: Evidence from Manding Languages." Ms., Université du Québec à Montréal.
———. 1989. "On Downstep in the Tonal System of Ojene Jula." In *Current Approaches to African Linguistics*. Vol. 7, edited by John Hutchison and Victor Manfredi, 1–14. Dordrecht: Foris Publications.
Bendor-Samuel, John T., editor. 1989. *The Niger-Congo Languages*. Lanham, Maryland: American Universities Press for Wycliffe Bible Translators/Summer Institute of Linguistics.
Borer, Hagit. 1983. "Parametric Syntax." Ph.D. dissertation, Massachusetts Institute of Technology, Cambridge. Published, Dordrecht: Foris Publications, 1984.

———. 1987. "Parallel Morphology." Paper presented at the Lexicon Project, MIT Center for Cognitive Science, Cambridge.

———. 1989. "The Syntax of Lexical Insertion." Paper presented at the Department of Linguistics, University of Massachusetts, Amherst, 31 March.

Capo, Hounkpati B.C. 1985. "Prelude to the Relationship between Gbè and Yoruboid, *Journal of the Linguistic Association of Nigeria* 3, 99–103.

Charette, Monik. 1988. "Some Constraints on Governing Relation in Phonology." Ph.D. dissertation, McGill University, Montreal.

———. 1990. "License to Govern." *Phonology* 7, 233–54.

Chomsky, Noam A. 1981. *Lectures on Government and Binding.* Dordrecht: Foris Publications.

Clark, Mary M. 1978. "A Dynamic Theory of Tone with Special Reference to the Tonal System of Ìgbo." Ph.D. dissertation, University of Massachusetts, Amherst. Distributed by the Indiana University Linguistics Club, Bloomington.

———. 1982. "On the Syntactic Distribution of the Associative Particle in Ìgbo: Implications for the Structure of the NP." Ms., University of New Hampshire, Durham.

———. 1989. *The Tonal System of Ìgbo.* Dordrecht: Foris Publications.

Clements, George N. 1979. "The Description of Terraced-Level Tone Languages." *Language* 55, 536–58.

———. 1981. "The Hierarchical Representation of Tone Features." *Harvard Studies in Phonology* 2, 50–108. Also in *Current Approaches to African Linguistics.* Vol. 1, edited by Ivan R. Dihoff, 145–76. Dordrecht: Foris Publications, 1983.

———. 1984. "Principles of Tone Assignment in Kikuyu." In *Autosegmental Studies in Bantu Tone*, edited by George N. Clements and John Goldsmith, 281–339. Dordrecht: Foris Publications.

Clements, George N. and Kevin Ford. 1978. "On the Phonological Status of Downstep in Kikuyu." In *Phonology in the 1980's*, edited by Didier L. Goyvaerts, 309–57. Ghent: Story-Scientia.

———. 1979. "Kikuyu Tone Shift and its Synchronic Consequences." *Linguistic Inquiry* 10, 179–210.

Courtenay, Karen. 1968. "A Generative Phonology of Yorùbá." Ph.D. dissertation, University of California, Los Angeles.

Éménanjo, E.Nwánọ̀lúẹ. 1971. "Aspects of the Phonology and Morphophonemics of Ọnịcha." Master's thesis, University of Ìbàdàn.

———. 1975a. "Aspects of the Ìgbo verb." In *Ìgbo Language and Culture*, edited by F.Chídòzíe Ọgbàlụ́ and E.Nwánọ̀lúẹ Éménanjo, 160–73. Ìbàdàn: Oxford University Press.

———. 1975b. "The Ìgbo Verbal: a Descriptive Analysis." Master's thesis, University of Ìbàdàn.

———. 1978. *Elements of Modern Ìgbo Grammar.* Ìbàdàn: Oxford University Press.

———. 1981. "Auxiliaries in Ìgbo Syntax." Ph.D. dissertation, University of Ìbàdàn. [Distributed by the Indiana Univertsity Linguistics Club, Bloomington, 1984. Page references to this work are to the unpublished version.]

———. 1984. "Ìgbo Verbs: Transitivity or Complementation?." Paper presented at the 5th Annual Conference of the Linguistic Association of Nigeria, Nsụ́ká, submitted to *Studies in African Linguistics.*

Fassi-Fehri, Abdelkader. 1987. "Generalized IP Structure, Case and VS word order." In *Actes du Premier Colloque International de la Société de Linguistique du Maroc*, 189–221.

Fromkin, Victoria. 1976. "A Note on Tone and the Abstractness Controversy." *Studies in African Linguistics.* Supplement 6, 47–62.

———. (ed.) 1978. *Tone: A Linguistic Aurvey.* New York: Academic Press.

Fujimura, Osamu. (ed.) 1974. *Three Dimensions of Linguistic Theory.* Tokyo: TEC.

Fukui, Naoki. 1986. "A Theory of Category Projection and its Application." Ph.D. dissertation, Massachusetts Institute of Technology, Cambridge.
Giegerich, Heinz J. 1985. *Metrical Phonology and Phonological Structure.* Cambridge: Cambridge University Press.
Goldsmith, John. 1976. "Autosegmental Phonology." Ph.D. dissertation, Massachusetts Institute of Technology, Cambridge. [Distributed by the Indiana University Linguistics Club, Bloomington. Published, New York: Garland, 1979.]
———. 1981a. "The Structures of Questions in Ìgbo." *Linguistic Analysis* 7, 367–93.
———. 1981b. "Complementizers and Root Sentences." *Linguistic Inquiry* 12, 541–74.
———. 1990. "The fallen angels." Ms., Department of Linguistics, University of Chicago.
Green, Margaret M. and G.Égembà Ìgwè. 1963. *A Descriptive Grammar of Ìgbo.* Berlin: Akademie.
Greenberg, Joseph H. 1963. *The Languages of Africa.* Bloomington: Indiana University Press.
Halle, Morris and Jean-Roger Vergnaud. 1982. "On the Framework of Autosegmental Phonology." In *The Structure of Phonological Representations*, edited by Harry van der Hulst and Norval Smith, 65–82. Also in *Proceedings of NELS 12*, edited by James Pustejovsky and Peter Sells, 97–115. Amherst, Mass.: GLSA.
Haraguchi, Shosuke. 1975. "The Tone Pattern of Japanese" Ph.D. dissertation, Massachusetts Institute of Technology, Cambridge.
Hayes, Bruce. 1986. "Inalterability in CV Phonology." *Language* 62, 321–51.
Higginbotham, James. 1985. "On Semantics." *Linguistic Inquiry* 16, 547–93.
Huang, C.-T. James. 1980. "The Metrical Structure of Terraced-level tones." In *Proceedings of NELS 10*, 257–70. Amherts, Mass.: GLSA.
Hyman, Larry M. 1972. "A Phonological Study of Fe?fe? Bamiléké." Supplement 4 to *Studies in African Linguistics.*
———. 1976. "The Great Ìgbo Tone Shift." In *Proceedings of the Third Conference on African Linguistics*, edited by Erhard Voeltz, 111–25. Bloomington: Indiana University Press.
———. 1978. "Historical Tonology." In *Tone: a Linguistic Survey*, edited by Victoria Fromkin, 257–69.
———. 1985. "Word Domains and Downstep in Bamiléké-Dschang." *Phonology Yearbook* 2, 47–83.
Hyman, Larry M. and Russell Schuh. 1974. "Universals of Tone Rules: Evidence from West Africa." *Linguistic Inquiry* 5, 81–115.
Hyman, Larry M. and Maurice Tadadjeu. 1976. "Floating Tones in Mbam-Nkam." In *Studies in Bantu Tonology*, edited by Larry M. Hyman, 57–111. Southern California Occasional Papers in Linguistics 3. Los Angeles: University of Southern California.
Íhìọ́nú, P.Ụ́zọ̀dínmá. 1988. "Tone and Specificity in Ìgbo." Paper presented to the Workshop on Tone, Accent and Locality in Niger-Congo, University of Massachusetts, Amherst, 14 November.
———. 1989. "The OV Syntax of Ìgbo." Paper Presented at the 3nd Niger-Congo Syntax and Semantics Workshop, Massachusetts Institute of Technology, Cambridge, 24 January.
Inkelas, Sharon, William Leben and Mark Cobler 1987. "The Phonology of Intonation in Hausa." In *Proceedings of NELS 18*, edited by James Blevins and Juli Carter, 327–42. Amherst, Mass.: GLSA.
Kamany, Honoré. 1988. "La structure syllabique du bamiléké." Master's thesis, Université du Québec à Montréal.
Kaye, Jonathan D. 1987. "Is There a Projection Principle in Phonology?" Paper presented at the 18th Conference on African Linguistics, Université du Québec à Montréal.
———. 1989. *Phonology: a Cognitive View.* Hillsdale (New Jersey): Lawrence Erlbaum.
Kaye, Jonathan D., Jean Lowenstamm and Jean-Roger Vergnaud. 1985. "The Internal Structure of Phonological Elements: a Theory of Charm and Government." *Phonology Yearbook* 2, 305–28.

Kaye, Jonathan D., Jean Lowenstamm and Jean-Roger Vergnaud. 1987. "Constituent Structure and Government in Phonology." *Phonology* 7, 193–232.
Kayne, Richard. 1984. *Connectedness and Binary Branching.* Dordrecht: Foris Publications.
Kiparsky, Paul V. 1974. "Phonological Representations." In *Three dimensions of Linguistic Theory*, edited by Osamu Fujimura, 5–86. Tokyo: TEC.
Koster, Jan. 1986. *Domains and Dynasties.* Dordrecht: Foris Publications.
Lániran, Yétúndé. 1991. "Intonation in Tone Languages: the Yorùbá Example." Ph.D. dissertation, Cornell University, Ithaka, NY.
Leben, William R. 1973. "Suprasegmental Phonology." Ph.D. dissertation, Massachusetts Institute of Technology, Cambridge. Published, New York: Garland Press.
Lieber, Rochelle. 1980. "On the Organization of the Lexicon." Ph.D. dissertation, Massachusetts Institue of Technology, Cambridge. [Distributed by the Indiana University Linguistics Club, Bloomington.]
Liberman, Mark Y. and Allan Prince. 1977. "On Stress and Linguistic Rhythm." *Linguistic Inquiry* 8, 249–336.
———. 1981. "Morphological Conversion within a Restrictive Theory of the Lexicon." In *The Scope of Lexical Rules*, edited by Teun Hoekstra, Harry van der Hulst, and Michael Moortgat, 161–200. Dordrecht: Foris Publications.
Manfredi, Victor. 1979. "Morphologization of Downstep in Ìgbo Dialects." Bachelor's thesis, Harvard University.
———. 1983a. "Surface Generalizations about Ìgbo Tone-bearing Units: Towards a Restriction on the Concept 'Tone Rule'." Paper presented at the 14th Conference on African Linguistics, Madison.
———. 1983b. "Èdo High-spreading and Ìgbo Downstep in Light of Each Other." Paper presented at the 4th Conference of the Linguistic Association of Nigeria, Benin-City.
———. 1984. "Abstractess and Ìgbo Verb Tone." Paper presented at the 5th Conference of the Linguistic Association of Nigeria, Nsuka
———. 1987. "Antilogophoricity as Domain Extension in Ìgbo and Yorùbá." In *Niger-Congo Syntax and Semantics.* Vol. 1, edited by Victor Manfredi, 97–117. Privately Published.
Meier, Paul, Ingé Meier and John Bendor-Samuel. 1975. *A Grammar of Izíì, an Ìgbo Language.* Normal, Okla.: Summer Institute of Linguistics/Wycliffe Bible Translators.
Nespor, Marina and Irene Vogel. 1986. *Prosodic Phonology.* Dordrecht: Foris Publications.
Nikiema, Emmanuel. 1988. "Onset-to-rime Government." Ms., Université du Québec à Montréal.
Nwáchukwu, P.Akujuoobì. 1966. "The Verb System of Èzínàíhìte West Dialect of Mbàisén in weré." Long Essay, University of Ìbàdàn.
———. 1976a. "Noun Phrase Sentential Complementation in Ìgbo." Ph.D. dissertation, University of London.
———. 1976b. "Stativity, Ergativity and the -rV Suffixes in Ìgbo." *African Languages/Langues africaines* 2, 119–42.
———. 1983. "Towards a Classification of Ìgbo verbs." In *Readings on the Igbo Verb.* Pilot edition, edited by P.Akujuoobì. Nwáchukwu, 17–42. Ònìcha: Africana-Far Eastern Publishers, for the Ìgbo Language Association.
———. 1985. "Inherent Complement Verbs in Ìgbo." *Journal of the Linguistic Association of Nigeria* 3, 61–74.
———. 1987. *The Argument Structure of Ìgbo Verbs.* Lexicon Project Working Papers 18. Cambridge: MIT Center for Cognitive Science.
Odden, David. 1982. "Tonal Phenomena in Kishambaa." *Studies in African Linguistics* 13, 177–208.
———. 1986. "On the Role of the Obligatory Contour Principle in Phonological Theory." *Language* 62, 353–83.
Oyèláràn, Olásopé O. 1970. "A Phonology of Yorùbá." Ph.D. dissertation, Stanford University.

Prunet, Jean-François. 1986. "Spreading and Locality Domains in Phonology." Ph.D. dissertation, McGill University, Montreal.
Pulleyblank, Douglas. 1983. "Tone in Lexical Phonology." Ph.D. dissertation, Massachusetts Institute of Technology, Cambridge. Published, Dordrecht: Reidel.
Ritter, Betsy. 1988. "A Head Movement Approach to Construct State Noun Phrases." *Linguistics* 26, 909–29.
Roberts, Ian. 1985. "Agreement Parameters and the Development of English Modal Auxiliaries." *Natural Language and Linguistic Theory* 3, 21–58.
Schachter, Paul. 1969. "Natural Assimilation Rules in Akan." *International Journal of American Linguistics* 35, 342–55.
Schachter, Paul and Victoria Fromkin. 1968. *A Phonology of Akan.* Working Papers in Phonetics 9. University of California, Los Angeles.
Schadeberg, Thilo C. 1986. "The Lexicostatistic Base of Bennett and Sterk's Reclassification of Niger-Congo with Particular Reference to the Cohesion of Bantu." *Studies in African Linguistics* 17, 69–83.
Stewart, John M. 1965. "The Typology of the Twi Tone System." Preprint from the *Bulletin of the Institute of African Studies (Legon)*, 1, 1–27.
———. 1971. "Niger-Congo: Kwa." In *Current Trends in Linguistics.* Vol. 7, *Linguistics in Sub-Saharan Africa*, edited by Thomas Sebeok, 179–212. The Hague: Mouton.
———. 1981. "Key Lowering (Downstep/Downglide) in Dschang." *Journal of African Languages and Linguistics* 3, 113–38.
———. 1983. "Downstep and Floating Low Tones in Adiukru." *Journal of African Languages and Linguistics* 5, 57–78.
Swift, Lloyd B., A. Ahághotù and E. Ùgóji [Ugorji]. 1962. *Ìgbo Basic Course.* Washington: Foreign Service Institute.
Tadadjeu, Maurice. 1974. "Floating tones, shifting rules and downstep in Dschang Bamiléké." In Supplement 5 to *Studies in African Linguistics* 283–90.
Travis, Lisa. 1988. *The Syntax of Adverbs.* McGill Working Papers in Linguistics Special issue on Comparative Germanic Syntax, edited by Denise Fekete and Zofia Laubitz, 280–310. McGill University, Montreal.
Uwaláàka, Marry A -A. 1982. "Ìgbo 'Consecutivization' Revisited." *Journal of the Linguistic Association of Nigeria* 1, 63–72.
Voorhoeve, Jan. 1971. *Tone Systems: the Theme Underlying the Variations* [trans. by F. Heny]. Leiden: Brill.
Voorhoeve, J., A.E. Meussen and K.F. de Blois. 1969. "New Proposals for the Description of the Ìgbo Completive Phrase." *Journal of West African Languages* 6, 79–84.
Welmers, William. E. 1963. "Associative a and ka in Niger-Congo." *Language* 39, 432–47.
———. 1970 "Ìgbo Tonology." *Studies in African Linguistics* 1, 255–78. [Reprinted in William E. Welmers. *African Language Structures.* Berkeley: University of California Press, 1973.]
Welmers, William. E. and Beatrice F. Welmers. 1968. *Ìgbo: a Learner's Manual.* Los Angeles: University of California at Los Angeles.
Williams, Edwin S. 1976. "Underlying Tone in Margi and Ìgbo." *Linguistic Inquiry* 7, 462–84.
Williamson, Kay R.M. 1970. "Some Alternative Proposals for the Ìgbo Completive Phrase." *Research Notes* (Ìbàdàn) 3, 83–90.
———. 1984. "Introduction." In *Ìgbo-English Dictionary* [2nd edition]. Benin City: Ethiope.
———. 1986. "The Ìgbo Associative and Specific Constructions." In *The Phonological representation of Suprasegmentals*, edited by Koen Bogers, Harry van der Hulst and Maarten Mous, 195–208. Dordrecht: Foris Publications.
———. 1989. "Niger-Congo Overview." In *The Niger-Congo Languages*, edited by John T. Bendor-Samuel, 3–45. Lanham, Maryland: American Universities Press for Wycliff Bible Translators and the Summer Institute of Linguistics.

Winston, Denis. 1973. "Polarity, Mood and Aspect in Ọhụhụn Ìgbo Verbs." *African Language Studies* 14, 119–78.
Wórùkwó, Glory. 1983. "The Verbal System of Ìkwére." Bachelor's thesis, University of Port Harcourt.

Dschang and Ebrie as Akan-type Total Downstep Languages

John M. Stewart

1. INTRODUCTION*

Meeussen (1970:270) coined the term "total downstep" some twenty years ago: "There seems to be a phenomenon which could be called 'total downstep', in which a high is not lowered just a little, but all the way to the next lower register." In this paper I distinguish between overt total downstep languages, which are immediately recognizable as such by Meeussen's criterion, and covert total downstep languages such as Akan, which Meeussen does not recognize as total downstep languages but which meet his criterion as soon as they are treated as having automatic downstep in the context [H_L] rather than in the context [L_H]: in the overt total downstep languages the [H$^!$H] drop is patently the same size as the [HL] drop, but in languages such as Akan there is no [HL] drop as [H$^!$L] occurs to the exclusion of [HL], and the [H$^!$L] drop is, as one would expect, twice the size of the [H$^!$H] drop.

Today's best-known and best-documented example of an overt total downstep language, and the one with which I shall be mainly concerned here, is Kikuyu, which Meeussen does not mention: recognition of downstep in Kikuyu came only with the work of Ford in the early 1970s, and the present pre-eminence of Kikuyu on the tonological scene only with Ford's subsequent collaboration with Clements. For references, and more on the history of Kikuyu tonology, see Clements (1984:281–2).

Clements (1983:166–7) endorses Meeussen's "total downstep", and goes on to posit a major typological division between "total" downstep languages such as Kikuyu and "partial" downstep languages such as Igbo and Akan: "The essential characteristic of languages with 'total' downstep is that pitch contours are much more narrowly specified than in 'partial' downstep systems. In particular, an adequate theory of 'total' downstep must account for the fact that all other factors being equal, there is *never* a systematic pitch difference between the sequences H-L and H-$^!$H,

---

* I have profited greatly from extensive comments by Larry M. Hyman and Constance Kutsch Lojenga on an earlier version of this paper, but I remain of course solely responsible for its deficiencies and for the views expressed.

or between the sequences L-L and L-$^!$H." It was in reaction to this that I first pointed out (Stewart 1983a:70–1) that the supposedly crucial difference between languages such as Kikuyu and languages such as Akan is reducible to differences in the tonal sequence structure conditions, those of Kikuyu allowing [HL] but not [H$^!$L] and those of Akan allowing [H$^!$L] but not [HL]; and that such differences do not warrant major differences in the descriptive apparatus such as those proposed by Clements (1983:167–8).

In my earlier (1983a) paper I extend to Akan-type languages what I see as the essence of Clements's (1983) treatment of total downstep languages, namely his analysis of downstep as a floating low tone. For Adioukrou, an Akan-type language, as well as for Akan itself, I propose an "H-lag" rule which applies wherever a linked L would otherwise occur in the inadmissible context H_; "H-lag" spreads the H to the TBU of the L (TBU = tone-bearing unit), dislodging the L and leaving it unlinked. As the unlinked L is realized as downstep, "H-lag" has the effect of creating not only non-automatic downsteps before H (as it gives [HH$^!$H] where we would otherwise have [HLH]), but also automatic downsteps before L (as it gives [HH$^!$L] where we would otherwise have [HLL]). This in itself, I suggest, invalidates the following claim made by Clements (1983:170) in support of his major typological division: "While it is natural enough to interpret the symbol [$^!$] as a floating Low tone in Kikuyu tonal representations, where we find no downdrift of a consistent nature, it would be totally unmotivated to treat [systematic] downdrift ([Stewart's(1965)] automatic downstep) in H-L-H sequences as a function of floating tones in languages like Igbo and Akan." (Note incidentally that Clements's notion of "systematic downdrift" (1983:154, 166), which he here identifies with my automatic downstep, is in fact incompatible with my notion of downstep and downdrift as binary and postbinary respectively.)[1]

---

1 My term "automatic downstep" originally represented a revision of Winston's "automatic downdrift", and reflected my disagreement with Winston as to the phonological status of the phenomenon; he writes as follows on the situation in Efik (1960:189): "Although downstep and automatic downdrift have a similar phonetic effect, they must be clearly distinguished from the point of view of distribution and function. Automatic downdrift is normal when peaks and valleys follow one another; it is conditioned by these circumstances and has no other significance. Downstep, on the other hand, occurs arbitrarily and normally distinguishes or helps to distinguish some particular meaning or syntactical relationship, or both." Here, "downdrift" (the "automatic" is redundant) is synonymous with "declination"; in those days it was never used in any other sense as far as I am aware.

Winston, despite his recognition of the "similar phonetic effect", had continued to subscribe to the then prevailing view that the phenomenon in question was simply a matter of downdrift and thus had no phonological status. I saw the fact that the phenomenon was

In the present paper I begin with a revised version of my (1983a) analysis of Akan as a total downstep language with automatic downstep in the context [H_L]. The main revision (already foreshadowed in Stewart 1983b:132–3) concerns the status of the floating low tone which is realized as a downstep: I now explicitly recognize it as a third tonal autosegment l, distinguished from its non-floating counterpart L̲ in terms of a binary feature category [stepping] and realized as a downward stepping of the tone level frame to the point at which a following H would be level with a preceding L̲. This makes it possible, for all the material examined in this paper, to formulate all the postlexical tone rules as automatic rules serving structure conditions; the "H-lag" rule, for instance, is replaced by two separate automatic rules: a low tone stepping rule which changes L̲ to l in the service of a purely tonal sequence structure condition which disallows HL̲, and a tone spreading rule which relinks to the preceding tone any TBU left unlinked by the change from L̲ to l (a [+stepping] tone cannot of course be linked) in the service of a structure condition which disallows an unlinked TBU after a linked TBU. (Note that although a [+stepping] tone cannot be linked, a [–stepping] tone can be unlinked; and that when it is an unlinked L̲ that is changed to l by the low tone stepping rule, no TBU is left unlinked.)

I go on to explore the applicability of my total downstep treatment to two tonally well-documented languages which resemble Akan in having (at least) the three-way contrast [0 down]/[1 down]/[2 down] after a high tone, but which differ from Akan in also having a three-way contrast [–2 down]/[–1 down]/[0 down] after a low tone; Akan, of course, while it has the three-way contrast [HH][0 down]/[H¹H][1 down]/[H¹L][2 down] after [H], has only the two-way contrast [LH][–1 down]/[LL][0 down] after [L]. The first of these two languages is Dschang, which, like Akan, is a downstep language by any definition, and the second Ebrié, which, although it has many of the characteristics of a downstep language, appears on the surface to be a discrete level tone language with three tone levels.

I suggest that the tone systems of these languages differ from that of Akan basically in that they do not have the tonal segment structure condition which in Akan disallows the [+high, +stepping] segment h, and that their [–2 down] is analysable as LhH [L$_i$H] ($_i$ = upstep) just

---

automatic as no obstacle to treating it as downstep, which, as Winston put it, had "fully 'phonemic' status" (1960:188); few if any phonemicists, after all, would have denied the phonological status of the **p** of English **empty** on the grounds that it was automatic in precisely this sense.

The original authors of the notion of systematic downdrift would appear to be Schachter and Fromkin (1968:106–9).

as their [2 down], like that of Akan, is analysable as HIL [H¹L]. I also suggest that these languages have not only automatic downstep (i.e. HIL to the exclusion of HL) but also automatic upstep (i.e. LhH to the exclusion of LH), that Ebrié [ML][1 down] (M = "mid" tone) is analysable as Hh(H)IL [-1 +2 = 1 down] ((H) = unlinked linking H), and that both Ebrié [LM][-1 down] and Dschang [-1 down] are analysable as Lh(H)lH [-2 +1 = -1 down].

Thus just as my earlier (1983a) paper challenges the recognition of a major typological division between languages such as Akan and "total downstep" languages in Meeussen's narrow sense and proposes a common descriptive apparatus, so the present paper challenges the recognition of a major typological division between languages such as Akan and Kikuyu on the one hand and, on the other, discrete level tone languages such as Ebrié, and shows that the descriptive apparatus devised for the former can accommodate the latter also.

2. AKAN

2.1. Total downstep, whole numbers, and integer-assigning algorithms

I adopt, though only as an illustrative device for showing the number of steps up or down at any point, the following modified version of Clements's (1983:167) integer-assigning algorithm for the "pitch interpretation" of total downstep languages:

(1)   a. Each tone level is numbered 1, 2, ..., n, starting from the highest;
        b. An increment of 1 is added to each tone for each stepping low tone to its left.

("Each stepping low tone to its left" replaces Clements's "each low dominating it in the tree"; his tree shows the depth of embedding of any tone within downstepped "registers", and the increments assigned by (1b) reflect this depth of embedding. His tree, like his algorithm, is an integral part of his descriptive apparatus but not of mine; any such tree would be incompatible with my claim that the floating/stepping low tone is realized not indirectly by a lowering effect on all the tones to the right but directly by a downward stepping of the tone level frame at the point in question). The following Kikuyu example illustrates:

Stewart: Dschang and Ebrié as Akan-type total downstep languages 189

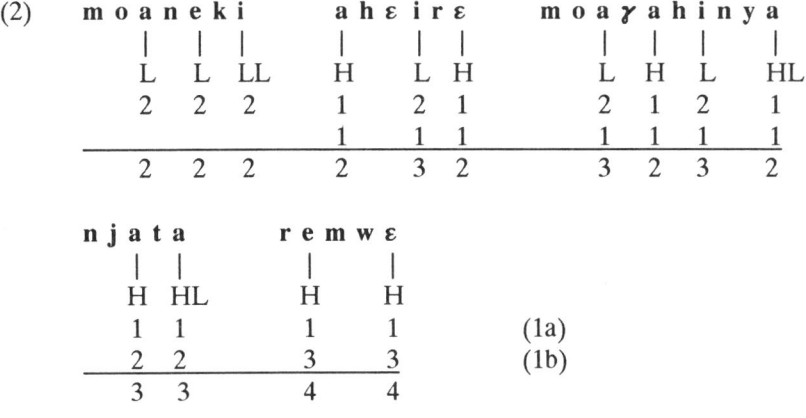

moànèkìˈ áhɛìrɛ́ moàɣáhìnyáˈ njátáˈ rémwɛ́
'Mwaniki gave   (the) weakling stars   once.'

Note that the appropriateness of the whole numbers is a consequence of the totality of the downstep, or, in other words, a consequence of the realization of the stepping low tone as a downward stepping of the tone level frame by an interval of the same size as that which separates the two tone levels; note in particular that the [LL] and [LᶦH] intervals are both [0 down], being made up in the latter case of the [LH] interval [−1 down] plus the downstep interval [1 down].

Compare the application of the same rules in the case of the following "hypothetical sequence which might occur in Igbo or Twi[-Akan]" cited by Hyman (1979:19):

(3) τ τ τ τ τ τ τ τ τ τ   (τ = tone-bearing
     | | | | | | | | | | unit)
     HL L HL HL L HL L HL HL L
     1 2 1 1 2 1 2 1 1 2   (1a)
        1 1 2 3 3 4 4 5 6   (1b)
     1 3 2 3 5 4 6 5 6 8

     Hᶦ L Hᶦ Hᶦ L Hᶦ L Hᶦ Hᶦ L

Note that the [HᶦL] interval is [2 down], or twice the size of the [HᶦH] interval, being made up of the [HL] interval [1 down] plus the downstep interval [1 down].

The following is a telescoped version of Hyman's own treatment of the same hypothetical sequence:

(4)
H	L	ꜜH	ꜜH	L	ꜜH	L	ꜜH	ꜜH	L
1	3	1	1	3	1	3	1	1	3
		1	2	2	3	3	4	5	5
1	3	2	3	5	4	6	5	6	8

Here note the following points:

(5) a. In the second row of integers an increment of 1 is added to each tone for each downstep to its left, just as in (1b) an increment of 1 is added to each tone for each stepping low tone to its left.
 b. In the first row of integers the low tone level is numbered 3, not 2, the interval between H and L being taken to be twice the size of the downstep interval.
 c. The bottom row, however, is identical to that of (3).

It will be seen that Hyman's second row of integers differs from mine purely as a consequence of the fact he posits [HLꜜH] sequences instead of [HꜜLH] sequences; and that if this is changed, the low tone level has to be numbered 2, not 3, under (5b), with the result that his first row of integers also becomes the same as mine.

It should be noted that if the hypothetical sequence in (3) and (4) had begun with L instead of H, the initial L would have been numbered 2 in (3) and 3 in (4), and the numbers in the bottom row in (4) would thus not have been identical to those in (3) but would have been 1 higher throughout. This, however, does not matter, as what matters is not the size of the numbers but the size of the differences between them.

One great advantage of rejecting Hyman's [HL$_Q$ꜜH] sequences in favour of [HꜜL$_Q$H] sequences (L$_Q$ = a maximum sequence of Ls) is that it allows us to say that just as Kikuyu, which has [HL] to the exclusion of [HꜜL], has an automatic rule of low tone deletion which applies wherever [HꜜL] would otherwise occur, so Akan and Adioukrou (though not all languages similarly analysable as having [HꜜL] to the exclusion of [HL]) have an automatic rule of low tone stepping which applies wherever [HL] would otherwise occur; see the next subsection.

2.2. Sequence structure conditions and the automatic rules which serve them

2.3. "Downstep Displacement" in Kikuyu

In Kikuyu, "High tones may be contrastively downstepped after either High or Low tones, while Low tones may be contrastively downstepped after Low tones" (Clements 1983:167); the only condition on downstep between two linked tones is the one we have seen already, namely that which excludes [H¹L]. Wherever this condition would otherwise be violated by the occurrence of an [L]-initial word after an [H¹]-final word, Clements and Ford's "Downstep Displacement" applies: "This process applies to any downstep occurring between a high tone and a low tone, and shifts the downstep rightward across the low tone, or low tone sequence, until the first high tone, or the end of the sentence, is reached; the low tones are concomitantly raised to high. ... Using the subscript-Q notation to indicate ... a maximal string of the designated item, and interpreting a rule change applying to such a string as carrying out the stipulated change individually on each member of the string, we may state this rule as follows:

Downstep Displacement $^!L_Q \rightarrow H_Q^! / H\_$

This rule has the effect of eliminating pitch drops of two intervals from representations ..." (Clements and Ford 1977:225–6).

I restate this in (6) in terms of three tonal autosegments and as two separate rules, each of them an automatic rule (A-rule) serving a structure condition (on the lines of proposals by Stewart 1983b and Schadeberg 1986):

(6) a. (Kikuyu) SC1:   NOT H1L̲   1 = stepping low tone
                                          L̲ = linking low tone

     b.   SC1A Low Deletion (LDel): L̲ → ∅ / H1_

     c.   SC2:   NOT τ τ̂   τ̂ = unlinked τ
                             |
                             T

     d.   SC2A Tone Spreading (TSpr): τ τ̂
                                                |⁄
                                                T

     SC = Structure Condition
     A = Automatic rule

(6a–b) says that H1L̲ is disallowed, and that wherever it would otherwise occur, the L̲ is deleted (by LDel). (6c–d) says that an unlinked TBU is disallowed after a linked TBU, and that whenever an unlinked TBU would otherwise occur in this context (as for instance in the wake of LDel), it is linked to the linking tone on the left (by TSpr). Where there is more than one L, each rule reapplies as often as is necessary:

192 *The representation of tonal register*

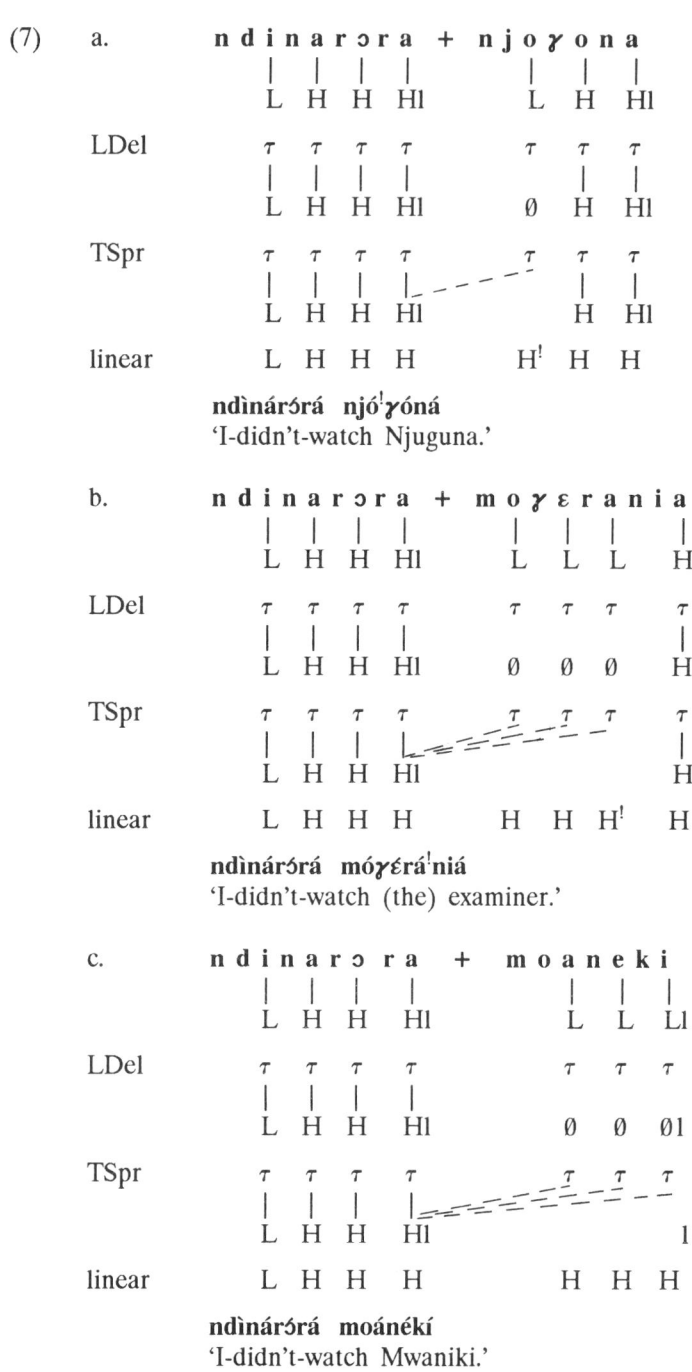

Note that as the phonetic realization of a stepping tone depends on there being at least one linked tone both before it and after it, the sentence-final l in (7a) and the sentence-final ll in (7c) have no phonetic realization. Note also that the context Hl_ is mentioned in (6b) only as an aid to clarity; the context is in fact simply that of the L̲ in (6a). Any such redundant material should of course be disregarded in the evaluation of the complexity of any A-rule.

2.3.1. Low tone stepping in Akan

Akan differs from Kikuyu firstly in that in Akan a downstep may not follow a low tone, and secondly in that whereas Kikuyu has [HL] to the exclusion of [H¹L], Akan has [H¹L] to the exclusion of [HL]. Downstep is thus contrastive only in the context [H_H] (where it is said to constitute non-automatic downstep), but also occurs non-contrastively in the context [H_L] (where it is said to constitute automatic downstep). The condition which disallows [HL] and the A-rule which serves it may be stated as in (8a–b):

(8)   a.   (Akan)   SC1: NOT HL̲

   b.   SC1A Low Stepping (LStep):   L̲ → 1 / H_

   c.   SC2: NOT τ τ̃
                        |
                        T

   d.   SC2A Tone Spreading (TSpr):   τ   τ̃
                                            |₋₋
                                            T

(8a–b) says that L̲ may not follow H, and that an L̲ which would otherwise violate this condition is replaced by l. (8c–d) says for Akan precisely what (6c–d) says for Kikuyu, namely that an unlinked TBU (such as typically results from the application of Kikuyu Low Deletion or Akan Low Stepping) is inadmissible after a linked TBU, and is linked by Tone Spreading to the linking tone on the left. The examples in (9a) and (9c) illustrate the operation of both A-rules at word boundaries:

194 *The representation of tonal register*

(9) a.

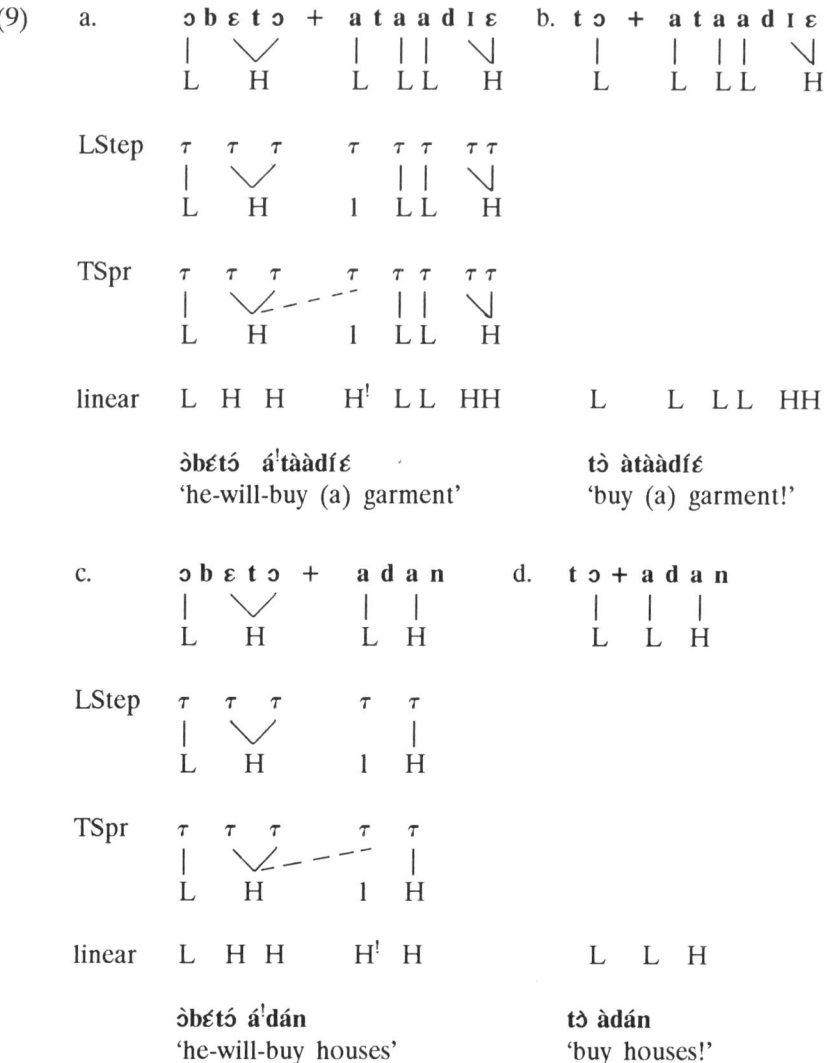

Note that LStep results in an [H¹L] sequence in (9a) and in an [H¹H] sequence in (9c).

Now consider (10), in which the object nouns, like those in (9), have linking low tone prefixes, but in which the prefixes, unlike those in (9), are unrepresented on the segmental tier:

(10) a. ɔbɛtɔ + kawa   b. tɔ + kawa
         | \/ | | | | |
         L H   L L H   L   L L H

LStep   L H   l L H   L   L H

linear   L H H ! L H   L   L H

         ɔ̀bɛ́tɔ́ ˈkàwá   tɔ̀ kàwá
         'he-will-buy (a) ring'   'buy (a) ring!'

c. ɔbɛtɔ + dan   d. tɔ + dan
    | \/ | | |
    L H   L H   L   L H

LStep   L H   l H   L H

linear   L H H ! H   L   H

         ɔ̀bɛ́tɔ́ ˈdán   tɔ̀ dán
         'he-will-buy (a) house'   'buy (a) house!'

Note that LStep applies regardless of whether the L is linked or not (though it can lead to TSpr only where the L is linked), and that it results in [H¹L] and [H¹H] sequences in (10a) and (10c) respectively just as it does in (9a) and (9c) respectively. Note also that, as (10b) and (10d) illustrate, an unlinked L which survives to the surface has no phonetic realization.

An unlinked L may survive to the surface only before or after L or pause; a condition which disallows it in the context l_H is served by an A-rule of Contour Formation (CForm) which links it to the TBU to the left, as we see in (11a):

(11) a. ɔtɔ + dan   Cf. b. ɔtɔ + kawa
         | | | | | | |
         L Hl   L H   L Hl   L L H

CForm   τ τ   τ
         | |⎯⎯⎯⎯⎯ |
         L Hl   L H

linear   L H͡L   H   L H ! L H

         ɔ̀tɔ́ˡ⸍ dán   ɔ̀tɔ́ ˈkàwá
         'he-buys (a) house'   'he-buys (a) ring'

196   *The representation of tonal register*

3. DSCHANG

3.1. The distribution of downstep and upstep

My analysis of automatic downstep in languages like Akan as obligatory l in the context H _ L leads me to challenge the assumption, shared by all previous writers on Dschang from Tadadjeu (1974) onwards, myself (1981) included, that Dschang does not have automatic downstep. By the alternative analysis which I now propose, Dschang has not only automatic downstep but also automatic upstep (i.e. obligatory h in the context L̲ _ H̲); and the alleged [HLH] sequences which have been generally accepted as evidence of the absence of automatic downstep are [H$^!$L$_i$H] sequences, in which the second [H] has the same pitch realization as the first not because it is not downstepped but because it is both downstepped and upstepped.

Hyman (1979:18), who is the leading writer on Dschang, claims that his integer-assigning algorithm for downstep languages is valid not only for languages such as Igbo or Akan (see the illustration in (4) above) but for Dschang also; he applies it essentially as follows to a hypothetical Dschang sequence:

(12) H   L $^!$H   L   H $^!$H   L $^!$H $^{!!}$H   L
      1   3   1   3   1   1   3   1   1   3
               1   1   1   2   2   3   5   5
      ───
      1   3   2   4   2   3   5   4   6   8

Note in particular that as in his treatment of automatic downstep languages such as Akan, he takes the interval between H and L to be twice the size of the downstep interval.

Compare the total downstep alternative which I now propose:

(13)   Hl   Lh   (H)   lHl   Lh   Hl   Hl   Lh   (H)   lHl   (H)   lHl   L
              1   2   1   2   1   1   2   1   1   2
       plus   1   2   3   3   4   5   6   8   9
              ──
              1   3   3   5   4   5   7   7   9   11
       minus   1   1   2   2   2   3   3   3
              ──
              1   3   2   4   2   3   5   4   6   8

                                                       (H) = unlinked linking H

Here, in the first row of integers, the low tone level is numbered 2, not 3, and in the second and fourth rows respectively the number for each non-stepping tone is +1 for each stepping low tone (l) to the left and −1 for each stepping high tone (h) to the left. The integers on the bottom row are the same as Hyman's. Unlinked linking tones are ignored.

My present analysis of the various intervals corresponds as follows to Hyman's:

(14) a. Found in Hyman's data on the associative construction

	Hyman	Stewart
[-2 down]	LH	LhH
[-1 down]	L¡H	Lh(H)lH
[0 down]	LL, HH	L(L), H
[1 down]	H¡H, L¡L	HlH, LlL
[2 down]	HL	HlL

b. Not found in Hyman's data on the associative construction

	Hyman	Stewart
[2 down]	H"H	Hl(H)lH
[3 down]	H¡L	Hl(H)lL

Note that my Hl(H)lH and Hl(H)lL (Hyman's H"H and H¡L), which Hyman (1979:15) shows to be comparable with each other, both fail to occur in the data on the associative "N_1 of N_2" construction on which most of the discussion of the Dschang tonal system has focussed up to now; I shall not consider them further here, but I would point out in passing that their comparability with each other is more clearly reflected in my analysis than in Hyman's own.

There is a four-way tonal contrast in nouns (including nominal infinitives) consisting of a low tone prefix plus a monosyllabic stem; it is as in (15a–d) after the lexical rules have applied:

(15) a. lə-tɔŋ   b. lə-tɔŋ   c. lə-tɔŋ   d. lə-tɔŋ
         | | | | | | | /\
         L L   L LhH   L hHlH   L LhH

linear   L L   L   L °   L   H   L   L̂ᵢH

         lətɔ̀ŋ   lətɔ̀ŋ°   lətɔ́ŋ   lətɔ̀ᵢ´ŋ
         'to reimburse' 'navel'   'to call'   'feather'

     e. -n a   f. -k a ŋ   g. -s ə ŋ
          | | |
          L L   L   LhH   L   hH

linear   L   L °   H

          nà   kàŋ°   sə́ŋ
          'animal'   'squirrel'   'bird'

In the linear representation the nouns are in their prepausal form; L° is a prepausal L (prepausal in linear terms, that is) which differs from an unmarked prepausal L in that it is non-falling, or "non-downgliding". Note, however, that I accord the linear representation no theoretical status, and that by the present analysis[2] the absence of "downglide" is merely a phonetic consequence of the fact that autosegmentally, the L is not prepausal but is followed by an h(H) sequence (which, of course, has no direct realization of its own).

The nouns in (15e–g) differ from those in (15a–d) in that their prefixes, like those of the Akan nouns seen in (10) above, are unrepresented on the segmental tier. In addition, the noun in (15g) differs from that in (15d) in that its stem has no initial L and thus no contour. Note that there are no nouns in which the prefix is unrepresented on the segmental tier and the stem has the sequence h(H)lH as it does in (15c).

Compare the output of the lexical rules in (15) with the output of one of Hyman's versions of the lexical rules (1985:48, 58–9):

---

[2] In my 1981 analysis downstep and "downglide" were treated as being in complementary distribution and as constituting different manifestations of a single phenomenon of "key lowering", with "downglide" occurring prepausally and downstep elsewhere; the L/L° distinction was accordingly represented as L!/L and recognized as having phonological status. This treatment reflected (a) an assumption about Akan which I made at the time but subsequently abandoned in my 1983a paper (see Introduction and section 2.1 above), namely that automatic downstep occurred in the context HL_H (and not in the context H_LH), and (b) a suggestion which I had made earlier that (in Akan) "key lowering can [generally] be considered to occur at the end of every low tone syllable which is not followed by another low tone syllable; where it is non-final it is manifested as lowering of the pitch of all the subsequent high tones, and where it is final it is manifested as a slight fall towards the end of the final syllable" (Stewart 1971:185). This suggestion appeared to offer the possibility of explaining automatic downstep in terms of "downglide"; I saw "a case for taking downglide to be the more basic of the two manifestations since, if we postulate it in both contexts in sub-surface phonology, we can plausibly treat the other manifestation, namely downstep, as secondary to it; we can say that in a HLH sequence the pitch interval which separates the end of the L from the following H is the same as that which separates the beginning of the L from the preceding H, but that the following H has a lower pitch than the preceding H as the LH interval starts from the bottom of the downglide at the end of the L. The fact that in surface phonology there is no downglide in this context can be covered by a surface rule deleting downglide in non-final position." (1971:185). Once it is accepted that automatic downstep occurs not in the context HL_H but in the context H_LH, of course, the possibility of deriving automatic downstep from "downglide" no longer exists, and in any case the analysis of "downglide" as ! could be retained only at the price of admitting an exception to the new generalization that (in Akan) ! occurs only after H.

(16) a. l ə - t ɔ ŋ   b. l ə - t ɔ ŋ   c. l ə - t ɔ ŋ   d. l ə -t ɔ ŋ
      | | | | | | | |
      L   L   L   LH   L   LH   L   H

     e.   n a   f.   k a ŋ   g.   s ə ŋ
             | | |
            L   LH   H

The LLH of (16c) is derived from LHL, in which the final L is unlinked like the final H in (16b), by a rule of "L-metathesis". The contour which I posit in (15d) but not in (15g) is absent in (16d) as Hyman derives it by a postlexical rule. The tone-only prefix which I posit in (15e–g) is likewise absent in (16e–g); Hyman posits the absence of any prefix.

Hyman's (1985:50–1) data on the tones in the "N_1 of N_2" associative construction are retranscribed in tables 1 and 2, with the omission of those combinations in which N_2 has the tone pattern L-Lh(H) illustrated in (15b) and (15f); the postlexical rules which apply in these combinations are exactly the same as those which apply in the corresponding combinations in which N_2 has the tone pattern L-L illustrated in (15a) and (15e). The lexical representations to the left of the arrows are autosegmental, with the autosegments L̲, H̲, l, h transcribed as ˋ, ˊ, ¦, ᵢ respectively to save space.

An accent which is not written over a TBU may represent either a tone which is linked to an adjacent TBU and which forms part of a contour (as for instance in à-sàᵢˊŋ 'tail'), or an unlinked linking tone; in the latter case ° is written between the accent and the adjacent TBU where there is no hyphen there already, thus: n̄-dzà°ᵢˊ 'axe', màm-ᵢˊ°¦bhú 'dogs'. The postlexical representations to the right of the arrows are linear. The prefixes of all the nouns in table 1, of all the nouns at N_1 in table 2, and of the L-hHlH noun V̀-ᵢˊ°¦mɔ́ 'child' at N_2 in table 2 are, like those of the nouns in (15a–d), represented on the segmental tier, while the prefix of the remaining nouns at N_2 is, like that of the nouns in (15e–g), unrepresented on the segmental tier. The associative marker è in 1–12 of each table is that of classes 1 and 9, and the associative marker á in 13–24 of each table is that of class 7.

I assume that the associative marker is the marker of an associative form of the second noun, and I have enclosed this associative form in brackets in Tables 1 and 2. The tone rules apply within the brackets in the first instance; the rules applying within the brackets and those applying after the removal of the brackets are discussed in the next two subsections respectively.

Table 1
24 tone combinations of bisyllabic nouns in the
"N₁ of N₂" associative construction

1. è-fɔ̀   + [è + màn-dzwì]   → èfɔ̀ màndzwì   'chief of leopards'
2. è-fɔ̀   + [è + màm-ᵢ´ᵒ¦bhʉ́] → èfɔ̀ màmbhʉ́   'chief of dogs'
3. è-fɔ̀   + [è + mà-tsɔ̀ᵢ´ŋ]   → èfɔ̀ màtsɔ̀ᵢ´ŋ   'chief of thieves'
4. ǹ-dzàᵒᵢ´   + [è + màn-dzwì]   → ǹdzà ¦àmàndzwì   'axe of leopards'
5. ǹ-dzàᵒᵢ´   + [è + màm-ᵢ´ᵒ¦bhʉ́] → ǹdzà ¦àmàmbhʉ́   'axe of dogs'
6. ǹ-dzàᵒᵢ´   + [è + mà-tsɔ̀ᵢ´ŋ]   → ǹdzà ¦àmàtsɔ̀ᵢ´ŋ   'axe of thieves'
7. ǹ-ᵢ´ᵒ¦dɔ́ŋ + [è + màn-dzwì]   → ǹ¦dɔ̀ŋ màndzwì   'horn of leopards'
8. ǹ-ᵢ´ᵒ¦dɔ́ŋ + [è + màm-ᵢ´ᵒ¦bhʉ́] → ǹ¦dɔ̀ŋ màmbhʉ́   'horn of dogs'
9. ǹ-ᵢ´ᵒ¦dɔ́ŋ + [è + mà-tsɔ̀ᵢ´ŋ]   → ǹ¦dɔ̀ŋ màtsɔ̀ᵢ´ŋ   'horn of thieves'
10. ɲ̀-ɲìᵢ´   + [è + màn-dzwì]   → ɲ̀ɲìᵢ´ ¦màndzwì   'machete of leopards'
11. ɲ̀-ɲìᵢ´   + [è + màm-ᵢ´ᵒ¦bhʉ́] → ɲ̀ɲìᵢ´ ¦màmbhʉ́   'machete of dogs'
12. ɲ̀-ɲìᵢ´   + [è + mà-tsɔ̀ᵢ´ŋ]   → ɲ̀ɲìᵢ´ ¦màtsɔ̀ᵢ´ŋ   'machete of thieves'
13. à-zɔ̀b   + [á + màn-dzwì]   → àzɔ̀b ɔ̀màn¦dzwì   'song of leopards'
14. à-zɔ̀b   + [á + màm-ᵢ´ᵒ¦bhʉ́] → àzɔ̀b ɔ̀mámbhʉ́   'song of dogs'
15. à-zɔ̀b   + [á + mà-tsɔ̀ᵢ´ŋ]   → àzɔ̀b ɔ̀mátsɔ́ŋ   'song of thieves'
16. à-làŋᵒᵢ´   + [á + màn-dzwì]   → àlàŋ àmàn¦dzwì   'stool of leopards'
17. à-làŋᵒᵢ´   + [á + màm-ᵢ´ᵒ¦bhʉ́] → àlàŋ àmámbhʉ́   'stool of dogs'
18. à-làŋᵒᵢ´   + [á + mà-tsɔ̀ᵢ´ŋ]   → àlàŋ àmátsɔ́ŋ   'stool of thieves'
19. à-ᵢ´ᵒ¦lá? + [á + màn-dzwì]   → àlá? ámán¦dzwì   'country of leopards'
20. à-ᵢ´ᵒ¦lá? + [á + màm-ᵢ´ᵒ¦bhʉ́] → àlá? ámám¦bhʉ́   'country of dogs'
21. à-ᵢ´ᵒ¦lá? + [á + mà-tsɔ̀ᵢ´ŋ]   → àlá? ámə́¦tsɔ́ŋ   'country of thieves'
22. à-sàᵢ´ŋ   + [á + màn-dzwì]   → àᵢsáŋ ámán¦dzwì   'tail of leopards'
23. à-sàᵢ´ŋ   + [á + màm-ᵢ´ᵒ¦bhʉ́] → àᵢsáŋ ámám¦bhʉ́   'tail of dogs'
24. à-sàᵢ´ŋ   + [á + mà-tsɔ̀ᵢ´ŋ]   → àᵢsáŋ ámə́¦tsɔ́ŋ   'tail of thieves'

Table 2
24 further "N_1 of N_2" tone combinations

1.	è-fɔ̀	+ [è + ˋ-nà]	→	èfɔ̀ nà	'chief of animal'
2.	è-fɔ̀	+ [è + V̀-ᵢ´ᵒˈmɔ́]	→	èfɔ̀ mɔ́	'chief of child'
3.	è-fɔ̀	+ [è + ˋ-ᵢsə́ŋ]	→	èfɔ̀ ᵢsə́ŋ	'chief of bird'
4.	ǹ-dzàᵒᵢ´	+ [è + ˋ-nà]	→	ǹdzà ˈnà	'axe of animal'
5.	ǹ-dzàᵒᵢ´	+ [è + V̀-ᵢ´ᵒˈmɔ́]	→	ǹdzà ˈàmɔ́	'axe of child'
6.	ǹ-dzàᵒᵢ´	+ [è + ˋ-ᵢsə́ŋ]	→	ǹdzà ásə́ŋ	'axe of bird'
7.	ǹ-ᵢ´ᵒˈdɔ́ŋ	+ [è + ˋ-nà]	→	ǹˈdɔ̀ŋ nà	'horn of animal'
8.	ǹ-ᵢ´ᵒˈdɔ́ŋ	+ [è + V̀-ᵢ´ᵒˈmɔ́]	→	ǹˈdɔ̀ŋ mɔ́	'horn of child'
9.	ǹ-ᵢ´ᵒˈdɔ́ŋ	+ [è + ˋ-ᵢsə́ŋ]	→	ǹˈdɔ̀ŋ ᵢsə́ŋ	'horn of bird'
10.	ɲ̀-ɲìᵢ´	+ [è + ˋ-nà]	→	ɲ̀ɲìᵢ´ ˈnà	'machete of animal'
11.	ɲ̀-ɲìᵢ´	+ [è + V̀-ᵢ´ᵒˈmɔ́]	→	ɲ̀ɲìᵢ´ ˈmɔ́	'machete of child'
12.	ɲ̀-ɲìᵢ´	+ [è + ˋ-ᵢsə́ŋ]	→	ɲ̀ɲìᵢ´ ˈsə́ŋ	'machete of bird'
13.	à-zɔ̀b	+ [á + ˋ-nà]	→	àzɔ̀b ɔ̀nà	'song of animal'
14.	à-zɔ̀b	+ [á + V̀-ᵢ´ᵒˈmɔ́]	→	àzɔ̀b ɔ́mɔ́	'song of child'
15.	à-zɔ̀b	+ [á + ˋ-ᵢsə́ŋ]	→	àzɔ̀b ɔ̀ᵢsə́ŋ	'song of bird'
16.	à-ləŋᵒᵢ´	+ [á + ˋ-nà]	→	àləŋ ə̀nà	'stool of animal'
17.	à-ləŋᵒᵢ´	+ [á + V̀-ᵢ´ᵒˈmɔ́]	→	àləŋ ə́mɔ́	'stool of child'
18.	à-ləŋᵒᵢ´	+ [á + ˋ-ᵢsə́ŋ]	→	àləŋ ə̀ᵢsə́ŋ	'stool of bird'
19.	à-ᵢ´ᵒˈláʔ	+ [á + ˋ-nà]	→	àláʔ áˈnà	'country of animal'
20.	à-ᵢ´ᵒˈláʔ	+ [á + V̀-ᵢ´ᵒˈmɔ́]	→	àláʔ áˈmɔ́	'country of child'
21.	à-ᵢ´ᵒˈláʔ	+ [á + ˋ-ᵢsə́ŋ]	→	àláʔ ásə́ŋ	'country of bird'
22.	à-sàᵢ´ŋ	+ [á + ˋ-nà]	→	àᵢsáŋ áˈnà	'tail of animal'
23.	à-sàᵢ´ŋ	+ [á + V̀-ᵢ´ᵒˈmɔ́]	→	àᵢsáŋ áˈmɔ́	'tail of child'
24.	à-sàᵢ´ŋ	+ [á + ˋ-ᵢsə́ŋ]	→	àᵢsáŋ ásə́ŋ	'tail of bird'

3.2. The tones of the associative form of the noun

The derivations in (17) illustrate all the tone rules which apply internally within the associative form of the noun. Where, as in (17a–f), the associative marker has low tone, no tone rules apply. Where, as in (17g–m), the associative marker has high tone, an HL sequence arises as the L of the nominal prefix invariably follows, and as we have already seen, this sequence is, as in Akan, inadmissible in any context. Where, as in (17g–j) and (17l), the nominal prefix is represented on the segmental tier, a Low Stepping (LStep) rule identical to that of Akan applies, and a Tone Spreading (TSpr) rule identical to that of Akan, and serving an identical condition, applies in its wake. Where, however, as in (17k) and (17m), the prefix is not segmentally represented and the L is thus unlinked, the H of the associative marker is deleted by a rule of Pre-Floater High Deletion (PFHDel); PFHDel serves the same condition as LStep, and bleeds LStep by deleting an initial H before an unlinked L. Where, as in (17j), LStep applies to an L followed by an LhH contour, (a) that contour, which is admissible only after a linked L, is simplified by a rule of Downstepped Contour Low Disassociation (DCLDis), which disassociates the L of the contour, (b) the resulting unlinked L is thereupon changed to l by a rule of Unlinked Low Stepping (ULStep) in the service of a condition which disallows unlinked L in the context l_h, and (c) the resulting lh sequence is thereupon deleted by a rule of Down-Up Deletion (DUDel) in the service of a condition which disallows that sequence in any context. Where, as in (17h) and (17l), LStep applies to an L followed by an hH sequence, (a) the resulting lh sequence is deleted by DUDel in the same way as an lh sequence resulting from ULStep, and (b) the HH sequence which results from that is reduced by a rule of High Degemination (HDegem), in the service of a condition which disallows that sequence in any context, to a single H linked with the same TBUs; where, as in (17l), the application of TSpr results in two consecutive TBUs each consisting only of a vowel being linked with the same tone, the second is deleted by a rule of Vowel Degemination (VDegem) serving a condition which disallows that situation.

(17) a.
```
        e + m ə n - d z w i          b.  e + m ə m - b h ʉ
        |     |       |                  |     |       |
        L     L       L                  L     L      hHlH
linear  L     L       L                  L     L       H
        2     2       2                  2     2       1

        è   mə̀ndzwì                      è   mə̀mbhʉ́
        'of leopards'                    'of dogs'
```

c.
```
        e + m ə - t s ɔ ŋ             d.  e +     - n a
        |     |     /\                    |         |
        L     L    LhH                    L   L     L
linear  L     L    LᵢH                    L         L
        2     2    2 0                    2         2

        è   mə̀tsɔ́ᵢ´ŋ                      è   nà
        'of thieves'                     'of animal'
```

e.
```
        e + V - m ɔ                   f.  e +     - s ə ŋ
        |   |   |                         |         |
        L   L  hHlH                       L   L    hH
linear  L   L   H                         L   ᵢ    H
        2   2   1                         2        0

        è   V̀mɔ́                          è  ᵢsə́ŋ
        'of child'                       'of bird'
```

g.
```
        a + m ə n - d z w i           h.  a + m ə m - b h ʉ
        |     |       |                   |     |       |
        H     L       L                   H     L      hHlH

LStep,  τ     τ       τ                   τ     τ       τ
TSpr    |_ _ _        |                   |_ _ _        |
        H     1       L                   H     1      hHlH

DUDel                                     H     0      ØHlH

HDegem                                    H            ØlH

linear  H     H !     L                   H     H !     H
        1     1       3                   1     1       2

        á    mán!dzwì                     á    mə́m!bhʉ́
        'of leopards'                    'of dogs'
```

204   *The representation of tonal register*

```
          j.   a  +  m  ə - t  s  ɔ  ŋ              k.  a  +       - n  a
               |     |      ∧                           |          |
               H     L      LhH                         H    L     L
PFHDel                                                  τ          τ
                                                                   |
                                                        ∅    L     L

LStep,         τ     τ      τ
TSpr           |_ _ _ _     ∧
               H     l      LhH

DCLDis         τ     τ      τ
               |_ _ _ _     ⚹∧
               H     l      LhH

ULStep         H     l      lhH

DUDel          H     l      ∅∅H

linear         H     H !    H              L              L
               1     1      2              2              2

               á     má'tsɔ́ŋ               à    nà
               'of thieves'                'of animal'

          l.   a  +  V - m  ɔ               m.  a  +       - s  ə  ŋ
               |     |   |                      |          |
               H     L   hHlH                   H    L     hH

PFHDel                                          τ          τ
                                                           |
                                                ∅    L     hH

LStep,         τ     τ      τ
TSpr           |_ _ _ _     |
               H     l      hHlH

DUDel          H     ∅      ∅HlH

HDegem         H            ∅lH

VDegem         a     ∅ - m  ɔ
               |         |
               H         lH

linear         H     !      H              L     ᵢ        H
               1            2              2              0

               á     'mɔ́                   à    ᵢsə́ŋ
               'of child'                  'of bird'
```

In (17g) as in the Akan example in (9a), LStep applies to the L̲ of a nominal prefix followed by an L̲-initial noun stem and creates an HlL [H¹L] sequence. Dschang has no H̲-initial noun stems such as those of Akan in (9c–d) and (10c–d), but unlike Akan, has (L̲)hH̲-initial noun stems such as those in (17j) and (17m) (cf. (15d) and (15g)); as was seen in (15), monosyllabic noun stems with linked H̲ preceded by h have LhH̲ or hH̲ according to whether or not the prefix is represented on the segmental tier, and as we have now seen in (17j), the application of LStep to the L̲ of a nominal prefix followed by a stem-initial LhH̲ contour results ultimately in an HlH [H¹H] sequence. Dschang has, in addition, h(H̲)lH̲-initial noun stems such as those in (17h) and (17l) (cf. (15c)); as was seen in (15), these noun stems never have a prefix which is unrepresented on the segmental tier, and as we have now seen in (17h) and (17l), the application of LStep to the L̲ of the prefix again results ultimately in an HlH [H¹H] sequence, though by a different route.

The A-rules SCLDis, ULStep, DUDel, HDegem and VDegem seen in (17) operate as follows:

(18) a. SC3:   NOT τ
                            $\wedge$
                           lLhH

b. SC3A Stepped Contour Low Disassociation (SCLDis): τ
                                                      $\not{\wedge}$
                                                     lLhH

c. SC4:   NOT l(L̲)h

d. SC4A Unlinked Low Stepping (ULStep): (L̲) $\rightarrow$ l /l_h

e. SC5:   NOT lh

f. SC5A Down-Up Deletion (DUDel): lh $\rightarrow$ ∅∅

g. SC6:   NOT H̲H̲

h. SC6A High Degemination (HDegem):
                                         τ_Q
                                         $\nearrow$
                              H̲ $\rightarrow$ ∅ /H̲ _

j. SC7: NOT τ^V τ^V τ^V = TBU consisting of a vowel
             $\vee$
              T

k. SC7A Vowel Degemination (VDegem): τ^V $\rightarrow$ ∅ / τ^V _
                                                              $\vee$
                                                               T

SCLDis unlinks the L of an LhH contour after l. ULStep changes an unlinked L̲ to l in the context l_h. DUDel deletes lh. HDegem deletes the second of two successive H̲s and transfers its TBUs to the first. VDegem deletes the second of two successive TBUs each consisting only of a vowel where both are linked with the same tone.

The rest of the A-rules seen in (17), namely LStep, TSpr and PFHDel, have fellow-conspirators that we have yet to see, and the formulation of the conspiracies in question is therefore held over to the next subsection.

3.3. The tones of the associative construction

The surface tone sequences of some of those combinations in tables 1 and 2 in which the associative marker has high tone are derivable without recourse to any tonal A-rules apart from those already seen, as the derivations in (19) illustrate:

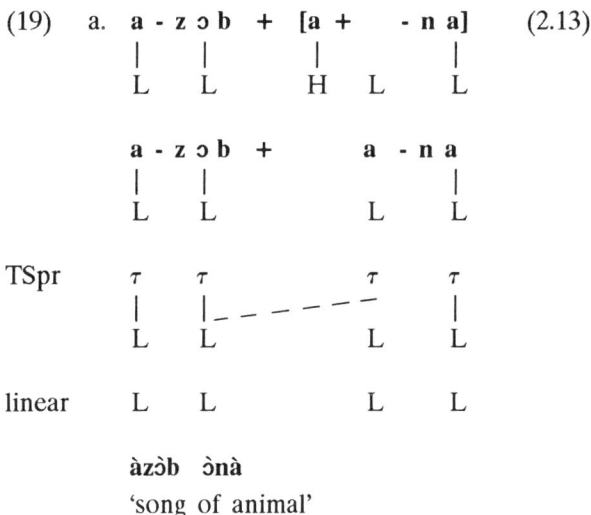

b. a - z ɔ b + [a +   - s ə ŋ]   (2.15)
    | | | |
    L   L   H   L   hH

    a - z ɔ b +   a - s ə ŋ
    | | | |
    L   L   L   hH

TSpr   τ   τ   τ   τ
       | |_ _ _ _ _ _ _ | |
       L   L   L   hH

linear L   L   Lᵢ   H

        àzɔ̀b ɔ̀ᵢsə́ŋ
        'song of bird'

c. a - l a ʔ + [a +   - n a]   (2.19)
    | | | | |
    L hHlH   H   L   L

    a - l a ʔ +   a - n a
    | | | | |
    L hHlH   L   L

LStep, τ   τ   τ   τ
TSpr | |_ _ _ _ _ _ | |
        L hHlH   l   L

linear   L   H   H!   L
         àláʔ   áʹnà
         'country of animal'

d. a - l a ʔ + [a +   - s ə ŋ]   (2.21)
    | | | |
    L hHlH   H   L   hH

    a - l a ʔ +   a - s ə ŋ
    | | | |
    L hHlH   L   hH

LStep,   τ   τ   τ   τ
TSpr | |_ _ _ _ _ _ |
         L hHlH   l   hH

DUDel   L hHlH   ∅   ∅H

HDegem   τ   τ   τ   τ
         | |_ _ _ _ _ _ _ _
         L hHlH   ∅

linear   L   H   H   H

         àláʔ   ásə́ŋ
         'country of bird'

e. a - l a ʔ + [a +   m ə n - d z w i]   (1.19)
    | | | | |
    L hHlH   H   L   L

    a - l a ʔ +   a m ə n - d z w i
    | | |_ _ _ _ |
    L hHlH   H   l   L

HDegem   τ   τ   τ   τ   τ
         | |_ _ _ _ _ _ _ _
         L hHlH   ∅   l   L

linear   L   H   H   H !   L

         àláʔ   ámə́n'dzwì
         'country of leopards'

Compare (19a,b) with (20a,b) respectively, which illustrate an A-rule of Pre-Floater Stepping High High Deletion (PFSHHDel), (19c,d) with (20c,d) respectively, which illustrate an A-rule of Weakened Contour Low Disassociation (WCLDis), and (19e) with (20e), which illustrates A-rules of Vowel-Only Low Deletion (VOLDel) and Non-Low Vowel Deletion (NLVDel):

(20) a. a - l ə ŋ + [a +   - n a]   (2.16)
         | | | |
         L   LhH   H   L   L

         a - l ə ŋ +   a - n a
         | | | |
         L   LhH   L   L

PFSHHDel   L   L∅∅   L   L

TSpr   τ   τ   τ   τ
           | |_ _ _ _ _ _ _ |
           L   L   L   L

linear   L   L   L   L

           àlə̀ŋ ə̀nà
           'stool of animal'

b. a - l ə ŋ + [a +   - s ə ŋ]   (2.18)
    | | | |
    L   LhH   H   L   hH

    a - l ə ŋ +   a - s ə ŋ
    | | | |
    L   LhH   L   hH

PFSHHDel   L   L∅∅   L   hH

TSpr   τ   τ   τ   τ
           | |_ _ _ _ _ _ _ |
           L   L   L   hH

linear   L   L   L!   H

           àlə̀ŋ ə̀ˈsə́ŋ
           'stool of bird'

c. a -s a ŋ + [a +   -n a]   (2.22)
    | ∧ | |
    L LhH   H   L L

    a -s a ŋ +   a -n a
    | ∧ | |
    L LhH   L   L

LStep,   τ τ   τ   τ
TSpr | ∧- - - - - - - | |
         L LhH   l   L

WCLDis   τ τ   τ   τ
         | ⩗ | |
         L LhH   l   L

linear   Lᵢ H   H! L

         àᵢsáŋ   á!nà
         'tail of animal'

d. a -s a ŋ + [a +   -s ə ŋ]   (2.24)
    | ∧ | |
    L LhH   H   L hH

    a -s a ŋ +   a -s ə ŋ
    | ∧ | |
    L LhH   L   hH

LStep,   τ τ   τ   τ
TSpr | ∧- - - - - - - | |
         L LhH   l   hH

DUDel   L LhH   ∅   ∅H

HDegem   τ τ   τ   τ
         | ∧──────────────────
         L LhH   ∅

WCLDis   τ τ   τ   τ
         | ⩗
         L LhH

linear   Lᵢ H   H   H

         àᵢsáŋ   ásə́ŋ
         'tail of bird'

e. e - f ɔ + [e +   m ə n - d z w i]   (1.1)
    | | | | |
    L   L   L   L   L

    e - f ɔ +   e m ə n - d z w i
    | | | | |
    L   L   L   L   L

VOLDel, τ   τ   τ   τ   τ
TSpr | |_ _ _ _ | | |
         L   L   ∅   L   L

NLVDel   e - f ɔ   ∅ m ə n - d z w i
         | | | |
         L   L   L   L

linear   L   L   L   L

         èfɔ̀   mə̀ndzwi
         'chief of leopards'

f. e - f ɔ + [e +   V - m ɔ]   (2.2)
    | | | | |
    L   L   L   L   hHlH

    e - f ɔ +   e V - m ɔ
    | | | | |
    L   L   L L   hHlH

VOLDel, τ   τ   τ τ   τ
TSpr | |_ _ _ _| | |
         L   L   ∅ L   hHlH

NLVDel   e - f ɔ   ∅ V - m ɔ
         | | | |
         L   L   L   hHlH

VOLDel, e - f ɔ   ∅   - m ɔ
TSpr, | | |
NLVDel   L   L   ∅   hHlH

linear   L   L   H

         èfɔ̀   mɔ́
         'chief of child'

PFSHHDel, like PFHDel and LStep, serves the condition which disallows HL; where both the H̲ and the L̲ are unlinked, PFSHHDel deletes the H̲, together with the h which necessarily precedes. WCLDis unlinks the L of an LhH contour where the H of the contour is linked with more than one TBU. VOLDel deletes an L̲ if it is linked only with a TBU consisting only of a vowel and that TBU is preceded by a TBU which constitutes a stem. NLVDel deletes a TBU which consists only of a non-low vowel where it is preceded by a TBU which constitutes a stem and both TBUs are linked with the same tone. The references to the stem in these informal outlines of VOLDel and NLVDel are unsatisfactory as the stem is not a phonological entity, but we shall disregard this problem for the moment. Note that VOLDel, TSpr and NLVDel apply twice each in (20f), bringing about first the deletion of the vowel of the associative marker and then the deletion of the vowel of the nominal prefix. Note also that I analyse the vowel of this particular prefix as non-low solely on the grounds that it undergoes NLVDel.

The A-rules WCLDis, VOLDel and NLVDel seen in (20) operate as follows:

(21) a. SC8: NOT $\tau\ \tau$ (Yields to SC10 (21e))
                        LhH

b. SC8A Weakened Contour Low Disassociation (WCLDis): $\tau\ \tau$
                                                                              LhH

c. SC9: NOT $s\tau\ \tau^V$ (Yields to SC1 (NOT HL))
                     |
                     L

          $s\tau$ = "solid" TBU (= stressed TBU?; see text)
          τ^V = TBU consisting of a vowel

d. SC9A Vowel-Only Low Deletion (VOLDel): $s\tau\ \tau^V$
                                                                                     |
                                                           L $\rightarrow$ ∅ / __

e. SC10: NOT $s\tau\ \tau^E$ τ^E = TBU consisting of a
                     ∨   non-low vowel
                     T

f. SC10A Non-Low Vowel Deletion: $\tau^E \rightarrow ∅ / s\tau$ __
         (NLVDel)   ∨
                                                                             T

What we specify here as a "solid" TBU is what we referred to earlier as a TBU which constitutes a stem. The term *solid* goes back to a "solid/fluid" distinction I drew in my earlier (1981) study to account for the fact that the available data on the associative construction showed that the tone rules operated differently according to whether a TBU constituted a stem on the one hand or, on the other, a nominal prefix or an associative marker. There is no information in the data on any corresponding phonetic distinction, but the possibility that there may be a difference in stress would appear to be worth investigating; see Clark (1991) for what she considers to be "empirical evidence that what is involved here is stress".

Note that SC8 is marked as yielding to SC10; this means that, as the examples in (22) illustrate, wherever there is a simultaneous violation of SC8 and SC10, the appropriate rule serving SC10, namely NLVDel, takes precedence over the appropriate rule serving SC8, namely WCLDis.

(22) a. ɲ- ɲ i + [e + m ə n - d z w i]   (1.10)
          | ∧ | | |
          L LhH   L   L   L

          ɲ- ɲ i +   e m ə n - d z w i
          | ∧ | | |
          L LhH   L   L   L

LStep,   τ   τ   τ   τ   τ
TSpr | ∧ - - - - ‾ | |
          L LhH   l   L   L

NLVDel   ɲ- ɲ i   ∅ m ə n - d z w i

linear   L   L̂ᵢH   !   L   L

          ɲɲìᵢ´ ˈmə̀ndzwì
          'machete of leopards'

b. ɲ- ɲ i + [e + - n a]   (2.10)
    | ∧ | |
    L LhH   L   L   L

    ɲ- ɲ i +   e - n a
    | ∧ | |
    L LhH   LL   L

LStep,   τ   τ   τ   τ
TSpr | ∧ _ _ _ _ _ |
         L LhH   1L   L

NLVDel ɲ- ɲ i   ∅ - n a
linear   L   L̂ᵢH   !   L

        ɲ̀ɲìᵢ´ ¹nà
        'machete of animal'

SC9 is similarly marked as yielding to SC1, the condition which disallows
H̲L̲, to indicate that, as the same examples illustrate, wherever there is
a simultaneous violation of SC1 and SC9, the appropriate rule serving
SC1, namely LStep, takes precedence over the appropriate rule serving
SC9, namely VOLDel.

We have so far seen three rules serving the condition which disallows
H̲L̲; a fourth, Downstepped High Deletion (DHDel), deletes the H̲ after l,
as in (23):

(23) a.   n - d ɔ ŋ + [e + m ə n - d z w i]   (1.7)
           | | | | |
           L hHlH   L   L   L

           n - d ɔ ŋ +   e m ə n - d z w i
           | | | | |
           L hHlH   L   L   L

DHDel   L hHl∅   L   L   L

SHHDel,   τ   τ   τ   τ   τ
LwLSpr | _ _ _ _ _ _ | | |
           L   ∅∅l   L   L   L

NLVDel   n - d ɔ ŋ   ∅ m ə n - d z w i

linear   L ǃ L   L   L

           ǹ¹dɔ̀ŋ   mə̀ndzwì
           'horn of leopards'

b. n - d ɔ ŋ + [e +   - n a]   (2.7)
    | | | |
    L hHlH   L   L   L

    n - d ɔ ŋ +   e - n a
    | | | |
    L hHlH   LL L

DHDel   L hHlØ   LL L

SHHDel,   τ   τ   τ   τ
LwLSpr | - - - - - _| |
            L   ØØl   LL L

NLVDel   n - d ɔ ŋ   Ø - n a

linear   L ! L   L

            n̍dɔ̀ŋ nà
            'horn of animal'

This triggers two further A-rules that we have not yet seen. Stepping High High Deletion (SHHDel) deletes the sequence h(H) in the context L _l((L))L provided the two outside Ls of the context are both linked. Leftward Low Spreading (LwLSpr), which bleeds TSpr in the service of the condition which disallows an unlinked TBU after a linked TBU, links the unlinked TBU with the tone to the right instead of the tone to the left; we shall see the conditioning factors later.

The application of DHDel results in a simultaneous violation of the conditions served by SHHDel and LwLSpr respectively, and SHHDel must apply first, as otherwise TSpr would apply instead of LwLSpr, and would, moreover, prevent the application of SHHDel. The condition served by TSpr and LwLSpr must therefore be marked as yielding to the condition served by SHHDel.

The rules serving the condition which disallows HL can now be seen to operate as follows:

(24) a. SC1: NOT HL

   b. SC1A1 Pre-Floater High Deletion (PFHDel): H → Ø /[_ (L)

   c. SC1A2 Pre-Floater Stepping High High Deletion (PFSHHDel):
      h(H) → ØØ /_ (L)

   d. SC1A3 Downstepped High Deletion (DHDel): H → Ø /l_ L

   e. SC1A4 Low Stepping (LStep):   L → l /H _

This says in effect that the L̲ is changed to l by LStep, the main rule, where the H̲ is not deleted by one of the three rules which bleed LStep: the H̲ is deleted by DHDel when it is preceded by l, as we have just seen, and, as we saw earlier, where the L̲ is unlinked, the H̲ is deleted by PFHDel if it is in initial position, and is deleted together with the preceding h by PFSHHDel if it is itself unlinked. Note that the order of the three H-deleting rules in relation to each other is arbitrary as their structural descriptions are mutually exclusive: the H̲ is deleted by PFHDel only in initial position, by PFSHHDel only where h precedes, and by DHDel only where l precedes.

SHHDel, which, as we saw, applies in the wake of DHDel in the examples in (23), operates as follows:

(25) a. SC11: NOT τ   τ
                     | |
                    L̲h(H̲)l((L̲))L̲

  b. SC11A Stepping High High Deletion (SHHDel):

                         τ   τ
                         | |
              h(H̲) → ∅∅ /L̲ _l((L̲))L̲

This says that the tone sequence specified in (25a) is inadmissible, and that SHHDel reduces it to L̲l((L̲))L̲. Note that if the sequence was admissible, its pitch realization would be the same as that of L̲L̲, namely [0 down], and that SHHDel may thus be regarded as a dissimilation rule. Note also that by the present analysis, SHHDel is the only source of L̲lL̲ sequences.

Three of the six of the derivations in (26), namely (26a–b) and (26e), illustrate a rule of High Disassociation (HDis) which disassociates H̲ in the context L̲h_lT if it is linked only with one or more "fluid" TBUs and both of the linking tones of the context are linked; see (21) above for our "solid/fluid" distinction. Note that where, as in (26a–b), the T of the context is H̲, the disassociation of the "fluidly linked" H̲ results in a L̲h(H̲)lH̲ [−1 down] sequence, and that this supports our original analysis of noun-internal [−1 down] as L̲h(H̲)lH̲. Also illustrated in (26) are two other new rules, Stepping High Insertion (SHIns), which inserts h in the context L̲ _ H̲ in the service of a condition which disallows L̲H̲, and Leftward High Spreading (LwHSpr), which, like Leftward Low Spreading (LwLSpr) which we have seen already in (23) and see again in (26c), bleeds TSpr in the service of the condition which disallows an unlinked TBU after a linked TBU:

(26) a.   a - z ɔ b + [a + m ə m - b h ʉ]   (1.14)
           | | | | |
           L   L   H   L   hHlH

           a - z ɔ b +   a m ə m - b h ʉ
           | | | └─┐ |
           L   L   H   l   H

SHIns   L   L   hH   l   H

HDis   τ   τ   τ   τ   τ
           | | ǂ ⫽ |
           L   L   hH   l   H

LwHSpr   τ   τ   τ   τ   τ
           | | ─ ─ ─ ─┘
           L   L   hH   l   H

TSpr   τ   τ   τ   τ   τ
           | |─ ─ ─ ─ ─ ─   ┘
           L   L   hH   l   H

linear   L   L   L   H   H

           àzɔ̀b ɔ̀məmbhʉ́   'song of dogs'

b.   a - z o b | [a + V - m ɔ]   (2.14)
     | | | | |
     L   L   H   L hHlH

     a - z ɔ b +   a - m ɔ
     | | | | |
     L   L   H   Hl H

SHIns L   L   hHl H

HDis   τ   τ   τ   τ
       | | ǂ |
       L   L   hHl H

LwHSpr τ   τ   τ   τ
       | | ─ ─┘
       L   L   hHl H

linear L   L   H   H

       àzɔ̀b ómɔ́   'song of child'

c.
```
         n - d z a + [ e  +  m ə - t s ɔ  ŋ]        (1.6)
             |       |   |       |     /\
             L      LhH  L       L    LhH

         n - d z a +      e m ə - t s ɔ ŋ
             |       |    |   |     /\
             L      LhH   L   L    LhH
```

LStep   L   LhH   l   L   LhH

SHHDel   L   LØØ   l   L   LhH

LwLSpr
```
           τ        τ           τ    τ     τ
           |        |            `--⌐      /\
           L        L           l    L    LhH
```

linear   L   L   ˈL   L   L͡ᵢH

    ǹdzà ˈàmə̀tsɔ̀ᵢ́ŋ 'country of dogs'

d.
```
         n - d z a + [ e  +  - s ə  ŋ]              (2.6)
             |       |       |    |
             L      LhH L    L   hH

         n - d z a +     e -  s ə  ŋ
             |       |   |    |
             L      LhH  LL  hH
```

LStep   L   LhH   lL   hH

ULStep   L   LhH   ll   hH

DUDel   L   LhH   lØ   ØH

LwHSpr
```
           τ        τ           τ         τ
           |        |            `-----⌐
           L       LhH          l         H
```

linear   L   L   H   H

    ǹdzà ásə́ŋ 'axe of bird'

e. a - z ɔ b + [a +   m ə n - d z w i]   (1.13)
    | | | | |
    L   L   H   L   L

    a - z ɔ b +   a   m ə n - d z w i
    | | | |
    L   L   H   l   L

SHIns   L   L   hH   l   L

HDis   τ   τ   τ   τ   τ
        | | ɫ̸——# |
        L   L   hH   l   L

SHHDel L   L   ØØ   l   L

TSpr   τ   τ   τ   τ   τ
        | |_ _ _ _ _ = |
        L   L   l   L

linear L   L   L   L   !   L

àzɔ̀b ɔ̀mə̀n'dzwì   'song of leopards'

f. n - d z a + [e + - n a]   (2.4)
    | | | |
    L   LhH L L   L

    n - d z a +   e - n a
    | | | |
    L   LhH   LL L

LStep   L   LhH   lL   L
SHHDel   LL   LØØ   lL   L

TSpr   τ   τ   τ   τ
         | |_ _ _ _ |
         L   L   lL   L

NLVDel   n - d z a   Ø - n a
linear   L   L   !   L

ǹdzà 'nà 'axe of animal'

The new rules seen in (26) operate as follows:

(27) a. SC12: NOT L̲H̲
      b. SC12A Stepping High Insertion (SHIns): Ø → h /L̲ _ H̲

c. SC13: NOT τ fτ_Q τ fτ = "fluid" TBU
                | | |
                Lh   H   lT

d. SC13A High Disassociation (HDis): τ fτ_Q τ
                                       | ╪ |
                                       Lh   H   lT

e. SC2: NOT τ $\hat{\tau}$ (Yields to SC1 (NOT $\underline{HL}$),
               | SC4   (served by ULStep),
               T   and SC11 (served by SHHDel))

f. SC2A1 Leftward High Spreading (LwHSpr): τ ($\hat{\tau}_Q$) $\hat{\tau}$ sτ
                                            | ↘↙
                                            Lh   (H) lH

g. SC2A2 Leftward Low Spreading (LwLSpr): τ $\hat{\tau}_Q$ fτ
                                           | ↘↙
                                           L   l($\underline{L}$) L

h. SC2A3 Tone Spreading (TSpr): τ $\hat{\tau}$
                                 |↙
                                 T

(27a–b) says simply that $\underline{LH}$ is inadmissible, and that SHIns changes it to $\underline{LhH}$. (27c–d) says that an H linked only with one or more "fluid" TBUs is inadmissible in the context indicated, and that HDis unlinks it. (27e) says that an unlinked TBU is inadmissible after a linked TBU, but that this condition yields to the three conditions listed on the right. (27f–h) says that where no other condition takes precedence, TSpr links the unlinked TBU with the tone of the preceding TBU if it remains unlinked after the two rules which bleed TSpr have applied; but that where one or more unlinked TBUs opposite an h(H)l sequence are preceded by a TBU linked with an L and followed by a "solid" TBU linked with an H, LwHSpr links the rightmost unlinked TBU with the H to the right; and that where one or more unlinked TBUs opposite an l or an l($\underline{L}$) sequence are preceded by a TBU linked with an L and followed by a "fluid" TBU linked with an L, LwLSpr links all the unlinked TBUs with the L to the right.

Note that as LwHSpr links only one unlinked TBU, it leaves any remainder to be linked by TSpr, as in (26a); and that as the structural description of LwLSpr specifies the linked TBU to the right as "fluid", it is TSpr and not LwLSpr that applies in (26e–f).

Our account of the tones in tables 1 and 2 is now complete. Table 3 shows the A-rules which apply in the derivation of each of the 48 combinations in these two tables after the completion of the derivation of the appropriate associative form of the second noun.

Table 3

The postlexical A-rules which apply in the 48 tone combinations of tables 1 and 2 after the completion of the derivation of the associative form of the noun.

	TONE COMBINATIONS IN TABLE 1	TONE COMBINATIONS IN TABLE 2
1.	VOLDel/TSpr/NLVDel (20e)	VOLDel/TSpr/NLVDel
2.	VOLDel/TSpr/NLVDel	VOLDel/TSpr/NLVDel/ VOLDel/TSpr/ NLVDel (20f)
3.	VOLDel/TSpr/NLVDel	VOLDel/TSpr/NLVDel
4.	LStep/SHHDel/LwLSpr	LStep/SHHDel/TSpr/NLVDel (26f)
5.	LStep/SHHDel/LwLSpr	LStep/SHHDel/LwLSpr/VDegem
6.	LStep/SHHDel/LwLSpr (26c)	LStep/ULStep/DUDel/ LwLSpr(26d)
7.	DHDel/SHHDel/LwLSpr/ NLVDel (23a)	DHDel/SHHDel/LwLSpr/ NLVDel (23b)
8.	DHDel/SHHDel/LwLSpr/NLVDel	DHDel/SHHDel/LwLSpr/NLVDel
9.	DHDel/SHHDel/LwLSpr/NLVDel	DHDel/SHHDel/LwLSpr/NLVDel
10.	LStep/TSpr/NLVDel (22a)	LStep/TSpr/NLVDel (22b)
11.	LStep/TSpr/NLVDel	LStep/TSpr/NLVDel/VOLDel/TSpr/ NLVDel/DUDel/HDegem
12.	LStep/TSpr/NLVDel	LStep/TSpr/NLVDel/ULStep/ DUDel
13.	SHIns/HDis/TSpr/SHHDel (26e)	TSpr (19a)
14.	SHIns/HDis/LwHSpr/TSpr (26a)	SHIns/HDis/LwHSpr (26b)
15.	SHIns/HDis/LwHSpr/TSpr	TSpr (19b)
16.	HDegem/HDis/TSpr/SHHDel	PFSHHDel/TSpr (20a)
17.	HDegem/HDis/LwHSpr/TSpr	HDegem/HDis/LwHSpr
18.	HDegem/HDis/LwHSpr/TSpr	PFSHHDel/TSpr (20b)
19.	HDegem (19e)	LStep/TSpr (19c)
20.	HDegem	HDegem
21.	HDegem	LStep/TSpr/DUDel/HDegem(19d)
22.	HDegem/WCLDis	LStep/TSpr/WCLDis (20c)
23.	HDegem/WCLDis	HDegem/WCLDis
24.	HDegem/WCLDis	LStep/TSpr/DUDel/HDegem/ WCLDis (20d)

Rule index:

DHDel (24d)	LStep (24e)	PFSHHDel (24c)	ULStep (18d)
DUDel (18f)	LwHSpr (27b)	SHHDel (25b)	VDegem (18k)
HDegem (18h)	LwLSpr (27g)	SHIns (27b)	VOLDel (21d)
HDis (27d)	NLVDel (21f)	TSpr (27h)	WCLDis (21b)

4. EBRIÉ

The above analysis of Dschang as an Akan-type total downstep language with not only automatic downstep (HlL to the exclusion of HL) but also automatic upstep (LhH to the exclusion of LH) suggests the possibility of similar analyses of at least some of those languages which appear on the surface to be discrete level tone languages with three tone levels. An obvious candidate for such an analysis is Ebrié, a language of the southeastern Ivory Coast classified by Stewart (1989:224) as a member of the Potou-Tano group, which also includes Akan. Kutsch Lojenga (1985), in a study of the tones of 256 "N_1's N_2" combinations in the Ebrié associative construction, finds that "the surface tone patterns of Ebrié utterances can be represented as sequences of the following four discrete level tones, just as if Ebrié were a straightforward discrete level tone language: H = high, M = mid, L = low, X = extra low", but that there are very severe restrictions on the distribution of X as well as significant restrictions on that of M:

(28) a. X occurs only as the second tone in a two-tone contour, and contours occur only prepausally. All the contours which occur, namely HM̂, HX̂, LX̂, are falls from H or L to M or X.

b. M does not occur postpausally or after another M.

In her 1985 article she analyses X as a floating low tone. Now, however, she regards the extra low pitch as a matter of phonetic realization (pers. com.), and her surface representations are accordingly amended here by substituting L° for her prepausal L, L for her prepausal contour LX̂, and HL̂ for her prepausal contour HX̂; L°, as in the linear representations of the tones of Dschang (see (15) above), is a prepausal L which differs from an unmarked prepausal L in that it is non-falling, or "non-downgliding". All that then remains of the restrictions in (28) is as follows:

(29) a. Contours occur only prepausally, and the only contours which occur are falls from H to M or L.

b. M does not occur postpausally or after another M.

She interprets M, whether after H or L, as a downstepped H (1985:2), and analyses downstep as a floating low tone (1985:5–7) just as I had done in my earlier (1983) work on Adioukrou (which, incidentally, is spoken immediately to the west of Ebrié) and Akan. She finds, however, that she has to make two major changes in the integer-assigning algorithm that I had proposed for Adioukrou and Akan. First, she takes the HL interval to be not [1 down] but [2 down], citing my own earlier (1981) treatment of Dschang as a precedent. Second, her floating low tone has the effect of lowering by one step not the whole of the remainder of the utterance but only the immediately following H.

I now propose to reinterpret (a) her floating low tone as the stepping low tone l already seen in the above treatment of Kikuyu, Akan and Dschang, (b) her HL [2 down] as the HlL already seen in the above treatment of Akan and Dschang, and (c) her LH [−2 down] as the LhH already seen in the above treatment of Dschang. There is then no longer any need for the first of the two changes which she makes in the integer-assigning algorithm, and we can go on to obviate the need for the second by reinterpreting [−1 down] as HhH where it corresponds to her [MH] (as distinct from her [LM]); (30a) illustrates not only this but also a further revision that I propose, one which requires that final [HM] be analysed not simply as HlH but as HlHh(H):

(30) a. **m-mye 'bwe**   Cf. b. (Kutsch Lojenga) **m-mye 'bwe**

```
       |    |    /\                              |    |    /\
       Hl   Hh   HlHhH                           HL   H    HLH
       1    1    1 1                             1    1    1 1
plus        1    1 2                      plus        1      1
       ─────────────                             ─────────────
       1    2    2 3                             1    2    1 2
minus            1 1                             [H   M    H M]
       ─────────────
       1    2    1 2
```

ḿ¹myé ¡'bwé¹ˊ 'girls' word'

The further revision just referred to is the consistent analysis of [M] as H in the context Hl_hH even where this means positing unlinked tones to make up the context. (30a) illustrates the case of [M] in final position; we shall see that the final h(H) posited is derivable from that of final Lh(H)representing [L°]. The only other cases are those of [LM][−1 down] and [ML][1 down], which I analyse as Lh(H)lH and Hh(H)lL respectively; as we shall see, these representations are in certain circumstances cost-free in the sense that no special rules are needed to generate them. The reader's special attention is drawn to the fact that the representation of Kutsch Lojenga's [LM] is then identical to my representation of Hyman's [L¹H] in the above treatment of Dschang.

With these revisions, Ebrié, like Dschang as treated above, has both automatic downstep (HlL to the exclusion of HL) and automatic upstep (LhH to the exclusion of LH).

There is a eight-way tonal contrast in monosyllabic noun stems; where the stem is coextensive with the noun and the noun is at N_2 in an "N_1's N_2" associative construction and is preceded by an N_1 which ends on a linked low tone in all contexts, the eight-way tonal contrast is as follows:

(31) a. 'bi   b. 'bwe   c. pɔ   d. yi
       | | ∧ |
       L   LhH   (h)HlL   (h)H

linear   L   L°   (ᵢ)H↑L   (ᵢ)H

      'bì   'bwè°   (ᵢ)pɔ́ᴸ   (ᵢ)yí
     'drum'   'word'   'body'   'thing'

e. gbu   f. ko   g. hrã   h. wɔ
   | | ∧ |
  L L   L LhH   L hHlL   L hH

linear   L   L°   ᵢH↑L   ᵢH

     gbù   kò°   ᵢhrã́ᴸ   ᵢwɔ́
    'gun'   'parrot'   'canoe'   'cat'

The brackets round the initial (h) of (31c–d) indicate that it does not belong to the lexical representation either of the noun represented or of the preceding noun, but is inserted by an A-rule of Stepping High Insertion (SHIns) identical to that of Dschang, serving the condition which disallows LH sequences. Apart from the initial (h) of (31c–d), the lexical representations of the eight nouns in (31) are exactly the same as the representations they have in (31). The nouns in (31e–h) differ in their lexical representations from those in (31a–d) in that they have an initial unlinked L, which, of course, has no phonetic realization; it will be seen that the tones of the nouns in (31e–f) have the same linear representations as those of the nouns in (31a–b). The nouns in (31g–h), in which the leftmost linked tone is H, differ further in their lexical representations from those in (31c–d) in that the H is preceded by h; if of course it was not preceded by h there would be a violation of the condition which disallows LH sequences.

The typical noun, when it is at N_1 in the "N_1's N_2" associative construction, is preceded by a marker which it lacks when it is at N_2 in that construction, and this marker invites comparison with the Dschang associative marker. In each language the marker in question precedes the "possessor" noun despite the fact that the "possessor" noun comes after the "possessed" noun in Dschang but before it in Ebrié. Moreover, the Ebrié marker has the same underlying phonological representation as one of the three different (grammatically conditioned) Dschang markers, namely á; conveniently, the Dschang marker in question is one of the only two which appear in Hyman's data. The Ebrié marker, however, can hardly be considered to be an associative marker as it occurs when the noun is in isolation; we shall call it an autonomy marker, and say that the associative construction is marked by the absence of the autonomy marker on the second, or "possessed", noun.

In (32) we see the derivations of the autonomous forms of the nouns in (31a–d), consisting of the autonomy marker plus the noun proper:

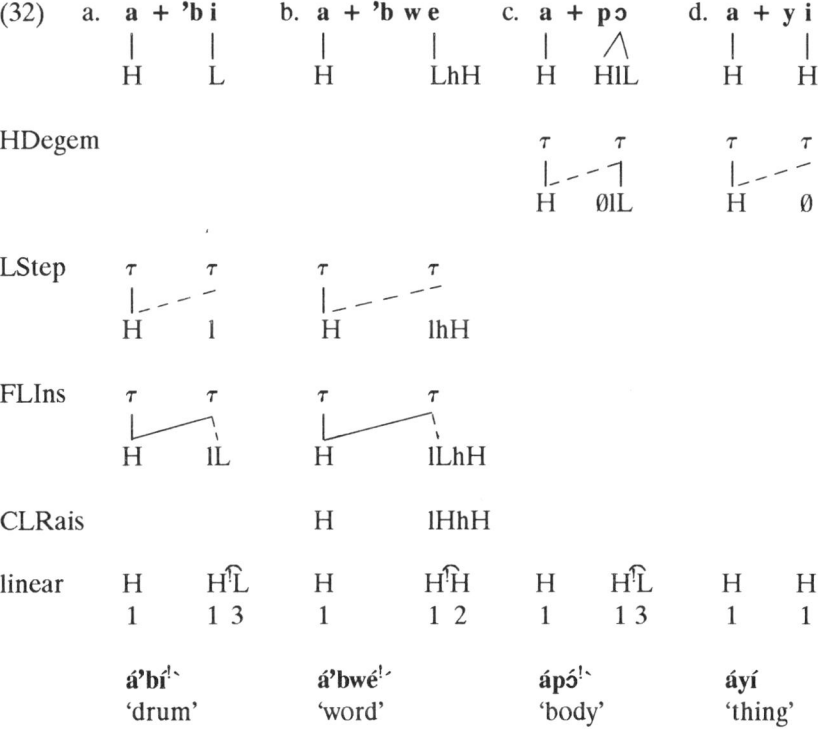

As we see here, the tone of the prefix is H, and where the stem begins with H, no rules apply apart from a High Degemination (HDegem) rule identical to that of Dschang. However, where the stem begins with L, there is a violation of the condition which disallows HL sequences, and in the context illustrated it is served by a Low Stepping (LStep) rule essentially identical to that of Akan and Dschang, but incorporating the linking to the H̲ of any TBU previously linked only to the L̲.

The application of LStep results in the violation of a condition which disallows an l where no linked tone follows. This condition, as (32a–b) illustrate, is served by an A-rule of Final Low Insertion (FLIns), which inserts L̲ after the l and links it to the final TBU:

(33) a. SC4: NOT l(h(H̲))]

      b. SC4A Final Low Insertion (FLIns):

$$\emptyset \rightarrow \underline{L} \ /Hl\_(h(\widehat{\underline{H}}))]$$

with τ linking to the inserted L.

The application of FLIns completes the derivation in (32a), but creates a further violation in (32b); Ebrié disallows an HlL contour which is not in final position on the tonal tier. In the context which (32b) illustrates, namely before hH̲, this condition is served by an A-rule of Contour Low Raising (CLRais), which changes the L of the contour to H. CLRais is one of two rules which serve the condition in question, the other being Contour Low Disassociation (CLDis), which, as we shall see later, unlinks the L of the contour before L̲:

(34) a. SC5: NOT τ
                                  /\
                                  HlLT

      b. SC5A1 Contour Low Raising (CLRais):

$$L \rightarrow H \ /Hl\_hH̲$$

      c. SC5A2 Contour Low Disassociation (CLDis): τ
                                                                                /≠
                                                                                HlLT

CLRais accounts for all instances of the prepausal contour $\widehat{HM}$ of (28) and (29) above.

In (32) we saw the derivations of the autonomous forms of the nouns in (31a–d); in (35) we see those of the nouns in (31e–h), which differ from the nouns in (31a–d) in that they have an initial unlinked L̲:

(35) a.
```
    a +  g  b  u           b.  a +    k  o
    |    |  |                  |      |  |
    H    L  L                  H      L  LhH
```

PFHDel
```
    τ       τ                  τ          τ
            |                              |
    Ø    L  L                  Ø      L  LhH
```

linear
```
    L    L                     L         L°
    2    2                     2         2

    àgbù                       àkò°
    'gun'                      'parrot
```

c.
```
    a +  h  r  ã           d.  a +    w  ɔ
    |    |    /\               |      |  |
    H    L    hHlL             H      L  hH
```

PFHDel
```
    τ       τ                  τ          τ
            /\                             |
    Ø    L  hHlL               Ø      L  hH
```

linear
```
    L       ᵢHⁱL               L         ᵢH
    2       0 2                2         0

    àᵢhrã⁽⁻                    àᵢwɔ́
    'canoe'                    'cat'
```

Here LStep is bled by an A-rule of Pre-Floater High Deletion (PFHDel) which, like that of Dschang, deletes the H of an HL sequence where the H is in initial position and the L is unlinked. The application of Ebrié PFHDel, like that of Dschang PFHDel, leaves a TBU unlinked without triggering any tone spreading rule; we assume that an unlinked TBU is admissible in initial position, and that it is realized just as if it had low tone. An obvious alternative, in the examples in (35) at least, would be to say that it was relinked with the unlinked L opposite, but we see no benefit which would offset the cost of the extra rule.

Whereas Akan has one A-rule serving the condition which disallows HL and Dschang has four, Ebrié has three; consider the examples in (36), which differ from those in (32) in that the initial consonant of the noun proper is one of the voiced fortes, which function in Ebrié as "(tone) depressor consonants":

(36) a. a + b ɛ   b. a + d r e   c. a + g w e   d. a + d ɔ̃
         | | | | | /\ | |
         H   L   H   LhH   H   HlL   H   H

HDegem   τ   τ   τ   τ
                                       |_ _ _ _\ |_ _ _ _
                                       H   ∅lL   H   ∅

SLIns   H 1 L   H 1   LhH
linear   H ! L   H !   L°   H   HL̂   H   H
         1   3   1   3   1   1 3   1   1
         á¹bɛ̀   á¹drè°   ágwé¹˜   ádɔ̃́
         'paddle'   'bead'   'fish hook'   'monkey
                                                            sp.'

Stepping Low Insertion (SLIns), which bleeds LStep where the HL lies across a voiced fortis consonant, inserts 1 opposite that consonant.

The conditions which disallow HL, LH and HH in any context, and the A-rules which serve these conditions, may now be stated as follows:

(37) a. SC1: NOT HL

   b. SC1A1 Pre-Floater High Deletion (PFHDel): H ⟶ ∅ /[_ (L)

   c. SC1A2 Stepping Low Insertion (SLIns):   τ   Dτ
                                                      | |
                                             ∅ ⟶ 1 /H _ L

      Dτ = TBU with initial depressor (i.e. voiced fortis) consonant

   d. SC1A3 Low Stepping (LStep):   τ_Q
                                              ⌐¹
                                        L ⟶ 1 /H _

   e. SC2: NOT LH

   f. SC2A Stepping High Insertion (SHIns): ∅ ⟶ h /L _ H

   g. SC3: NOT HH

   h. SC3A High Degemination (HDegem):   τ_Q
                                        ⌐¹
                                   H ⟶ ∅ /H _

A prefix consisting of a toneless nasal consonant may occur immediately before the stem of the noun; it often marks the plural. It is homorganic with the following consonant, and a following voiced lenis consonant becomes a nasal after it:

(38) a. N- + 'b ye   b. N- + 'd w ɛ   c. N- + ɟ r w ã
             | | |
             LhH   L   LhH   LhH

assim   m-m ye   n-n w ɛ   ɲ-ɟ r w ã
rules | | | |
             LhH   L   LhH   LhH

           'girls'   'snail'   'twins'

As the following derivations of the autonomous forms illustrate, the nasal prefix never has any effect on the tone pattern:

(39) a. a + m-m y e   b. a + n-n w ɛ   c. a + ɲ-ɟ r w ã
        | | | | | | |
        H   LhH   H   L   LhH   H   LhH

NIncorp am   m y e   an   n w ɛ   aɲ   ɟ r w ã
         | | | | | | |
         H   LhH   H   L   LhH   H   LhH

IVDel   Øm   m y e   Øn   n w ɛ   Øɲ   ɟ r w ã
         / | / | | / |
         H   LhH   H   L   LhH   H   LhH

PFHDel   n   n w ɛ
                                                     |
                                      Ø   L   LhH

SLIns   H   l   LhH

LStep,   m   m y e
FLins |_ _ _ _ _ ˋ
         H   lLhH

CLRais   H   lHhH

linear   H   H͡H   L   L°   H   !   L°

         m̀myé⸜   'girls'   ǹnwɛ̀°   'snail'   ɲ́'ɟrwã̀° 'twins'

By Nasal Incorporation (NIncorp), a syllabic nasal is incorporated into a preceding syllable in the service of a condition which allows syllabic nasals only in initial position. Where, as in all three of these examples, this results in a VN syllable, the vowel is forthwith deleted by Initial Vowel Deletion (IVDel) in the service of a condition which disallows VN syllables, and the nasal becomes syllabic again. Apart from the effective substitution of the syllabic nasal of the prefix for the vowel of the autonomy marker by these two rules, the three derivations proceed exactly as in (32b), (35b) and (36b) respectively. We have shown the two segmental rules as applying first, but there is no ordering which needs to be specified. Note in (39b) that after the deletion of the initial H by PFHDel, nothing remains of the autonomy marker, and the representation of the autonomous form of the noun is identical to the underlying representation of the noun proper; note in particular that in each case there is an initial unlinked TBU opposite an initial unlinked L.

24 of Kutsch Lojenga's 16 x 16 = 256 tone combinations of nouns in the "N_1's N_2" associative construction are retranscribed in table 4. The unwieldy total is cut down in the first instance to 8 x 8 = 64 by taking only those combinations in which neither noun has a stem with an initial unlinked L. The remaining eight at N_1 are then cut down to six by excluding the two which have a stem with an initial H and a depressor consonant; these pattern in exactly the same way in all contexts as their counterparts with non-depressor consonants. The four at N_2 with stem-initial H are cut down to one, the postlexical rules which apply being exactly the same in the case of all four; and the four at N_2 with stem-initial L are cut down to three by taking only one of the two with a depressor consonant, the postlexical rules which apply being the same in both cases. As in the case of the Dschang data in tables 1 and 2, the lexical representations to the left of the arrows are autosegmental, with the autosegments L, H, l, h transcribed as ˋ, ˊ, ˈ, ˌ respectively to save space and with accents representing unlinked linking tones separated by ° from the adjacent TBU, and the postlexical representations to the right of the arrows are linear. The linear representations immediately to the right of the arrows are followed by Kutsch Lojenga's representations of the tones in terms of her H, M and L. The autonomy marker is bracketed with N_1 to indicate that the postlexical rules apply in the first instance as if the enclosed constituent, which is of course the autonomous form of the noun, was in isolation.

Table 4
24 tone combinations of nouns, none of which has a stem with initial L, in the Ebrié "N_1's N_2" associative construction

1.	[á + 'cɔ̃]	+ 'bì	→ á'cɔ̃ ᵇbì	HHL	'fish's drum'
2.	[á + 'cɔ̃]	+ bɛ̀	→ á'cɔ̃ ˈbɛ̀	HHL	'fish's paddle'
3.	[á + 'cɔ̃]	+ 'bwè°ᵢ´	→ á'cɔ̃ ᵇbwè°	HHL°	'fish's word'
4.	[á + 'cɔ̃]	+ yí	→ áᵇcɔ̃ ᵢyí	HMH	'fish's thing'
5.	[á + grò]	+ 'bì	→ áˈgrò 'bì	HLL	'in-law's drum'
6.	[á + grò]	+ bɛ̀	→ áˈgrò bɛ̀	HLL	'in-law's paddle'
7.	[á + grò]	+ 'bwè°ᵢ´	→ áˈgrò 'bwè°	HLL°	'in-law's word'
8.	[á + grò]	+ yí	→ áˈgrò ᵢyí	HLH	'in-law's thing'
9.	[á + m-myè°ᵢ´]	+ 'bì	→ ḿˈmyé ᵢ'bíˈˋ	HMHL̂	'girls' drum'
10.	[á + m-myè°ᵢ´]	+ bɛ̀	→ ḿˈmyé bɛ̀	HML	'girls' paddle'
11.	[á + m-myè°ᵢ´]	+ 'bwè°ᵢ´	→ ḿˈmyé ᵢ'bwéˈˊ	HMHM̂	'girls' word'
12.	[á + m-myè°ᵢ´]	+ yí	→ ḿˈmyé ᵢyí	HMH	'girls' thing'
13.	[á + ɲ-jrwã̊ᵢ´]	+ 'bì	→ ɲˈjrwã̊ ᵢ'bíˈˋ	HLHL̂	'twins' drum'
14.	[á + ɲ-jrwã̊ᵢ´]	+ bɛ̀	→ ɲˈjrwã̊ bɛ̀	HML	'twins' paddle'
15.	[á + ɲ-jrwã̊ᵢ´]	+ 'bwè°ᵢ´	→ ɲˈjrwã̊ ᵢ'bwéˈˊ	HLHM̂	'twins' word'
16.	[á + ɲ-jrwã̊ᵢ´]	+ yí	→ ɲˈjrwã̊ ᵢyí	HLH	'twins' thing'
17.	[á + 'ká͂ˈˋ]	+ 'bì	→ á'ká͂ ᵇbì	HHL	'monkey's drum'
18.	[á + 'ká͂ˈˋ]	+ bɛ̀	→ á'ká͂ ˈbɛ̀	HHL	'monkey's paddle'
19.	[á + 'ká͂ˈˋ]	+ 'bwè°ᵢ´	→ á'ká͂ ᵇbwè°	HHL°	'monkey's word'
20.	[á + 'ká͂ˈˋ]	+ yí	→ áᵇká͂ ᵢyí	HMH	'monkey's thing'
21.	[á + m-myɔ́]	+ 'bì	→ ḿmyɔ́ 'bíˈˋ	HHHL̂	'children's drum'
22.	[á + m-myɔ́]	+ bɛ̀	→ ḿmyɔ́ ˈbɛ̀	HHL	'children's paddle'
23.	[á + m-myɔ́]	+ 'bwè°ᵢ´	→ ḿmyɔ́ 'bwéˈˊ	HHHM̂	'children's word'
24.	[á + m-myɔ́]	+ yí	→ ḿmyɔ́ yí	HHH	'children's thing'

232   *The representation of tonal register*

Many of the surface tone sequences in table 4 are derivable without recourse to any A-rules apart from those already seen, as the derivations in (40) illustrate:

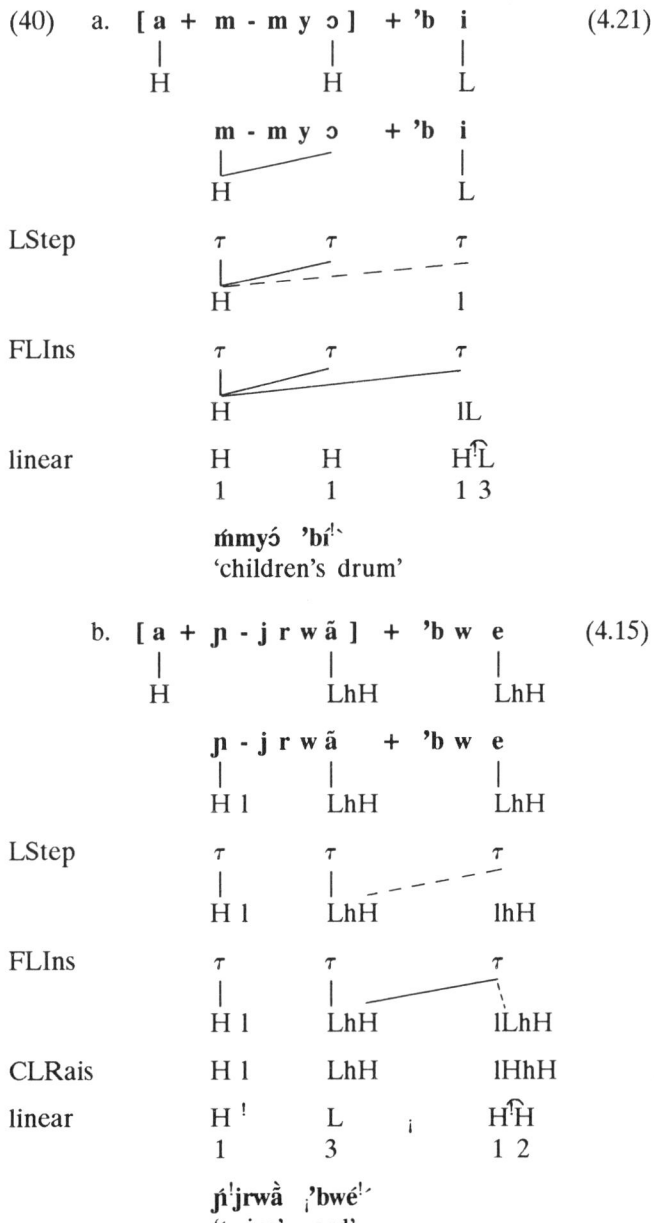

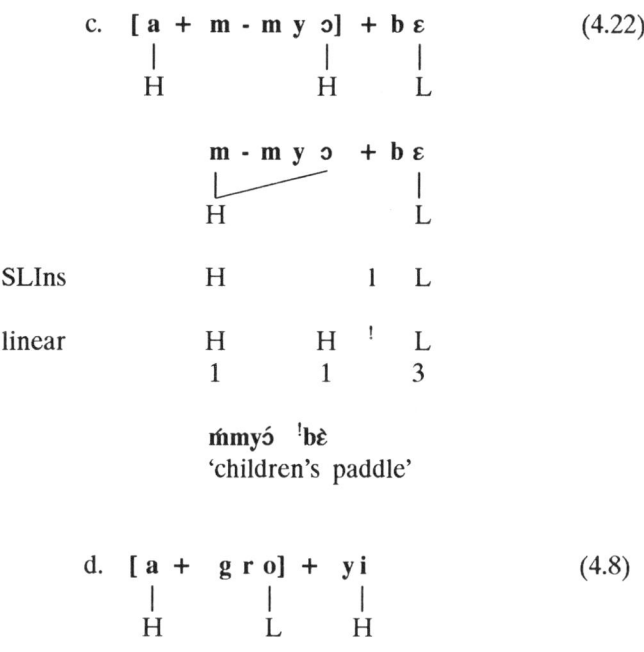

The derivations in (41) illustrate Contour High Disassociation (CHDis), which disassociates the first H of an HlH contour in the service of a condition which disallows that contour on a non-final TBU, and which has the effect of changing final [HM̂] contours into level [M] tones as soon as they lose their final status:

(41) a.   [a + m - m y e] + 'b i   (4.9)
           | | |
           H   LhH   L

         m - m y e   + 'b i
         └────┐ \ |
          H   lHhH   L

CHDis   τ   τ   τ
         └──╫─┐ \ |
          H   lHhH   L

LStep,   τ   τ   τ
FLIns | \   ──┐
           H   lHhH   lL

linear   H !   H   ᵢ H͡L
          1   2   1 3

         ḿ!myé ᵢ'bǐ
         'girls' drum'

       b.   [a + m - m y e] + y i   (4.12)
             | | |
             H   LhH   H

           m - m y e   + y i
           └────┐ \ |
            H   lHhH   H

CHDis   τ   τ   τ
           └──╫─┐ \ |
            H   lHhH   H

HDegem   τ   τ   τ
             | \   ──┐
             H   lHhH   ∅

linear   H !   H   ᵢ H
            1   2   1

           ḿ!myé ᵢyí
           'girls' thing'

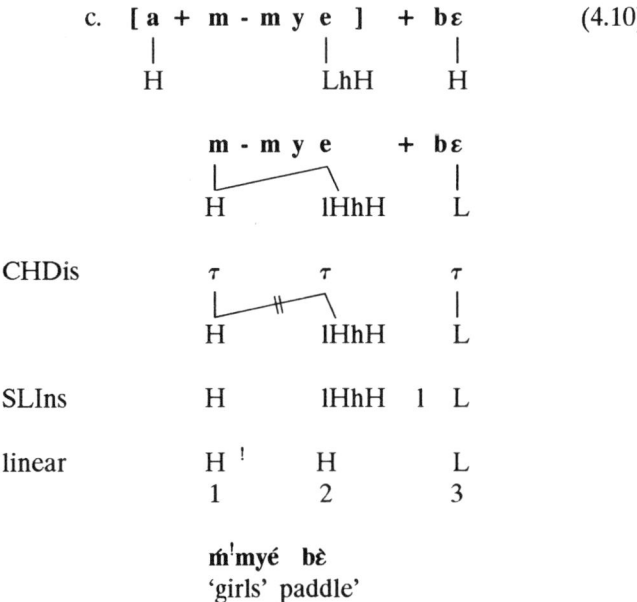

ḿ¹myé bɛ̀
'girls' paddle'

Note that the final unlinked H of the first noun, while it becomes linked on the application of LStep and HDegem in (41a) and (41b) respectively, remains unlinked in (41c), in which the second noun begins with a depressor consonant on the segmental tier and with L on the tonal tier, and ultimately forms part of a Hh(H)lL sequence realized as [1 down][ML]. Recall that by the present analysis, [M] is invariably analysed as H in the context Hl_hH, and [ML] is invariably analysed as Hh(H)lL.

CHDis and the condition it serves may be formulated as follows:

(42) a. SC7: NOT τ τ
              ∧
              HlH

      b. SC7A Contour High Disassociation (CHDis): τ τ
                                                    ⫽∖
                                                    HlH

The derivations in (43) illustrate the application of CHDis in the wake of the creation by Contour Low Raising (CLRais) of an HlH contour on a non-final TBU:

236   *The representation of tonal register*

(43)   a. [a + 'c ɔ̃] + y i (4.4)   b. [a + 'k ã] + y i (4.20)
            | | | | | ∧ |
            H   L   H   H   H   HlL   H

                a -'c ɔ̃   + y i   a -'k ã   + y i
                └─┐ | └─┐ |
                H   lL   H   H   lL   H

SHIns   H   lL h H   H   lL h H

CLRais   τ   τ   τ   τ   τ   τ
                └─┐ ∖ | └─┐ ∖ |
                H   lH h H   H   lH h H

CHDis   τ   τ   τ   τ   τ   τ
                └─╫─┐ | └─╫─┐ |
                H   lH h H   H   lH h H

linear   H ! H ᵢ H   H ! H ᵢ H
                1   2   1   1   2   1

                áᵇcɔ̃̃ ᵢyí   áᵇkã́ ᵢyí
                'fish's thing'   'monkey's thing'

We have already formulated CLRais and the conspiracy in which it serves as follows, in (34):

(44)   a.   SC4: NOT   τ
                       ∧
                      HlLT

       b.   SC4A1 Contour Low Raising (CLRais):   τ
                                                    ∧
                                        L → H /Hl_hH̲

       c.   SC4A2 Contour Low Disassociation (CLDis): τ
                                                       ∧̸
                                                      HlLT

Note that whereas CHDis (42b) is triggered when the contour in question is non-final on the *segmental* tier, CLRais (44b) is triggered when the contour in question is non-final on the *tonal* tier; (32b) above illustrates the triggering of CLRais in the absence of any following TBU.

Contour Low Disassociation (CLDis) (44c), which disassociates the L of a tonally non-final HlL contour but which is bled by CLRais (44b), is illustrated in (45):

(45) a. [a + 'c ɔ̃] + 'b i (4.1)   b. [a + 'k ã] + 'b i (4.17)
        | | | | ∧ |
        H   L   L   H   HlL   L

        a- 'c ɔ̃   + 'b i   a- 'k ã   + 'b i
        └─╲ | └─╲ |
        H   lL   L   H   lL   L

CLDis   τ   τ   τ   τ   τ   τ
        └─╳ | └─╳ |
        H   lL   L   H   lL   L

linear   H   H   !   L   H   H   !   L
         1   1   3   1   1   3

        á'cɔ̃ ᵎbì   á'ká ᵎbì
        'fish's drum'   'monkey's drum'

An A-rule of Dissimilatory Low Raising (DLRais), serving a condition which disallows the sequence Lh(H)lL, which would of course be realized as [0 down][LL], raises the first L to H and thereby creates an Hh(H)lL sequence realized as [1 down][ML] (cf. (41c) above), as (46) illustrates:

(46) [a + ɲ-j r w ã] + b ɛ   (4.14)
        | | |
        H   LhH   L

             ɲ-j r w ã   + b ɛ
              | | |
              Hl   LhH   L

SLIns   Hl   LhH l   L

DLRais   Hl   HhH l   L

linear   H!   H   L
              1   2   3

              ɲ'jrwá́ bɛ̀
              'twins' paddle'

DLRais, which serves a condition identical to the Dschang condition served by Stepping High High Deletion (25b), which creates an L̲L̲ sequence, operates as follows:

(47) a. SC8: NOT L̲h(H)L̲

   b. SC8A Dissimilatory Low Raising (DLRais): L̲ ⟶ H / _ h(H)L̲

Our account of the tones in table 4 is now complete. Table 5 shows the A-rules which apply in the derivation of each of the 24 tone combinations of table 4 after the completion of the derivation of the autonomous form of the first noun.

Table 5
The postlexical A-rules which apply in the 24 "autonomous noun + non-autonomous noun" combinations of table 4 after the completion of the derivation of the autonomous noun

1–3.	CLDis (45a)	14.	SLIns/DLRais (46)
4.	SHIns/CLRais/CHDis (43a)	15.	LStep/FLIns/CLRais(40b)
5–7.	(no rules)	16.	HDegem
8.	SHIns (40d)	17–19.	CLDis (45b)
9.	CHDis/LStep/FLIns (41a)	20.	SHIns/CLRais/CHDis (43b)
10.	CHDis/SLIns (41c)	21.	LStep/FLIns (40a)
11.	CHDis/LStep/FLIns/CLRais	22.	SLIns (40c)
12.	CHDis/HDegem (41b)	23.	LStep/FLIns/CLRais
13.	LStep/FLIns	24.	HDegem

Rule index:

CHDis (42b)	CLRais (34b)	FLIns (33b)	LStep (37d)	SLIns (37c)
CLDis (44c)	DLRais (47b)	HDegem (37h)	SHIns (37f)	

It remains to consider those of Kutsch Lojenga's combinations which involve nouns with stem-initial unlinked (L); it will be recalled that these combinations could not be conveniently accommodated in table 4.

Where the second noun has stem-initial unlinked (L), the rules which apply are essentially the same as those which apply in Dschang where the second noun has an unlinked (L) prefix; compare the Ebrié derivations in (48a) and (48b) with the Dschang derivations in (19c) and (19d) respectively:

(48) a. [a +   wɔ] +   k o   b. [a +   wɔ] +   h r ã
         | | | | | /\
         H   L hH   L LhH   H   L hH   L hHlL

PFHDel [τ   τ]   [τ   τ]
                   | |
         ∅   L hH   ∅   L hH

         a-   wɔ +   k o   a-   wɔ +   h r ã
                | | | /\
             L hH   L LhH   L hH   L hHlL

LStep   L hH   l LhH   L hH   l hHlL

DUDel   L hH   ∅ ∅HlL

HDegem   τ   τ   τ
                                                   |_ _ _ _ _ ┐
                                               L hH   ∅lL

linear   Lᵢ   H   !   L°   Lᵢ   H   H͡L
             2   0   2   2   0   0 2

             àᵢwɔ́ !kò°   àᵢwɔ́ hrã́ !˺
             'cat's parrot'   'cat's canoe'

The Ebrié Down-Up Deletion (DUDel) rule is identical to the Dschang rule of the same name, which, as we saw in (18e–f), deletes an lh sequence in any context; in Ebrié, however, as (32b) illustrates, the condition served by DUDel yields to that served by FLIns, with the result that DUDel can apply only where a linked tone follows.

No other postlexical tone rules apply to these (L)-initial nouns when they are at N_2, but Nasal Incorporation (NIncorp) applies on the segmental tier when they have a nasal prefix:

240   *The representation of tonal register*

```
(49) a. [ a  +   w  ɔ]  + m- m r a       b. [ a  + n- t e]  + m- m r a
         |       |        |     |            |      |         |     |
         H       L  hH    L     L            H      L   L     L     L
```

NIncorp   [an +   t e]

IVDel   [Øn +   t e]

PFHDel [τ +   τ]   [τ   +   τ]
             |
         Ø   L hH   Ø   L   L

```
            a-  w  ɔ +  m- m r a              n-  t e  + m- m r a
            |   |      |     |                |   |      |     |
            L   hH  L  L                      L   L      L     L
```

NIncorp   a- w ɔ m   m r a   n- t e m   m r a
            | | | | | |
            L   hH L L   L   L   L   L

LStep   L   hH l   L

linear   Lᵢ H   !   L   L   L   L
            2   0   2   2   2   2

            àᵢwɔ́m ꜝmrà   ǹtèm mrà
            'cat's sponge'   'father's sponge'
```

Note that NIncorp applies just as it does when the nasal is preceded by the autonomy marker, as for instance in the first noun in (49b), but that as the result in the circumstances under consideration is not a VN syllable in initial position, Initial Vowel Deletion (IVDel) does not apply as it does in the first noun in (49b).

Where the first noun has stem-initial ⓁhH and the second has no stem-initial Ⓛ, the same rules apply as in combinations 17–24 in table 4 except that PFHDel applies in addition in the derivation of the autonomous form of the first noun. Where the first noun has stem-initial ⓁL and the second has no stem-initial Ⓛ, in most cases the same rules apply as in combinations 5–8 and 13–16 in table 4 except that PFHDel applies instead of Stepping Low Insertion (SLIns) in the derivation of the autonomous form of the first noun. Of course PFHDel applies even if the stem-initial consonant is not a depressor consonant as it is in combinations 5–8 and 13–16; the differences between the latter combinations on the one hand and 1–4 and 9–12, in which the stem-initial
```

consonant is not a depressor consonant, on the other, arise from the difference in the consonant, and a depressor consonant can have no effect on the tones unless the tone preceding the tone with which its TBU is linked is H̲.

In the counterparts of two of the relevant combinations of table 4 (i.e. the combinations other than 1–4 and 9–12), namely 14 and 20, we encounter [−1 down][LM] sequences for the first time. The derivations in (50a) and (50b) should be compared with those of 4.20 and 4.14 in (43b) and (46) respectively:

(50) a. [a +   h rã]   + y i   b. [a + n-n w ɛ] + b ɛ
         | /\ | | | | |
         H   L hHlL   H   H   L   LhH   L

         a-   h rã   + y i   n-n w ɛ   + b ɛ
                   /\ | | |
              L hHlL   H   L LhH   L

SHIns,   τ   τ   τ
CLRais,   ⋆\ |
CHDis   L   hHlH   h H

SLIns,   τ   τ   τ
DLRais | |
                                         L   HhH   l L

SHIns   Lh   HhH   l L

HSLIns   τ   τ   τ
                                                 | |
                                        LhHl   HhH   l L

linear   L   H   ᵢ H   L   H   L
             2   1   0   2   1   2
            àhrã́   ᵢyí   ǹnwɛ́   bɛ̀
            'canoe's thing'   'snail's paddle'

In the case of (50a) our analysis of [LM] as L̲h(H̲)lH̲ is cost-free in that that is precisely the representation generated by our existing rules. In (50b), however, in which we encounter an [LML] sequence for the first time, we find ourselves obliged to posit a new rule, a rule of High Stepping Low Insertion (HSLIns), which inserts H̲l in the context h_ HhH̲ in the service of a condition which disallows hH̲hH̲:

(51)   a. SC9:   NOT hH̲hH̲

       b. SC9A High Stepping Low Insertion (HSLIns):
           ∅ ⟶ (H̲)l /h_ HhH̲

5. CONCLUSION

We find, then, that Dschang and Ebrié are both analysable autosegmentally as having the same four tonal autosegments, namely two [−stepping], or linking, tones L̲, H̲ which may be linked or unlinked, and two [+stepping] tones l, h which are never linked and which are realized as downstep and upstep respectively. We find, moreover, that the two languages are analysable as sharing an impressive number of essentially identical tone rules: LStep ((24e) and (37d)), SHIns ((27b) and (37f)), HDegem ((18h) and (37h)), DUDel ((18f) and (48b)), and even PFHDel ((24b) and (37b)).

By this analysis Dschang and Ebrié, while they differ from Akan in having one tonal autosegment that Akan lacks, namely h, resemble Akan not only in having automatic downstep (H̲lL̲ to the exclusion of H̲L̲) but also in that they eliminate inadmissible H̲L̲ sequences, arising at word boundaries for instance, mainly by means of the low tone stepping rule LStep, which changes L̲ to l after H̲.

The Akan tone system, with its two linking tones plus downstep, and the Ebrié system, which many would describe as having three linking tones and no downstep, are representative of the two most common types of tone system found among the Niger-Congo languages of West Africa. The analysis proposed here, whereby Ebrié has two linking tones plus downstep plus upstep, suggests a tentative answer to the vexed question of the historical relationship between the two types of system: systems like that of Ebrié developed from systems like that of Akan by the introduction of upstep. This is particularly plausible if it is correct, as is commonly supposed, that systems like that of Akan themselves developed from simple two-tone systems by the introduction of downstep: the introduction of downstep results in a system with a gap in it, and this gap is sometimes subsequently filled by the introduction of upstep.

On the theoretical side, we have followed Clements (1983) in his bid to accommodate downstep within autosegmental theory by treating it as a floating low tone, and have accordingly made a distinction between a stepping tone and an unlinked linking tone similar to his (1984:321) distinction between a floating low tone which acts as a downstep operator and a floating low tone which does not. This has allowed us to keep the tonal representation within the bounds of a single tier.

The above analyses of Dschang and Ebrié meet our requirement that a postlexical tone rule should always be an automatic rule serving a structure condition, and should thus never have a structural description which does not violate any structure condition. All previous analyses of these languages have failed to meet this requirement. In my own earlier (1981) analysis of Dschang I had, for instance, instead of LStep, an "H-lag" rule which spread the H of an HL [2 down] sequence to the following L-toned syllable, dislodging the L and converting it to !; and I also had a "Downstep Deletion" rule which deleted the resulting ! before L at a later stage, providing the preceding H had survived to that stage. (Under the present LStep proposal there is of course no need for a deletion rule as the ! created by LStep survives in surface H!L [H!L] just as it does in Akan.) This fails twice over to meet our requirement. In the first place, the HL [2 down] of the structural description of "H-lag" is an admissible sequence; in fact HL [2 down] results wherever "Downstep Deletion" applies. In the second place, the H!L [3 down] of the structural description of "Downstep Deletion" is likewise an admissible sequence; as we have seen, the language does allow H!L [3 down] (the H!(H)!L of the present analysis) despite the fact that it is not found in the associative construction. Pulleyblank's (1983, 1986) "H-spread" and "L-deletion", to cite a parallel from one of the theoretically less alien of the other previous analyses of Dschang, are essentially the same as my "H-lag" and "Downstep Deletion", and open to the same objections.

It seems highly unlikely that the structure violation requirement could be met in either Dschang or Ebrié if the inadmissibility of the sequence HL was not recognized.

POSTSCRIPT

The above treatments of both Dschang and Ebrié would almost certainly benefit from revision in the light of a recent observation by Clark (1991, section 4.4) on Hyman and Tadadjeu's (1976) analysis of Dschang L° (i.e. prepausal non-downgliding L) as L followed by a floating H which protects the L from downgliding:

> In the framework I am assuming, floating tones are not allowed to remain in the representation ...; thus the high tone at the end of the non-downgliding [low-stemmed] nouns [of Dschang] cannot be a floating tone, but must be part of a contour.

Our own treatment retains Hyman and Tadadjeu's floating H in the form of an unlinked linking H, and it is true that our unlinked linking tones, although they are allowed to remain in the representation, have no effect on the realization apart from the blocking of downglide by a prepausal unlinked linking H; now if we were to analyse L° as the contour L!H, in which the L!H interval [0 down] is made up, as it is in Kikuyu (see section 2.1. above), of the [LH] interval [−1 down] plus the downstep interval [1 down], we could adopt what we see as the essence of Clark's theoretical assumption, and claim that unlinked linking tones have no effect whatsoever on the realization.

REFERENCES

Clark, Mary M. 1991. "The Representation of Downstep in Dschang Bamileke." This volume.
Clements, George N. 1983. "The Hierarchical Representation of Tone Features." In *Current Approaches to African Linguistics* Vol. 1, edited by Ivan R. Dihoff, 145–76. Dordrecht: Foris Publications.
———. 1984. "Principles of Tone Assignment in Kikuyu." In *Autosegmental Studies in Bantu Tone*, edited by George N. Clements and John Goldsmith, 281–339. Dordrecht: Foris Publications.
Clements, George N. and Kevin C. Ford. 1977. "On the Phonological Status of Downstep in Kikuyu." In *Harvard Studies in Phonology*. Vol. 1, edited by George N. Clements, 187–272. Cambridge, Mass.: Science Center.
Hyman, Larry M. 1979. "A Reanalysis of Tonal Downstep." *Journal of African Languages and Linguistics* 1, 9–29.
———. 1985. "Word Domains and Downstep in Bamileke-Dschang." *Phonology Yearbook* 2, 47–83.
Hyman, Larry M. and Maurice Tadadjeu. 1976. "Floating Tones in Mbam-Nkam." In *Studies in Bantu Tonology*, edited by Larry M. Hyman, 57–111. Southern California Occasional Papers in Linguistics 3. Los Angeles: University of Southern California.
Kutsch Lojenga, Constance. 1985. "The Tones of the Ebrié Associative Construction." *Journal of African Languages and Linguistics* 7, 1–22.
Meeussen, A.E. 1970. "Tone Typologies for West African Languages." *African Language Studies* 11, 266–71.
Pulleyblank, Douglas George. 1983. *Tone in Lexical Phonology*. Ph.D. Dissertation, Massachusetts Institute of Technology, Cambridge.
———. 1986. *Tone in Lexical Phonology*. Dordrecht: Reidel.
Schachter, Paul and Victoria Fromkin. 1968. *A Phonology of Akan: Akuapem, Asante and Fante*. Working Papers in Phonetics 9. Los Angeles: University of California at Los Angeles.
Schadeberg, Thilo C. 1986. "A Note on Segment Inventories, Redundancy Conditions and A-rules." In *The Phonological Representation of Suprasegmentals*, edited by Koen Bogers, Harry van der Hulst and Maarten Mous, 307–15. Dordrecht: Foris Publications.
Stewart, John M. 1971. "Niger-Congo, Kwa." In *Linguistics in Sub-Saharan Africa*, edited by T. Sebeok et al., 179–212. The Hague: Mouton.
———. 1981. "Key Lowering (Downstep/Downglide) in Dschang." *Journal of African Languages and Linguistics* 3, 113–38.
———. 1983a. "Downstep and Floating Low Tones in Adioukrou." *Journal of African Languages and Linguistics* 5, 57–78.
———. 1983b. "Akan Vowel Harmony: the Word Structure Conditions and the Floating Vowels." *Studies in African Linguistics* 14, 111–39.
———. 1989. "Kwa." In *The Niger-Congo Languages*, edited by John Bendor-Samuel, 217–45. Lanham: University Press of America.
Tadadjeu, Maurice. 1974. "Floating Tones, Shifting Rules, and Downstep in Dschang-Bamileke." In *Papers from the Fifth Annual Conference on African Linguistics*, edited by William R. Leben. Supplement 5 to *Studies in African Linguistics*, 283–90.
Winston, Denis. 1960. "The 'Mid Tone' in Efik." *African Language Studies* 1, 185–92.

Tonal Register in East Asian Languages

Moira Yip

1. INTRODUCTION*

The term register has been used in several senses. In this paper I will explore the relationship between these different kinds of register, and try to assess whether they are phonologically one and the same, or whether we must distinguish between them. The three kinds of register that will be discussed here are:

I.   Tonal register, dividing the pitch of the voice into 2 ranges, called [+upper] register and [−upper] register.
II.   Phonation register, giving laryngeal characteristics such as murmur or creaky voice.
III   Intonation register, determining the level on which a lexical tone is actually realized in an utterance.

I will first investigate the properties of each of these in turn. Then I will discuss the relation between the three, and conclude that they cannot all be reduced to a single feature.

2. REGISTER AS A TONAL FEATURE

The model of tonal features I will present here is laid out in Yip (1980) and modified in Yip (1989). For useful discussion see also Pulleyblank (1986, whose terminology I adopt here), and Hyman (1986, this volume). Four level tones are given by the structures in (1), where the register feature [upper] divides the pitch range into two halves, and these are then further refined by the subsidiary feature [raised];[1,2]

---

* Previous versions of this paper have been given at NELS, Carnegie Mellon University, November 1989, and at Cornell University. I would like to thank the audiences at those talks for their comments. Thanks also to Nick Clements, Harry van der Hulst and Larry Hyman for comments and suggestions. All errors are of course my own.
1   The numbers below each tone show the approximate notation for each tone in Chao's (1931) system of numbering used by most workers on Chinese tone; 5 denotes high pitch, 1 denotes low pitch, and contour tones are shown by their starting and ending points.
2   Hyman (1986, and this volume) uses the term register for the secondary feature, but I will use it consistently for the major division of the pitch range.

(1) [+upper]   [+upper]   [−upper]   [−upper]
        | | | |
     [+raised] [−raised] [+raised] [−raised]
       55   44/33   33/22   11

Contour tones still have a single specification for [upper], but it dominates a sequence of two specifications for [raised]. This gives four possible contour tones, shown in (2); I have substituted the shorthand H, L for [+/− raised] respectively, and will continue this practice throughout the paper.

(2)   [+upper]   [+upper]   [−upper]   [−upper]
        /\   /\   /\   /\
       L H   H L   L H   H L
        35   53   13   31

In general I will show tones in this form, as a complex of tonal features headed by [upper], which acts as a tonal root node and associates to the segmental tier. Where I depart from this practice for some reason, I will make my reasons clear. I will refer to [upper] as a tonal register feature, and L, H as the melodic features.

The evidence for a tonal register feature, [upper], is of two types. First, there are rules which delete the subsidiary L, H tones, but leave the register behind. Tones may then spread from a neighboring segment, and the result will be a surface tone whose level is a composite of the underlying register, and the neighboring tone. My first example of this is drawn from Taiwanese; for a fuller discussion see Yip (1980:168–9) and references therein.[3]

2.1. Taiwanese

On sonorant-final syllables, Taiwanese has five citation tones which surface unchanged pre-pausally; in non-final position they are reduced to four, two of which are [+upper] register (55, 53) and two of which are [−upper] register (21, 33). There is a third set of allotones which surface before the diminutive suffix a^{53}. This set has only two members, (55 and 33). The data are given in (3):

---

[3] This dialect was called Amoy in Yip (1980) but I have changed the name to Taiwanese in accordance with current practice.

Yip: Tonal register in East Asian Languages

(3)
Citation:	53	21	33	13	55
Non-final:	55	53	21	33	
Before a^{53}:	55		33		

It is this final set that is of interest here. The usual non-final forms are replaced by tones that retain their register, but lose all other contrasts of contour and height. Both [+upper] tones are now [+upper, H] (55), and both [−upper] tones are now [−upper, H] (33). This suggests that the subsidiary H, L tones have been deleted in this environment, leaving the register behind. The suffix which causes these changes, a^{53}, is [+upper, HL], so the H tone that surfaces on the preceding syllable can be attributed to spreading leftwards from the suffix.

(4)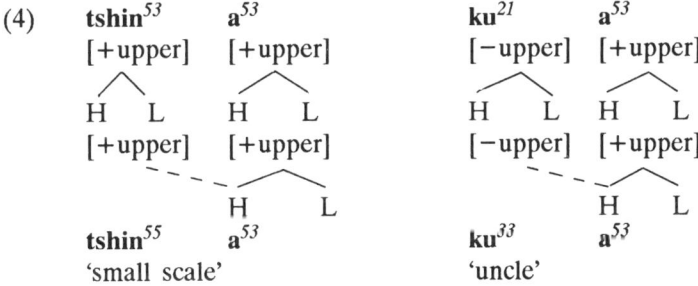

2.2. Suzhou

A second, similar example is found in the Wu dialect of Suzhou. Shih (1986:72 ff.) reports on Suzhou, giving data from Ye (1979). Suzhou has two registers, with three or four tones in each:

(5)   [+upper]   44   52   412   5
      [−upper]   13   31   3

In compounds, initial syllables retain their citation tones. Medial syllables keep only their register; they lose their tones and become level, either [+upper] 44 or [−upper] 33. Final tones are neutralized still further.

This kind of phenomenon provides evidence for separating out overall tonal register from the finer distinctions of height and contour denoted by subsidiary H, L.

2.3. Fuzhou

The second kind of evidence for the separation of register and melody comes from processes which spread register, but leave the subsidiary tones unaffected. My example here comes from Fuzhou. For details see Yip (1980:170–71). Fuzhou has a complex set of tonal changes affecting non-final syllables in combination. Here I will consider just one pair, 1̲3̲–22 → 35–22.[4] The initial syllable keeps its rise, but changes register from [−upper] to [+upper]. Since 22 can be shown to be [+upper] in the system because it groups with the [+upper] tones in its effects on vowel height, the change in 1̲3̲ can be seen to result from spreading [+upper] rightward from the final syllable, and the initial syllable keeps its rise, but changes register.[5]

(6)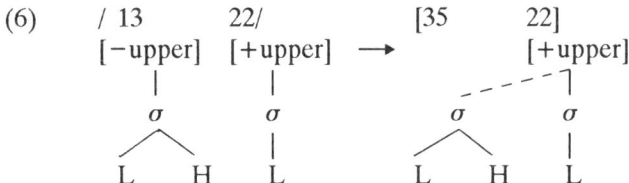

2.4. Cantonese

My last piece of evidence for the independence of register and melody comes from Cantonese. The data here come from Law (1990), although I depart from her on some elements of the analysis. Cantonese has six tones (a seventh, 53, is reported for some speakers): four level tones and two rising tones.

---

4 The underscore denotes a final glottal stop.
5 There is a technical problem here in the feature geometry argued for in Yip (1989). If the H, L tones are dependents of [upper], spreading of [upper] should carry the dependent tones along with it, and yet this is exactly what does not happen in Fuzhou, where the first syllables keeps its LH rise. For this reason in (6) I have shown the two tonal features separately associated to the syllable node, in line with Yip (1980). A better model for these facts would be that of Shih (1986:22), in which register and melody are sister nodes which can each spread independently. This problem does not affect the main point here, which is that register can spread.

(7)   55 [+upper, H]
      33 [+upper, L]
      22 [−upper, H]
      11 [−upper, L]
      35 [+upper, LH]
      13 [−upper, LH]

There are a number of sentence-final particles in the language, and also two utterance-final boundary tones, L and H, which have no register of their own. The effect of adding one of these, say the H tone, which has a "weakening" semantic flavor, is that it shows up with the underlying register of the preceding sentence particle, as shown in (8):

(8)   a 11   →   a 13   ke 33   →   ke 35
      [−upper]   [+upper]
      |⁻ ⁻ ⁻ |⁻ ⁻ ⁻ ⁻
      L   H   L   H

The Fuzhou and Cantonese facts provide further evidence for a register feature, and in conjunction with the Taiwanese facts show that we must recognize tonal register as distinct from melody.

3. REGISTER AS A PHONATION FEATURE

The second type of register I shall be concerned with is closely related to, but distinct from, purely tonal register. Some languages show differences in voice quality in vowels, such as breathy voice (murmur) or creaky voice (laryngealized). Such phonation differences frequently affect the observed pitch of the syllable, and behave phonologically in ways similar to tone. Shanghai provides my first example.

3.1. Shanghai

Shanghai contrasts murmured and plain syllables, with murmured syllables showing a lower pitch overall. The tonal inventory of Shanghai is as follows (data from Xu, Tang and Qian 1981, 1982, 1983):

(9)   Clear: T1 T2 T4   Murmured: T3 T5
               53 24 <u>55</u>   13 <u>13</u>

Tones T3 and T5 occur only on syllables with voiced onsets accompanied by a murmured release, apparently a kind of breathy voice. Sherard (1972:84–7) quotes Ladefoged in support of the view that the term "voiced aspiration" is not appropriate here, and we shall see that phonologically murmur and aspiration behave quite differently in Shanghai. Murmured release occurs on *all and only voiced* obstruents, but it is contrastive on sonorants, including liquids, nasals, glides, and the so-called "zero initial", where it surfaces as "smooth murmured onset" (Sherard:, p. 87), in contrast to the glottal stop found with non-murmured zero initials. It is important to note that murmur is not fully predictable from voicing, at least in the sonorants. Although murmured sonorants predominate, plain ones are reasonably common. Zee and Maddieson (1980:67) give contrasting sets, including seven lexical items in the non-murmured tones 1, 2 and 4, and minimal pairs. Sherard gives contrasting pairs, including five in the non-murmured tones, and they are all different from Zee and Maddieson's. Some examples are given below: **h** denotes murmur. [6]

(10)   **nyhə**   'cow'   **nyə**   'to pinch'
        lhyng   'order'   **lyng**   'carry'
        wha?   'slippery'   **wa?**   'to pick'

Sherard (1972:88–91) has tables of occurring syllables, but no frequency counts. The impression one gets is that nasals and liquids, except **m**, are rare in "high" (unmurmured) tones, but glides and zero are about as common as they are in "low" (murmured) tones.

Given this distribution of murmur, it cannot be predicted from voicing on the onset. However, voicing *can* be predicted from murmur: if the syllable is murmured, then the onset is voiced. There is no need for a distinctive feature [voice] underlyingly in Shanghai.

Shanghai, like the other Wu dialects, is known for its left-dominant tone sandhi. In polysyllabic words the tones of all but the first syllable are deleted, and the tone of the first syllable spreads over the rest of the utterance. The details will not concern us here; see Zee and Maddieson (1980), Yip (1980), Duanmu (1988), Lu (1986), Selkirk and Tong (1988) for treatments of various styles of speech. What is of interest is the behavior of murmur. I will argue that murmur has a closer affinity to the tonal features of Shanghai than it does to the laryngeal properties of the onset. This is because it too deletes on non-initial syllables, whereas voicing and voiceless aspiration remain intact.

---

6   **y** is a lower high front rounded vowel. **ə** is a mid central vowel with lip compression.

Sherard carefully describes the facts as they occurred in the speech of his informants, who were typically around 30 in 1970, when his field work was conducted. They came from urban Shanghai, but were interviewed in Hong Kong. He states (p. 80) that the murmured onsets are always fully voiced, both initially and medially, and contrasts this with other Wu dialects where they have been described as devoiced initially. He also says that medially the murmur is lost, and in support of this he cites neutralizations that take place between murmured and plain sonorants in non-initial position:[7]

(11) **the hu**   'contraband'
      chOng hhu > chong hu '(auto)accident'

We may thus analyze Shanghai as follows. (I am indebted to Duanmu (1988) for several aspects of this analysis; I differ from him in taking murmur to be tonal, rather than a property of the onset).

I. On non-initial (which probably equals unstressed) syllables, delete both tone and murmur.

II. Associate the remaining tone and murmur one-to-one, left-to-right, with the word (see Goldsmith 1976; Pulleyblank 1986 on universal association principles); since there is only a single specification for murmur, this will always surface on the first syllable only. There may however be two tones (eg LH for the rising tones), and these will associate with the first two syllables.

III. Associate excess tones with the final syllable.

IV. Remaining syllables surface as 33 by default, with a drop on the final syllable to 31.

Note that there is no spreading in Shanghai, either of tone or of murmur; the effect of spreading results from association of up to two tones with a polysyllabic domain. Murmur appears to be fixed on the onset syllable solely because there is only one remaining specification for murmur.

As an illustration, consider the patterns of tones 2 and 3 on different numbers of syllables:[8]

---

[7] Duanmu (1988) discusses an apparently different dialect, in which initial onsets are devoiced, and medially murmur is retained. He argues that in this dialect murmur is a property of the onset, and not of the tone.

[8] I use the notation familiar to workers on Chinese tone. Sonorant final syllables are typically shown with two digits, e.g. 22, even when the tone is level. Note that the digits may be spuriously precise, in that what is crucial about 13 versus 24 is that both are rising, and one is higher than the other. The 24 tone might instead have been notated as 34 (e.g.

(12) T2: 24   T3: 13
   Clear 33 44   Murmur 22 44
          33 55 31   22 55 31
          33 55 33 31   22 55 33 31
          33 55 33 .. 33 31 22 55 33 .. 33 31

Both tones are LH, but T3 is also [+murmur]. On monosyllables [murmur] affects the entire syllable with which it is associated, and the entire LH rise is lower. On polysyllables, [+murmur] is associated only with the first syllable, which it lowers, so that we get 22 versus 33 on the first syllable. On the second syllable, the H is unaffected by murmur, so both tones 2 and 3 rise to 5. Below I show the representations for the murmured tone 3 on one and three syllables; the final syllable gets its tones by default.

(13)   [+murmur]   [+murmur]
           | |
           σ   σ   σ   σ
          /\ | |
         L H   L   H
         13   22 55 (31)

So far I have talked of "murmur" and used a feature [+murmur], and I have argued that this feature is tonal rather than being a property of the onset. The implication is that the feature, whatever it is, belongs with the other tonal features in the feature geometry, and not with the laryngeal features. I am assuming a model of feature geometry along the lines of Clements (1985), Sagey (1986). There are three main candidates for what "murmur" is:

I.   A laryngeal feature(s), maybe the complex [voice, +spread gl.]

II. A tonal feature, maybe [−upper]

III. A feature with affinities to both tonal and laryngeal nodes

I is the least plausible of these. Its advantage is that it alone directly explains the fact that "murmur" conditions onset voicing. However, it makes the deletion of murmur in non-initial syllables impossible to

---

Lu 1986), 25 or 35. This being so, the variation between 24, 33 44, 33 55 on domains of different lengths bearing T2 seen in (12) is not significant. What matters is that T3 is lower than T2 throughout on one syllable, but on two or more syllables the first syllable is always lower, and the second syllable is always the same.

explain. To see this, note that deletion affects both tone and murmur, but *not* voicing, or aspiration on voiceless onsets. If murmur is voiced aspiration, this generalization clearly cannot be captured.

II, that murmur and [−upper] are one and the same, was essentially the position taken in Yip (1980). It directly explains the deletion of both tone and murmur, and the failure to affect voicing and aspiration, but leaves two problems. First, there is no obvious reason why [−upper] (murmur) should condition onset voicing. In other tone languages, such as Cantonese, this is not the case. Second, it fails to distinguish between the phonetic realization of [−upper] in Shanghai as both lowered pitch and murmur, and [−upper] in Taiwanese or Cantonese as just lowered pitch.

Both these problems are part of a more general issue: what is the relationship between laryngeal features and tonal features? On the one hand they can be quite independent from one another, as in most African tone languages, or in Cantonese; on the other hand there is a clear historical relationship (see Yip 1980; Kingston and Solnit 1988; and references cited therein), and even a synchronic one in some cases. Shanghai is an instance of this split personality: murmur occupies the middle ground. It deletes like tone, but unlike laryngeal features it conditions voicing on the onset in obstruents, as if it were itself laryngeal.

This leaves us with the third possibility: murmur is a feature which partakes of both laryneal and tonal characteristics. I propose to capture this directly as shown below, by making "murmur" a dependent of both the tonal and the laryngeal nodes. Underlyingly, it is tonal, but it attaches to the laryngeal node as well, and in the process causes obstruent voicing:[9,10]

(14)   Tonal Root Node (TRN)   Root Node
                                     |
                                  Laryngeal
         L   H
                         [murmur]   [+spread glottis]

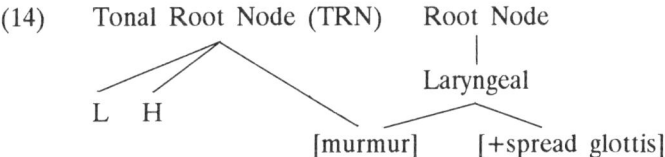

---

9 On tonal root nodes, see Archangeli and Pulleblank (1986), Hyman (1986), Yip (1989).
10 Since this paper went to press, Pat Keating has suggested to me that [murmur] should be identified with [+slack vocal cords], and that this would correctly characterize the phonetic effects.

In non-initial position the tonal root node and its contents, including [murmur], delete; since obstruents remain voiced, this deletion must follow the default rule that determines voicing.

(15) a. [murmur] ⟶ [voice]
     b. TRN ⟶ ∅, contents delete too

This proposal is a radical departure from standard notions of feature geometry in that [murmur] does not have a unique constituency. I would suggest, though, that it may be a useful way to think about the kind of interim stage we find in Shanghai, where an erstwhile segmental laryngeal feature is becoming tonal, but has not yet completed the transition and severed all ties to its host laryngeal node.[11,12]

3.2. Tibetan[13]

Tibetan is of interest because it resembles Shanghai in having a doubly-dependent feature, [murmur], but whereas in Shanghai the TRN deletes, taking murmur and tone with it, in Tibetan the Laryngeal node deletes, taking murmur, voicing and aspiration with it. In other words, murmur is only licensed if *both* its superordinate nodes are present; if either one deletes, it disappears too.[14]

On long V[+son] syllables, non-falling tones contrast with falling tones in both Lhasa and Tsang dialects. Non-falling syllables rise phonetically, but may be level phonologically; see figure 1 for F_0 tracings.

---

11 It is also true that tone and phonation register may co-exist. See the discussion on Mpi and other cases in Maddieson (1979), and references cited therein.
12 Larry Hyman (p.c.) has pointed out that unrelated features *may* all delete together. For example, in Mandarin neutral toned stressless syllables vowel tenseness and onset aspiration are both lost at once. However, Cheng (1973:82) argues that a single feature [±tense] is responsible for both these changes. In any case, it is clear that a rule which deletes a constituent is simpler and thus more natural than a rule that does not. To the extent that phonation register cross-linguistically deletes with either tone or other laryngeal features it should thus be treated as a constituent with them.
13 The data in this section comes from a variety of sources, including Dawson (1980), Ossorio (1982), Mazaudon (1977), Hari (1979), Kjellin (1975, 1976), Shih (1986). I would particularly like to thank Scott Meredith for useful discussion. Hari disagrees with my other sources on a number of points; I have taken the dialects described by the others as the basis for my discussion.
14 Requiring (instead of allowing) double dependency will solve some but not all of the problems pointed out by Pulleyblank (1986:13), and brought to my attention by Nick Clements.

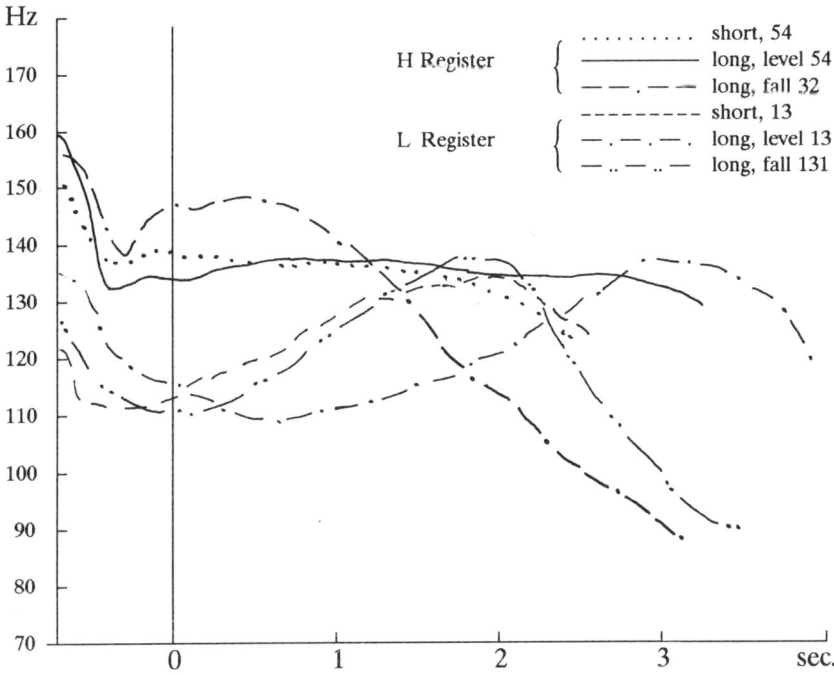

Figure 1. The average curves plotted together. Note that the curves seem to gather toward one high and one low frequency level with or without movements between them.

Hari (1979) finds this contrast on short syllables too, but the other reports disagree. There is also a high/low register difference, giving four tones, as shown below:

(16)   Level/Rise   Falling
     High   **phüü** 54 'offer'   **phee** 52 'come'
     Low   **thee** 13 'mule'   **thuu** 131 'six'

The digits are for comparison with other sources only; they are not a close match to the F_0 tracings.

The high/low register contrast is limited to sonorants and voiceless aspirates (including fricatives). Voiced obstruents are always low; plain voiceless stops are always high:

(17)　　High　　　　　　　　　　Low
　　　　ma 54　'wound'　　　　**ma** 13　'mother'
　　　　tha 54　'end'　　　　　**tha** 13　'now'
　　　　sa 54　'place'　　　　　**sa** 13　'eat'
　　　　see 52　'know'　　　　**see** 131 'three days from now'
　　　　see 54　'crystal'　　　**soo** 13　'deceit, pretense'

The high/low contrast is accompanied on monosyllables by a "phonation register" difference:

(18)　　*High register*: "tense":

　　　　• glottal stop on vowel-initial syllables
　　　　• strong aspiration
　　　　• voicelessness of plain stops and affricates, and sometimes slight aspiration
　　　　• pharyngealization of checked syllables

　　　　Low register:

　　　　• absence of above
　　　　• always/sometimes breathy

Having surveyed the basic facts, now I turn to the behavior of tone and register in compounds. In compounds, the first syllable loses its level/falling contrast (neutralized in favor of level); it keeps the high/low register contrast:

(19)　　If the first syllable is:

　　　　a.　H level: **cen** 54　'eye, pol'　　**cencu** 54 54　　'tear, pol'
　　　　　　H fall: **tshoa** 52 'meeting'　　**tshoakang** 54 54 'meeting hall'

　　　　b.　L level: **maa** 13　'butter'　　**maarin** 13 54　　'price paid for butter'
　　　　　　L Fall: **tee** 131　'rice'　　　**teešing** 13 54　　'rice field'

The second syllable loses the high/low register contrast, neutralized in favor of H; it keeps the level/falling contrast:

(20) If the second syllable is:

a. H level: ngee 54 'bad,evil'   tshingee 54 54 'bad language'
   L level: ming 13 'name'   chööming 54 54 'name given
                                                  by monks'

b. H fall: nii 52 'two'   cunñii 54 52 'twelve'
   L fall: rii 131 'nationality' phorii 13 52 'Tibetan race'

The second syllable also loses the "phonation register" contrast, and finally the second syllable loses any aspiration and voicing contrasts on the onset; medial onsets are all more or less plain voiced. It is worth noting that the loss of register/tone in compounds is not stress conditioned. Stress falls on the first long vowel, otherwise on the first syllable.

I will focus here on the changes in the second syllable. Let us assume, as in Shanghai, that [murmur] is a feature dominated by both laryngeal and tonal nodes. This directly explains the relationship to voicing and phonation, and to pitch. On the second syllable, the laryngeal node deletes, taking [murmur] with it. All laryngeal and phonation contrasts disappear, but the tonal contrast of level/falling is retained. This is the opposite of Shanghai, where the TRN deletes. The result of deleting [murmur] is that syllables surface as H register by default, showing clearly that [murmur] is the marked feature, even in the case of sonorants.

Returning to the first syllable, where the level/fall contrast is lost, let us assume that since this contrast is restricted to long syllables, the TBU is the mora; tonal contrasts will thus be captured as given below:

(21) Level   Falling   Short Syllables:
     m   m   m   m   m
     | | | |
     H   H   H

On the first syllable of compounds, then, the tone (H) deletes. Everything else remains intact.

As in Shanghai, I have suggested that it is possible for a single feature to be dominated by both laryngeal and tonal nodes, and that this directly captures languages in an intermediate stage between contrasts being born by onset consonants, and a truly tonal language. A crucial difference between Shanghai and Tibetan is that in Shanghai the tonal root node deletes, carrying its contents, including murmur, with it; however other laryngeal features remain intact. In Tibetan, on the other hand, the

Laryngeal node and its contents, including [voice], delete, leaving other tonal contrasts intact.

I have argued for a tonal register feature, [upper], and a somewhat different developmental stage when a single feature may be dominated by both laryngeal and tonal nodes. I now turn to register and intonation, and the connection between what has been called register in intonation and the entities discussed in the preceding sections. Despite the title of this paper, my first example is not East Asian, but African: Hausa.

4. REGISTER AS AN INTONATION FEATURE

If intonation involves the addition and manipulation of the tonal register feature [upper], what kind of phenomena would we observe? Setting aside temporarily the phonetic implementation of register, we might find rules which insert and spread [+upper], and rules which insert and spread [−upper]. In a language which has a lexical contrast in [±upper], rules like this would neutralize the contrast: one set of tones would be unaffected, but the other set would merge with them. In a language without a lexical contrast, addition of some value of [upper] would create a distinction where none existed before. The latter situation pertains in non-tonal languages, like English, where intonation typically introduces contrastive pitch to the system. (See for example various works of Pierrehumbert, Liberman and Beckman.) However, there is no way of telling what tonal feature is involved in such systems, since it interacts with no others and creates only a 2-way contrast.

The most common reported effects of intonation on tones are:

(22) a. All tones raise (lower) somewhat.
      b. The pitch range expands (contracts), with high tones raising and low tones lowering.

Neither of these effects can be described as a phonological rule operating on [upper]; however, they can be understood as phonetic implementation rules (Liberman and Pierrehumbert 1984; Pierrehumbert 1980; Pierrehumbert and Beckman to appear) governing the realization of [upper].[15] Following Shih (1988), (22a) resets the reference line ("an abstract line that corresponds to the mid pitch range") higher, raising all tones. (22b) "scales tonal targets away from the reference line". This latter, pitch

---

15 Or any other tonal feature. The sources cited here do not take a stand on what the tonal features are, but use L, M, H, and som times H+, L± etc. as primitives.

range expansion, (22b) is a particularly clear example of a process which afffects the realization of [upper], rather than of the melodic L, H (i.e. [raised]) feature.

In order to get a clearer understanding of register in intonation we need to look at tonal languages, and the interaction of intonation and lexical tone. My first example comes from Hausa.

4.1. Hausa

Inkelas, Leben and Cobler (1987) argue convincingly that Hausa *yes-no* question intonation can be understood as the addition and spreading of a H Register tone; that downdrift involves the insertion and spreading of a L Register tone, and that emphasis involves the addition of a H register tone. Hausa already has two lexical tones, and the register tones are superimposed on this system, so that a H tone with H register attached surfaces as extra-high, and a L tone with L register attached surfaces as downdrifted L. The Inkelas, Leben and Cobler analysis is interesting because it appears to show clear manipulation of a tonal register feature for the purposes of intonation. However, it turns out that their notion of register differs in important ways from the notion needed in the phonology of East Asian languages, and a single feature, say [upper], cannot be used to account for both sets of facts. In my summary of their account I use H and L register tones, following their terminology; later I will discuss the relationship between these entities and [±upper].

Hausa has downdrift, a process whereby all tones are lowered following a L tone. Inkelas, Leben and Cobler analyze this as the addition of a register L to all lexical L tones, followed by rightward spreading of the register L to a following H tone. They say (p. 330) "a register tone *shifts* the register, so that it affects not only the tone it is associated with, but all the remaining tones in the phrase as well". Thus downdrift involves only local spreading, but the effect perpetuates itself across the phrase.

In *yes-no* questions, three effects of interest here are felt:

I.   downdrift is suspended in the final intonational phrase;

II. phrase-final H become extra-high;

III. boundary L becomes raised L.

These three effects are attributed to the addition of a register H, which associates to the final H of a question, and spreads iteratively leftward.[16] Its presence on H tones blocks the spreading rightward of register L's that would usually cause downdrift, accounting for I above. The extra-high and raised-low tones in II and III are the direct interpretations of lexical H and L associated with H register. An example is given below (Inkelas, Leben and Cobler (10)); % marks the Intonational Phrase boundary:

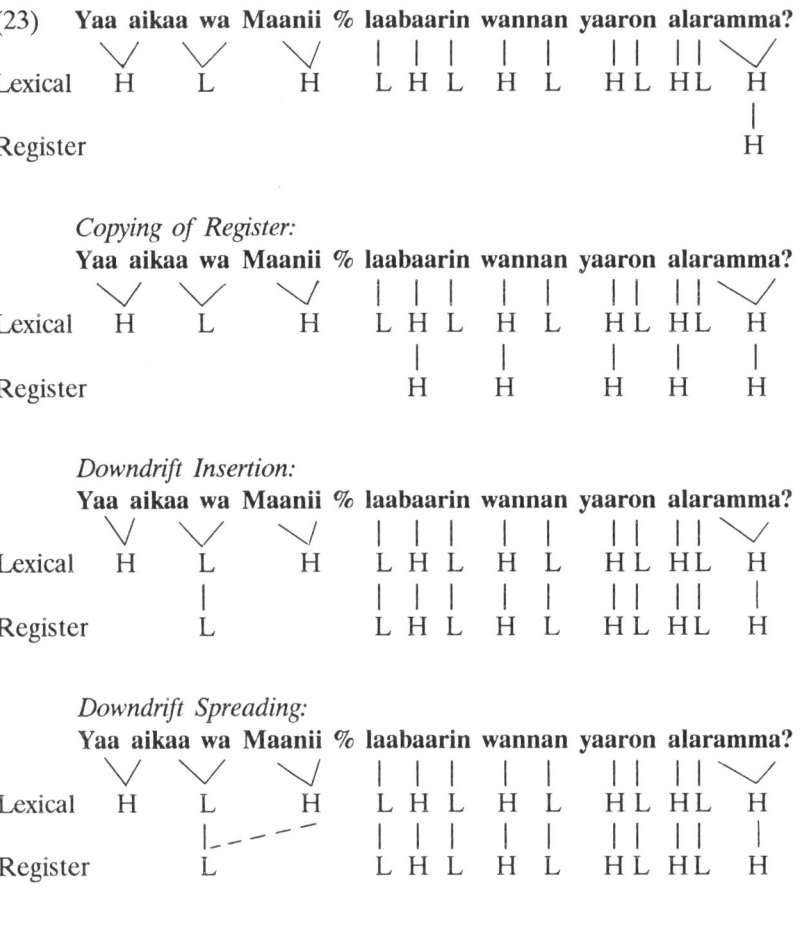

---

[16] Actually, Inkelas, Leben and Cobler (1987) have to state this rule as a copying rule, because they wish to leave the intervening Ls free to accept a L register tone. The resulting alternation of H and L register resets the register repetitively back to its original position, resulting in the perceived level effect.

Now let us consider whether we can equate H and L register tones with [+/-upper].[17] There are two striking differences that suggest we cannot.

I. Inkelas, Leben and Cobler's register tones reset the register *permanently*, but [±upper], like Inkelas, Leben and Cobler's lexical tones, do not. In Hausa, a sequence of LHLH gets a register L on each L, and these spread to the following Hs. The result is that the register is reset lower twice, giving downdrift:

(24)

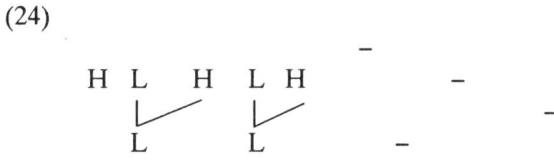

In Chinese languages, a comparable sequence would be two low register rising tones, and each of these would have essentially the same register, with no successive lowering:[18]

(25)   [−upper]   [−upper]

         L   H   L   H   [13] [13]

II. There is some connection between lexical and register tones in Hausa, such that lexical Ls get L register (in downdrift) and lexical Hs get H register (both in questions and in emphasis). There is no such general connection between [+upper] and H, and [−upper] and L, in East Asian languages. Cantonese, for example, has all four possible combinations underlyingly. Because of this connection, in Hausa the effect of register is in some sense to expand the pitch range, raising Hs and lowering Ls (although the spreading of downdrift *does* lower Hs too). We will see other cases of pitch range expansion later.

---

17 Inkelas, Leben and Cobler themselves consider their proposal to be in the spirit of Yip (1980) and Hyman (1986), but although it is, I think, rather close to Hyman's concept of register, it is rather different from that of Yip (1980).
18 See for example Shih's (1987:10) data on Mandarin sequences of two higher register rising tones, tone 2. (Sequences of two low rising tones, tone 3, do not surface because of the third-tone sandhi rule.) Shih gives F_0 values at the beginning and end of each syllable as follows: in a sequence of two tone 2s, first syllable: 216–257 Hz; second syllable: 217–249 Hz. If [+upper] resets the register permanently, we would expect updrift here; instead the two syllables are almost identical.

It seems unavoidable to conclude that Inkelas, Leben and Cobler's register tones are not the same creature as the feature [upper] needed for East Asian languages. To further check this conclusion, I turn to intonation and emphasis in the East Asian languages themselves.

5. INTONATION IN EAST AASIAN LANGUAGES

5.1. Shanghai

The only reports of Shanghai intonation that I am aware of are two brief mentions of the effects of focus. Sherard (1972:170) says that stressed (i.e. emphasized) syllables tend to be louder, longer, and raised in pitch. He also says there is an "audible juncture" after stressed syllables. Selkirk and Tong (1988) say that focussed syllables have a "wider-than-normal pitch range". They also say that after the focussed element there is compression of the pitch range, and a lowering of the entire pitch register. These two statements only partially agree on the effect on the focussed syllable itself. It seems clear that high tones raise, but Sherard implies that low tones do too, whereas Selkirk and Tong imply that they remain either static, or lower. Whichever is the case, it is clear that there is no merger of the two registers under focus; the effect is one of the two types of phonetic effect noted in (20).

5.2. Mandarin

In two elegant papers, Shih (1987, 1988) presents detailed results of her work on Mandarin tone and intonation. Mandarin has four lexical tones, given here in feature terms from Yip (1980):[19]

(26) Tone 1 [+upper], H
      Tone 2 [+upper], LH
      Tone 3 [−upper], L
      Tone 4 [+upper], HL

---

[19] Tone 4 is often shown numerically as 41, which would appear to cross registers. However, Shih confirms earlier impressionistic reports to the effect that tone 4 never reaches a final L level if another tone follows (1987:10): "Tone 4 in the non-sentence final position is actually HM". This is consistent with a [+upper, HL] tone, and the extra low end-point observed in final position may result from final lowering (Hirschberg and Pierrehumbert 1987).

Tone 3 has two variants, a low rise in utterance final position, and low level elsewhere. A sequence of two tone 3 syllables undergoes a sandhi rule, the first changing to tone 2, high rising.

Shih shows that Mandarin exhibits downdrift (she uses the term catathesis), so that L tones have a lowering effect on the following H tone. The effect is more noticeable with tone 3 than with tones 2 and 4, raising the possibility that the effect is caused by [−upper] register rather than L tone; however, the existence of some catathesis even after tones 2 and 4 seems to suggest that L tone itself, or the complete tonal complex, may be the cause.

Shih then discusses the effects of prominence (=focus). Prominence raises high targets, and leaves alone or lowers low ones. Duration and intensity also increase. After prominence, things are scaled back again and normal values are found.[20] This is similar to Shanghai, and very different from Hausa. In Hausa, everything raises under focus, leading Inkelas, Leben and Cobler to analyze this as the addition of H register. However, in Mandarin low targets do not raise, so this is an instance not of general raising but of pitch range expansion (22b).

Given that we are dealing with a phonetic implementation rule which scales tones, what phonological feature(s) does it take as its input? In principle it is possible to tell whether phonetic scaling operates on one tonal feature only, or on a complex. For example, if [+upper] is scaled up, and [−upper] scaled down, then in Mandarin tones 1, 2, 4, which are [+upper], should be raised throughout, including both the L and H targets of tones 2 and 4. Tone 3 should be lowered throughout. On the other hand if scaling operates on the L, H melodies (i.e., raises H and lowers L), then the H of tones 1, 2, 4 should raise, but the L of tones 2, 4 should lower. The result would be a stretching out of the contour tones over a wider range. Finally, if the entire complex is scaled, the [+upper], L targets should be more or less unchanged, since the [+upper] will be scaled upwards but the L will be scaled downwards. (There are no [−upper, H] targets in Mandarin; if there were, they also would be unchanged.)

These predictions are tabulated below:

---

[20] Gårding (1987) also gives data on focus in Mandarin. Her data is inconclusive as to the effect of focus on L; some speakers seem to raise L slightly, others seem to lower it. In her text Gårding claims, like Shih, that focus expands the frequency range, but the data does not really support her conclusion. Note also that even question intonation does not really affect F_0 of L tones for three of the speakers. Only one shows a noticeable rise (from 90–110 Hz).

(27) a. *Scaling of [upper] alone*
Tones 1, 2, 4   Raise throughout; shapes unchanged
Tone 3   Lower throughout, shape unchanged

b. *Scaling of [raised] (L, H) alone*
Tone 1   Raise throughout
Tone 2, 4   Ends stretched apart; greater rise, fall
Tone 3   Lower throughout

c. *Scaling of whole complex*
Tone 1   Raise throughout
Tone 2, 4   Start of T2, end of T4 unchanged
                End of T2, start of T4 higher
Tone 3   Lower throughout

(28)   Base   Register   Tone   Complex
                        Scaling   Scaling   Scaling

                                                  ―
                                     ―
                         ―
         H   ―
[+upper]
         L   ―   ―
                                                  ―
                                     ―

         H   ―   ―
[−upper]
         L   ―   ―
                                     ―
                         ―
                                                  ―

The differences, then, will be found in the effects of pitch range expansion on tones 2 and 4. Note that (27) and (28) assume that pitch range expansion is symmetrical, lowering the bottom line as much as it raises the top line.

(29) a. jin1 tian1   b. ming2 tian1

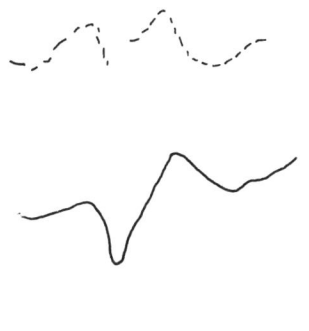
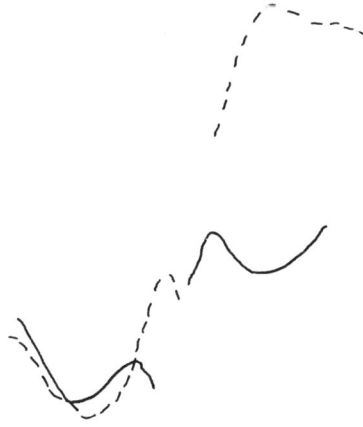

c. mei3 tian1   hou4 tian1

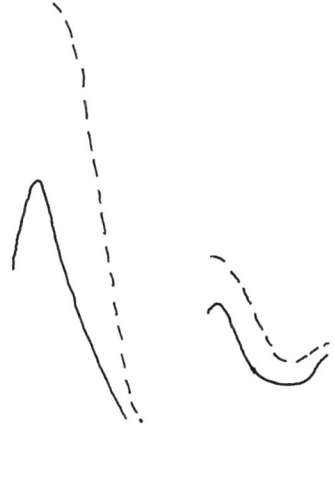

In (29) I give a figure from Shih (1987) which shows the effect of prominence on all four tones. (b) and (d) show tones 2 and 4, and in both cases the H portion is raised, but the L is unaffected. This is consistent with (27c), scaling of the entire feature complex, and inconsistent with (27a), scaling of the register alone, which would predict overall raising of the whole contour. It is less clear whether it is inconsistent with (27b), scaling of the tones alone. This is because it could be the case that although the tones are scaled apart, the L tone stays put while the H tone moves away. Notice, in (29c), that tone 3, which is also L, does not lower either.[21]

I conclude that focus in Mandarin cannot be a phonological operation on a register feature, and that the phonetic implementation process that expands the pitch range acts not on register alone, but probably on the whole tonal complex, although I leave open the possibility that it operates on just the melodic tonal features L, H ([raised]).

6. CONCLUSION

I have shown that it is necessary to recognize a tonal register feature, [upper], and that laryngeal features may doubly attach under laryngeal and tonal root nodes to create what I have referred to as phonation register. I have also shown that intonation register is not a phonological operation on the same feature (although it may be an operation on a different feature, if Inkelas, Leben and Cobler are right), but rather a way of realizing one or more tonal features phonetically. What is more, it is not possible to limit intonational effects to the realization of tonal register, since in Mandarin either all tonal features, or the melodic tones alone, must be involved.

REFERENCES

Archangeli, Diana and Douglas Pulleyblank. 1986. "The Content and Structure of Phonological Representations." Ms. University of Arizona and University of Southern California. To appear at Cambridge, Mass.: MIT Press.
Chao, Y-R. 1931. "A System of Tone Letters." *Le Maitre Phonetique*.
Cheng, C-C. 1973. *A Synchronic Phonology of Mandarin Chinese*. The Hague: Mouton.
Clements, George N. 1985. "The Geometry of Phonological Features." *Phonology Yearbook* 2, 225–52.

---

[21] Tone 3 is already extremely L, and it may be that it is articulatorily impossible to lower it any more for many speakers.

Dawson, W. 1980. "Tibetan Phonology." Ph.D. Dissertation, University of Washington.
Duanmu, San. 1988. "Shanghai Tone: Representation and Spreading." Ms. Massachusetts Institute of Technology, Cambridge.
den Dikken, Marcel and Harry van der Hulst. 1988. "Segmental Hierarchitecture." In *Features, Segmental Structure, and Harmony processes*. Part I, edited by Harry van der Hulst and Norval Smith, 1–78. Dordrecht: Foris Publications.
Gårding, E. 1987. "Speech Acts and Tonal Pattern in Standard Chinese: Constancy and Variation." *Phonetica* 44, 13–29.
Goldsmith, John. 1976. "Autosegmental Phonology." Ph.D. Dissertation, Massachusetts Institute of Technology, Cambridge. Published by Garland Publishing, New York 1980.
Hari, A. (1979) "An Investigation of the Tones of Lhasa Tibetan." Language Data: Asian Pacific Series 13. Dallas: Summer Institute of Linguistics.
Hirschberg, J. and J. Pierrehumbert. 1986. "The Intonational Structuring of Discourse." In *Proceedings of ACL*, 136–44. New York.
Hombert, J-M. 1978. "Consonant Types, Vowel Quality and Tone." In *Tone: A Linguistic Survey*, edited by Victoria Fromkin, 77–112. New York: Academic Press.
Hu, Tan. 1979. "Study on Tibetan Tones." Paper presented at the 12th International Conference on Sino-Tibetan Languages and Linguistics.
Hyman, Larry M. 1986. "The Representation of Multiple Tone Heights." In *The Phonological Representation of Suprasegmentals*, edited by Koen Bogers, Harry van der Hulst and Maarten Mous, 109–152. Dordrecht: Foris Publications.
———. this volume. "Register Tones and Tonal Geometry."
Inkelas, Sharon, William Leben and M. Cobler. 1987. "The Phonology of Intonation in Hausa." In *Proceedings of NELS 17*, edited by James Blevin and Juli Carter, 327–42. Amherst, Mass.: GLSA.
Îto, Junko and Armin Mester. 1989. "Feature Predictability and Underspecification: Palatal Prosody in Japanese Mimetics." *Language* 65, 258–93.
Kingston, J. and D. Solnit. 1988. "The Tones of Consonants". Ms. Cornell University, Ithaka, and the University of Michigan.
Kjellin, O. 1975a. "Progress Report on an Acoustical Study of Pitch in Tibetan." *Annual Bulletin of Research Institute of Logopedics and Phoniatrics* 9, 137–50. University of Tokyo.
———. 1975b. "How to Explain the 'Tones' in Tibetan." *Annual Bulletin of Research Institute of Logopedics and Phoniatrics* 9, 151–66. University of Tokyo.
———. 1976. "A Phonetic Description of Tibetan." *Annual Bulletin of Research Institute of Logopedics and Phoniatrics* 10, 127–43. University of Tokyo.
Law, Sam-po. 1990. "The Syntax and Phonology of Cantonese Sentence-Final Particles." Ph.D. Dissertation, Boston University.
Liberman, M. and J.B. Pierrehumbert. 1984. "Intonational Invariance Under Changes in Pitch Range and Length. In *Language Sound Structure*, edited by Mark Aronoff and Richard Oerhle, 157–233. Cambridge, Mass.: MIT Press.
Lu, Zhiji. 1986. "Tonal Changes: Interplay Between Tone and Tone Sandhi A Case Study of the Shanghai Dialect." *Studies in the Linguistic Sciences* 16, 97–111.
Maddieson, I. 1979. "Universals of Tone." In *Universals of Language: Phonology*, edited by Joseph Greenberg, 335–67. Stanford, Stanford University Press.
Mazaudon, M. 1977. "Tibeto-Burman Tono-Genetics." *Linguistics of the Tibeto-Burman Area* 3.
Ossorio, J. 1982. "Tsang Tibetan Phonology". Ph.D. Dissertation, University of Colorado.
Pierrehumbert, J.B. 1980. "The Phonology and Phonetics of English Intonation". Ph.D. Dissertation, Massachusetts Institute of Technology.
Pierrehumbert, J.B. and Mary Beckman. 1988. "Japanese Tone Structure." Cambridge, Mass.: MIT Press.
Pulleyblank, Douglas. 1986. *Tone in Lexical Phonology*. Dordrecht: Reidel.

Sagey, Elisabeth G. 1986. "The Representation of Features and Relations in Non-Linear Phonology". Ph.D. Dissertation, Massachusetts Institute of Technology, Cambridge.

Selkirk, Elisabeth and Tong Shen. 1988. "Prosodic Domains in Shanghai Chinese." To appear in *The Phonology-Syntax Connection*, edited by Sharon Inkelas and Draga Zec. CSLI Monograph.

Sherard, M. 1972. "Shanghai Phonology". Ph.D. Dissertation, Cornell University, Ithaka.

Shih, Chi-Lin. 1986. "The Prosodic Domain of Tone Sandhi in Chinese." Ph.D. Dissertation, Univrsity of California at San Diego.

———. 1988. "Tone and Intonation in Mandarin." *Working Papers of the Cornell Phonetics Lab*, 83–109.

———. 1987. "The Phonetics of the Chinese Tonal System." *AT&T Bell Labs Technical Memo*.

Sprigg, R.K. 1954. "Verbal Phrases in Lhasa Tibetan I." *Bulletin of the School of Oriental and African Studies* 16, 134–56.

———. 1955. "The Tonal System of Tibetan (Lhasa Dialect) and the Nominal Phrase." *Bulletin of the School of Oriental and African Studies* 17, 133–53.

Xu, B.H., Z.Z. Tang and N.R. Qian. 1981–83. "Xing bai Shanghai fang yan de lian du bian diao (Tone Sandhi in New Shanghai)". *Fangyan* 1981:2, 145–55; 1982:2, 115–28; 1983:3, 197–201.

Ye, X.L. 1979. Tone Sandhi in Suzhou. *Fangyan* 1, 30–46; 4, 30–47.

Yip. Moira. 1980. "The Tonal Phonology of Chinese". Ph.D. Dissertation, Massachusetts Institute of Technology, Cambridge.

———. 1989. "Contour Tones." *Phonology* 6, 149–74.

Zee, E. and I. Maddieson. 1980. "Tones and Tone Sandhi in Shanghai: Phonetic Evidence and Phonological Analysis." *Glossa* 14, 45–88.

Index of Authors

Abney, Steven A. 150, 162, 179
Áhághotù, A. 167, 183
Akinlabí, Akinbìyí 82, 105, 82, 105, 133, 135, 179
Amáyó, Aírén 135, 137, 174, 179
Anderson, Steven R. 2, 3, 24, 105
Archangeli, Diana 7, 24, 72, 77, 105, 253, 266
Armstrong, Robert G. 82, 105, 179
Arnold, G.F. 115, 127, 132
Aronoff, Mark 26, 72, 106, 132, 267
Awóbùlúyì, Oládélé 135, 179
Baker, Mark C. 151, 161, 179
Bamba, Moussa 21, 24, 133, 134, 140, 146, 157, 176, 179
Bannert, R. 131
Bao, Zhiming 16, 24
Bearth, Thomas 2, 24
Beckman, Mary, E. 9, 17, 24-26, 30, 72, 110, 111, 113, 114, 116, 119-132, 258, 267
Bendor-Samuel, John T. 107, 179, 182, 183, 244
Berg, Rob van den 110, 116, 121, 130
Bergman, Richard 78, 106
Bergmann, Gunther 116, 132
Bezooijen, Renée 114, 130
Blevins, James 25, 181
Blois, K.F. de 183
Bogers, Koen 25, 106, 107, 183, 244, 267
Bolinger, Dwight 114, 115, 125, 130
Borer, Hagit 150, 162, 179
Botne, Robert D. 107
Brown, Gillian 120, 121, 130
Bruce, Gösta 109, 116, 125, 126, 130, 131, 181
Capo, Hounkpati B.C. 134, 180
Carlson, Robert 17, 24, 63, 64, 72, 101, 106
Carrell, Patricia L. 36, 72
Carter, Juli 25, 106, 181, 267
Chan, Marjorie K.M. 6, 24, 78, 103, 106

Chang, Kun 2, 24
Chao, Y.-R. 245, 266
Charette, Monik 21, 24, 134, 146, 180
Cheng, C.-C. 25, 254, 266
Chomsky, Noam A. 4, 24, 150, 180
Clark, Mary M. 17, 20, 21, 24, 29, 39, 42, 43, 45, 49, 50, 63, 64, 72, 88, 106, 133, 134, 160, 165, 174, 178, 180, 213, 243, 244
Clements, George N. 1, 3, 4, 6, 7, 9-11, 13, 20, 21, 24, 31, 32, 71, 72, 75, 77, 79, 84, 124, 131, 135, 136, 138, 140, 143, 176, 180, 185, 186, 188, 191, 103, 106, 111, 116, 242, 244, 245, 252, 254, 266
Cobler, Mark 23, 25, 29-31, 36, 71, 72, 79, 107, 181, 259-263, 266, 267
Cohen, A. 116, 131
Collier, René 116, 131
Connell, Bruce 109, 116, 131
Cooper, William 112, 131
Cope, A.T. 13, 24
Courtenay, Karen 180
Crystal, David 115, 131, 256
Currie, Karen 130
Dawson, W. 254, 267
Dihoff, Ivan R. 24, 106, 131, 180, 244
Dikken, Marcel den 7, 24, 267
Docherty, G.J. 130, 132
Dolphyne, Florence, A. 71, 72
Duanme, San 4, 16, 24, 250, 251, 267
Elugbe, Ben 147
Éménanjo, E.Nwánòlúe 160, 167, 168, 170, 172, 175, 180
Ewen, Colin 105
Fassi-Fehri, Abdelkader 150, 180
Flik, Eva 2, 24
Ford, Kevin C. 32, 72, 103, 106, 135, 138, 140, 143, 180, 185, 191, 244
Fromkin, Victoria A. 24, 25, 106, 137, 138, 180, 181, 183, 186, 244, 267

Fujimura, Osamu 180, 182
Fukui, Naoki 150, 161, 181
Gage, William 91, 115, 131
Gårding, Eva 116, 131, 263, 267
Giererich, Heinz J. 173, 181, 183
Goldsmith, John 4, 24, 36, 72, 94, 106, 133, 135, 160, 176, 180, 181, 244, 251, 267
Goyvaerts, Didier L. 180
Green, Margaret M. 160, 172, 181
Greenberg, Joseph H. 26, 134, 181, 267
Gruber, Jeffrey 2, 24
Gussenhoven, Carlos 110, 130, 131
Haïk, Isabelle 106
Halle, Morris 4, 16, 24, 133, 181
Halliday, M.A.K. 115, 131
Haraguchi, Shosuke 176, 181
Hari, A. 254, 255, 267
Hart, Johan 't 116, 131
Hayes, Bruce 128, 131, 133, 181
Higginbotham, James 150, 181
Hirschberg, J. 262, 267
Hockett, Charles F. 127, 131
Hoekstra, Teun A. 182
Hollenbach, Barbara E. 2, 24
Hombert, J.-M. 267
Hu, Tan 251, 267
Huang, Cheng-Teh James 10, 21, 25, 31, 71, 72, 111, 130, 131, 140, 181
Hulst, Harry van der 1, 7, 16, 24-26, 72, 106, 107, 133, 181-183, 244, 245, 267
Hung, Tony T.N. 130, 131
Hutchison, John 179
Hyman, Larry M. 1, 2, 7, 9, 10, 18, 19, 21, 25, 29, 31, 34-39, 44, 46, 51, 57, 59, 62, 67, 70, 72, 75-77, 79, 80, 82, 84, 87-90, 92-94, 105, 106, 133, 135, 139, 144, 145, 149, 151-154, 156, 157, 160, 181, 185, 189, 190, 196-199, 223, 225, 243-245, 253, 254, 261, 267
Igwè, G.Égembà 160, 172, 181
Ihìónú, Uzòdínmá 160, 175, 181
Inkelas, Sharon 7, 9, 11, 21, 23-25, 29-31, 36, 71, 72, 75, 77, 79, 80, 84, 87, 89, 106, 107, 140, 181, 259-263, 266, 267, 268
Itô, Junko 267
Jack, M. 131
Jacobson, Leon C. 106
Jensen, John 72, 131
Johnson, C. Douglas 9, 25
Johnson, Kyle 161, 179
Kamany, Honoré 181

Katamba, Francis 92, 106
Kaye, Jonathan 21, 25, 78, 106, 134, 146, 177, 181, 182
Kayne, Richard 146, 182
Kenstowicz, Michael 84, 107
Kenworthy, Joanne 130
Kidda, Mairo 84, 107
Kingdon, Roger 115, 131
Kingston, John 24, 25, 131, 132, 253, 267
Kiparsky, Paul V. 42, 43, 72, 139, 182
Kjellin, O. 254, 267
Koopman, Hilda 2, 15, 25, 106
Koster, Jan 146, 182
Kubozono, Haruo 110, 112, 130, 131
Kutsch Lojenga, Constance 21, 25, 185, 222, 223, 230, 238, 244
Ladd, Robert 20, 24, 25, 109-113, 115, 116, 119, 121, 122, 124, 128-132
Ladefoged 250
Láníràn, Yétundé 21, 25, 138, 146, 179, 182
Lahiri, Aditi 128, 131
Laubitz, Zofia 183
Laver, J. 131
Law, Sam-po 231, 233, 248, 267
Leben, William R. 4, 5, 7, 23-25, 29-31, 36, 71, 72, 75, 79, 107, 134, 181, 182, 244, 259-263, 266, 267
Leroy, Jacqueline 89, 90, 107
Li, Charles N. 25, 106, 157, 158
Liberman, Mark 17, 20, 26, 30, 72, 110, 116, 125, 127, 132, 179, 258, 267
Lieber, Rochelle 151, 161, 182
Longacre, Robert E. 2, 26
Lowenstamm, Jean 21, 25, 133, 134, 146, 177, 181, 182
Lu, Zhiji 250, 251, 267
Maddieson, Ian 2, 26, 250, 254, 267, 268
Maeda, Shinji 116, 132
Magaji, Daniel 2, 25
Manfredi, Victor 1, 21, 26, 133, 140, 149, 151, 154, 179, 182
Mazaudon, M. 254, 267
McCarthy, John 7, 26
McDonough, Joyce 72, 107
McHugh, Brian 84, 107
Meeussen, A.E. 94, 106, 185, 188, 244
Meier, Ingé 182
Meier, Paul 182
Mester, Armin 267
Mohanan, Kate P. 34, 43, 72
Moortgat, Michael 182

Index of authors

Mountford, Keith W. 101, 107
Mous, Maarten 25, 106, 107, 183, 244, 267
Mutaka, Ngessimo 105, 107
Napoli, Donna Jo 106
Nemers, Julie 101, 107
Nespor, Marina 173, 178, 182
Newman, Paul 81, 107
Newman, Roxana Ma 3, 26, 82, 107
Nikiema, Emmanuel 134, 141, 182
Nwáchukwu, P.Ákujuoobi 167, 168, 172, 173, 175, 182
O'Connor, J.D. 115, 127, 132
Odden, David 17, 26, 63, 71, 72, 99, 101, 104, 107, 134, 146, 147, 164, 182
Oehrle, Richard T. 26, 72, 106
Ogbàlú, F.Chídòzíe 180
Olson, Howard, Stanley 94, 107
Ossorio, J. 254, 267
Oyèláràn, Olásopé 154, 182
Palmer, Harold 115, 132
Peters, Ann M. 9, 26
Pierrehumbert, Janet E. 9, 17, 20, 24, 26, 30, 72, 109-111, 113, 114, 116, 119-130, 132, 258, 262, 267
Pike, Kenneth L. 4, 9, 26, 115, 132
Plunkett, Bernadette 72, 107
Poser, William J. 110, 132
Prince, Alan 179
Prunet, Jean-François 141, 183
Pulleyblank, Douglas George 7, 9, 18, 24-26, 32, 33, 36, 37, 40, 72, 77, 79, 82, 88, 104-107, 133, 139, 149, 152, 183, 243-245, 251, 254, 266, 267
Pustejovsky, James 181
Qian, N.R. 249
Rietveld, Toni 110, 130, 131
Ritter, Elisabeth 150, 151, 183
Roberts, Ian 142, 161, 179, 183
Russell, Jann M. 3, 26
Sagey, Elisabeth G. 6, 7, 26, 252, 268
Schachter, Paul 9, 26, 137, 183, 186, 244
Schadeberg, Thilo C. 94, 99, 107, 134, 183, 191, 244
Scherer, K.R. 116, 132
Schlindwein, Deborah 105, 107
Schuh, Russell G. 106, 181
Sebeok, Thomas 26, 107, 183, 244
Selkirk, Elisabeth 250, 262, 268
Sells, Peter 181
Sherard, M. 250, 251, 262, 268

Shih, Chi-Lin 23, 26, 247, 248, 254, 258, 261-263, 266, 268
Silverman, Kim 116, 132
Smith, H.L. 115, 132
Smith, Norval 24-26, 72, 107, 181, 267
Snider, Keith L. 1, 3, 7, 9-12, 14, 16, 26, 75, 77, 79, 93, 107
Solnit, D. 253, 267
Sorensen, John 112, 131
Sportiche, Dominique 2, 15, 25, 106
Sprigg, R.K. 268
Stahlke, Herbert 3, 26, 79, 107
Stevens, Kenneth N. 16, 114, 132
Stewart, John M. 9, 21, 22, 26, 34, 72, 84, 107, 136, 138, 139, 145, 183, 185-187, 191, 197, 198, 222, 244
Swift, Loyd B. 167, 183
Tadadjeu, Maurice 39, 45, 57, 59, 62, 67, 72, 80, 89, 106, 133, 138, 139, 144, 149, 152, 157, 181, 183, 196, 243, 244
Tang, Z.Z. 249
Thomas, Elaine 85-89, 107
Thorsen, Nina 112, 132
Tolkmitt, Frank 116, 132
Tong, Shen 250, 262, 268
Trager, George L. 115, 132
Travis, Lisa 151, 183
Tuller, Laurice 25, 106
Ugoji, E. [Ugorji] 167, 183
Ùwaláàka, Marry A.-A. 148, 183
Vergnaud, Jean-Roger 21, 25, 133, 134, 146, 177, 181, 182
Vogel, Irene 173, 178, 182
Voorhoeve, Jan 89, 108, 133, 139, 145, 152, 160, 161, 183
Walusimbi, Livingstone 92, 106
Wang, W. 3, 4, 26
Warnier, Jacqueline [Leroy] 89, 108
Wedekind, Klaus 2, 26
Welmers, Beatrice 168, 183
Welmers, William E. 9, 26, 75, 78, 106, 108, 149, 160, 168, 183
Williams, Carl E. 114, 132
Williams, Edwin S. 4, 27, 133, 160, 161, 183
Williamson, Kaye R.M 133, 134, 139, 160, 166, 168, 183
Winston, Denis 9, 27, 168, 184, 186, 244
Voeltz, Erhard 181
Woo, Nancy 4, 5, 27
Wórùkwó, Glory 184

Xu, B.H. 249
Yang, I.-S. 72
Ye, X.L. 247, 268
Yip, Moira J. 5-9, 14, 16, 22, 23, 27, 36, 39, 42, 73, 77-79, 81, 103, 108, 245, 246, 248, 250, 253, 261, 262, 268
Zee, E. 250, 268
Zemp, Hugo 2, 24

Index of Languages

Àbó 82, 151
Adioukrou 22, 26, 186, 190, 222, 223, 244
African 5, 8, 10, 24-27, 62, 72, 75-78, 81, 84, 103, 105-108, 111, 114, 130, 131, 133, 179-184, 244, 253, 258, 268
Aghem 84
Akan 21, 22, 71, 137, 140, 183, 185-188, 190, 193, 196, 198, 202, 205, 222, 223, 226, 227, 242-244
Amo 92
Asian 5, 22, 77, 78, 81, 108, 245, 258, 259, 261, 262, 267
    East 5, 22, 77, 78, 108, 245, 258, 259, 261, 262
    Southeast 81
Babanki 84
Bamileke 17, 29, 36, 39, 72, 79, 80, 82-84, 87-90, 94, 103, 106, 244
    Dschang 17, 18, 21, 22, 25, 29, 31-34, 36, 39, 42, 44, 59, 61, 62, 65, 70-72, 79, 80, 82, 83, 89, 90, 94, 103, 106, 107, 149, 181, 183, 185, 187, 188, 196, 197, 205, 222-227, 230, 238, 239, 242-244
    Fe'fe' 84, 87, 88, 106
    Mankon 19, 76, 84, 86, 87, 89, 90, 92, 94, 100, 102, 103, 107, 108
    ɣɔmaláʔ-Yamba 21, 134, 135, 137-140, 144, 145, 147-152, 161-163, 176, 178
Bantu 9, 84, 89, 93, 94, 99, 103, 106, 133, 149, 180, 181, 183, 244
    Eastern 84, 89
    Grassfields 103, 133
Benue-Congo 134, 176
Benue-Kwa 21, 134, 135, 176, 177
Cahi 94, 95, 100, 102
Cantonese 36, 248, 249, 253, 261, 267
Chadic 84
Chaga 80, 84, 89, 107
    Kirua (= Vunjo) 107
    Vunjo (= Kirua) 107
Chicahuaxtla 2
Chinese 23, 24, 26, 27, 42, 73, 106, 108, 131, 176, 177, 245, 251, 261, 266-268
Copala 2, 24, 25
Dagbani 82
Dan 2, 24
Danish 132
Danyang 24, 106
Dutch 110, 130
Ebrié 21, 22, 25, 185, 187, 188, 222, 223, 225-227, 231, 238, 239, 242-244
Èdó 135-137, 139, 146, 147, 179, 182
Efik 27, 186, 244
Ehugbo 149
Engenni 19, 76, 84-90, 92, 94, 100, 107
English 20, 24, 26, 30, 72, 73, 109-111, 113, 114, 122, 128, 130-132, 149, 161, 172, 179, 183, 186, 258, 267
    American 26, 107, 115, 131, 132, 179, 183
    British 131
Esimbi 106
European 128, 130, 131
Ewe 106, 140
Fuzhou 23, 248, 249
Ga'anda 3, 26, 82, 107
Gbè 134, 180
ɣekoyó (= Kikuyu) 135, 136, 138-140, 143, 145, 148
Grebo 107
Gwari 2, 25
Hausa 23, 25, 29, 30, 107, 181, 258, 259, 261, 263, 267
Ìgbo 17, 21, 24, 26, 27, 63-65, 71, 72, 82, 88, 106, 133-135, 137-140, 146, 147, 149, 151, 160-162, 164, 166, 170, 172, 173, 178, 180-186, 189, 196
Igede 2, 78, 106
Ikwére 184

Ìzîi 149
Japanese 24, 26, 30, 72, 110, 120-124, 130-132, 176, 181, 267
Jukun 78
Kagwe 2, 15, 25
Kikuyu (= ɣekoyó) 63, 72, 77, 84, 106, 140, 180, 185, 186, 188, 190, 191, 193, 223, 243, 244
Kinande 105, 107
Kirimi 19, 76, 84, 87, 94
KiShambaa 17, 26, 63, 65, 71, 72, 99, 101, 104, 107, 146, 147, 164, 182
Kom 82, 84, 87
Krachi 9, 11, 15, 26, 107
Kru 25, 78, 81, 106, 134
Kwa 9, 21, 26, 107, 134, 135, 154, 174, 176, 177, 183, 244
Lhasa 254, 267, 268
Llogoori 9
Luganda 92, 106
Mandarin 23, 254, 261-263, 266, 268
Mbàisén 148, 167, 168, 170, 171, 174, 175, 182
Mbam-Nkam 72, 106, 181, 244
Miao-Yao 2, 24
Moba 3, 26
Mpi 254

Ngamambo 79, 82-84, 94
Ngemba 84, 89, 107
Niger-Congo 22, 26, 107, 134, 149, 179, 181-183, 242, 244
Nigerian 107
Nneewi 170
Ògbakịrị 167, 174, 175
Òweré 167
Potou-Tano 222
Qirwana 94
Shanghai 23, 249-251, 253, 254, 257, 262, 263, 267, 268
Supyire 17, 63-65, 72, 101, 106
Suzhou 23, 247, 268
Swedish 130, 131
Taiwanese 23, 246, 249, 253
Tangale 84, 107
Temne 101, 107
Tibetan 23, 254, 257, 267, 268
Trique 2, 24-26
Tsang 254, 267
Twi[-Akan] 26, 183
Wu 247, 250, 251
Yala Ikom 36, 82, 105
Yorùbá 20, 21, 25, 82, 105, 131, 133-139, 146-148, 179, 180, 182
Zulu 13, 24

Index of Subjects

Agreement
    alternations 161
    chain 151
    class 151
    morphology 149
    parameters 183
    prefix 149, 151
    suffix 67
Association
    convention 42, 135
    No Association Convention 42
    domain 135, 136, 155, 157, 162, 166, 178
    Linguistic Association of Nigeria 133, 179, 180, 182, 183
    of a feauture 42
    of all Ls as register tones 93
    re- 155, 156
    rule 135
    rules of leftward H 136
    tone 135, 136, 151, 162, 178, 251
    universal principles of 251
Associative construction
    absence of Downstep Deletion in 243
    in Dschang 18, 44, 197, 199-201, 206ff
    in Ebrié 25, 222, 230, 231, 244
    head noun of 50
    lack of L-Spread in 153
    marker 224, 225
    phonetic alternations in 155
    relevance of status TBU 213
    relevance of syntax for 178
    resemblance with Construct State or Nominal Compound 149, 162
    rising-tone and low-toned nouns indistinguishable in 58
    in ɣɔmalaʔ-Yamba 161
Baseline 116-120, 123, 129
Bracket Erasure Convention 34
Catathesis 120-122, 263
Cliticization 57, 58, 155, 156, 162, 163, 178
Configurations

    accentual 124
    Levels vs. 130
Construct state 149, 150, 162, 183
Contour
    composite 6
    downstepping 111
    falling 59, 67, 69, 135
    falling-rising 78
    fundamental frequency 109, 114, 117
    intonation 114, 132
    non-downstepping 111
    prepausal 222, 226
    rising 42, 58, 83
    rising-falling 78
    short 42
    Simplification 48-50, 52-55, 57, 58, 61, 62, 67-70
    tonal 135
    tone 135, 222
    two-tone 15, 21, 22, 148, 222, 242
    unitary 6
Contour formation
    at level I
        blocked by Principle of Left-Right Application 49
        creating a short contour 46
        divided per level 61, 62
        exemplified 45, 51-53, 55, 68
        shifting H tone 53
    at level II
        exemplified 44, 49, 50
        not to melody LM 42
        statement of 41
    at end of word 35
    linking TBU to the left 195
    simultaneous with Lowered H Deletion and Assimilation 45
    word division needed for 38
Contour Low Disassociation 202, 205, 209, 212, 226, 236, 237
Contour Low Raising 226, 235, 236

Cumulative 9, 11, 12, 136
Declination 8, 110, 112, 131, 132, 186
Delinking 83, 84, 99, 100, 136-138, 145
Depressor consonant 230, 235, 240, 241
Determiner Phrase (DP) 149, 150, 162
Downdrift
  as automatic downstep 9, 144, 186
  in Ga'anda 26
  in Hausa 259
  in opposition with spreading 149
  intonational 79
  not in Kikuyu 186
  not in Dschang 33
  or spreading 149
  partial 139, 144
  predictable from tonal representation 17
  register lowering as 8, 75, 82, 101
  relation with downstep 71, 87
  representing on register tier 29-31
Downglide 72, 183, 198, 243, 244
Downstep
  accent-level 20
  accent-to-accent 125
  automatic 9, 21, 22, 136-138, 142, 144, 185-188, 193, 196, 198, 222, 223, 242
  creation rules 37
  double 18, 69
  environment 18, 66, 71
  intervening 17, 31, 172
  intonational 20, 109, 130
  lexical 104
  linear theory of 128
  local 139
  nested 112, 120-122, 124, 128
  nesting of 20
  nonautomatic 9, 136, 137, 193, 136
  overt 21
  partial 134, 138-140, 142-144, 146-149, 162, 164, 168-170, 185
  phonetic model of 123
  phonological 121, 110
  phrase-internal 120, 121
  phrase-level 20
  phrase-to-phrase 125
  successive occurrences of 9
  tonal 21, 25, 89, 103, 106, 244
  total 134, 138-140, 142-144, 147-149, 153, 154, 157, 185-188, 196, 222
  true 37, 44, 128

  unpredictable 104
Downstepped Contour Low Disassociation 202
Falling Contour Simplification 67, 69
Feature
  binary 187
  geometry 6, 7, 25, 26, 76, 105, 106, 140, 248, 252, 254
  laryngeal 16, 252-254, 257, 266
  [constricted] 16
  [spread] 16
Focus 126, 130, 262, 263, 266
Government
  metrical 135, 141, 144, 147, 148, 169, 170, 179
  phrasal 135, 179
  proper 134
  prosodic 134, 149, 163, 173, 174
  syllabic 135, 179
  syntactic 141, 146, 156
  tonal 141, 142, 144, 146-148, 179
Identical Tone Merger 41, 42, 45, 47-52, 54, 55, 57, 58, 60-62, 68, 70, 71
Implementation 9, 10, 82, 87, 89, 100-103, 258, 263, 266
Initial Tone Association Rule 135, 136
Integer 188, 196, 222, 223
Intermediate phrase 122, 123, 125-128
Locality 133, 135, 139, 146, 157, 181, 183
Minimality 134, 142, 147, 173
Murmur 23, 245, 249-254, 257
Node
  high-toned 59
  laryngeal 39, 40, 42, 46, 56, 253, 254, 257, 258, 23, 257, 258
  place 39
  supralaryngeal 39
  target 42, 46, 60, 61
  tonal 7, 11, 12, 18, 39, 40, 42, 46, 48, 53, 54, 56, 60, 61, 69, 77, 80, 102, 103, 253
  tonal root 18, 77, 80, 103, 246, 253, 254, 257
  vowel height 105
  vowel root 105
Obligatory Contour Principle (OCP) 12-14, 17, 21, 32, 42, 65, 87, 101, 104, 107, 134, 141, 146, 154, 156, 157, 173, 174, 178, 182

Index of subjects 277

Paralinguistic 20, 109, 113-118, 120-130
Phonology
   autosegmental 4-6, 24, 72, 133, 181, 267
   charm-and-government 141
   cognitive approach to 168
   dependency 105
   intonational 109, 110, 115, 126, 131, 132
   lexical 26, 43, 45, 47, 49, 52, 53, 70, 72, 107, 183, 244, 267
   metrical 112, 129
   phrasal 67-69, 134
   phrase-level 138
   pitch 109
   postlexical 61
   tonal 27, 73, 108, 109, 268
   word level 45, 51, 57
Pitch
   level 12, 91, 104, 115, 116, 138, 144
   of the voice 22, 134, 142, 174, 198, 245, 249
   phonology 109
   range
      advantage of baseline approach for analysis of 118
      changes in 26, 72, 132, 267
      dividing the 245
      expansion of 258, 259, 261, 263, 264, 266
      expressing emotions 114, 129
      modification of 20, 130
      narrowing (compressing) of 20, 262
      of focused syllables 262
      overall 117, 125, 126
      paralinguistic account of 120, 121, 124-128, 129
      phonetic modeling of 20, 109
      resetting of 23
      rising to top of 30
      variation in 113, 116
Prefix
   á- 67
   agreement 149, 151
   boundary with stem 34
   noun 35, 37, 38, 43, 46, 68
   Ñ- 61
   tone 91, 156, 197
Reassociation 155, 156
Reduplicate 6
Reduplication 174
Register shift
   accentual in Gekoyó 140, 191
   controlled by register trees 20, 109
   cumulative nature of 9, 10, 12

   definition of 1, 79
   influence on downstep 119
   metrical and linear 130
   modeled in terms of tonal height 129
   not with contours 8
   phonological or phonetic account? 9, 10, 15, 118
   pre-cyclic 135
   reestablishing of phonetic pitch 1,8
   spreading of 259
Rhythm 164
Space
   tonal 116-120, 123, 124, 126, 129, 130
Spreading
   and government 142, 145, 147, 148
   assimilation by 81, 82
   automatic 103, 133
   characterization of 56, 141
   combinations with delinking 137
   constraints on 46, 139, 140, 142, 145, 147, 148, 260
   directionality of 42, 137, 247, 248
   in Cahi 94
   in Fuzhou 248
   interaction with downstep 12, 134, 136, 139, 140, 142, 146
   interaction with downdrift 29, 259, 260, 261
   lacking in associative construction 153, 154
   lacking in Shanghai 251
   of H with question intonation 259
   ordering of 62
   parametrization of 135
   rule-governed 133, 134
   Rules of 94, 148, 187, 193, 202, 215, 216, 220, 227
   yielding contours 5, 46, 136
Strict Cycle Condition 41-43, 62
Structure preservation 134, 176
Suffix
   agreement 67
Tier
   skeletal 5-7, 141, 163
   tonal 5, 7, 11, 18, 21, 29, 30, 43, 156, 226, 235, 236
   tone 6
Tone
   abstract 20, 21, 109, 110, 112, 138, 139, 145, 147, 258
   contour 19, 46, 89
   extra-low 36
   falling 6, 7, 78, 88, 100, 102, 135, 136

features 4, 6, 21, 24, 76, 77, 79, 103, 106, 131, 177, 180, 244
floating 65
floating high 32, 57
heights 2, 4, 25, 76-79, 85, 106, 267
high-toned 40, 44, 50, 58, 59
identical 69
level 24, 76, 85, 88, 106, 131, 180, 187, 188, 222
lexical 23, 39, 40, 109, 134, 136, 140, 170, 174, 245, 259
linking 191, 193, 199, 242
low-toned 39, 40, 44, 56-59
nuclear 115
rising 23, 53, 78, 81, 154
Tone Bearing Unit (TBU) 4, 5, 7, 8, 11, 12, 14, 76-78, 81, 82, 84, 86-88, 90, 91, 99, 101, 103, 104, 137, 186, 187, 191, 193, 195, 199, 205, 212, 213, 215, 216, 220, 226-228, 230, 233, 235, 236, 241, 257
Upstep
    as tonal government 148
    automatic 22, 188, 196, 222, 223
    characterization of 101, 102
    constraints on 94
    differences between Dschang/Ebrié and Akan 22, 187, 242
    in Engenni 19, 76
    in Kirimi 19, 76, 94ff
    in Mankon 19, 76
    in Zulu 13

morphological upstepping rule 88
non-local 11
ordering of 85, 88
phoneme 87
related to downstep 10, 13-15, 22
unpredictable 85
upstepping operator 76, 90
Voice
    breathy 249, 250
    creaky 23, 245, 249
    distinctive feature in Shanghai 250
    long-term characteristics 119, 129
    pitch of the 22, 134, 142, 174, 198, 245, 249, 22, 30
    quality 114, 132, 249, 16
    raised 114, 124, 126
    raising the 20
    voiceless aspirates 255
    voiceless aspiration 250
    voiceless onsets 253
    voiceless stops 255
Voiced
    aspiration 250, 253
    fortis 228
    lenis 228
    obstruents 250, 255, 254
    onsets 250
Weakened Contour Low Disassociation 168, 209, 212
Well-formedness Condition (WFC) 133, 135, 136, 163

Hounkpati B. C. Capo

A Comparative Phonology of Gbe

1991. 24 x 16 cm. XXIV, 238 pages. Cloth. DM 138,–
ISBN 3-11-013392 X
(Publications in African Languages and Linguistics 14)

(Foris Publications · Berlin · New York)

The Gbe language unit, spoken in Ghana, Togo, Bénin and Nigeria, comprises more than fifty lects including such well-known members as Eue, Fon, Gen-Mina and Aja. This book presents the first comparative study of this unit and proposes an internal classification based upon the author's firsthand investigation of nineteen present-day lects.

On the basis of this documentation, a reconstruction of the major features of Proto-Gbe segmental phonology, including its phoneme inventory and major syllable structure constraints and phonological rules, is proposed. This monograph will be of interest not only for its specific contributions to linguistic reconstruction in West Africa, but also for its innovative approach to comparative methodology, which draws upon some of the results of contemporary phonology including distinctive feature theory. One of the author's major conclusions is that the Proto-Gbe phoneme system included nasal vowels but no nasal consonants, these arising as variants of oral consonants before nasal vowels, leading to the present-day system of "paired" oral and nasal consonants.

The present monograph constitutes an important new addition to the field of Gbe studies and West African comparative linguistics, and will provide a valuable reference work and resource for future researchers.

mouton de gruyter

Berlin · New York

Robert K. Herbert
Language Universals, Markedness Theory and Natural Phonetic Processes

1986. 14.8 x 22.8 cm. X, 299 pages. Cloth.
ISBN 3 11 010973 5

(Trends in Linguistics. Studies and Monographs 25)

This research monograph has as its goal the explication of the relationship between diachronic and synchronic universals in phonology.

It first presents an exhaustive categorization of the various types of half-nasal consonants which occur among the world's languages. The data comes from a wide variety of sources and a wide variety of language families so that the validity of the generalizations can be demonstrated. The complex interactions obtaining between nasal and oral consonants which abut upon one another, and, in particular, those realized as surface units, i.e. prenasalized and postnasalized consonants, are dealt with in detail.

mouton de gruyter
Berlin · New York